Inequality in Early America

Reencounters with Colonialism:
New Perspectives on the Americas

editors (all of Dartmouth College)
Mary C. Kelley, AMERICAN HISTORY
Agnes Lugo-Ortiz, LATIN AMERICAN STUDIES
Donald Pease, AMERICAN LITERATURE
Ivy Schweitzer, AMERICAN LITERATURE
Diana Taylor, LATIN AMERICAN AND LATINO STUDIES

Frances R. Aparicio and Susana Chávez-Silverman, eds., *Tropicalizations: Transcultural Representations of Latinidad*

Michelle Burnham, *Captivity and Sentiment: Cultural Exchange in American Literature, 1682–1861*

Colin G. Calloway, ed., *After King Philip's War: Presence and Persistence in Indian New England*

Carla Gardina Pestana and Sharon V. Salinger, eds., *Inequality in Early America*

Susana Rotker, *The American Chronicles of José Martí: Journalism and Modernity in Spanish America*

Renée L. Bergland, *The National Uncanny: Indian Ghosts and American Subjects*

Inequality

IN

Early America

Carla Gardina Pestana and
Sharon V. Salinger, editors

Dartmouth College

Published by University Press of New England

Hanover and London

Dartmouth College

Published by University Press of New England, Hanover, NH 03755

© 1999 by The Trustees of Dartmouth College
Printed in the United States of America 5 4 3 2 1

CIP data appear at the end of the book

 To Gary

Contents

CONCEPTUALIZING INEQUALITY

AFTERWORD

Illustrations

Abbreviations Used in the Notes

AHR   *American Historical Review*
CMHS   *Collections of the Massachusetts Historical Society*
JAH   *Journal of American History*
NEQ   *New England Quarterly*
WMQ   *William and Mary Quarterly*

Inequality in Early America

Carla Gardina Pestana and Sharon V. Salinger

INTRODUCTION: INEQUALITY IN EARLY AMERICA[1]

> Race inequality, often splicing together with class and gender inequality, has proved extraordinarily resistant in the quest to achieve the democratic ideas that American society has long professed.
>
> — GARY B. NASH[2]

 THIS VOLUME BRINGS together the work of scholars with a wide variety of interests, all of whom find that the concept of inequality influences their view of the past. The theme of inequality offers an opportunity to address a range of topics central to early American history; at the same time, it permits us to honor the work of Gary B. Nash. Colonial American society was shaped by inequities imported from Europe as well as relations of power and subjugation fashioned in the "New World." Interactions among various social groups—elites, white servants, women, African and African-American slaves, Native Americans—reflected the dynamics of power: how it was exercised, accommodated, and resisted. The revolution that brought an end to British colonial rule was fought in the name of justice and an end to hereditary privilege; while it overturned certain traditional inequities, it led to the creation of a new political system that legitimated, even strengthened, others. In this volume, a dozen scholars examine the issue of inequality as it touched the lives of early Americans from the first period of English colonization until the early decades of the new United States. The essays that follow further our knowledge of the experiences of ordinary Americans and of the world in which they lived, and they contribute to the ongoing discussion of how best to study inequality.

Gary Nash holds a central place in the field of American history. His large and distinguished body of published work, as well as his service as director of the National Center for History in the Schools and president of the Organization of American Historians, offers clear testimony that, for him, the writing of history is part of a larger project. His historical research has confirmed his suspicions that America has not lived up to the promise of equality for everyone and that historians have largely ignored the issue. He has been continuously drawn to the themes of inequality, from his first book, *Quakers and Politics*, through his groundbreaking studies of radicalism in the American Revolution, to his more recent work in African-American history. Nash also has been devoted to influencing the way history has been written, and he has been concerned throughout his career with educational reform and with the presentation of history in American classrooms. We therefore chose the theme of inequality for a conference honoring the work of Nash that took place at the Huntington Library in January 1997; this volume, which has its roots in that gathering, continues our effort to grapple with the role of inequality in early American history and historiography.

Nash's career thus far spans three decades that have seen major changes in the writing of history as well as more modest but perhaps ultimately more profound changes in the composition of the historical profession. The prevailing scholarship of the early 1960s, when Nash began his career,[3] overlooked social and political inequalities to focus on the commonalties that were said to characterize early American society. This trend in American historiography, eventually dubbed the consensus school, concentrated on political and intellectual history in such works as Edmund S. Morgan and Helen M. Morgan's *The Stamp Act Crisis* (1953), Clinton Rossiter's *The Seedtime of the Republic* (1953), and Robert E. Brown's *Middle-Class Democracy and the Revolution in Massachusetts, 1691–1780* (1955). Although the ostensible American penchant for consensus politics was occasionally decried, as it was by Louis Hartz in his 1955 study, *The Liberal Tradition in America*, it was more often celebrated. Such was the case in Daniel J. Boorstin's *The Americans: The Colonial Experience* (1958), which won the prestigious Bancroft Prize in 1959.[4]

Politics, defined as the workings of the official political system and the elites who dominated it, was central to history written at the time.[5] The most strenuous historiographical controversy in the years just prior to 1965 debated the extent of democracy in early America; sparked by Robert Brown's 1955 study of prerevolutionary Massachusetts, this argument animated the pages of the *William and Mary Quarterly* in the late 1950s and early 1960s in much the same way that the republicanism debate would in the late 1970s and early 1980s. A collection of essays, *Reinterpretations of*

Early American History, in 1966 included three thematic chapters on political, imperial, and diplomatic history, a list that suggests the prevailing parameters of historical inquiry.[6] As a result, introductory history courses generally proceeded chronologically through noteworthy political events. African-American slaves entered these narratives solely as the cause of political crises, such as the three-fifths compromise at the Constitutional Convention; their own experiences as enslaved people did not warrant notice. Women were, if anything, more thoroughly absent from the standard accounts of early American history.

By the mid-1960s some scholars, many of them recent Ph.D.s, were pursuing new directions, and the outlines of new trends in scholarship were becoming visible. A number of studies appeared at mid-decade challenging the focus on institutional Puritanism, especially the ministerial elite, that was typical of New England history in the wake of Perry Miller's campaign to revitalize that region's intellectual history. Darrett B. Rutman's *Winthrop's Boston: Portrait of a Puritan Town, 1630–1649* (1965) depicted a society animated less by religious piety than by material concerns. In the same year, John Demos published an article on early Plymouth life that anticipated the New England town studies that he and others would publish in 1970. These works of "new social history" had a profound impact on the writing of American history of all eras, turning scholarly attention to local studies of ordinary people.[7] The impact of these town histories was so great initially that the primacy of New England studies, which had been the focus of colonial American history since the inception of historical inquiry in the nineteenth century, was temporarily reconfirmed.

A second strand of history-writing emerged that emphasized the common people. The historiographical trend would be labeled "New Left" for its association with the radical politics of the late 1960s and 1970s. (As with other cultural trends, scholarship that came to be synonymous with "the sixties" did not appear until the second half of the decade.) An early effort in this direction, Staughton Lynd's 1961 essay, "Who Should Rule at Home? Dutchess County, New York, in the American Revolution," revived progressive historian Carl Becker's phrase about the radical impulses within the revolution. Not until 1968, when Jesse Lemisch published his article "The American Revolution Seen from the Bottom Up," did "history from the bottom up" and "the inarticulate" enter the historian's shared vocabulary.[8] Nash's own decision to move beyond the history of elites in favor of an approach that integrated various groups occurred around mid-decade, under the combined pressure of the civil rights movement and the challenges of teaching UCLA students drawn from more diverse backgrounds than his Princeton classmates and students had been. Other New Left historians were similarly influenced by their experiences during this era of protest.[9] This scholarship, particularly that associated with the New Left, reinvigorated the progressive tradition, returning to an early emphasis on conflict and social divisions. It moved beyond the Progressives' narrow economic determinism, however, trying both to write ordinary colonists, African Americans, women, and Native Americans into the history and to grant them an agency previously reserved for elite white men.[10]

The historical profession of the mid-1960s was similarly on the verge of change, but at that moment the changes were not yet in evidence. The professoriate remained overwhelmingly male, white, and educated at a handful of elite institutions. Along with Nash's own dissertation advisor, Wesley Frank Craven, who was nearing retirement at Princeton, Oscar Handlin at Harvard, Carl Bridenbaugh at Brown, Daniel J. Boorstin at Chicago, and Edmund S. Morgan at Yale were among the leading senior scholars in the study of colonial history. Bernard Bailyn had been elevated to the rank of professor at Harvard in 1961. The up-and-coming young men in the profession, such as Jack P. Greene and Richard S. Dunn, earned praise, as would Nash for his first book, for looking at traditional topics in new ways; Greene examined the institutional history of the legislative assemblies in the southern colonies to illuminate the preconditions for the independence movement, while Dunn studied the Winthrop dynasty over three generations to chart the changing nature of colonial New England politics within its imperial context.[11] While the profession continued to be dominated by men, the number of women receiving Ph.D. degrees at American universities was on the rise after 1965, following a long postwar hiatus. In part as a result of the temporary decline in female university faculty, neither the Organization of American Historians nor the American Historical Association had elected a woman president for at least two decades prior to the mid-1960s.[12] An African American would not hold the position of president in either organization until John Hope Franklin became the first in each, serving the OAH in 1974–75 and the AHA in 1979. A homogeneous and perhaps somewhat complacent profession, unsurprisingly uncovered historical actors much like itself.

Nash's graduate training occurred in this setting, but he would be among those who worked to bring about change. Nash recalls two assignments in his first graduate seminar with Frank Craven that helped guide the direction of his approach to history. He read Cotton Mather's *Magnalia Christi Americana* (1702) in preparation for an oral presentation and was struck by the way Mather described a scene that occurred in 1637. The Puritans, allied with the Narragansett, destroyed an entire Pequot village: "in a little more than *one hour*, five or six hundred of these barbarians were dismissed from a world that was burdened with them." Nash was captivated by Mather's "brilliantly unambiguous display of divine intervention, demonstrating that the Puritans were the historical agents of God's design for mankind's redemption."[13] Nash also remembers being assigned Douglas Leach's *Flintlock and Tomahawk: New England in King Philip's War* (1958) and his amazement that the book had been warmly received by reviewers. Nash responded viscerally to statements in the preface by Samuel Eliot Morison. Morison sought to use the past for understanding modern events, and he drew insights from the defeat of the Wampanoags and their allies by New England soldiers in 1675–76. He related this history to "our recent experiences of warfare, and of the many instances today of backward peoples getting enlarged notions of nationalism and turning ferociously on Europeans who have attempted to civilize them." Reading Mather and Morison helped Nash to see that historians' unexamined assumptions shape the history they produce; his reaction to these interpretations pushed him to look at the past from a different perspective.[14]

Nash learned two fundamental lessons about sound scholarship from his mentor, the "warm-hearted, wry, and orderly" Craven: begin by reading everything on the project, and be thoroughly grounded in the sources. Nash notes that the first rule enables scholars to envision the development of historical thinking on a topic. The second rule "is too obvious to require comment, though examples are hardly wanting these days of books written from the armchair, not the archive." Nash's work embodies these standards. All of it is firmly situated within the historiography. Beginning with his first book, in which he used long-available manuscript sources to uncover the social structure of early Pennsylvania, Nash mined exhaustively sources not previously identified as important for the study of early America. He took seemingly dry sources, such as estate inventories and tax lists, and brought the histories of ordinary men and women to life.[15]

Nash's attention to class conflict, cultural interaction, and the struggles of non-elites fueled the transformation of early American scholarship. Nash's interest in such issues dates back to his earliest published work. As might be expected of a 1964 Princeton graduate, Nash did not explicitly describe inequality in *Quakers and Politics*, the monograph that was based on his doctoral dissertation. Yet his argument clearly pointed in that direction. Previous histories of colonial Pennsylvania, Nash remarked, had tended to celebrate how the Quakers, traditionally characterized as an industrious, lower-middle-class, egalitarian community, fled religious oppression and a corrupt England to establish a free and pure society in the New World.[16] In Nash's hands the story of early Pennsylvania became a struggle for political stability and maturity. He noted that Penn had intended to create a government that balanced power and offered settlers of middling wealth a place alongside the elites. Instead, Penn endorsed a design that accorded the wealthy a greater share in government. By the middle of the third decade of the eighteenth century, residents of southeastern Pennsylvania exhibited an increasingly unequal distribution of wealth. Nash detailed a decline in the economic strength of the lower orders and argued that this trend continued through the eighteenth century.[17] Because of the centrality of economics to his interpretation of Pennsylvania politics, Nash intended to include the term in his book title. Given the prevailing unpopularity of such an approach, his graduate school mentor opposed the idea, and *Quakers and Politics* went to press without a mention of its economic theme in the title.

Almost immediately after *Quakers and Politics* appeared, Nash published a collection of essays and documents in which he clarified how the theme of stratification in society affected his thinking. He studied the distribution of wealth to understand the origins and extent of inequality as well as its effects on "the political, social, economic, and cultural life of the people." By the time this volume appeared, the study of social structure was commanding the attention of a small yet growing number of historians who were focusing on how alterations in the socioeconomic profile of a society not only reflected economic shifts but "precede and are causally linked to political movements."[18] Here Nash articulated what would become another recurrent theme in his work, the link between the reallocation of power and political change. He saw the historical profession as deeply divided between those who saw American history as essentially "middle class," with little conflict arising from inequities in the social structure, and those who emphasized the growing stratification that carried with it new social attitudes. To help resolve the conflict among scholars, he urged them to devote their efforts to empirical study, to incorporate the new social science methodologies that would enable them to measure social structure. The collection, part of the new series by Prentice-Hall called Interdisciplinary Approaches to History, included essays that did just that.

With *Red, White, and Black* (1974), Nash moved beyond inequality within the white community to a broader view that encompassed the various peoples who met in early North America. A largely synthetic book designed primarily for undergraduates, *Red, White, and Black* launched a two-pronged critique aimed at the writing of American history. Nash noted that traditional early American scholarship was ethnocentric. While this tradition had, by the early 1970s, been challenged and historians were busy offering a corrective, Nash deemed these attempts insufficient. Revisionists had only substituted white heroes with new "figures whose skin is not so pale." This antidote was certainly necessary, Nash conceded, but as history it did not serve us very well.[19]

For Nash only a total reexamination of the story would suffice. Historians did not have to cease studying how Europeans transplanted their cultures to the New World. New chapters had to be added, however. Societies,

Nash wrote, had been in North America for thousands of years, and native peoples, along with the Africans who were forced to the colonies, "were actively and intimately involved in the process of forging a new, multi-stranded culture" that would become the United States. He proposed that much in the historical arsenal had to change. Scholars could no longer characterize colonization and settlement as an inevitable triumph. They had to reconceive Africans and Indians, not as victims but as people who actively and powerfully affected the course of historical change. To follow this advice, historians must abandon a vocabulary in which cultures were described as inferior or superior and people were identified as savage or civilized. They would have to place Indian and African people within their own diverse societies, with rich and complex histories, rather than lumping all Indians or all Africans together as undifferentiated masses. In addition, scholars ought to see the members of these groups as historical actors in their own right, actors who responded to life in North America and contributed to the course of European settlement. Nash also called upon historians to reconceptualize early American history. No longer a tale of English colonization along the "continent's eastern seaboard," it must become the history of the "peoples of North America" and the study of the interactions among various cultural groups.

Red, White, and Black made a dramatic entrance onto the scholarly scene and altered the study of the formative years of American society. The work brought home the fact that racial inequalities, evident in the United States of the 1970s, had not existed from the moment Europeans colonized North America. Historians could no longer evoke the inevitable march of progress nor the superiority of the Christian religion to explain the relationship between red and white, nor could they claim that the status of chattel slaves meant that Africans played no role in hammering out the relationship between white and black. *Red, White, and Black* figured prominently in Nash's goal of reaching a broad student audience with his scholarship. It also inspired a generation of historians, who responded to contemporary ethnic inequalities and gave voices to previously silenced individuals and groups. At the conference honoring Nash's work in January 1997, many participants acknowledged the significance of *Red, White, and Black* for their own intellectual development.

In the 1970s, Nash also set the groundwork for what is now his classic study in a series of important articles. *The Urban Crucible* constituted a major reinterpretation of early American history.[20] Nash blended the social, economic, and political history of Philadelphia, Boston, and New York and highlighted the political consequences of changes in society and the economy. He was not satisfied with previous interpretations of the origins of the revolution, in which social and economic structure were disassociated from political ideology. For Nash, the revolution was best understood "if ideological principles and economic interests are seen as intimately conjoined." To accomplish this, Nash returned to the theme of urban poverty, acute in Boston and more uneven in Philadelphia and New York. Increasing inequality led to discontent within the lower classes and the development of a radical popular politics. Where previous historians had focused on the dramatic events traditionally associated with the revolution—the Stamp Act riots, the Boston Massacre, the Boston Tea Party, and nonimportation—Nash argued that the tensions from underlying social and economic inequalities helped to create a space in which revolution was possible.[21]

Nash returned to the scene of his first explorations, Philadelphia, in *Forging Freedom*. He presented the social and economic profile of the African-American community and reconstructed the economic and demographic realities of black urban life in the eighteenth and early nineteenth centuries. Although "not a single document remains to inform us how Philadelphia's slaves and free blacks might have viewed their world," he worked to recapture individual and community consciousness. In Nash's telling, black Philadelphians perceived their world from their immediate past as slaves rather than from the perspective of the limitations placed on mobility, the degrees of poverty, or the horrors of racism. No obstacles, he concluded, were sufficient to take away the empowerment that accompanied freedom.[22]

The optimism Nash displayed in *Forging Freedom* disappeared in the two books that followed. *Race and Revolution* was based on the three inaugural Merill Jensen Lectures in Constitutional Studies that Nash delivered at the University of Wisconsin in 1988. The essays comprising the first portion of the book offered an impassioned argument about the contradictions between republican ideology and self-interested politics, especially as they related to the issue of slavery. Nash found considerable fault with the founding generation for its unwillingness to abolish slavery and its inability to uphold the ideal that the United States was a land of liberty. The second portion of the book contains a collection of documents that invite students to draw their own conclusions about the controversies over slavery in the new nation. In *Freedom by Degrees*, Nash continued to explore the issue of abolition. The movement toward abolition, he and co-author Jean Soderlund argued, occurred in fits and starts, and claims that the North was motivated by loftier concerns than those of the South arose from a misreading of the process. Pennsylvania's Emancipation Act of 1780, for example, freed no slaves, and the Pennsylvania Abolition Society, although well meaning, accomplished little. Again, self-interest more than ideology determined who would free their slaves. Without a concerted effort by white society, much of the burden for achieving freedom fell upon the shoulders of African Americans.[23]

Nash restated his conviction that historians have a responsibility to help realize the promise of a just America in his presidential address at the national meeting of the Organization of American Historians in March 1995, an address that was later published in *The Journal of American History*. Nash chronicled two parallel yet discordant themes in American history. Countless examples exist of men and women, from the first settlement at Jamestown through today, whose personal/sexual relationships crossed racial and ethnic boundaries. At the same time, the creation and development of a "virulent racial ideology that arose among the dominant Euro-Americans" was intended to maintain racial purity. In the early twentieth century, for example, racial intermingling was seen as analogous to committing national suicide, and people of mixed race were defined as degenerate. Nash called for a reexamination of "America's Achilles heel of race" in order to create and maintain "an antiracist sensibility that can help achieve America's foundational principles of freedom, equality and social justice."[24]

Nash's quest to expose the existence of inequality in American life has had an enormous impact on the field of early American history. Testimony to his influence is contained in this volume. Moreover, his effect has been felt beyond the world of professional historians. Beginning with *Red, White and Black*, Nash directed a substantial corpus of work toward student audiences. He co-edited a college-level textbook that appeared in 1986; in 1991 he was one of four authors involved in a twelve-book series for grades K through 8; and he was sole author of a high school history text.[25] Around the same time, Nash became involved in the creation of guidelines for teaching history nationwide. The National History Standards emerged out of a 1989 initiative by President George Bush and the nation's governors to develop educational standards. Charlotte Crabtree and Nash, as director and associate director, respectively, of the National Center for History in the Schools at UCLA, submitted a proposal to "administer a national consensus-building project to develop national history standards." The chair of the National Endowment for the Humanities, Lynne Cheney, announced in January 1992 that the center's proposal had been approved, and "National History Standards Project was launched." A national council that set policy included twenty-eight individuals representing presidents of organizations involved with teaching history, supervisory staff from county and city school districts, classroom teachers, and distinguished scholars. To broaden the range of participants further, the center also organized a national forum "with representatives from twenty-four major education, parent-teacher and public interest associations having a stake in history in the schools." In addition, nine focus groups were formed to provide "advisory, review, and consulting services."[26]

In 1994, when the National History Standards were published, Nash was propelled into his most public role. The swirling of invective around the standards was situated within an age-old struggle about who owns the past. Critics proclaimed that the guidelines represented no less than "the end of history."[27] Few seemed to notice that the standards were intended to supplement, not replace, history textbooks. Another of the battle lines formed around the claim that Nash was their sole author, so his name became virtually synonymous with the standards. Jack Diggins, for example, criticized *The Urban Crucible* as a means to discredit the standards. Since Nash was known for promoting a radical position in his own scholarship, conservatives assumed he had forced his view of history on the standards.[28] Nash always countered the accusation by describing the collective process of their creation.

Nash's willingness to participate in the creation (and subsequent defense) of the standards was consistent with his commitment to educational reform. For him, the project initially appeared particularly challenging because it represented an opportunity to bring school curriculum in line with current scholarship. He was not unaware of the inherent dangers, however. Historians discuss each other's work as part of the scholarly process. When these arguments enter the public sphere, such debates have a "history of becoming politically divisive." Still, the "culture wars" that accompanied the publication of the standards reached a level that even Nash had not predicted. Although his scholarly work had previously been impugned by those unwilling to concede the existence of class, gender, and racial inequality, the heated response to the standards took the attack outside the academy, into the public arena, and it reached a feverish pitch. Recently, Nash authored a number of accounts of the battle, including one with Crabtree and Ross Dunn.[29]

The attack on his role in writing the standards reflects how enormously successful Nash has been as a scholar and as an advocate of a more inclusive view of American history. The debates highlight the seemingly insurmountable chasm that separates the views of most historians, who have for more than a generation included the lives of ordinary people, with those of conservative critics, who remain suspicious of an approach to history that does not focus exclusively on the white male elite and the inevitable march of progress. Although conservatives fear that this more inclusive approach to history necessarily involves a repudiation of fundamental American values, Nash, for one, has been motivated out of his faith in the promise of those values. His conviction that a history that includes ordinary people will inspire students and encourage them to work for the freedom and equality rooted in the founding of this nation have spurred him to become involved in educational reform. Far from bringing about an end of history,

Nash has always worked for its broadest dissemination and widest relevance. The changes that Nash has helped to foster in scholars' understanding of the past and his efforts to introduce this new understanding into the classroom arose from this desire to recover the situation of ordinary people in the past and to improve their situation in the present.

Over the span of Nash's career as a member of the UCLA history faculty, the study of early American history has been transformed. By the late 1990s, scholars have come to acknowledge the importance of race, class, and gender for understanding early America. In that respect, conservative pundits are correct: the profession now believes early American history is best understood from a vantage point that includes the lives of ordinary people as well as elites and that explores how various social tensions shaped the experiences of all groups. The consensus among students of the past is that colonial America was a more complex, fractious, and ultimately, interesting place than was once imagined. The themes of race, class, and gender affected the historiography of early America sequentially, with interest focusing first on issues of class, followed rapidly by race and more slowly by women's history (later broadened to gender). After early articles by Lemisch and others, class—especially the impact of economic inequalities on the American Revolution—became a focal point of much research. The privileged position initially accorded to class can be seen in the volume edited by Alfred F. Young, *The American Revolution: Explorations in the History of American Radicalism* (1976). Two of three sections in that collection (or eight of eleven essays) are devoted to some aspect of the challenge mounted by the "lower orders." The other three essays, in the closing section (tellingly entitled "Outsiders") dealt with women, blacks, and Indians.[30] Nash's *Urban Crucible* culminated over a decade of interest in the relationship of economic inequality to the revolution. More recently, books by Stephen Innes, Marcus Rediker, Sean Wilentz, and a number of the graduate students trained by Nash have continued to explore the impact of the economic inequality on early American society and specific occupational groups.[31]

The efforts to recapture the history of blacks and Indians in the colonial period bore fruit somewhat more slowly, as the selections in the Young collection suggest. In this endeavor, the first survey authored by Nash was a significant early text: James Axtell called *Red, White, and Black* the "first ethnohistorical textbook." After its publication, works about Indians and African Americans increased dramatically. For the period from 1970 to the late 1980s, for instance, *Books about Early America* lists forty-nine books about Indians (up from eleven titles in the period prior to 1970) and from 1965 to the late 1980s, fifty-two about blacks and slavery (as compared to five). With a new generation of scholars studying ethnographic methods, a host of significant works on various Native American communities appeared in the 1980s, revolutionizing that subfield.[32] The study of slavery in the colonial period initially concentrated on the slave trade and the origins of racism. In *Black Majority* (1974), however, Peter Wood produced an early study that located blacks at the center of the social and economic development of South Carolina. More recent efforts have similarly attempted to recover the experience of African Americans—both slave and free. Following the suggestion made by Nash in *Red, White, and Black*, some works have treated the interaction of all three groups that met in North America; Daniel H. Usner Jr.'s *Indians, Settlers, and Slaves* offers a good example.[33]

Women's history in early American historiography depended heavily on articles until the 1980s, when a number of important books appeared. Works by Nancy Cott, Mary Beth Norton, Linda Kerber, and Laurel Thatcher Ulrich, all published within a five-year period, examined women's roles in Puritan New England, the American Revolution, and the early nation. Shortly afterward, Carol Karlsen reassessed the phenomenon of witchcraft prosecutions in early New England, revealing the centrality of gender. Attention to early American women may have suffered initially from the concern in the broader field to illuminate the movement for improvements in women's status, which tended to direct scholars to the nineteenth century and the campaign for women's rights. Alternatively, the view that the colonial past represented a "golden age," widely held by progressive women's historians, posited an uncomplicated past that did not invite greater scrutiny.[34] Many of the early efforts to recount the history of women revolved around the question of whether their status was improved or hampered by such events as the American Revolution, just as early modern women's history queried whether the Protestant Reformation helped or hurt women. Our understanding of such issues has become increasingly sophisticated. With the appearance in the past few years of books by Norton, Cornelia Hughes Dayton, and Kathleen M. Brown, the profound importance of gender roles and identities has become clear.[35]

The vast majority of histories about early America reflect a new sensibility that arises from attention to the different inequalities that shaped the past. The dramatic changes that have overtaken the field are nicely captured in a collection that appeared in 1997: more than half of the thirteen essays in *Through a Glass Darkly: Reflections on Personal Identity in Early America* deal primarily with Native Americans, blacks, or women; the others invariably locate the individual "self" within a society that struggled with issues of difference and inequality. The issues occupying these scholars differ dramatically from the questions that challenged their predecessors in the field three decades ago. Attention to women's history and to the history of slaves, Native Americans, and the inarticulate of whatever race has grown phenomenally in the past few decades.[36]

The teaching of history has been similarly transformed. Undergraduate survey courses no longer move chronologically through political events without regard for larger social trends or cultural shifts. Textbooks reflect faculty preference for a more multilayered approach, and textbook publishers often market two or three different texts to offer faculty a choice of emphases in their survey courses. Slave experience is as important in many of these texts as the political implications of the institution of slavery for sectional controversies. Women and urban laborers, as well as family structure and survival strategies, similarly receive attention in texts and courses, marking a major departure from the traditional political narrative. A text is more likely to open not with the founding of Jamestown in 1607 but with native culture on the eve of colonization.

The composition of the professional community also has changed since the mid-1960s, although perhaps not as much as popular perceptions suggest. The numbers of women and minorities earning the Ph.D. degree and entering the ranks of the professoriate has risen. Members of these groups have held the prestigious Omohundro Institute of Early American History and Culture fellowship in recent years. In accordance with their rising numbers, women are more likely to be asked to review books for major journals than they had been thirty years ago. The profession is plagued by a new gender inequality, however, with women disproportionately represented among part-time and temporary faculty.[37] Still, at the upper level of the profession women as well as people of color are earning recognition for their contribution.[38] The faculty hired to teach in universities and colleges across the country are no longer drawn primarily from a handful of eastern schools. Students trained in graduate programs across the nation, but particularly Berkeley, University of Pennsylvania, UCLA, Michigan, and Wisconsin, have competed successfully against students from institutions that once enjoyed a virtual monopoly. In building up the early American graduate history program at UCLA, Nash did as much as anyone to expand the opportunities for nontraditional students to earn advanced degrees and win employment in academia. Socially as well as intellectually, the historical profession of today is a different place from what it was thirty years ago.

The essays that follow reflect these changes in history writing while continuing to push at the margins of the field. Each author was asked to prepare an essay on an aspect of early American inequality, some initially for presentation at the conference in honor of Nash (January 1997 at the Huntington Library) and others for inclusion in this volume. The wide range of subject matter covered reveals the myriad ways in which scholars currently think about inequality. The volume is divided into three sections. The first

two are largely historical, examining how inequality was sustained and resisted in early America; the third considers how inequality is currently
being conceptualized. In addition, Richard S. Dunn's afterword offers a
personal perspective on Nash's career.

Inequality was sustained by a wide range of contemporary customs and
attitudes, as authors in the first section demonstrate. In "'Either Married
or to Bee Married': Women's Legal Inequality in Early America," Mary
Beth Norton argues that the legal terms *feme sole* and *feme covert* are not
particularly useful for understanding the position of women in early
American society. Confining her analysis to the period before 1670, Norton examines court procedures for a time when historians claim women
had the fewest constraints on their legal actions. What she finds, however,
is that, whether married or not, few women acted alone. Men spoke even
for single women. Norton concludes that because women had no independent legal identities in early American society, they were simply erased
from society's consciousness.

Thomas N. Ingersoll considers how conservatives warned of the dangers of violent social leveling whenever they objected to social or political
movements in early America. "'Riches and Honour were Rejected by
Them as Loathsome Vomit': The Fear of Leveling in New England" moves
from Puritan New England to the early republic, canvassing the exaggerated rhetoric of social critics bent on maintaining their own exalted position. J. Richard Olivas's analysis of inequality takes him to Boston during
the Great Awakening. In "Partial Revival: The Limits of the Great Awakening in Boston, Massachusetts, 1740–1742," Olivas contrasts the promise
that the awakening would have no boundaries with the reality that church
membership was available on only a limited basis. Many who desired membership were passed over by Boston's revivalist clergy; the vast majority of
the new communicants had family ties to the churches.

For Sylvia R. Frey, an examination of the role of evangelical religion in
the postrevolutionary South reveals a lost opportunity for the new
American nation. Had the evangelical Protestant gospel of spiritual equality of all Christians been realized, a new social order would have emerged.
Protestant theology, while articulating a theoretical equality between men
and women, enforced the patriarchal ordering of society in which women
were subordinated to men. In addition, while some evangelical congregations became biracial and voiced their ambivalence about the institution of
slavery, the social order was left undisturbed. Indeed, Frey argues, the postrevolutionary orthodoxy in the South was more gendered and racialized
than had been the case in the colonial period.

The essays in section 2 explore the relationship between inequality and
resistance in early America. In "'I Loved the Place of My Dwelling': Puritan

Missionaries and Native Americans in Seventeenth-Century Southern New England," Neal Salisbury examines how Christianity figured into the lives of Native Americans in the regions of Martha's Vineyard, Massachusetts Bay, and Plymouth in the seventeenth century. Colonization wreaked havoc on the Indians of this region, and Salisbury argues that for some Christianity offered one means for reordering their lives—spiritually, materially, and politically. By turning to Christianity, however, Indians did not abandon their cultural identity. Indeed, Salisbury underscores that their version of Christianity offered them a means of surviving and of rebuilding their societies.

The next two selections treat resistance by African Americans. Through a close reading of runaway advertisements, Billy G. Smith measures the temporal and regional differences in the behavior of slave women. Smith reviews a host of factors that contributed to a slave's decision to abscond. He argues that family, friends, geography, gender, and opportunity all played a role and that slaves occasionally fled with goals other than simply establishing their permanent freedom or escaping the immediate consequences of their masters' wrath. Sterling Stuckey reconsiders the idea of a "spiritual holocaust" among African-American slaves during the colonial period in "African Spirituality and Cultural Practice in Colonial New York, 1700–1770." Looking at the celebration of Pinkster in Albany, he argues that evidence of African dance and drumming at such festivals indicates the continuing importance of African cultural traditions that closely linked dance and religion. He notes that even as whites borrowed black dance they misunderstood its larger significance within the context of African-American culture and as a form of resistance.

Laurel Thatcher Ulrich unlocks the relationship between two seemingly disparate strands of women's labor, spinning and embroidery, to explore the complex familial ideology in which poor women spun and elite women stitched. Ulrich revisits an important early article in which Nash attributed the failure of the Boston spinning factory to women's unwillingness to leave their homes to work for a wage. Ulrich disagrees. Economic factors, she argues, embedded in the gendered system that ordered power and defined labor destroyed the factory's chances of success.

The authors in section 3 offer ways to reconceptualize the study of inequality in early America. Ronald Schultz begins his essay "A Class Society? The Nature of Inequality in Early America" with the assumption that inequality took many forms and was a pervasive feature of all societies in the early modern Atlantic world. Schultz explores the colonial economies to determine how useful the concept of class is as a descriptor and an analytical tool for discussing inequality in early America. It would be inaccurate, he writes, to claim that early America was a thoroughly class-dominated society. Although class helped define power relationships in isolated middle and northern urban and commercial farming areas as well as in the plantation economies, not until well after the Civil War did class surpass other forms of inequality in defining the exercise of political, social and economic power.

Peter H. Wood declares that despite a proliferation of studies of American slavery, historians, the students we teach, and the culture at large have so far failed to come to terms with the enormity of the slave experience. Concerned with the recent public discussion of race relations, Wood likens slavery to child abuse, in that both have long-term psychological consequences that must be confronted. Many voices described the horrors of slavery, Wood writes, but they were largely unheard. To confront the legacy of slavery and to understand its implications for American racism, Wood asks that historians adopt a different analytical framework: jettison the idea of the plantation because it conjures images of gentility and elegance without regard to the human costs, and replace it with the slave labor camp. As a modern phenomenon that generated many firsthand accounts, the gulag could be compared to American slavery, since both were forced labor systems with devastating consequences.

Philip D. Morgan presents a major review of the historiography of slavery. His discussion is predicated on the view that "slavery was a fundamental, acceptable, thoroughly New World institution" that profoundly shaped the lives of all early Americans. Noting that slave studies have proliferated in recent decades, his essay canvasses that literature, focusing on themes: where, when, how, with whom, and so what? Morgan's extensive bibliography stands as testimony to the growing importance of the study of slavery in early American historiography.

Finally, Gary Nash's essay, "The Concept of Inevitability in the History of European–Indian Relations," returns him to a theme that first caught his attention in graduate school. The essay explores how a framework of inevitability has shaped historians' analysis of relations between Europeans and Native Americans. Early New Englanders, for example, described conflicts between Indians and Puritans as predestined and English victories as divinely ordained. Inevitability took on a more secular cast through the nineteenth and twentieth centuries without, however, softening its effect. Historians claimed that larger forces, environmental and geographic, moral and political, or economic and social, dictated the ways in which individuals acted. As Nash describes it, humans could not be held responsible for their actions, no matter how deplorable, because discussions of conquest and conflict were predicated on the assumption that historical events were out of human hands. The essay reflects Nash's interest in history education in the schools, for he notes that successive generations of textbooks presented American schoolchildren with this inevitability theme. Only in very recent years has this refusal to acknowledge and explore human culpability been overturned.

These essays, the conference where many of them were first presented, and the work of Nash that they are intended to honor indicate how far the study of early American history has come in the past three decades. We now have a far more sophisticated understanding of the lives of ordinary people and the interactions between people of different cultures than we once did. In spite of the conservative outcry in recent years, it seems impossible that we might return to a time when history could be written as if the only historical actors who mattered were elite men with political and economic power. Historical study would be profoundly impoverished by a return to such a limited and limiting perspective, as the rich and varied essays presented here attest.

Notes

1. We would like to thank Joyce Appleby, Saul Cornell, Leila Rupp, and Carole Shammas for their comments on an earlier draft of this introduction; Lorena Walsh and Gregory Nobles, who, as readers for the press, offered useful critiques of the entire volume; and Roy Ritchie (director of research at the Huntington) for hosting the conference out of which this volume grew.

2. *Race, Class, and Politics: Essays on American Colonial and Revolutionary Society* (Urbana, Ill., 1986), xvii.

3. Nash received his Ph.D. degree at Princeton in 1964, joining the faculty at University of California, Los Angeles, in 1966.

4. Edmund S. Morgan and Helen M. Morgan, *The Stamp Act Crisis: Prologue to Revolution* (Chapel Hill, N.C., 1953); Clinton Rossiter, *The Seedtime of the Republic: The Origins of the American Tradition of Political Liberty* (New York, 1953); and Robert E. Brown, *Middle-Class Democracy and the Revolution in Massachusetts, 1691–1780* (Ithaca, N.Y., 1955); Louis Hartz, *The Liberal Tradition in America: An Interpretation of American Political Thought since the Revolution* (New York, 1955); and Daniel J. Boorstin, *The Americans: The Colonial Experience* (New York, 1958). Rossiter's book also won a Bancroft prize (1954). Boorstin explicitly linked his writing and teaching on the "unique virtues of American democracy" to his efforts to fight communism, as he told the House Committee on Un-American Activities in 1953; see Peter Novick, *That Noble Dream: The "Objectivity Question" and the American Historical Profession* (New York, 1988), 328. Hartz linked the problem with consensus to the sort of Red scare Boorstin so eagerly embraced; see *Liberal Tradition*, 10–13.

5. That is, politics understood in a traditional way as opposed to the more recent use of the term, which casts it more broadly to indicate that many aspects of life are structured by power relations. This later sense is captured in a myriad of book titles, such as Joan Wallach Scott's *Gender and the Politics of History* (New York, 1988).

6. Alan Simpson, "How Democratic Was Roger Williams?" *WMQ* 3d ser., 13 (1956): 53–67; Roy N. Lokken, "The Concept of Democracy in Colonial Politics,"

WMQ 3d ser., 16 (1959): 568–80; Richard C. Simmons, "Freemanship in Early Massachusetts: Some Suggestions and a Case Study," *WMQ* 3d ser., 19 (1962): 422–28; George D. Langdon Jr., "The Franchise and Political Democracy in Plymouth Colony," *WMQ* 3d ser., 20 (1963): 513–26; Richard Buel Jr., "Democracy and the American Revolution: A Frame of Reference," *WMQ* 3d ser., 21 (1964): 165–90; David Syrett, "Town-Meeting Politics in Massachusetts, 1776–1786," *WMQ* 3d ser., 21 (1964): 352–66. Also see J. R. Pole, "Historians and the Problem of Early American Democracy," *AHR* 67 (1962): 626–46. For Gordon Wood's comment that the republicanism debate became "something of a monster that has threatened to devour us all," see "Author's Postscript," in *In Search of Early America: The William and Mary Quarterly, 1943–1993*, ed. Michael McGiffert (Richmond, Va., 1993), 76; Ray Allen Billington, ed., *Reinterpretations of Early American History* (San Marino, Calif., 1966). Of 132 books published prior to 1965 listed among the 715 thematic titles in *Books about Early America: 2001 Titles*, ed. David L. Ammerman and Philip D. Morgan (Williamsburg, Va., 1989), 52 were drawn from the topics of politics, the economy, religion, and science and technology (that is, four of the twenty-three categories surveyed accounted for nearly half of the older books deemed worthy of inclusion in the volume).

7. See Perry Miller's *The New England Mind*, vol. 1, *The Seventeenth Century* (New York, 1939), and *The New England Mind*, vol. 2, *From Colony to Province* (Cambridge, Mass., 1953); and *Errand into the Wilderness* (Cambridge, 1956). Darrett B. Rutman, *Winthrop's Boston: Portrait of a Puritan Town, 1630–1649* (Chapel Hill, N.C., 1965). John Demos, "Notes on Life in Plymouth Colony," *WMQ* 3d ser., 22 (1965): 264–86. For a survey of New England Puritan historiography in the 1960s, see Michael McGiffert, "American Puritan Studies in the 1960s," *WMQ* 3d ser., 27 (1970): 36–67. The major social histories published in 1970s were Demos, *A Little Commonwealth: Family Life in Plymouth Colony* (New York, 1970); Philip J. Greven Jr., *Four Generations: Population, Land, and Family in Colonial Andover, Massachusetts* (Ithaca, N.Y., 1970); and Kenneth A. Lockridge, *A New England Town, The First Hundred Years: Dedham, Massachusetts, 1636–1736* (New York, 1970). Interestingly, in spite of their shared efforts to get away from history dominated by the ministerial elite, none of these studies depart from the declension model of early New England history.

8. Staughton Lynd, "Who Should Rule at Home? Dutchess County, New York, in the American Revolution," *WMQ* 3d ser., 18 (1961): 330–59. Lemisch called for a new history of the "inarticulate" in "The American Revolution Seen from the Bottom Up," in *Towards a New Past: Dissenting Essays in American History*, ed. Barton Bernstein (New York: 1968), 3–45. At the same time, his "Jack Tar in the Streets: Merchant Seamen in the Politics of Revolutionary America" provided an example of how such a history might be written; see *WMQ* 3d ser., 25 (1968): 371–407.

9. See Nash's autobiographical statement in Alfred F. Young, ed., *The American Revolution: Explorations in the History of American Radicalism* (DeKalb, Ill., 1976), 4. Lynd, for instance, was influenced by his stint teaching at Spellman College during the civil rights movement. See his *Living Inside Our Hope: A Steadfast Radical's Thoughts on Rebuilding the Movement* (Ithaca, N.Y., 1997), chap. 2.

10. For progressive histories of women, see especially Julia Cherry Spruill, *Women's Life and Work in Early America* (Chapel Hill, N.C., 1938), and Mary Beard, *Women as a Force in History: A Study in Traditions and Realities* (New York, 1946). A number of histories on "Negroes" in colonial America had appeared up to 1965: Lorenzo J. Greene, *The Negro in Colonial New England, 1620–1776*

(New York, 1942); Benjamin J. Quarles, *The Negro in the American Revolution* (Chapel Hill, N.C., 1961); and Thad W. Tate, *The Negro in Eighteenth-Century Williamsburg* (Williamsburg, Va., 1965). The Progressive historians of the colonial era had been largely uninterested in Native American history; see the essay by James Axtell "The Ethnohistory of Early America: A Review Essay," *WMQ* 3d ser., 35 (1978): 110–44, for the development of that interest after 1946.

11. Craven took his Ph.D. degree at Cornell in 1928, while Bridenbaugh (1936), Handlin (1940), and Morgan (1942) were all trained at Harvard. Boorstin was educated at Harvard, Oxford, and Yale but did not receive the equivalent of a Ph.D. until 1968 (when he earned a Litt. D. from Cambridge). This prosopography has been compiled with the help of *Directory of American Scholars* vol. 1, *History*, 5th ed. (New York, 1969). Gary B. Nash, *Quakers and Politics: Pennsylvania, 1681–1726* (Princeton, N.J., 1968); Jack P. Greene, *The Quest for Power: The Lower Houses of Assembly in the Southern Royal Colonies, 1689–1776* (Chapel Hill, N.C., 1963); Richard S. Dunn, *Puritans and Yankees: The Winthrop Dynasty of New England, 1630–1717* (Princeton, N.J., 1962).

12. Women earned 13% of the Ph.D. degrees in history awarded between 1930 and 1950, 10.4% from 1960 to 1969, 15.8% from 1970 to 1974, 26% from 1975 to 1980, 33% from 1981 to 1988, and 34.6% from 1989 to 1992. Recent years have shown a decline, with 20.8% in 1993 and 21.3% in 1995. See Carla Hesse, "Report on the Status and Hiring of Women and Minority Historians in Academia," *Perspectives: American Historical Association Newsletter*, 34, no. 3 (March 1996): 36; and [no author], "History Ph.D.'s Lose Edge in Latest NRC Survey," 35, no. 7 (October 1997): 3. In the 1930s the OAH had voted in Louise P. Kellogg (1930–31); in the 1940s, the AHA had chosen Nellie Neilson (1943). The next women to be selected would be Gerda Lerner in 1981–82 (OAH) and Natalie Zemon Davis in 1987 (AHA), a gap of fifty and forty-four years, respectively.

13. Nash, *Race, Class and Politics*, xv–xvi.

14. Ibid., xvi.

15. Ibid., xvi–xvii.

16. Nash, *Quakers and Politics*.

17. See also James T. Lemon and Gary B. Nash, "The Distribution of Wealth in Eighteenth-Century America," *Journal of Social History* 2 (1968): 1–24.

18. Gary B. Nash, *Class and Society in Early America* (Englewood Cliffs, N.J., 1970), 1, 3–4.

19. Gary B. Nash, *Red, White, and Black: The Peoples of Early America* (Englewood Cliffs, N.J., 1974), 1–2. The title played on that of Craven's recently published study, *White, Red and Black: The Seventeenth-Century Virginian* (Charlottesville, Va., 1971). Also see Nash, "The Image of the Indian in the Southern Mind," *WMQ* 3d scr., 29 (1972): 197–230.

20. Gary B. Nash, *The Urban Crucible: Social Change, Political Consciousness, and the Origins of the American Revolution* (Cambridge, Mass., 1979). See "Slaves and Slaveowners in Colonial Philadelphia," *WMQ* 3d ser., 30 (1973): 223–56; "The Transformation of Urban Politics, 1700–1764," *JAH* 60 (1973): 605–32; "The Failure of Female Factory Labor in Colonial Boston," *Labor History* 20 (1979): 165–88; "Urban Wealth and Poverty in Prerevolutionary America," *Journal of Interdisciplinary History* 4 (1976): 545–84; and "Social Change and the Growth of Prerevolutionary Urban Radicalism," in Young, ed., *The American Revolution*, 3–36.

21. See the review of *The Urban Crucible* by Raymond Mohl, *JAH* 67 (1980): 390–91.

22. Gary B. Nash, *Forging Freedom: the Formation of Philadelphia's Black Community, 1720–1840* (Cambridge, Mass., 1988); see also Thomas P. Slaughter, "From Slavery to 'Freedom': A Review Essay," *Pennsylvania Magazine of History and Biography* 113 (1989): 89–94.

23. Gary B. Nash, *Race and Revolution* (Madison, Wis., 1990); Gary B. Nash and Jean R. Soderlund, *Freedom by Degrees: Emancipation in Pennsylvania and Its Aftermath* (New York, 1991).

24. Gary B. Nash, "The Hidden History of Mestizo America," *JAH* 82 (1995): 950, 962. This theme is further developed in his *Forbidden Love,* due out in 1999.

25. Gary B. Nash, Julie Roy Jeffrey, et al., *The American People: Creating a Nation and a Society* (New York, 1986). It is currently in its fourth edition. The twelve-book series was published by Houghton Mifflin. It covers K–8 with variant Grade 4 and 6 volumes. Nash was the sole author of *American Odyssey: A History of Twentieth Century United States* published for high school students (Lake Forest, Ill., 1992).

26. Gary B. Nash, Charlotte Crabtree, and Ross E. Dunn, *History on Trial: Culture Wars and the Teaching of the Past* (New York, 1997), 156–60.

27. Lynne Cheney, "The End of History," *Wall Street Journal,* October 20, 1994. Also see Nash, Crabtree, and Dunn, *History on Trial,* 3–5.

28. See especially John Patrick Diggins, "The National History Standards," *American Scholar* 65 (1996): 495–522.

29. See Nash, Crabtree, and Dunn, *History on Trial,* as well as Nash, "Early American History and the National History Standards," *WMQ* 3d ser., 54 (1997): 579–600.

30. Young, ed., *The American Revolution.* Blacks, women and Indians (particularly blacks) are mentioned in a number of other essays, but the focus of all but those by Ira Berlin, Francis Jennings, and Joan Hoff Wilson is on struggles within the white community. This emphasis reflects the state of the field after almost a decade of New Left scholarship. For a recent call to return to consensus, see Arthur M. Schlesinger Jr., *The Disuniting of America* (New York, 1992), and a rejoinder by Lawrence W. Levine, *The Opening of the American Mind: Canons, Culture, and History* (Boston, 1996), esp. chap. 10.

31. Stephen Innes, *Labor in a New Land: Economy and Society in Seventeenth-Century Springfield* (Chapel Hill, N.C., 1988); Marcus Rediker, *Between the Devil and the Deep Blue Sea: Merchant Seamen, Pirates, and the Anglo-American Maritime World, 1700–1750* (New York, 1987); Sean Wilentz, *Chants Democratic: New York City and the Rise of the American Working Class, 1788–1850* (New York, 1984). Books by students that would fall into this category include Joyce Goodfriend, *Before the Melting Pot: Society and Culture in Colonial New York City, 1664–1730* (Princeton, N.J., 1992); Sharon V. Salinger, *"To Serve Well and Faithfully": Labor and Indentured Servants in Pennsylvania, 1682–1800* (New York, 1987); and Billy G. Smith, *The "Lower Sort": Philadelphia's Laboring People, 1750–1800* (Ithaca, N.Y., 1990).

32. Axtell, "Ethnohistory of Early America," 128. Another central early work, Francis Jennings's *The Invasion Within: Indians, Colonialism and the Cant of Conquest* (Chapel Hill, N.C., 1975), appeared the year after *Red, White, and Black.* Publishing trends in this field to 1989 can be followed in *Books about Early America: 2001 Titles,* ed. Ammerman and Morgan. Ethnohistorical methods shaped the works of Neal Salisbury, *Manitou and Providence: Indians, Europeans, and the Making of New England, 1500–1643* (New York, 1982); James Merrell, *The*

Indians' New World: Catabawas and Their Neighbors from European Contact through the Era of Removal (Chapel Hill, N.C., 1989); Daniel Richter, *The Ordeal of the Longhouse: Peoples of the Iroquois League in the Era of European Colonization* (Chapel Hill, N.C., 1992); Richard White, *The Middle Ground: Indians, Empires, and Republics in the Great Lakes Region, 1650–1815* (New York, 1991). Salisbury was among the first Ph.D. students trained by Gary Nash.

33. The essay by Philip D. Morgan in this volume treats these historiographical developments more extensively. The origins debate recently has been revisited in the January 1997 *WMQ.* Peter H. Wood, *Black Majority: Negroes in Colonial South Carolina from 1670 through the Stono Rebellion* (New York, 1974). Daniel H. Usner Jr., *Indians, Settlers, and Slaves in a Frontier Exchange Economy: The Lower Mississippi Valley before 1783* (Chapel Hill, N.C., 1992). Also see T. H. Breen and Stephen Innes, *"Myne Owne Ground": Race and Freedom on Virginia's Eastern Shore, 1640–1676* (New York, 1980); Allan Kulikoff, *Tobacco and Slaves: The Development of Southern Cultures in the Chesapeake, 1680–1800* (Chapel Hill, N.C., 1986); Philip D. Morgan, *Slave Counterpoint: Black Culture in the Eighteenth-Century Upper and Lower Souths* (Chapel Hill, N.C., 1998).

34. Nancy Cott, *The Bonds of Womanhood: "Women's Spheres" in New England, 1780–1835* (New Haven, Conn., 1977); Linda K. Kerber, *Women in the Republic: Intellect and Ideology in Revolutionary America* (Chapel Hill, N.C., 1980); Mary Beth Norton, *Liberty's Daughters: The Revolutionary Experience of American Women, 1750–1800* (Boston, 1980); and Laurel Thatcher Ulrich, *Good Wives: Image and Reality in the Lives of Women in Northern New England, 1650–1750* (New York, 1982). Carol F. Karlsen, *The Devil in the Shape of a Woman: Witchcraft in Colonial New England* (New York, 1987). The historiography of this early period is surveyed by Mary Beth Norton in "The Evolution of White Women's Experience in Early America," *AHR* 89 (1984): 593–619.

35. Mary Beth Norton, *Founding Mothers and Fathers: Gendered Power and the Forming of American Society* (New York, 1996), Cornelia Hughes Dayton, *Women before the Bar: Gender, Law, and Society in Connecticut, 1639–1789* (Chapel Hill, N.C., 1995), and Kathleen M. Brown, *Good Wives, Nasty Wenches, and Anxious Patriarchs: Gender, Race, and Power in Colonial Virginia* (Chapel Hill, N.C., 1996).

36. Ronald Hoffman, Mechal Sobel, and Fredrika J. Teute, eds., *Through a Glass Darkly: Reflections on Personal Identity in Early America* (Chapel Hill, N.C., 1997). Mary Beth Norton surveyed articles about women in three leading journals over the past twenty-five years, finding a remarkable rise in coverage of this topic in each. According to Norton, *WMQ*'s coverage rose from 5 articles in women's history in the 1970s to 12 in the 1980s and 8 in the years 1990–96; for the *JAH*, the figures were 6, 22, 16; and for the *AHR*, 7, 7, 21 (comment delivered at the annual meeting of the Organization of American Historians, San Francisco, 1997, in the session "The *WMQ*, 1972–1997: A Past into the Future").

37. Minority earning of the Ph.D. degree in history has shown "an absence of sustained improvement since 1975," according to a recent National Research Council Report summarized in Hesse, "Report," 36. The number of women reviewing books for the *WMQ* remained steady in 1960 (8%), 1970 (6.5%), 1980 (8.6%), and 1990 (8%), with an increase by the mid-1990s to 30% in 1995. For books on the history of the Americas (later divided into United States, Canada, and Latin America) in the *AHR*, the percentage of women reviewers rose from 3 in 1965 to 22 in 1995. For all books reviewed in the *JAH*, the comparable figures are 3% (1965) and 18% (1995). For both book reviewers and prize winners (see note following) the gender

of the writer or winner was determined on the basis of the first name; those (especially reviewers) who used initials only or whose first name was not readily identifiable were assigned to an "unknown" category. About 3% of all review writers fell into this category.

38. As of 1997, the OAH has had four white women and two African Americans (one of them a woman) as president; the AHA has had a total of five women but no additional blacks since Franklin held the post in 1979. The number of women book-prize winners also has risen. The Beveridge Prize (established in 1939) was given to a woman first in 1964; from 1985 through 1996, the prize has been given to women five times. Women won the Turner Prize in 1973, 1983, and 1997. The Bancroft Prize (established in 1948) has gone to women in 1956, 1960, 1963, 1973, 1981, 1982, 1985, 1986; and, in 1991, women won both of the Brancrofts bestowed in that year. Since its inception in 1917, the more popular Pulitzer Prize in history has been given to women in 1942, 1943, 1960, 1963, 1991, and 1995.

◩ *Sustaining Inequality*

Mary Beth Norton

"EITHER MARRIED OR TO BEE MARRIED": WOMEN'S LEGAL INEQUALITY IN EARLY AMERICA

IN THE FIRST treatise in English on the legal status of women, published in 1632, an anonymous lawyer signing himself "T. E." proclaimed in his first pages, "All of them [women] are understood either married or to bee married."[1] Contemplating the implications of that statement, which is simultaneously familiar and unfamiliar in its characterization of women's legal standing, has led me to question the thrust of previous scholarship and to formulate three new questions about the status of free women in the Anglo-American colonies.

T. E.'s declaration highlights the importance of marital status under the common law. Indeed, because of common-law rules the legal position of colonial "women" as a whole cannot be systematically analyzed. Rather, one must divide women, as T. E. did, into two groups: single (*femes sole*) and married (*femes covert*). To date, most scholarly discussions of colonial women's legal status have focused on *femes covert* and on a question first asked by Richard B. Morris in 1930: Did American wives in the seventeenth and eighteenth centuries enjoy more legal freedom than either their nineteenth-century descendants or their contemporaries who remained in England?[2] A number of historians have identified the ways in which lawmakers and judges at times failed to apply the full restraints of marriage law to female residents of the colonies.[3] Still, few have explored the full legal implications of marriage from a wife's perspective.[4] Thus, the first question not yet sufficiently examined in the historical literature: What were the practical consequences for a woman whose identity was subsumed by law into her husband's identity?

At the same time that T. E. distinguished the two sets of women, his singular phrasing—"either married or to bee married"—in effect linked rather than separated them. T. E.'s assertion that *femes sole* were defined by their marriageability implies that scholars have perhaps too readily accepted the notion that married and single women had widely disparate standings under the law. So, the second question: How different was the legal experience of single colonial women from that of their married counterparts?

The third query derives from combining the first two with the universality of T. E.'s statement. "All" women, he insisted, fit into these two categories.[5] Might, then, the significance of colonial wives' legal status extend beyond the courtroom to affect other aspects of their lives? Can echoes of wives' legal dependency be found in women's experiences elsewhere in colonial society?

Scholars now tend to concur that in the early years of settlement, when T. E. wrote his treatise, rules governing the activities of *femes covert* were treated more flexibly than they were in the eighteenth century, when colonial law became more formulaic and was applied more rigidly.[6] Accordingly, answers to these three questions can most profitably be sought in colonial courtrooms before 1670. An analysis of the first Anglo-American decades should reveal the conditions of women's standing during an era characterized by maximum possible freedom from legal restraints. In later years, women would have been subjected to further restrictions.

"Married"

Answering the first question about the practical consequences of coverture requires identifying the specifics of married women's status in early modern English law. Sir William Blackstone's words from the 1760s are those most commonly cited: "By marriage, the husband and wife are one person in law: that is, the very being or legal existence of the woman is suspended during the marriage, or at least is incorporated and consolidated into that of the husband: under whose wing, protection, and *cover*, she performs every thing. . . . Upon this principle, of an union of person in husband and wife, depend almost all the legal rights, duties, and disabilities, that either of them acquire by the marriage." More than a century earlier, T. E. also described the "identitie of person" of husband and wife after marriage. He remarked that a woman's personalty came absolutely to her husband when they wed, that her real estate became his to manage, that she could not make a will or contract with her husband, and that "it is seldom, almost never, that a marryed woman can have any action to use her writt onely in her owne name."[7]

One of the most immediate results of such dependent legal status was the relative absence of married women from the court records of colonial English America. Some striking numbers illustrate the point.[8] In a data set comprising nearly 2,400 Chesapeake civil suits (drawn from a universe of more than 5,900 total legal actions reported in published records), just 322 wives appeared as plaintiffs or defendants. Fewer than one third of them (99) came to court without their husbands. It might be assumed that the imbalanced sex ratio in the Chesapeake produced such remarkable results. But in New England similar patterns prevailed. In a sample of 340 civil cases (representing a universe of over 1,000 lawsuits) from Suffolk County, for example, just 56 wives appeared as litigants, only 7 of them alone. Or to look at the data in another way: wives composed less than two fifths of all female civil litigants in either New England or the Chesapeake, even though the vast majority of adult women in the colonies were married at any given time.[9]

That the paucity of married women acting independently in such cases resulted to a considerable extent from their status in English law is demonstrated when these examples are contrasted to similar data drawn from the published records of the New Amsterdam courts. There, married women acting alone comprised an overwhelming majority of female litigants: 83 percent of female litigants of known marital status were married. Also striking is the fact that it proved impossible to determine the marital status of a majority of the female litigants in the New Amsterdam courts: under the civil law, applied there as in the Netherlands, a woman's marital status did not so dramatically affect her access to the courts, and consequently clerks did not consistently record such biographical information. (In the Chesapeake, by contrast, only about 10% of all female civil litigants were of unknown marital status.)[10]

The presence of married Dutch women in the courts of New Amsterdam was in large part due to their traditional role in commerce in the Netherlands.[11] Even so, the contrasting rates of married women's participation in litigation in the Dutch and English colonies raise a question that can be best posed in counterfactual fashion. If common-law rules had not been applied, would English wives have had reason to sue or be sued in their own names? In other words, is there evidence of economic or other sorts of activities on their part in lawsuits filed by their husbands?

The answer is yes; and that response points to a significant piece of evidence allowing the assessment of the impact on women of the Anglo-American law of marriage. Because of the legal rules defining coverture, a wife had to rely on her spouse to file suits on her behalf or to defend her from legal attack. A man could fulfill that responsibility either as a sole litigant or as a party to a joint action.[12] But in either case, the need for her

husband's involvement meant that a woman lacked the capacity to act independently in the courts. And that suggests another question: Do surviving
records supply any evidence that wives and husbands did not always have
the same priorities with respect to women's interests? Again, the answer is
yes, although the evidence is more fragmentary.

Admittedly, most actions brought or defended against by husbands on
behalf of or in conjunction with their wives were suits for debt involving
the estates of their wives' previous husbands. Because of high mortality
rates in the Chesapeake, such civil actions were especially common there.[13]
Yet an appreciable number of case records show that a wife's own interests
could be at stake in the courtroom. Several times, for example, a male
trustee's failure to turn property over to a female orphan who had reached
maturity led that woman's new husband to file suit to obtain possession of
it. Conversely, a man whose wife unlawfully detained property from another was potentially liable for damages. In Plymouth in 1644, for instance,
Arthur Howland filed a successful claim against Robert Mendam, proving
that although Goody Mary Mendam had carried some items from England
for him, she "did not deliv[er] them, but sould them, and converted the
money to her owne use."[14]

Even more common was litigation revolving around work, especially
nursing and other healing activities, that wives had completed but for
which they had not been paid. One type of lawsuit merely requested
money due "for his Wifes Waiges" without specifying the nature of the
tasks that had been performed; others identified the labor at issue: "for the
washing of the linnen of the said Ellis by the plfs wife," "for my wifes attan-
dance of him and his wife in theire sickness."[15] Many such actions, as might
be expected, involved midwifery, wet nursing, or childbed nursing, not the
standard gatherings of women for childbirth itself but the extended care
required in complicated cases. In Maryland in 1654, for example, Thomas
Gregory sued David Thomas for eight weeks' pay due his wife, Anne, for
tending David's wife "whilst She lay in Child bed."[16]

Wives' healing activities were not confined solely to infants and parturi-
ent mothers. Women tended both women and men on their deathbeds,
cured "dangerously" ill menservants, and cared for men with sore legs (one
even "did chirurgery upon" such a leg). All this information was disclosed
in lawsuits brought by one man against another; women's names appeared
in the details, not in the forms of action.[17] In a 1663 Charles County, Maryland, suit, *Hugh O'Neale v. William Bowles*, "for the Cure" of the defendant, the sparse case record does not reveal the involvement of O'Neale's
wife Mary as the healer in question. Rather, that crucial piece of information emerges from the context of a series of five lawsuits dating back to the
fall of 1661, all revolving around her medical activities. Two were filed by

the widow Mistress Mary Doughty Vanderdonck before her marriage to O'Neale: she sued one man for payment for her work in curing his servants of sore legs and sore mouths (they probably had scurvy) and also sought compensation from a planter to whom she had "administred Phisick." After their wedding, Hugh O'Neale appeared for her in two lawsuits that also stemmed from her medical practice, and she herself asked for damages from a man who defamed her by accusing her of poisoning a female patient. Were it not for this extensive litigious history, O'Neale's 1663 suit against Bowles could not be recognized for what it is: the sixth in a string of similar cases deriving from the work of an active female healer.[18]

Although seventeenth-century colonial legal records contain some lawsuits brought by women like Mistress Vanderdonck prior to her second marriage, suits in which it is obvious that women's activities or interests were themselves at issue,[19] the common-law rules of marriage and their consequences for the standard form of civil suits serve as a barrier to historians seeking to uncover married women's economic roles. Had it not been for the detailed record keeping of some court clerks, it would be impossible today to identify certain cases as involving the work of women. The surviving records of many jurisdictions (e.g., the often-used published volumes of Essex County materials) are frequently too laconic and fragmentary to permit this sort of analysis. In such documents, a clerk's sparse notation— John Doe v. James Roe, debt, judgment for plaintiff—and the absence of file papers may well conceal the involvement of Jane Doe or Mary Roe. Even the form John and Jane Doe v. James and Mary Roe does not reveal much because, as already indicated, many such suits derived from debts owed by or to women's previous husbands.

The key point is not the problems the rules of coverture cause for twentieth-century historians but rather the difficulties those rules created for seventeenth-century wives. Sometimes, it is true, wives could use the common law to their own advantage, cleverly employing their subordination to hide from civil suits or even from monetary penalties for criminal behavior.[20] Yet at base, wives' submerged legal identity largely denied them access to the fruits of their own labor and enriched their husbands. Indeed, not only did husbands legally own or control their spouses' property, they also occasionally—when men purchased maidservants in order to marry them—literally owned their wives as well. How much say did female servants have in such transactions? No surviving source supplies an answer to that question.[21]

And consider, for example, lawsuits brought by men for their wives' work as wet nurses. No more intimate or personal labor could be imagined; moreover, wet nursing could be carried out only by women who had recently given birth and who were also suckling their own babies (or who had just lost or weaned them). Men received large sums for this essential service: among the fees at issue in such lawsuits were barrels of corn, hogsheads of tobacco, and livestock. George Willis, an ex-servant in Virginia, earned income from his wife's lactation over an extended period. In April 1642 he requested payment for her care of a baby whose parents had both died more than a year earlier. After authorizing the compensation, the county court ordered the baby, who was still nursing, moved elsewhere. Presumably, Goody Willis was again pregnant (it was thought imperative for a pregnant woman to cease nursing a previous child), because a year later George was back in court once more, this time claiming that he was due "one heifer with Calfe a payre of shoes and stockings and a shirt Cloath" for his wife's wet nursing the baby of yet another deceased mother.[22]

It is impossible to know the internal dynamics of these colonial households and to determine whether husbands such as George Willis allowed their wives to dispose of any or all of the income they earned from wet nursing or other work. Some seventeenth-century men did give their wives property for their own personal use or respected their claims to inherited estates.[23] Yet probably more common was the attitude of the Maryland planter who in 1659 replied to a debt suit by insisting that the sum he owed had been partially repaid "by his wife for helping the sayd Plantives wife to wash and milke." The Marylander's proprietary posture toward his wife's labor was equivalent to that of Humphrey Chadbourne of Maine, who at first refused to sell an animal he described as "his wives horse and for her riding" but who then could not resist an attractive offer from a wealthy purchaser.[24]

Another instructive example comes from New Haven in the mid-1650s. Goodwife Elizabeth Wheeler owned a cow, a ewe, and their offspring, a fact that her husband Thomas repeatedly acknowledged to neighbors. After Edward Parker inquired about buying a three-year-old steer, for instance, Thomas responded, "It was none of his, but his wives." Parker recounted that "Goodwife Wheeler said to her husband, You must not sell my steere, so he went away and left it." Likewise, when Robert Hill sought to purchase a ewe, Thomas said it "was his wives," and that deal too fell through. Yet Thomas killed and sold a calf born to his wife's cow; and when she "asked her husband for the money it was sould for," he inquired in return, "Who must paye for wintering the cow"? Elizabeth's reply— "Her milke will paye for that"—hints at an ongoing marital dispute over the distribution of the costs and benefits of her separate ownership of the animals, especially since another neighbor reported that Thomas had asked on a different occasion about who would pay for wintering the steer. After Thomas's death, Elizabeth complained that her cow and ewe had been inventoried as part of his estate, rather than having been recognized as hers by the court-appointed appraisers. Moreover, under questioning from the justices, she disclosed what had eventually happened to the steer Thomas refused to sell to Edward Parker: "it was killed, and they paid rates [taxes] with it; she said also ther was a cow of that stock sold for wampome, wch her husband also had to use aboute his occasions."[25]

The experiences of Elizabeth Chadbourne and Elizabeth Wheeler illustrate the crucial importance of men's ultimate control over their wives' possessions. Even when husbands admitted that their spouses had separate property, they could still legally dispose of that property when it was in their interest to do so. Humphrey Chadbourne gave in to pressure from a high-status neighbor who coveted his wife's horse and who sweetened the deal by throwing in a pair of pistols as part of the transaction. Thomas Wheeler had to pay taxes and needed funds for "his occasions" (that is, his daily business affairs). He repeatedly complained about having to bear the cost of wintering his wife's livestock and undoubtedly convinced himself that he was taking no more income from the offspring of her cow than was properly due him. Goody Chadbourne's response to her husband's sale of her riding horse is unknown. Goody Wheeler tried to protect her property during her marriage, although she did not always succeed. And in her widowhood she had to contend with appraisers who assumed that her animals had belonged to her husband, as well as with judges whose response to her claim to ownership of the beasts was not recorded by the New Haven town clerk.

Another widow, the Marylander Mistress Katherine Hebden, complained not about her husband's handling of her property during their marriage but about his disposition of it in his will. Mistress Hebden, whose work as a healer in the 1640s is nearly as well documented as that of Mistress Mary Vanderdonck O'Neale a decade and a half later, formally challenged her husband's will in court. In 1647, Thomas Hebden (who was evidently childless) drafted a will leaving everything outright to his wife, but two years later, shortly before his death, he changed his mind, allotting her only a life interest in the estate. At her death, he provided, she could dispose of just one third of it. He named trustees not only to supervise her handling of the estate but also eventually to disperse the other two thirds for religious or charitable purposes. Mistress Hebden was furious when she learned about the new will. According to a witness, she "complaine[d] to her Husband for that hee had made away the Estate wch hee had with her, and of his unkindnes to her therein." She tried to persuade him to destroy his 1649 testament; but although Thomas initially agreed to do so, he did not fulfill his promise. She failed in her attempt to overturn his second will, but nevertheless—according to the trustees, who sued to try to stop her—"pr[e]tended power to dispose of the said Estate and had disposed and wasted part thereof."[26]

Elizabeth Wheeler and Katherine Hebden thus explicitly opposed their spouses' decisions concerning their property, and it is hard to imagine that Goody Chadbourne remained silent when she learned that her husband had sold her horse. Other civil actions exposed similar conflicts between spouses over the control of a wife's property or the pursuit of her interests.[27] Sometimes a certain amount of reading between the lines is required to tease out the implications of the lawsuits in question. Often, as in *O'Neale v. Bowles*, the cases can be fully understood only within the context of other legal actions. Three particularly revealing complaints were filed by Maryland women after their husbands' deaths; each involved events that had occurred during their spouses' lifetimes.

In October 1658 the Maryland widow Mistress Jane Fenwick sued William Boreman for the value of two horses "belonging to the plfs owne proper estate" that had been lent to him (by whom is not recorded: perhaps her husband?). She claimed that the horses had been "heated & killed" through his "carelessnes" while he was using them to free two mired heifers owned by his employer. Boreman replied to the charge by disclosing that Mistress Fenwick's husband Cuthbert (who had died more than three years earlier) had been "in company with" him while he was working to free the heifers. Cuthbert Fenwick had never filed suit in the matter, and his widow lost the case.[28]

In September 1656, Mistress Jane Eltonhead, Jane Fenwick's widowed sister-in-law, filed suit against Edmund Scarborough, who, she claimed, had never supplied her with three servants she had paid for six years earlier, during her marriage. Her husband William failed to pursue such a claim prior to his death in March 1655, but Mistress Eltonhead energetically sought compensation once she was widowed, going to court four more times before her death in 1659 and eventually winning partial repayment.[29]

At the Charles County Court session of September 1661, the widow Joan Mitchell took the unusual step of filing four simultaneous lawsuits against high-status neighbors she said had defamed her by terming her a witch. Her targets included a local minister, the Reverend Francis Doughty, and his son Michael—the father and brother of Mistress Mary Vanderdonck O'Neale. Two years earlier, Joan's husband, Thomas Mitchell, had asked for the recording of two depositions specifying "abusful reproaches" of the same sort against his wife by another high-status neighbor, but he did not pursue a formal case against his wife's detractors.[30]

These civil actions shared three significant characteristics: first, a wife was wronged during her marriage; second, her husband did little or nothing (at least nothing evident in the court records) to right that wrong; and third, after her husband's death, when she was at last free to act on her own, the widow vigorously pursued her own interests in court. The logical inference is that in each case husband and wife had disagreed during their marriage about the utility of seeking a legal remedy for the wrong, that the husband had refused his wife's request to file suit in the matter, and that, once she regained *feme sole* status, the woman felt strongly enough about the issue to press her claim in the courts.

The three female plaintiffs met with mixed results; only Jane Eltonhead was even partly successful. Jane Fenwick lost, probably because her husband's presence in the swamp and his subsequent lack of protest indicated his implicit consent to Boreman's treatment of the horses. Three of Joan Mitchell's suits were dismissed for lack of evidence, after which she dropped the fourth. Yet her dramatic action—taken within a few months of her husband's death—suggests that she was far more troubled by the slander than he and furthermore that he had hesitated to challenge publicly the leaders of Charles County society. He had gone no further than asking the court clerk to record two depositions; his wife, by contrast, stung by the widespread gossip and movingly describing to the court her deep distress at the loss of her "good name," took swift and decisive action to halt the "table talke" about her supposed witchery. Even though she lost her cases, she may have succeeded in her aim: for six more years she continued to participate in Charles County litigation but without any indication of further slanderous remarks being spread about her.

In other instances as well Thomas Mitchell disregarded his wife's interests—indeed, her legal rights. Under the common law, the one legal occasion on which a wife had to be consulted independently of her husband was when he wanted to sell or transfer real estate, because of the transaction's potential impact on her dower right in his estate after his death. In England, spouses engaged in a complex procedure called "fine and recovery" in order to obtain a wife's approval for such sales. Colonial jurisdictions dispensed with the technicalities but generally enforced a rule requiring a wife to consent to the sale in question, through her signature on the deed, her public acknowledgment in court, or her agreement expressed during a separate examination by the proper officials. The widowed Joan Mitchell appears to have learned about this requirement when in March 1662/3 Humphrey Attwicks, wishing to clear his title to property he planned to resell, summoned her to court to acknowledge her consent to his 1659 purchase of land from her husband. She did as Attwicks requested, but then four months later filed suit against another man who had also bought land from her husband, seeking to recover her dower right in the property. At least twice, then, Thomas Mitchell, who had also failed to take decisive steps to protect his wife from widespread slander, neglected to fulfill the legal requirement of obtaining her consent to land sales.[31]

Joan Mitchell did not succeed in establishing her dower right, but other women did. In both Essex and Suffolk Counties, Massachusetts, widows persuaded courts to allot them a one-third life interest in real estate their husbands had sold during their marriages without their formal consent. A Maryland widow likewise convinced the Kent County Court that her third husband had illegally leased a plantation belonging to her child from an earlier marriage, thereby regaining custody of the land and its improvements. And one Chesapeake wife, too ill to travel to court but nonetheless resolute, informed the men dispatched to obtain her consent to her husband's transfer of three hundred acres that she "utterly refuseth to acknowledge the said sale or to signe the Covenant." Probably more common, however, was the experience of another female Marylander, who announced when she arrived in court in October 1658 that "she will not voluntarily & freely acknowledge a fine" but who "after a little space" returned and indicated that "shee is willing & doth freely of her owne accord" consent to her husband's sale of the property.[32]

What can be concluded from this analysis about the impact of the law of coverture on colonial wives? Clearly, the cost to married women of their dependent legal status was significant. Their husbands controlled their property, their earnings, even their ability to seek legal redress for wrongs done to them. Although husbands might acknowledge their wives' ownership of separate property, men's priorities for the use of that property ultimately prevailed. Recall Goody Wheeler's steer slaughtered to pay the taxes and her cow sold to meet daily expenses. Recall, moreover, the men who, like Thomas Mitchell, sold real estate without obtaining their wives' separate consent. It was the *purchasers* of such property, not the sellers, who generally insisted on the fulfillment of legal requirements: they wanted to ensure that their titles were clear and uncontestable.[33] Further, husbands' legal (as perhaps opposed to actual) domination of their wives was so complete as to raise the second question formulated at the beginning of this essay. Did the definition of coverture extend to women who were still unmarried?

"To Bee Married"

More remarkable than the absence of wives as litigants from colonial court records is the absence of female litigants of *any* description. More widows than wives appeared in civil suits, largely because of their activities in settling their dead husbands' estates; even so and even in the Chesapeake, where high mortality rates produced many widows, fewer than 500 widows participated in civil litigation in the sample drawn to represent nearly

6,000 civil cases. In New England, fewer than 200 widows participated in a sample representing more than 2,000 cases. The figures for the never-married are even smaller: single women composed only about 20 percent of all female litigants in both regions (whereas widows made up between 50% and 60% of that group) and a minuscule proportion of litigants as a whole.[34]

What accounts for the relative absence of single women from the ranks of civil litigants? Here technical legal status was not at issue, but other factors did come into play. In the Chesapeake, for example, the imbalanced sex ratio meant that many of those widows remarried quickly—so quickly, indeed, that some never appeared in court as *femes sole* at all but in succeeding court sessions (three to six months apart) were married to different men. Accordingly, most women made only one or two appearances as *femes sole* before their new husbands assumed the responsibility of managing their previous spouses' estates. For their part, never-married women throughout the colonies had the legal right to come to court on their own but at the same time had little reason to do so: mostly very young, they lived as dependents in the households of their parents or masters and mistresses and rarely owned property or needed to pay or collect debts.[35]

Still, the phenomenon is striking. Some young women did have grievances that required a judicial resolution, a fact evident from the details of suits filed by their new husbands. It appears, accordingly, that they did not think of going to court by themselves prior to their weddings but instead waited until they had married men who could represent their interests.[36] Although young men also rarely filed lawsuits (especially against fathers, step-fathers, or the estates of either), when they did so, they did not ask others to appear with them in court: they pursued their complaints in person.[37]

Never-married women were not just absent from the courtroom as civil litigants: they rarely appeared as witnesses either, even in lawsuits in which their own interests were at issue.[38] The only appreciable number of young *femes sole* who entered colonial courtrooms in any role other than that of accused criminal—usually in fornication or bastardy prosecutions—came as the victims of crimes.[39] Such victims were primarily maidservants who complained of abuse by their masters and mistresses, but they could also be young free women who had been assaulted or sexually molested. Even in such cases the women themselves seldom came into court on their own in-itiative. Information about the ill treatment of maidservants, for example, emerged not from cases in which the servants stepped forward with formal charges but rather from prosecutions of the young women for such offenses as running away. An accused maidservant would then describe the abuses to which she had been subjected as explanations or justifications for her behavior. For their part, free daughters tended to be represented by their fathers rather than speaking for themselves. The pattern is unmistakable: although no law prevented these *femes sole* from filing their own complaints, they usually did not do so. Young men, even servants, showed no comparable hesitation.[40]

The same was true even of *femes covert*: if victimized by crime, they rarely approached court officials independently but instead relied on their husbands (or occasionally their fathers) to report the offense. So in western Massachusetts in 1658, Thomas Roote told a local magistrate that Robert Bartlett had hit his wife "with a long stick to her great prejudice"; and in New Haven six years later, Thomas Morris accused John Brookes of "throwing downe his wife &c & makeing great disturbance." A woman whose husband refused to take such legal steps on her behalf was, like one Goody Fancy of New Haven in 1646, out of luck: when William Fancy resisted telling the authorities about his wife's employer's repeated sexual assaults on her, she too kept silent for many months. In the end, when the story finally came out because of a remark she made to a third party, she and her husband were whipped for their failure to report the crimes in timely fashion.[41] Only when their own husbands had abused them—and thus could not be expected to speak on the wives' behalf—were married women likely to complain directly to the authorities.[42]

Similar patterns held for witnesses as well. Assessing the proportion of testimony offered by female witnesses is difficult because clerks in many jurisdictions did not systematically note the names of witnesses in either civil or criminal cases. Yet where that information is available, the evidence is clear: women of all ages and marital statuses were much less likely than men to be called as witnesses in any sort of court proceeding. New Haven's published court records (both colony and town) are particularly full, so this phenomenon can be readily examined for that jurisdiction. Of approximately 150 civil cases in which witnesses were called, women appeared in fewer than one third (46). And of more than 200 criminal prosecutions in which witnesses testified, women appeared in only about one quarter (44). Furthermore, the female witnesses were more likely than not the sole members of their sex to testify in a given case, whereas most male witnesses appeared in groups of two or more.[43]

A conclusion that elides the legal significance of the *feme sole/feme covert* distinction thus appears unavoidable. At a fundamental level, it did not matter in the courts whether women were married or single: Men spoke on behalf of women in legal matters even when the law did not require them to do so, and when presented with a choice, men (both officials and litigants) preferred male over female witnesses. Inside the realm of the courts, all women, not just wives, were largely silenced.[44]

Outside the Courtrooms

The common law of marriage accomplished the goal of subordinating wives to their husbands by, in effect, erasing a wife's legal persona, a strategy with serious adverse consequences for single women as well. In theory, subordination does not require such erasure; colonial servants, for example, were unquestionably subordinate to their masters, yet a servant's legal identity was not obliterated in the same fashion as was that of a wife. In assessing the relationship of wives' legal status and women's overall standing in colonial society, therefore, the two can usefully be distinguished, thus differentiating between women's subordination in general and the particular *legal* form that subordination took. Finding elsewhere the erasure evident in the law of marriage thus discloses the impact of wives' legal status on other aspects of women's existence.

The following examples point to the significance of wives' legal status in the religious realm—perhaps the one area of early American life in which women were formally viewed as both equal to and independent of men. Historians studying women's role in colonial religion have paid little if any attention to wives' legal status, yet these incidents imply the relevance of common-law definitions even in such a seemingly disparate context. They thus supply suggestive evidence that Anglo-American marriage law affected women in a variety of hitherto unrecognized ways.[45]

The first example involves the erasure of wives' independent religious identity. In autumn 1644, the residents of the new town of Wenham, Massachusetts (then recently created from a part of Salem), engaged in a process repeated many times in seventeenth-century New England: organizing their church.[46] The minister, the Reverend John Fiske, kept detailed notes of the discussions that ensued. In the context of a lengthy debate about the church's decision to ask prospective female members to give public accounts of the state of their souls (a potentially contentious matter since many congregations excused them from that requirement), a question arose as to which people present had the capacity to object to the newly formulated policy. The issue was, in short, who should be regarded as the founding members of the new church? Although Fiske's notes do not say so explicitly, it can be inferred that the official document releasing church members from their obligation to Salem (known as a "dismissal") had listed only men by name. After a consensus insisting on public examinations of faith for both sexes had apparently been reached, the men were polled first. Then the congregation's leaders asked for objections from "any of the sisters present, the wives of those who were dismissed from Salem being of the church there and conceived to be dismissed with their husbands (as Mr. [Edward] Norris and Mr. [Samuel] Sharp [the Salem elders] conceived because women are supposed to go with their husbands)."

The matter, then, seemed simple enough: the Wenham husbands had been properly authorized to form a new church, and their wives were automatically encompassed in the dismissal document, just as they would have been had it been a legal action of some sort. Therefore, in December, when Joan White asked Elder Sharp to be formally dismissed from Salem so that she could join the Wenham congregation, he replied, in accordance with his guiding assumption, "that he and the church looked at her and the other sisters as already dismissed." Yet Fiske recorded that the question caused "some agitation" among the Wenham "brethren," for whom Sister White's petition raised an intriguing dilemma. White's husband had not joined the Salem church, the men realized: so how could Salem's dismissal "reach to these sisters whose husbands were not members?" Not only that: someone pointed out that "these sisters did not join in that request at first"; and another man indicated that "for some reasons" of their own two other women were "not yet free"—that is, uncertain of whether they should commune with the new congregation. After some discussion, the church dispatched two men to speak to "such sisters as do not, or have not desired it [that is, membership in the Wenham congregation]" and to ask them to declare themselves "pro or con, and give their answer unto the church." Both the reluctant women then expressed their doubts about the proceedings, and the Wenham church decided to consult the Salem elders.

In response to the puzzled inquiries, Samuel Sharp and Edward Norris explained that the Salem church had intended to dismiss everyone who wanted to be dismissed, and that those whose names had been omitted from the earlier document had only to ask for separate dismissals, which would routinely be granted. That Joan White did, and she was formally admitted to the Wenham congregation in April 1645. The other two women continued to hesitate.

This tale reveals far more than some of the complex negotiations that could surround the establishment of a new Massachusetts congregation; it also exposes the unstated assumptions that guided men's thinking about women's lack of independent standing in the community. Wives went with their husbands; it was as straightforward as that. Yet as Sister Joan White's case showed, such an assumption was not straightforward at all. Not all wives could automatically be subsumed into their husbands' religious identity. Because a wife could be a church member although her husband was not, the common-law rules did not accurately apply to religion, despite men's tendency to think in those terms.

The second example, which occurred in Rhode Island in early 1638, involved a young couple, Joshua and Jane Verin, raising different issues but ones no less bound up with wives' legal status.[47] Roger Williams, the founder of the tiny, religiously tolerant colony, had ordered that "no man should be molested for his conscience." Joshua Verin, Williams reported to Massachusetts Bay's leader, John Winthrop, "refused to heare the word with us," and the authorities "molested him not," in accordance with their principles. Yet Jane Verin, whom Williams described as "modest and gracious," resisted her husband's "ungodlines," preferring to attend religious services frequently. Joshua responded to his wife's piety with what Williams called "furious blowes" that endangered her life, treating her "tyrannically and brutishly." Both Jane and the community endured the beatings for what Williams termed a "long" period, but finally Joshua Verin was called to account for his actions in a meeting of the colony's governing body, composed of all male household heads.

There one of their number, William Arnold, declared that when he had agreed to Williams's policy of toleration, "he never intended it should extend to the breach of any ordinance of God, such as the subjection of wives to their husbands." When another man responded, "[I]f they should restrain their wives, etc., all the women in the country would cry out of them," Arnold replied, "Did you pretend to leave the Massachusetts, because you would not offend God to please men, and would you now break an ordinance and commandment of God to please women?" Vigorously defending Joshua Verin, he pointed out that penalizing Verin "was against their own order, for Verin did that he did out of conscience; and their order was, that no man should be censured for his conscience."

In recounting this story, both John Winthrop and the Reverend William Hubbard, one of New England's first historians, revealed that they sided with Arnold. Winthrop wrote of Arnold's "good solid reasons," and Hubbard declared that his position reflected "the very light of nature, and dictates of right reason" as well as "the express word of God." Even the Rhode Islanders—people widely known for their interest in attending "all religious meetings, though never so often, or though private, upon the week days"—did not adopt the solution some proposed, which was to divorce Jane and Joshua and thereby allow her to find another husband who would respect her piety. Instead, they simply disfranchised Joshua; as Williams put it, they "discard[ed] him from our Civill Freedome." The official order held out to Verin the possibility of reinstatement should he change his mind.

Thus, in Providence in 1638 wifely subjection and religious freedom clashed directly—and the former won. Confronted with a wife whose religious beliefs led her to defy her husband, even the most tolerant of all the New England colonies opted for maintaining the marriage and imposing on the offending husband only a symbolic penalty. Clearly, John Winthrop and William Hubbard were not alone in their belief that William Arnold correctly analyzed the proper solution to the problems in the Verin household. When Joshua's conscience conflicted with Jane's, his *had* to prevail, despite the fact that hers was more fully in accord with that of the colony's leaders.

Two decades later in Maryland, religion and marriage clashed in a different way. In October 1658 the Catholic priest Francis Fitzherbert was accused of several violations of Maryland's 1649 Act for Religious Toleration. Among other offenses, he was said to have threatened to excommunicate Thomas Gerard, a Catholic, if Gerard did not force his Protestant wife and children to attend Catholic services. Gerard, unlike Joshua Verin, chose to allow his wife freedom to practice her own religious beliefs and to extend that freedom to their children as well. Maryland's leaders signaled their acquiescence in Gerard's stance by filing charges against the meddling priest.[48]

Two aspects of the Gerard and Verin incidents link them inextricably. First, each raised the question of the extent of a husband's authority over his wife, and in each case the husband's interpretation was upheld. Thomas Gerard chose not to impose his religious beliefs on his wife; Joshua Verin did the opposite. Both were confirmed in their decisions by local officials, who declined to interfere in the marital relationships. Second, both incidents occurred in colonies with formal policies of toleration, thus implying that in colonies without such protections wives probably had little or no recourse against husbands who asked them to violate their consciences. Precisely such an instance surfaced in a 1646 New Haven prosecution, when Mistress Lucy Brewster disclosed that she opposed making public contributions to the local church, declaring that "it was as going to masse or going up to the high alter." Asked by a female friend why she then had complied with the custom, Mistress Brewster replied, "because her husband had comanded her." The guiding principle was therefore always the same: a husband's will prevailed. If he gave his wife religious freedom, fine; if he did not, that was his decision, and the authorities would not intervene on her behalf.[49]

All three examples, admittedly, pertain to wives rather than to single or widowed women, and two of the three involved some sort of action by secular authorities. Can more instances of similar thinking be found in church records? Were the same assumptions that wives should be subject to their husbands in religious matters made about daughters and their fathers as well? The answers to such questions lie not in legal documents but rather in the records of church proceedings kept by such clergymen as John Fiske.

Consequently, examinations of women's legal status in the Anglo-American colonies must, on the one hand, go beyond the hitherto easy distinction between *feme covert* and *feme sole* and, on the other, move outside the courtroom in the search for answers. Seventeenth-century women's dependence on men extended far beyond the legal confines of coverture and far outside the courtroom walls. Although no law prevented single women from acting independently in the courts, few did so, with the limited exception of widows forced to settle the estates of their dead husbands. Women and men both expected that men would speak for women of different ages and marital statuses in a variety of settings. Even in matters of religion and individual conscience and even in colonies known for their religious toleration, wives (as the Salem church elders remarked) were "supposed to go with their husbands." Some men, like Thomas Gerard, might choose not to exercise the authority they gained from what William Arnold termed "an ordinance and commandment of God," but that was their choice. Not only were seventeenth-century Anglo American wives subordinated to husbands, their independent identities were literally erased from society's consciousness. The consequences of that erasure for all women were momentous.

Notes

1. T. E., *The Lawes Resolutions of Womens Rights; or, the Lawes Provision for Woemen* (London, 1632), 6. T. E. and this article refer only to free women; colonial law defined enslaved and indentured women quite differently.

2. Richard B. Morris, *Studies in the History of American Law, with Special Reference to the Seventeenth and Eighteenth Centuries* (New York, 1930). See also Mary R. Beard, *Woman as Force in History* (New York, 1946); and Roger Thompson, *Women in Stuart England and America: A Comparative Study* (London and Boston, 1974). A critique of Morris is Marylynn Salmon, "The Legal Status of Women in Early America: A Reappraisal," *Law and History Review* 1 (1983): 129–51.

3. See, for example, Joan Gundersen and Gwen Gampel, "Married Women's Legal Status in Eighteenth-Century New York and Virginia," *WMQ* 3d ser., 39 (1982): 114–34.

4. A recent exception is Deborah A. Rosen, "Women and Justice in Colonial New York: Examining the Practical Reality of Common Law Restraints" (paper presented at the Columbia University Seminar on Early American History and Culture, New York, May 1997). One of the few published works of historical scholarship to address this question in the same sense I pose it is Carole Shammas, "Early American Women and Control over Capital," in *Women in the Age of the American Revolution,* ed. Ronald Hoffman and Peter Albert (Charlottesville, Va., 1989), 134–54. By surveying the value of property owned by decedents and the value of men's bequests to wives and daughters (as opposed to sons), Shammas demonstrates the extent to which colonial women were precluded by their legal and social status from exercising much control over property, thus revealing the severely negative financial impact of their standing as *femes covert* (or *femes covert* to be).

5. But of course they did not. Widows, who *had been* married, were anomalies in his schema. See my discussion of this point in *Founding Mothers and Fathers:*

Gendered Power and the Forming of American Society (New York, 1996), chap. 3.

6. See Marylynn Salmon, *Women and the Law of Property in Early America* (Chapel Hill, N.C., 1986); and Cornelia Hughes Dayton, *Women before the Bar: Gender, Law, and Society in Connecticut, 1639–1789* (Chapel Hill, N.C., 1995). Gundersen and Gampel (n. 3 above) date the decline of women's relative independence several decades later than does Dayton, though noting the same trend. An exception is Laurel Thatcher Ulrich, who has stressed married women's relative freedom from legal restraints as late as the early nineteenth century. See Ulrich, *Good Wives: Image and Reality in the Lives of Women in Northern New England, 1650–1750* (New York, 1982), chap. 2; and *A Midwife's Tale: The Life of Martha Ballard Based on Her Diary, 1785–1812* (New York, 1990); compare Mary Beth Norton, "Eighteenth-Century American Women in Peace and War: The Case of the Loyalists," *WMQ* 3d ser., 33 (1976): 386–409.

7. William Blackstone, in *Commentaries on the Laws of England* (Oxford, 1764–69), 1:430, as cited in Salmon, *Women and the Law of Property*, 200, n.1; and T. E., *Lawes Resolutions of Womens Rights*, 119, 204 (see, in general, pp. 79–90, 116–229).

8. These data sets were created for Norton, *Founding Mothers and Fathers;* see Appendix, pp. 409–10, for a description of the sampling and coding methods.

9. The percentages are as follows: wives made up 31% of female Chesapeake plaintiffs and 42% of female Chesapeake defendants; 31% of female New England plaintiffs and 38% of female New England defendants.

10. The percentage in the text represents 63 of 76 female civil litigants; the marital status of 89 such women in New Amsterdam could not be ascertained.

11. See Linda Biemer, *Women and Property in Colonial New York: The Transition from Dutch to English Law, 1643–1727* (Ann Arbor, Mich., 1983).

12. I developed the term *passive participant* to describe the wife's role in the first sort of lawsuit and the phrase *legal couple* to describe the second. These definitions apply only to cases in which the evidence makes it clear that the matter in dispute pertained solely to the wife (omitting, for example, cases in which both were defamed or were responsible for running up a debt). In the many cases in which full information is not available it was impossible to make such distinctions about the impetus for the suit. Even so, the evidence is sufficiently substantial to be highly suggestive. As reported in Norton, *Founding Mothers and Fathers*, 84, more than 80% of colonial civil suits involving wives included their husbands as well, thus fulfilling the common-law rules.

13. For example, *County Court Records of Accomack-Northampton, Virginia, 1640–1645*, ed. Susie M. Ames (Charlottesville, Va., 1973), 2:68, 183–84, 186–87, 198. A particularly complex suit of this sort is *Archives of Maryland*, ed. William Hand Browne et al. (Baltimore, 1883–1972), 49:78, 80–81, 87, 89–90, 95, 115, 120, 146, 170, 192, 245. Cases in which both plaintiff and defendant were settling estates of their wives' previous husbands were not uncommon: for example, *Archives of Maryland*, 60:500; *County Court Records of Accomack-Northampton*, 2:455–56.

14. Quotation: *Records of the Colony of New Plymouth in New England*, ed. Nathaniel B. Shurtleff and David Pulsifer (Boston, 1855–61), 20:77–78. Suits for property detained from wives: *Records of the Colony and Plantation of New Haven, 1638–1649*, ed. Charles J. Hoadly (Hartford, Conn., 1857), 1:142; *Province and Court Records of Maine*, ed. Charles Thornton Libby and Robert E. Moody (Portland, Maine, 1928–47), 2:47; *Archives of Maryland*, 41:74–75. See also suits by physicians for wives' unpaid medical bills: *Records of . . . New Plymouth*, 7:84; *Province and Court Records of Maine*, 2:168.

15. *Archives of Maryland,* 54:451, 4:223, 54:417.

16. Ibid., 10:403. See also 41:179–80, 249, 54:503; *County Court Records of Accomack-Northampton,* 2:269–70, 426–27.

17. Quotations: *Archives of Maryland,* 60:248, 4:268. Also 53:85, 92–93, 190–91, 605–6; 54:230, 466–67, 41:163.

18. This history may be traced in *Archives of Maryland,* 53:145–49, 215, 229–31, 240–41, 248, 261–63, 329, 367. Nowhere is there any indication that Hugh O'Neale had any medical competence. Another high-status female healer in Maryland whose activities are traceable because of her movement between marriage (when her husband filed suits on her behalf) and widowhood is Mistress Katherine Hebden; *Archives of Maryland,* 4:268, 359, 400–401, 10:122, 415. See also *Records and Files of the Quarterly Courts of Essex County Massachusetts,* ed. George F. Dow (Salem, Mass., 1911–21), 2:226–32; 3:298.

19. For example, *Archives of Maryland,* 4:446, 478–79, 41:332–33; *County Court Records of Accomack-Northampton,* 1:15. Other sorts of notations also reveal similar information; for example, *Archives of Maryland,* 4:483, 54:320, 328, 481, 60:141; *Ancient Town Records: New Haven Town Records, 1649–1684,* ed. Franklin B. Dexter (New Haven, Conn., 1917, 1919), 2:195.

20. Norton, *Founding Mothers and Fathers,* 85–87, cites some examples. See also *Archives of Maryland,* 49:236.

21. For examples of men's purchases of indentured maidservants as their wives: *Archives of Maryland,* 10:215, 268, 509, 41:468–70; *County Court Records of Accomack-Northampton,* 2:6, 185–86.

22. *County Court Records of Accomack-Northampton,* 2:160, 269–70; also 1:34, 149, 2:67–68, 426–27; *Archives of Maryland,* 54:548. For a rare instance of a direct payment to a married woman for wet nursing, see *Archives of Maryland,* 60:106, 144 (but compare p. 229).

23. See examples cited in Norton, *Founding Mothers and Fathers,* 427–28 n. 70; and *Archives of Maryland,* 41:264, 60:312–13; *Records and Files . . . of Essex County,* 3:338; *New Haven Town Records,* 1:328–29.

24. *Archives of Maryland,* 53:39; *York Deeds,* ed. William Sargent (Portland, Maine, 1888), vol. 5, pt. 1, n. 82.

25. *New Haven Town Records,* 1:304, 307–8.

26. *Archives of Maryland,* 4:511–12, 519–20, 548, 10:37, 46, 418–19 (her eventual accommodation with the trustees). On her work as a healer, see n. 18, above.

27. Or her recognition of her obligations. In 1666 in Somerset County, Maryland, Sarah Ballard, the widow of John Elzey and Thomas Jordan, repeatedly acknowledged to neighbors that her first husband had held in trust two cows belonging to his younger brother Peter and that she wanted her third husband, Charles Ballard, to return those cows and their offspring to Peter Elzey. Yet Charles Ballard refused to fulfill that obligation until forced to do so by Peter Elzey's successful lawsuit. (*Archives of Maryland,* 54:623, 625–28.)

28. Ibid., 41:167. Mistress Fenwick valued her horses; for a later case in which she vigorously and successfully pursued a claim to the ownership of a disputed horse, see 41:185, 194, 217–20, 277–79.

29. Ibid., 10:461, 523, 41:3, 199, 279.

30. Ibid., 53:54–55, 142–45, 156. Thomas Mitchell was still alive in late October 1660 (ibid., 92); his widow may have filed her first complaint as early as July 1661 (ibid., 139). Another set of suggestive cases involved husbands who filed suit on behalf of their wives long after the women could first have laid legal claim to

inherited property. (See, for example, ibid., 41:265, 372–73, 57:246–49, 304, 381.)

31. Ibid., 53:344–45, 372; for examples of property transfers in which wives' consent was properly obtained, see also 41:602, 53:525, 54:237; *Records of . . . New Plymouth,* 2:118–19; *York Deeds,* 1, pt. 1, pp. 3, 18, 32. See Salmon, *Women and Law of Property,* chap. 2, for a general discussion.

32. Quotations: *Archives of Maryland,* 49:420, 41:143–44; the other Maryland case, 54:201–2, 204. New England successes: *Records and Files . . . of Essex County,* 2:251–52, 3:186–89, 4:53–54; *Records of the Suffolk County Court, 1671–1680,* 2 vols. (33 amd 34) published separately as *Collections of the Colonial Society of Massachusetts,* ed. Samuel Eliot Morison (Boston, 1933), 2:755. But compare Morison, 1:536–37; *Province and Court Records of Maine,* 2:89–90.

33. For an example of such a suit to clear a land title, see *Archives of Maryland,* 49:473, 505.

34. The numbers represent cases with female litigants of such descriptions, rather than individuals. Since some widows made numerous court appearances while administering their husbands' estates, the number of individual women involved was considerably lower. One litigious never-married woman in Maryland (Mistress Margaret Brent) alone accounts for most of the appearances of single females in the Chesapeake. See Norton, *Founding Mothers and Fathers,* 282.

35. Accordingly, in both New England and the Chesapeake, suits filed by young women acting alone are exceedingly rare; see, for example, *Archives of Maryland,* 41:317, 54:386.

36. For example, *Archives of Maryland,* 10:433, 442, 49:441–42, 493–94, 54:512; *Records of . . . New Plymouth,* 7:146, 149; Morison, ed., *Records of Suffolk County,* 2:792–93.

37. See Norton, *Founding Mothers and Fathers,* 128, 434 nn. 68, 69; *Records and Files . . . of Essex County,* 3:229–35, 6:151–62; *Records of . . . New Plymouth,* 7:205–9.

38. For example, *Minutes of the Council and General Court of Colonial Virginia 1622–1632, 1670–1676,* ed. H. R. McIlwaine (Richmond, Va., 1924), 27. A unusual case in which two young women did testify is in *Archives of Maryland,* 41:169–74.

39. For discussions of the prosecution of female criminals, see Norton, *Founding Mothers and Fathers,* chap. 7, and Norton "Gender, Crime, and Community in Seventeenth-Century Maryland," in *The Transformation of Early American History,* ed. James Henretta et al. (New York, 1991), 122–50, 286–94.

40. See Norton, *Founding Mothers and Fathers,* 120–23, and "Gender, Crime, and Community," 126–34. A rape complaint brought by a father on behalf of his daughter, who seems to have concealed the assault for some months, is in *Archives of Maryland,* 10:499–500, 531–33. Fathers also occasionally complained on behalf of young sons who had been assaulted, but male servants usually came forward on their own to complain of mistreatment. For fathers' complaints on behalf of sons, see *New Haven Town Records,* 1:436–37, 2:188; *Province and Court Records of Maine,* 3:206. A few of many examples of men's complaints of assaults may be found in *Archives of Maryland,* 4:317–18, 10:31, 41:474–75; *Province and Court Records of Maine,* 1:278–79, 3:231; *New Haven Town Records,* 1:151–53.

41. *Colonial Justice in Western Massachusetts (1639–1702): The Pynchon Court Record,* ed. Joseph H. Smith (Cambridge, Mass., 1961), 237; *New Haven Town Records,* 2:109; see Norton, *Founding Mothers and Fathers,* 52–54, for a more detailed discussion of the Fancys. See also *Records and Files . . . of Essex County,* 3:33–34; *Province and Court Records of Maine,* 3:82–83; *Archives of Maryland,*

54:466. For a father's action on behalf of a (defamed) married daughter: *New Haven Town Records*, 1:389–90.

42. See, for example, *Province and Court Records of Maine*, 2:263, 460; *Court Records of Suffolk County*, 1:524, 2:1063. Some incidents of wife abuse also came to light because of the complaints of others; see the discussion in Norton, *Founding Mothers and Fathers*, 78–81, and *Province and Court Records of Maine*, 1:288, 3:76, 142.

43. The total number of cases solely involving men is approximated because my database for them is a sample. All cases involving women (including those with female witnesses) were coded. Slightly more than 50% of female witnesses were the only women to testify in civil suits (exactly 50% in criminal cases). Only about 30% of men, though, appeared without other male witnesses in both types of cases.

44. Cornelia Dayton, who comments on the declining proportion of women in court during the period from the mid-seventeenth century to the late eighteenth century, remarks not on the relatively low proportion to begin with (she found women to be about one third of those appearing in court in any capacity in the early days of New Haven) but focuses on the decrease after that time; see *Women before the Bar*, 1.

45. For example, Amanda Porterfield, *Female Piety in Puritan New England* (New York, 1992), considers the importance of marriage in Puritan doctrine and practice but does not address questions arising from wives' status.

46. Quotations in this and the following paragraph are taken from "The Notebook of the Reverend John Fiske," ed. Robert G. Pope, *Publications of the Colonial Society of Massachusetts* 47 (1974):6, 14–16, 19, 30. See also a list of "the members of the church of Newbury" in 1671 that names only men in *Records and Files . . . of Essex County*, 4:36.

47. The quotations in this and the next two paragraphs are from *The Journal of John Winthrop, 1630–1649*, ed. Richard S. Dunn et al. (Cambridge, Mass., 1996), 276–77; *Winthrop Papers, 1498–1649* (Boston, 1929–1947), 4:31; and William Hubbard, "History of New England from the Discovery to 1680," *CMHS* ser. 2, 6 ([1817]), 2:337–38. On the early governance of Rhode Island, see Norton, *Founding Mothers and Fathers*, 300–302. The disfranchisement order is recorded in *Records of the Colony of Rhode Island and Providence Plantations*, ed. John Russell Bartlett (Providence, R.I., 1856–65), 1:16.

48. *Archives of Maryland*, 41:144–46. The case against Fitzherbert was not resolved for another four years, at which time the charges were dismissed after the priest contended that his statements were themselves protected by the toleration act: "preacheing & teacheing is the free Exercise of every Churchmans Religion," he argued successfully (41:566–67).

49. *New Haven Town Records*, 1:244. See also a 1708 incident in Virginia involving a Quaker husband and a formerly Quaker (now Anglican) wife, "Religious Differences Between George Walker and Wife," in *Virginia Magazine of History and Biography* 16 (1908–1909): 79–81. In that case, the husband allowed his wife her freedom of conscience but insisted that he be able to determine their children's religious future; the local court likewise supported his decision.

Thomas N. Ingersoll

"RICHES AND HONOUR WERE REJECTED BY THEM AS LOATHSOME VOMIT"[1]: THE FEAR OF LEVELING IN NEW ENGLAND

 DEFENDERS OF THE social hierarchy worried about the effects of inequality in early America. Popular antagonism to the sway of the well-born and impudent social climbing by individuals exploiting commercial opportunities in the New World threatened to subvert the dogma that inequality and hierarchy were natural and necessary. To reinforce their authority, upper classes in early America deployed safeguards against dangerous behavior and ideas among the common people. Above all, they needed a general-purpose ideological bludgeon, a horrific image to wield against any challenge to the fundamental order, in which they enjoyed a privileged position. By the seventeenth century, a variety of radical sectarians, such as Familists and Anabaptists, had developed ideas that seemed to challenge not just hierarchical order but private property and the conjugal family. Conservatives caricatured these ideas to fashion a nightmare image of a "leveled" society. Anyone who strayed beyond the pale of acceptable discourse and comportment to challenge the establishment was accused of questioning the very principles of private property and hierarchy. In New England, as in regions where inequality was more marked, the fear of leveling was keen from the beginning of the colonial era. The terrible, instructive image of a community of goods and women did yeoman service in the antiradical cause in the land of Puritans and Yankees, an image that was rejuvenated in the 1790s by Jacobinism.

Even if New England societies were relatively homogeneous, peopled from the middle ranks of England's social structure and comparatively less unequal, the so-called better sort feared popular social forces in new and volatile American settlements.[2] Servants and other subordinate white people caused concern because they seemed willing to challenge the restricted rights and privileges of the lower orders. Exactly how much true leveling spirit existed in New England, however, is a question for another essay. Here the point is that magistrates and clergy with traditional convictions believed they saw overwhelming evidence that lower-class commitment to the social structure was weak.

Common people enjoyed a special advantage in the colonies owing to the dearth of laborers. The demand for labor was so intense that William Wood had to reassure prospective immigrants in England that, "whereas it is generally reported, that servants and poore men grow rich, and the masters and Gentrie grow poore," the latter was not true. Moreover, the friendly Indians were likely to bring in the "many lazie boyes that have runne away from their masters." Other sources suggest that Wood was too sanguine. John Winthrop's works alone provide many examples of rebellious servants, like the indentured man in Roxbury who angrily wished himself in hell rather than in service to his master, for he "sawe, that if he had beene at libertye, he might have had greater wages." Winthrop's daughter Mary complained that a newly arrived English maidservant at first "carried her selfe dutifully as became a servant," but in Boston's atmosphere she soon "got such a head and is growen soe insolent that her carriage towards vs, especially myselfe, is vnsufferable." Free workmen demanded "excessive rates of wages" and had to be restrained from frequenting too many church lectures, "to the great neglect of their affairs." The trouble with servants and workmen became worse after the outbreak of the first English civil war dried up the sources of immigrants. According to Winthrop, "the warres in England kept servantes from comminge to vs, so as those we had, could not be hired when their tymes were out, but vpon vnreasonable termes."[3] Disfranchised servants acted individually and posed no organized threat to the social structure, but magistrates conflated this group with the common people who had the right to vote and the political potential to undermine deference more methodically.

The ordinary freemen of Massachusetts, mostly small farmers and artisans, were able to demonstrate their power collectively. In the election of 1634, "the infearior sorte" of Boston voted out Winthrop's party of magistrates "as fearinge that the richer men would give the poorer sorte no great proportions of lande." Winthrop had to give way, reluctantly and in several phases of struggle, to an expansion of popular participation in government (based on the royal charter of the Massachusetts Bay Company) and a law code, all because the people demanded it. By the end of the colony's first phase, especially in the largest towns, like Boston, where inequality was greatest, there was "a long history of undeferential behavior among plebian sorts."[4]

Besides the threat from the ordinary people, the traditional hierarchy was under pressure by other forces, especially by humble but busy small entrepreneurs who balked at limits on their profits and social horizons. Guardians of hierarchy and deference were more concerned about the respect of common people for their betters than they were about covetousness in the marketplace. Nonetheless, ambitious traders, artisans, shopkeepers, jobbers, and hucksters presented a special challenge to traditional ideas. These industrious men and women were energized by both commercial opportunities in the New World and the Calvinist doctrine of the calling, according to which "the fulfilment of duty in worldly affairs [w]as the highest form which the moral activity of the individual could assume." It was a potent combination that might propel any person rapidly up the social scale, confounding the weight accorded to breeding, wealth, and religious orthodoxy.[5]

In the minds of nervous magistrates and ministers, the problem of heterodoxy was what linked the assertiveness of the lower orders and the aspirations of individuals who would exploit the marketplace to scamper up the social pyramid. As Louise A. Breen has recently argued, the social context drove theological debate. Breen shows how the traditionalists' fears of both the mass of undeferential common people, on one hand, and individual upwardly mobile tradespeople and craftsmen, on the other, grew in tandem. Members of both groups tended to associate with sectarians outside the Puritan mainstream, and both types were ambitious (covetous of their neighbors' property) and subversive, albeit in different ways. "Just as radicals believed in the irresistibility and boundlessness of the spirit," she argues, defenders of capitalist profit making and social climbing enunciated "a mysterious, unsystematized, and cosmopolitan mercantile ethos that resisted the worldly control of local authorities," inspiring the latter to launch fierce charges of leveling against both groups. Contrary to the traditional schema of a social hierarchy outlined in Winthrop's "Model of Christian Charity," Breen suggests that "few Puritans lived without the temptation to free themselves from the confining intellectual and social bonds" of Winthrop's model.[6] Poor servants, the mass of the common yeomen and artisans, and hustling traders all put great pressure on the social structure, which the guardians of the traditional hierarchy struggled to protect.[7]

Although no advocate of the community of goods ever seems to have spoken in the region, New England patriarchs charged every single kind of sectarian or social critic with the folly of utopian equality. From the Antinomians to the Gortonists to the Quakers to the witches to the land bankers, the bugbear of a socialist revolution served hostile local authorities well: they consistently accused their supposed populist enemies of an intent to destroy property itself. Curiously, the Indians could be seen as an exception. They were widely regarded as antagonists or obstacles to the colonists' religion and society, but, according to Matthew Mayhew, that was precisely because they were not levelers but had, like the Europeans, the strength of hierarchy: a monarchical aristocracy "maintained in great magnificence" by "yeomen" and "villains." Remarkably, the Indians were the (unwitting) allies of traditionalists in maintaining white society in its customary form. Officers of the standing order needed allies in their attacks on nonconformists, however spurious these alliances might be. Defenders of the status quo focused attention on exaggerated caricatures of radical sectarians. Of the various epithets, "Familists" (for the Family of Love sect) and "Libertines" were Winthrop's favorites; both suggested that the accused expounded beliefs that led to a leveled social structure.[8]

The most compelling image of social leveling, one that arguably lay at the root of many epithets, was the Münster commune of the 1530s.[9] Capping two decades of increasing religious and peasant radicalism in northern Europe, the German town of Münster was convulsed by an Anabaptist revolution that was suppressed in 1535 by the nobility and clergy following a long siege. One century later, the much-embellished "history" of this event, published by enemies of radicalism, was still fresh and powerful. Defenders of the standing order could all agree that "communism" (as it would come to be called in the nineteenth century) was a horrible thing. All a writer or preacher had to do to rouse the reader or auditor to full alert was to invoke Münster or Germany.

What really happened at Münster is still open to interpretation. Historians agree that the political-religious movement that gradually gained control of the town was not primarily a lower-class phenomenon, for one finds "an astonishing normality in distribution of wealth among the Münster Anabaptists." Although it is true that the poor flocked to the standard of rebellion after the urban Anabaptist leaders seized the town, the leaders were sufficiently dedicated to social stratification that nothing like absolute equality was ever likely.[10] However that may be, rebel leaders did adopt radically communitarian policies as a defensive measure on account of the siege.[11] In all, it was a dramatic upheaval. Subsequently, antagonists exploited the drama to create a frightful myth of Münster.

What is most telling about the myth of Münster is the readiness with which conservative Protestants and Catholics united to condemn Anabaptist leveling. The leading scriptural passages used by radicals in justifying their cause, in Acts (especially 4:32–37), describe the revolutionary practices of early Christians: "They had all things common . . . and distribution was made unto every man according as he had need."[12] Mainstream Christians who desired a reformation without a social revolution rejected the radical reading of these passages, fearful of their implications. Conservative Catholic and Protestant leaders might agree on little else, but they could agree that Münster had been a kind of hell on earth and that the experiment must not be repeated.

That view of Münster was dominant among the English when their colonial movement began. Thus, the next to last of the Thirty-Nine Articles of the Church of England pronounced: "The Riches and Goods of Christians are not common, as touching the right, title, and possession of the same, as certain Anabaptists do falsely boast."[13] Anglican objections to the ideal of Christian communalism arose less from a specifically religious concern than from a social conviction that have-nots resented haves and would take their property if they could, by the fraudulent means of some high-flown principle of equality. They believed that such a grotesque principle necessarily arose from sin, the sin of covetousness, one that came to have a particularly detestable reputation in conservative rhetoric. The socially conservative men who dominated the leadership of early New England were similarly fearful that the great Puritan colonial experiment could succumb to a spirit of leveling, and they erected an ideological battery against it.

A typical tactic was to accuse a social misfit of being even more baneful than the rebels of 1534. John Winthrop repeatedly accused Anne Hutchinson and her party of being considerably worse than the spirits responsible for "the Tragedy of Munster," for the Massachusetts magistrates "had not to doe with so simple a Devill, as managed that businesse. . . but Satan seemed to have commission now to use his utmost cunning to undermine the Kingdom of Christ here." Hutchinson was no simple-minded fanatic like John of Leiden (the quintessential Münster rebel), and she seemed to exercise a special influence over the common people as well as women of all ranks and merchants who were not members of local churches. Even after the Hutchinsonians were either expelled or silenced, the effects of their poisonous beliefs lingered. In 1641, Thomas Shepard warned that austere Puritan gentlemen in England would not support the New England experiment because they were under the impression that "no men of worth are respected" in the colonies, where "men will live as they list, without any over them, and unfit to rule themselves."[14]

Edward Winslow's furious attack on Samuel Gorton and his followers epitomized the social strategy of defenders of the traditional order. With great scorn he pictured Gortonists as "unlearned men, [for] the ablest of them could not write true English, no not in common words," so it was a great presumption for them to expound on weighty issues. But the ultimate aim of their teachings was what inevitably condemned their theology. By its lights every man was fit for magistracy, "whether rich or poore, ignorant or learned, then every Christian in a Common-wealth must be King," which could lead only to "the establishment of all confusion, and the setting up of Anarchy worse than the greatest Tyranny." More specifically, they would set up a society in which "they will put no manner of difference between houses, goods, lands, wives, lives, blood, nor any thing will bee precious in their eyes."[15] No matter how strongly they denied these views, they lied. Winslow's readers knew that it had happened once before, in Münster in 1534.

Münster was given a fresh seventeenth-century face by the English Revolution. In the 1640s and 1650s, a small number of English sects actually advocated and practiced a community of goods and other principles that form the prehistory of modern socialism. The most effective popular oganization, however, was that of the Levellers (branded with that name by their enemies), who had one of their deepest roots in Anabaptism. They advocated a broadening of the franchise and diminution of privilege but stopped far short of absolute equality or a redistribution of wealth. John Winthrop was misinformed by a sometime New England preacher writing from London, nonetheless, that the Levellers planned "to bringe allmost a parity upon all persons in the kingdome," to the applause of "innumerable approvers & abettors."[16] Despite Oliver Cromwell's success in quelling the Leveller movement, in the rhetoric of conservatives he came to be associated with all the radicals of the 1650s, especially the Levellers. To monarchists, moreover, he embodied horrendous regicide and the abolition of monarchy in 1649.

In New England in the years following the death of Cromwell, religious separatists still bore the main brunt of fears of leveling. Conservatives focused their attacks chiefly on those belonging to sects with origins in the English Revolution, like the Quakers, or those who had played important roles in the radical theater of that event, especially Baptists. Responding to an influx of Quaker missionaries in to the colony in the late 1650s, John Norton penned a tract, commissioned by the General Court, lambasting that sect. In a fierce assault on the Quakers and others who sympathized with "the Enthusiasts in Germany [Münster], & Libertines," Norton condemned their beliefs as more disgusting "than the Frogs that sometime annoyed Egypt." He acknowledged that their outlandish notions were inevitable, considering "[h]ow potent a temptation, [is] the opening of an opportunity to the irregenerate & hungry multitude, of changing places with their superiours, and possessing themselves with their power, honour & estates." Cataloguing a list of notorious movements and their leaders in recent history, of which the most malefic was John of Leiden (1509–36), who had crowned himself "king" at Münster in memory of David, Norton heaped scorn on those who had "seduced the inferior sort, especially such as were pinched with penury," into leveling the social structure. He would be echoed over many decades by similar attacks on Quakers because the fundamental result of their beliefs was to "make them Equal with *God Himself.*"[17]

At the close of the tract, Norton inserted what appears at first glance to be merely tacked on. Shifting completely out of the religious discourse in which he had been engaged throughout a lengthy sermon, he makes a fiery statement about political economy. New Englanders must remember that the founders had a religious mission and did not mean to establish "a plantation of Trade." He worried, as he fretted about the destruction of the property relation itself by levelers, that the mission to be "like a light upon a Hill" might "go out in the snuff" of trade. New England's fields were groaning with wealth, its towns growing into cities; it was becoming "a place of merchandize" full of commercial temptations.[18] This peculiar eruption at the end of Norton's pamphlet shows how the two kinds of leveling were closely associated in the minds of conservatives: both organized, ideological sectarians and excessive upward social mobility by trading individuals represented threats to the social structure. The attack on destabilizing social ambitions drew on rhetoric aimed at usury and covetousness, which were sinful and unneighborly, contrary to the communal values of Winthrop's "Model." More profoundly, overrapid social mobility based on profit making was a direct threat to a stable social structure. Norton and others like him were intent on creating a society into which a person was born at a given level, a level one might transcend only gradually by accumulation of wealth based on diligence and piety rather than shrewdness, pride, and covetousness. For, if moneymaking alone could make a man, all men were theoretically equal, and that could not be.

The specter of Münster was revived in 1668, as part of an attack on a newly gathered Baptist church in Massachusetts. New England merchant Joshua Scottow translated and published the superb tract on Münster by the sixteenth-century Low Countries Protestant activist, Guy De Brès, called *The Rise, Spring and Foundation of the Anabaptists, Or Re-baptized of Our Time.* Scottow's publication renewed the Münster legend. For Scottow and de Brès, what made radical evangelicals like the Anabaptists so threatening, so disproportionately important relative to their numbers, was their social policy, not their theology as such. "These Anabaptists would put all the world in a confusion by their community of goods, and that they might enjoy other men's labours." De Brès took quite seriously his duty to explain away ancient precedents for communal practices. In general, he argued, "Christians possessed proprieties, and . . . some very rich, who left not their riches to put them into a common stock," for "Christ's speech, Mat. 25. 35 fully teaches us propriety in goods." Moreover, the levelers of Münster were hypocrites: "Riches and Honour were re-jected by them as loathsome vomit (at least, as they made shew of)." Their supposed equality had led to immorality (in the form of polygamy), intol-erance (the burning of all books but the Bible), and general misery for the common people.[19]

The hydra of absolute equality also appears in a sermon by Urian Oakes in 1673, again in tandem with an attack on unrestrained capitalism and so-cial climbing. Oakes thanks God that he had never "in displeasure left us [New Englanders] to be Levelers and Libertines, to do every man what seems good in his own eyes." In the context of the sermon, however, this is more nervously prescriptive than descriptive. Oakes also briefly condemns "Griping, and Squeezing, and Grinding the faces of the poor" by those grasping men who attached too much importance to property. But he quickly draws the subversive teeth of that exhortation by turning on the poor, complaining that they can not afford the quality of the clothes they wear, seemingly bent on spoiling the role of clothing "to distinguish and put a difference between persons according to their Places and Condi-tions." They are akin to those who chased after the phantom of "Liberty of Conscience: that they may hold and practise what they will in Religion." They were in thrall to the pagan moon goddess Diana, protector of hunts-men but also of the lower classes in general, "and great is the Diana of the Libertines of this age."[20]

Down to the eighteenth century, a near consensus prevailed among con-servatives that the lower orders' insolent posture and some individuals' profit seeking and upwardly mobile self-interest were twin threats to the social order. Cotton Mather was the last major traditionalist willing to con-demn leveling by both the common people in general and those over-shrewd, social-climbing persons who trafficked in the marketplace. Busy in defense of hierarchy, he developed a rich commentary on class distinctions as a crucial barrier to leveling. Fear of Anabaptist leveling inspired him to cheer as the parson and reputed Baptist George Burroughs was hanged for witchcraft in 1692. Burroughs was not merely doctrinally unsound, he was a fiend from hell, seducing the innocent into covetousness; a spirit-afflicted young woman claimed that he had "caried me up to an exceeding high mountain and shewed me all the kingdoms of the earth and tould me that he would give them all to me if I would writ in his book." Those the devil tormented were often tempted by his offers of great wealth.[21]

Despite the executions in 1692, Mather continued to worry about Satan tempting the lowly. In 1696 he lamented that "the Proud Hearts of many Servants, make them discontented, at the Lowness of their present Station, and at the Lowliness which they must Express in their Station" and warned them "[t]hat this Pride was the sin of the Devils; the Devils could not bear to be Servants in such a station as the Almighty God had appointed for them."[22] Mather felt compelled to warn servants "[v]ehemently" not to steal from masters one "[p]enny as long as you live." Turning to slaves he justified their status by the precedent in the Bible, assured them that they were better cared for than "if you were your Own men," and warned them not to make themselves "infinitely Blacker than you already are." In an-other sermon he addressed slaves similarly, lamenting that there was "a Fondness for Freedom in many of you, who live comfortably in a very easy Servitude." More discreetly and with much less heat, he censured the avid-ity of men who enslaved and sold free Africans (as opposed to those who were already slaves in Africa and therefore legitimately held in slavery in the New World).[23] In Mather's moral universe, striving and discontented lower orders were still more worrisome than grasping entrepreneurs.

Historians often imply that the clergy was evenhanded in condemning both the restless poor and the excessive aspirations of men of commerce, but close attention to the structure of sermons suggests otherwise. Invoca-tions of the ghost of Münster or more general images of the leveling spirit were frequently and prominently featured in sermons, often in the conclu-sion or coda of long arguments seemingly preoccupied with theological is-sues. These discussions indicate that the conservative clergy were most alarmed by the ambitions of both white and black people who had to work with their hands: they might level society even without a revolution simply by refusing to accept the hierarchy as it existed and by insisting on a princi-ple of equality. Watchmen guarding the social hierarchy had to counter that insidious threat by the awful image of "those obstreperous Folks in Ger-many, who by the wrongs they did unto the Reformation, have left their name as execration to Posterity."[24] Good Protestants of all sects, including Mather's most ardent rivals for theological authority, united in agreement that it was essential to avoid a repeat of that event.

The authority of clerical leaders like Cotton Mather on social (as op-posed to moral) matters gave way in the eighteenth century to the author-ity of political economists, a change that is still too little studied. The years between the close of the seventeenth century and Mather's death in 1728 mark the beginning of the "rationalization" of economic life, in tandem with the eighteenth-century ideological revolution, after which "self-interest was construed as dependable and constructive" by a majority, even though the values of "commonwealth" hostile to self-interest would always remain strong.[25] By 1700 the commercial development of New England had advanced to the point that fretting about it openly seemed not just old-fashioned but ill-advised. A preacher in a trade-oriented maritime town risked alienating an important minority of church members by condemn-ing entrepeneurial ambition and self-enrichment as covetousness, so even the weak injunctions found in Mather's works were seldom heard. This was all the more true in Massachusetts after 1691 because Congregationalist preachers had to compete with Anglican clergy for the adherence of wealthy churchgoers. Perry Miller noticed a strategic shift. He discovered that Cotton Mather actually advised his colleagues to play dumb, to affect to be too ignorant "to pronounce any Judgement upon that Spirit of Over-trading and Over-doing that some suppose very much threatens us."[26] Mather continued to admonish the grasping rich on occasion, but his special target was always the dissatisfied and assertive poor man. Spicing his discourse with an American touch, he wrote of the latter, "what the *Indian* said of the *Spaniard*, that may be said of this Miserable; Hold up a piece of Eight, and say, This is his *God!*"[27] Mather went out of this world wagging a disapproving finger at those whose prideful ambition led them to strain against their assigned places in the social structure. He exhorted the common people to "[a]cquiesce in your Portion. . . . All your present Poverty is but the Inconvenience" of this life, for "[t]he Grave, the Grand Leveler, will quickly bring the Rich and the Poor to be upon Equal Terms."[28]

The transition to a more openly class-based discourse on leveling is seen most clearly in the century-long debate in Massachusetts about establishing a land bank. Land banks responded to the worst problem plaguing the ambitious lower-middle-class elements in the rising commercial empire of New England: the shortage of circulating capital. Rich merchants exported virtually any hard money and bullion they could obtain to buy commodities at wholesale in the Old World. As a consequence, small traders and commercial farmers tried to finance their ambitions by inflationary means hateful to mercantile fiscal conservatives, their wealthy creditors: they tried to establish a land bank, to back up paper currency issues with mortgages on real estate. It was not a class confrontation as such, for the leaders of land bank schemes were property owners, but it was definitely a clash between two different conceptions of how unequal society should be. Wealthy and conservative merchants believed that the degree of inequality created by the supremacy of hard money was natural and even necessary to maintain a social order they dominated. People who had land, talent, ambition, and little else saw the iron rule of hard money as an unfair advantage to a privileged few that stymied their own economic dynamism.

In the era following the imperial wars of Louis XIV, when many expected that commerce would boom, ruling New England patriarchs reacted ferociously to the "leveling" threat of land banking. Massachusetts attorney-general Paul Dudley could not have been more explicit about the most foolish idea that had ever "entred into the reason of any Man out of Eutopia." His entire analysis was secular; he wasted no breath on the sin of covetousness. The only consequence of public credit based on the mortgage of land would be "to Confound the People, and make Money Vile and Contempt-ible; and as much as in them lies, to Alter and Destroy the very Nature of Money," the essential mark of leveling. Why was there a shortage of money in the first place? It was especially because "the Ordinary sort, are fallen into [extravagance], far beyond their Circumstances . . . in their whole way of Living."[29] Dudley threw in the various ways land banking would offend "the Prerogative," "the Constitution," and so on, but his main point was that the social hierarchy was threatened, which all decent people must be expected to disapprove.[30]

Conservative clergy, allied with the silver-banking, antiradical men like Dudley, trained their moralistic fire on the dangerous dishonesty of com-mon people rather than on the subversive nature of pursuing profits. The change is epitomized in Peter Thacher's remarkably artful (or confused?) performance of 1720. Although the sermon includes an awkward attempt to play the traditional, now problematic theme about the sharpness of some merchants, Thacher pours his real passion into the subtext concern-ing the misbehavior of the lower orders. Their principal ambition seems to be "to feed on other men's Bread" and indulge in "excessive expence for Apparel and Drink." Worst of all were the lowest of the low: "Oh! how Criminal is the Fault of the Unfaithful Day-Labourers! . . . Guilty of a foul way of stealing." To feed their appetites even more gluttonously, the com-mon people made "[o]utcries for a [paper] Medium of Trade," a land bank.[31] That leading Congregational ministers attacked the land bank sig-naled a decline in their authority among insubordinate, increasingly self-conscious popular forces, as they forged an alliance with hard-money men. Because of that alliance, commercial covetousness could no longer be con-demned as sinful, and a harder, more strictly ideological critique of lower-class leveling emerged.

The same realignment of forces is clear in the struggle over the establish-ment of a central town market in the 1730s. The effort to establish a fixed, regulated market with stalls in Boston, which at one point sparked an arson attempt aimed at foiling the project, engendered angry rhetoric about class subversion.[32] Benjamin Colman explained the importance of the market in moral and social terms. Above all, a superintended public market would prevent the common country people, servants, and children "that bring in Provisions, hawking and sauntring about Town," having their morals cor-rupted. He launched his sharpest attack on the popular objection that re-stricting the outlet of commodities to a market would raise prices and dis-criminate against common consumers. He bears quoting in full: "They that are poorer in worldly state should and must give way to the Rich. Who but they ordinarily should buy the dearest and best of the kind? Providence means it for them. It is the Government of Heaven; let us submit to it.

GOD has given unto their hand more abundantly. Let not thine Eye be evil. Now & then we that are poorer may tast of the best too and be thankful."[33] The populist touch in the last line is distinctly off-key and unconvincing; normally, ministers did not think of themselves as belonging to the lower orders. They agreed with Reverend Samuel Willard when he snorted that "[m]inisterial gifts [are not] (ordinarily) acquired in a Shoemakers shop," and those of Colman's stature tasted of the best more often than "now and then." Colman was defending inequality and deference with rare candor but with dubious theology and primitive sociology: The poor who infringe the privileges of the rich rebel against divine will; and if they would be patient, they could enjoy instead whatever might trickle down from the groaning tables of the righteous rich. The crudity and condescension of such arguments exposed Colman and his colleagues to ridicule. Antagonists of the standing order, like land bankers, began to lash back at such charges of "leveling" social mobility. "What, they must have brick Houses must they?" as one satirized the arrogant indignation of the rich; "no, a groat a day is enough for them."[34]

Being men of property themselves, however, leading land bankers were also likely to invoke the possibility of a Münster-like result should their opponents suppress the land bank. Citing Francis Bacon, they suggested that when "[p]overty, and broken Estates in the better sort [that is, the organizers of the land bank], be join'd with want and necessity, in the mean people, the danger is Eminent and Great." Chaos in the social structure was near: "The whole Province is in a Flame at this time. Every Man's Hand is against his Brother." Still, the anti–land bankers seemed to have the more frightening and compelling argument: land banks would ruin social order by permitting debtors to despoil creditors. After all, the colonists had seen the inflationary effects of the paper money Massachusetts issued to finance wars with the French between 1689 and 1713.

The hard-money opposition to paper money remained remarkably consistent over the course of the eighteenth century, but conservative pamphleteers became more colorful and forceful writers. Again, despite the rhetorical tirades, it does not appear that the contest between the two groups was ever class antagonism per se; in fact, land bankers appear to be categorized most reliably by church membership lists: they were primarily New Lights in the 1740s. Nonetheless, opponents of the land banks tried their best to convince the general public that it was a class war by the have-nots to rob the haves or that paper money would inevitably lead to such a war. The trend begun by Paul Dudley in 1714 culminated in the works of William Douglass, who opposed the land bank that was briefly set up in the 1740s. This disastrous experiment occurred only because "the Popular or Democratick Part of the Constitution are generally in debt" and had agitated for a "depreciating Currency" to pay their creditors out of sheer "leveling and licentiousness." Douglass went so far as to compare land bankers to African blacks "who sell their Progeny into Slavery." He also threw in the scientific argument that "it is a natural Instinct in Animals to provide for Posterity," so land bankers were "unnatural" by creating misery for future generations. But his main point was always that land banking represented an attempt to put the honest rich "upon a level with the Idle and Extravagant."[35]

An anonymous popular writer counterattacked in full force in 1750, the year the Massachusetts currency was firmly established on a silver basis and the land bankers were ruined. By a striking ironic inversion, the author charged the silver bankers with leveling, that is, with a conspiracy to reduce everyone else to a level at which they were all in debt to the hard-money men. "Whenever you see any Sett, or Party of Men prosper," the writer warned, "they immediately grow haughty [and] imperious, and spurn at all beneath them, that [are not alr]eady their immediate Slaves." And "the Sons of Lucre" were well organized to defeat any political initiative "that in any manner of way tends to interfere and clash with their Views of Interest." That was because they were "[e]nemies to all Communities . . . sons of Plutus, who sacrifice[d] only to MAMMON."[36] The writer embellishes his work with biblical references at the end of the pamphlet for good measure but offers basically a secular argument every bit as hard-nosed as those presented by Douglass. *Massachusetts in Agony* is a key document in the history of American radical thought. It reveals how frustrating it was for reformers to be accused of hostility to property when their actual goal was to increase wealth and the number of people who could amass it and enjoy its fruits. The colonial phase of the debate about landbanking ended in the 1750s in a complete rout of the land bankers by the powerful creditor minority, whose leader was the same man who would contribute so much to provoking rebellion in the province in the 1760s and 1770s, Thomas Hutchinson.

So powerful was the charge of leveling that it represented the most serious threat to the New England rebels of 1776, when their loyalist enemies sought to associate them with the long tradition of social radicalism in Europe and America. On the eve of the War of Independence, the cause of defending American rights against the British government depended on an uneasy coalition of popular radicals and that portion of the upper classes who felt more threatened by the mother country than by the risk that a political rebellion would be socially subversive. These people of significant property were skittish, however, and would abandon the cause if it seemed to be tacking toward an upheaval against the local class structure and the deference that held it together. For this reason, loyalists did their utmost to tar the whole colonial resistance movement with the brush of leveling, in hopes of scaring social conservatives into submission to their sovereign. Even a moderate New England Tory who never would become a loyalist exile condemned, on the eve of the Battle of Lexington and Concord, "a spirit of levelism and fierceness, which with a blind fiery zeal, pulls down government, rulers, church, state, science, and morals, into one general and common ruin." By early 1775 a social conservative like John Adams was nearly apoplectic in his response to Tory needling that he and other rebels were akin to the Levellers in the New Model Army of the English Revolution.[37] For this reason, after republican independence became the explicit goal, rebel leaders almost never appealed to the republican precedent of 1649 for fear of promoting the militant subversive spirit associated with the abolition of the monarchy and the House of Lords.[38]

Egalitarian ideology was given a stimulus by the American Revolution, however, and after the war with Great Britain was over, the charge of leveling was resurrected by socially conservative American republicans in the service of conformity of thought and hostility to radical innovation. Not surprisingly, the old quarrel about paper money immediately reared its ugly head, and hard-money conservatives rallied to the defense of traditional deflationary policy. The issue in Massachusetts was particularly embittered because the poor farmers who advocated liberal policies of extended credit and inflationary currency were directly threatened with ruin and because the creditor class was obstinately determined not to follow the example of other colonies and make modest postwar adjustments to protect those at greatest risk.[39] When Shays's Rebellion broke out and was violently suppressed, conservatives loudly denounced Shaysites as fanatical levelers. Since the event occurred amid the gathering drive by nationalists to replace the existing Constitution and erect a stronger federal government, they found this supposed evidence of the evils of weak state government very convenient grist for their mill.

Nationalist leaders seized upon Shays's Rebellion to promote the campaign for a constitutional convention in 1786–87, and reactionary New Englanders were in the forefront, like George Washington's future secretary of war, Henry Knox. General Knox did not hesitate to misrepresent Shays's men as supposedly acting on the creed "[t]hat the property of the United States has been protected from the confiscations of Britain by the joint exertions of all," so private property should be abolished. He followed up a few weeks later with an even more intemperate exaggeration of Shaysite goals, again warning that the insurgents intended "a division of property by means of the darling object of most of the States[:] paper money." George Washington was the communication's nexus for the nationalist cause, and through him the rumor of fanatical leveling in Massachusetts was spread far and wide. When he wrote James Madison, he emphasized what he saw as Knox's key allegation: the insurgents were levelers aiming to flatten the social structure, men who believed the national wealth "ought to be the common property of all" and that their opponents "ought to be swept from the face of the Earth" and their property redistributed by "Agrarian Laws."[40]

The debate about money in Massachusetts in the 1780s made no pretence of a theological context, although Fisher Ames threw the faggott of sectarianism on the fire for good measure by noting that "[s]ince the days of Cromwell there has not been an instance of such general infatuation." But his analysis was basically social: the rebels were not sinners but "a ragged banditti," "Hottentots," and "bankrupts and sots who have gambled or slept away their estates." In one blazing newspaper attack after another he excoriated the leveling implications of paper money secured by land mortgages and movables: "An Act making paper or swine a tender, is a confiscation of my estate." He ignored the conflicting evidence offered by Nathaniel Ames, who explained that the rebellion was brought on by "taxes called for that bear very unequally upon the people, and all property accumulating with greater rapidity than ever known into a few people's hands."[41]

By this time (the 1780s) writers rarely made specific references to dusty old Anabaptist Münster anymore. Historical memory does not last indefinitely without a concerted effort, and many people now lacked a frame of reference for the Münster of 1534. A new phantasm of a leveled and miserable society was needed and was provided by "Jacobinism" in the 1790s. Surprisingly, most of conservative New England supported the French Revolution, at least formally in its early stage, even as the government in Paris became progressively radicalized.[42] But the rise of religious skepticism and the organization of Democratic-Republican societies in the United States by 1795, provided the catalyst for the conservatives to rise up and attack leveling Jacobins at home and abroad. The most colorful prose flowed from the pen of the English immigrant William Cobbett in Pennsylvania, but the New England rhetoricians were the most bitter and best organized. Their single-minded purpose was to show not that American radicals were covetous and disorderly sinners or anarchists but that they would create a different social order, in which the privilege and deference traditionally owing to wealth and white skin would be eliminated.[43]

Naturally, Fisher Ames was among those in the forefront of antileveling polemics, warning furiously that New England Jacobins were "despicable" and would "overturn, and overturn, and overturn, till property shall take wings." The popular, often cited *Remarks on the Jacobiniad*, by John S. J. Gardiner, is a crude satire describing the chaotic scene in a Democratic-Republican club, presided over by a mere cobbler, in which the members debate the prospective membership of a black man. The fact that supposed scientific authorities regard blacks as closer to the orang-utan than to the human species is greeted by "a severe invective against larning," and the applicant is accepted according to the principle of absolute equality. The passions stirred up in this decade were still being vented one century later by antiradical historians who heaped ridicule on the "leveling principles" of all Jeffersonian Democrats.[44]

No rational discourse on inequality and the nature of a just society could emerge in early America because the slightest effort to address the issues was greeted by accusations of leveling. Anyone who questioned the fairness of the distribution of wealth was incriminated as a fanatic hostile to private property itself. Likewise, those individuals who sought wealth and status with too much zeal were likely to be labeled by conservatives as subverters of traditional social stratification. Since the colonists enjoyed a remarkable degree of freedom to exploit rich natural resources and thereby to achieve economic independence and perhaps even social mobility, private property was no less sacrosanct in America than it was in the Old World—virtually no one wanted to be perceived as hostile to property and inequality as such. As a result, charges of leveling obscured the issues, silenced critics, and perpetuated a social structure dominated by those best positioned to malign as levelers anyone who seemed to threaten their interests.

Afterword

The bogey of Jacobinism served its purpose well in nineteenth-century American polemics. It is no surprise, for example, that the Radical Republicans of the 1860s were branded as Jacobins by fellow New Englanders who opposed their effort to reconstruct the nation. They were parodied as planning to seize not just the slaves and infrastructure of the South but the lands as well, to "develop them by the hands of our artisan armies."[45] By this time, however, the era of Napoleon III, the charge of Jacobinism was losing its punch, so it was being gradually replaced by its modern equivalent. That process is visible in the congressional debates over the Homestead Act, arguably the most leveling piece of legislation in nineteenth-century America, one supported by many ordinary land-hungry New England families and bitterly opposed by conservative forces in the Atlantic states. Supporters of the act had to face charges of "Jacobinism, Red Republicanism, and so on."[46] In the wake of the revolutions of 1848, when socialists tried to inaugurate a truly new era in European politics, "red republicanism" referred to a political economy of limitations on the rule of wealth and a redistribution of the estates of the aristocracy. Imaginative

American reactionaries were already seizing on redness (and its later derivatives, like "pink"), fashioning it into a new version of an old specter to frighten all who would listen.

Notes

1. [Guy de Brès, or "de Brez"], *The Rise, Spring and Foundation of the Anabaptists, Or Re-baptized of Our Time,* trans. [Joshua Scottow] (Cambridge, 1668), 10. Originally published as *La racine, source et fondement des Anabaptistes: réfutation très curieuse des doctrines de cette secte* (1565).

2. They might have taken heart from the history of early Plymouth, where an experiment in communal social organization failed, especially because "[t]he aged and graver men to be ranked and equalized in labours and victuals, clothes, etc., with the meaner and younger sort, thought it some indignity and disrespect unto them." Besides, the young men "did repine that they should spend their time and strength to work for other men's wives and children without any recompense." See William Bradford, *Of Plymouth Plantation, 1620–1647,* ed. Samuel E. Morison (1856; reprint, New York, 1952), 121.

3. *New England Prospect* (London, 1634), 60, 80. Reprinted in *A Library of American Puritan Writings: The Seventeenth Century,* vol. 9, *Histories and Narratives,* ed. Sacvan Bercovitch (New York, 1986). *The Journal of John Winthrop, 1630–1649,* ed. Richard S. Dunn, James Savage, and Laetitia Yeandle (Cambridge, Mass., 1996), 93, 102, 316, 573. Mary Dudley to Margaret Winthrop, 1636, in "The Winthrop Papers," vol. 3, *CMHS* 5th ser., 1 (1871), 68.

4. *The Journal of John Winthrop,* 138. Edmund S. Morgan, *The Puritan Dilemma: The Story of John Winthrop* (Boston and Toronto, 1958), 101–14, 166–73, 203. Gary B. Nash, *The Urban Crucible: Social Change, Political Consciousness, and the Origins of the American Revolution* (Cambridge, Mass., 1979), 9; see chap. 1 for a more empirical description of what is referred to variously in the present essay as the "social structure" or "hierarchy."

5. On the subversive character of the entrepreneurial spirit, see Max Weber, *The Protestant Ethic and the Spirit of Capitalism,* trans. Talcott Parsons, foreword by R. H. Tawney (1904–5; reprint, New York, 1958), 80; Frederick Engels, "Socialism: Utopian and Scientific," in *Karl Marx and Frederick Engels: Selected Works* (New York, 1986), 387–89; and Stephen Foster, *Their Solitary Way: The Puritan Social Ethic in the First Century of Settlement in New England* (New Haven, Conn., 1971), 99–126. The best-known story of the confrontation between traditional values and the spirit of capitalist entrepreneurial spirit concerns the not very representative rich merchant Robert Keayne. See Bernard Bailyn, "The Apologia of Robert Keayne," *WMQ* 3d ser., 7 (1950): 568–87.

6. Louise Breen, "Religious Radicalism in the Puritan Officer Corps: Heterodoxy, the Artillery Company, and Cultural Integration in Seventeenth-Century Boston," *NEQ* 68 (1995): 6, 42, 14–15. For the related argument that, "[p]aradoxically, the triumph of Puritan communalism ultimately depended upon a highly individualistic process of geographic mobility within New England," see Virginia Dejohn Anderson, *New England's Generation: The Great Migration and the Formation of Society and Culture in the Seventeenth Century* (New York, 1991), 92. For Winthrop's model, in which "the rich and mighty should not eat up the poor, nor

the poor and despised rise up against their superiors and shake off their yoke," see *The Puritan Tradition in America, 1620–1730,* ed. Alden T. Vaughan (Columbia, N.Y., 1972), 139.

7. For a different interpretation, according to which the clergy sought a general reformation that "was not, in New England at least, a class struggle," see Richard P. Gildrie, *The Prophane, the Civil, and the Godly: The Reformation of Manners in Orthodox New England, 1679–1749* (University Park, Pa., 1994), 44 and passim. Gildrie emphasizes the seeming even-handedness with which the clergy attacked the covetousness of those who were not members of the lower orders. See, for example, pp. 4, 35, 39, 89.

8. Matthew Mayhew, *A Brief Narrative of the Success which the Gospel Hath Had, Among the Indians* (Boston, 1694), 7. See, for example, *The Journal of John Winthrop,* 248.

9. The imprecision of these labels as well as the central role of Münster, which "had sent a thrill of horror through the respectable classes all over Europe," is emphasized by Christopher Hill, in *Society and Puritanism in Pre-Revolutionary England,* 2d ed. (New York, 1967), 240, and *The World Turned Upside Down: Radical Ideas during the English Revolution* (New York, 1972), 21–22.

10. James M. Stayer, *The German Peasants' War and Anabaptist Community of Goods* (Montreal, 1991), 130. In the years before 1534, ordinary Anabaptists were likely to pool community resources to achieve economic equality for the sake of "a full expression of the love ethic," but they never intended to overthrow either the civil or clerical authority that defended private property as such. See Peter J. Klassen, *The Economics of Anabaptism, 1525–1560* (London, 1964), 115. Some Marxist analysts have seen the event as one reflecting the aspirations of a bourgeois-democratic animus against autocracy, rather than primarily a poor people's uprising. See Karl Kautsky, *Communism in Central Europe in the Time of the Reformation,* trans. J. I. and E. G. Mulliken (1897; reprint, New York, 1959).

11. Rebel leaders seized all money and jewels and prohibited any medium of exchange; they seized and redistributed the property of non-Anabaptist emigrés; and they declared the principle of economic equality. Nothing further was done, however to affect the distribution of wealth. See Stayer, *The German Peasants' War,* 130–38. The rebels attracted joyful adherents from the surrounding region, but far more women than men flowed into the city; the result was an official inauguration of polygamy to preserve the patriarchal moral order. See Kautsky, *Communism in Central Europe,* 268.

12. All quotations are from the authorized King James version of the Bible. See also Christopher Hill, *The English Bible and the Seventeenth-Century Revolution* (New York, 1993), 161.

13. Irvin B. Horst, *The Radical Brethren: Anabaptism and the English Reformation to 1558* (The Hague, 1972), 43. Münster's political use was evident early on. The English Bible translator William Tyndale noted that his opponents (the "holy prelates") feared the Bible might move the people "to rise against their princes, and to make all common, and to make havoc of other men's goods." See *The Obedience of a Christian Man,* cited in Hill, *The English Bible,* 3.

14. *A Short Story of the Rise, Reign, and Ruine of the Antinomians, Familists & Libertines* in *The Antinomian Controversy, 1636–1638: A Documentary History,* ed. David D. Hall, 2d ed. (Durham, N.C., 1990), 275–76. Quoted in Philip F. Gura, *A Glimpse of Sion's Glory: Puritan Radicalism in New England, 1620–1660* (Middletown, Conn., 1984), 79.

15. Edward Winslow, *Hypocrisie Unmasked: By A True Relation of the Proceedings of the Governour and Company of the Massachusets against Samuel Gorton* (London, 1646), 7, 44, 58. Reprinted in *A Library of American Puritan Writings: The Seventeenth Century*, vol. 10, *Tracts Against New England*, ed. Sacvan Bercovitch (New York, 1985).

16. Thomas Harrison to Winthrop, April 2, 1648, in "The Winthrop Papers," vol. 2, *CMHS* 4th ser., 7 (1865): 439. Hill, *World Turned Upside Down*, chap. 7 and passim. H. N. Brailsford, *The Levellers and the English Revolution*, ed. Christopher Hill (Stanford, Calif., 1961), 31–34, 524–27.

17. John Norton, *The Heart of N[ew]-England Rent at the Blasphemies of the Present Generation, Or, A Brief Tractate Concerning the Doctrine of the Quakers* (Cambridge, Mass., 1659), 2, 40. Peter Pratt, *The Prey Taken from the Strong: Or, An Historical Account of the Recovery of One from the Dangerous Errors of Quakerism* (New London, Conn., 1725), v.

18. Norton, *The Heart of N[ew]-England Rent*, 58.

19. De Brès, *Rise, Spring and Foundation of the Anabaptists*, 52, 5, 10–32 (quote on p. 10). De Brès was careful to keep his critique of Anabaptist ideology within the discourse on sin: "but it is worse for them to bind all men unto it [i.e., adult baptism] upon pain of damnation" (p. 52). For the context in which it was published in Boston, see Carla Gardina Pestana, *Quakers and Baptists in Colonial Massachusetts* (New York, 1991), 55–58.

20. Urian Oakes, *New-England Pleaded With, And Pressed to Consider the Things which Concern Her Peace at Least in this Her Day* (Cambridge, 1673), 28, 32, 34, 53. Norton and Oakes were echoed, for example, by James Fitch, who attacked those who "by their Apparel do shew that parity is pleasing to their Pride," and, on the other hand, those men of trade who left aside godliness "to seek worldly Wealth by unrighteous means." See *An Explanation of the Solemn Advice, Recommended to the Council in Connecticut Colony, To the Inhabitants in that Jurisdiction. Respecting the Reformation of those EVILS Which have been the Procuring Cause of the Late Judgements Upon New-England* (Boston, 1683), 43, 44.

21. *The Salem Witchcraft Papers: Verbatim Transcripts of the Legal Documents of the Salem Witchcraft Outbreak of 1692*, ed. Paul Boyer and Stephen Nissenbaum, 3 vols. (New York, 1977), 1:169. See also Carol F. Karlsen, *The Devil in the Shape of a Woman: Witchcraft in Colonial New England* (New York, 1987), 127–28.

22. Cotton Mather, *A Good Master Well Served: A Brief Discourse on the Necessary Properties & Practices of a Good Servant* (Boston, 1696), 35. Moreover, some common people were "so proud, fond and foolish, that they won't let their children go out to service." See Benjamin Wadsworth, *Vicious Courses, Procuring Poverty, Described and Condemned: A Lecture Sermon* (Boston, 1719), 10.

23. Mather, *A Good Master Well Served*, 44, 53. Cotton Mather, *Tremenda: The Dreadful Sound with which the Wicked are to be Thunderstruck* (Boston, 1721), 27; *Theopolis Americana: An Essay on the Golden Street of the Holy City, Publishing a Testimony Against the Corruptions of the Market-Place* (Boston, 1710), 21. For an interesting, desperate attempt by Cotton's father to find some biblical authority to prove that the killing of a master by a servant was somehow worse than other murders, see Increase Mather, *The Wicked Man's Portion, Or A Sermon Preached at the Lecture in Boston in New-England the 18th Day of the 1 Moneth 1674 when Two Men were Executed, Who had Murthered their Master* (Boston, 1675).

24. [Cotton Mather], *Baptistes, or, A Conference About the Subject and Manner of Baptism* ([Boston], 1705), 25.

25. Joyce Appleby, *Economic Thought and Ideology in Seventeenth-Century England* (Princeton, N.J., 1978), 248. In regard to the timing, the central figure in Weber's analysis is Benjamin Franklin, a New Englander who was maturing just as Mather died. See Weber, *The Protestant Ethic*, 53–65.

26. Nash, *The Urban Crucible*, 80; quoted in Perry Miller, *The New England Mind*, vol. 2, *From Colony to Province* (1953; reprint, Boston, 1961), 307.

27. Cotton Mather, *A Very Needful Caution: A Brief Essay to discover the Sin that Slayes Its Ten Thousands* (Boston, 1707), 29.

28. Cotton Mather, *Some Seasonable Advice unto the Poor* [Boston, 1726], 8.

29. Paul Dudley, *Objections to the Bank of Credit Lately Projected at Boston* (Boston, 1714), 9, 22, 24.

30. As quoted in [Samuel Lynde et al.], *A Vindication of the Bank of Credit* ([Boston], 1714), 2. For the proposal, published originally in London in 1688, see [Anonymous], *A Model for Erecting a Bank of Credit* (Boston, 1714).

31. Peter Thatcher, *The Fear of God Restraining Men from Unmercifulness and Iniquity in Commerce* (Boston, 1720), 18, 19, 11.

32. For a description, see Nash, *The Urban Crucible*, 129–36.

33. Benjamin Coleman, *Some Reasons and Arguments Offered to the Good People of Boston and Adjacent Places, For the Setting Up Markets in Boston* (Boston, 1719), 5, 12.

34. Samuel Willard, *Ne Sutor Ultra Crepidam: Or Brief Animadversions Upon the New-England Anabaptists Late Fallacious Narrative* (Boston, 1681), 26. [Elisha Cook Jr.?], *A Letter to An Eminent Clergy-Man in the Massachusett's Bay* ([Boston], 1720), 7, 11.

35. Rosalind Remer, "Old Lights and New Money: A Note on Religion, Economics, and the Social Order in 1740 Boston," *WMQ* 3d ser., 47 (1990): 566–73. [William Douglass], *A Discourse Concerning the Currencies of the British Plantations in America* (Boston, 1740), 20, 29, 37; *An Essay, Concerning Silver and Paper Currencies, More Especially with Regard to the British Colonies in New-England* (Boston, [1738]), 9; *A Letter to Merchant in London Concerning a Late Combination in the Province of the Massachusetts-Bay in New-England* ([Boston], 1741), 9.

36. [Anonymous], *Massachusetts in Agony: Or, Important Hints to the Inhabitants of the Province: Calling Aloud for Justice to be Done to the Oppressed; And Avert the Impending Wrath Over the Oppressors, by "Vincent Centinel"* (Boston, 1750), 6–9, 4, 12, 13–14. This pamphlet may have been written by Samuel Adams Jr., son of a major projector of the land bank of the 1740s, future rebel leader in 1776. This hypothesis is based on a comparison of the syntax and word choice to that in the work known to be written by Adams.

37. Samuel Williams, *A Discourse on the Love of Our Country, Delivered on a Day of Thanksgiving, December, 1774* (Salem, Mass., 1775), 14. "Letter of Novanglus," January 23, 1775, in *Papers of John Adams*, vol. 2, ed. Gregg L. Lint et al. (Cambridge, Mass., 1977), 232; also pp. 300–301. These respond to [Daniel Leonard] *Massachusettensis* (Boston, 1775), 18–19, 61–62.

38. This generalization is based on a reading of all political pamphlets and newspapers during the years of the War for Independence (1775 to 1783). One key measure is revealing. Whereas the early annual "Boston Massacre" orations recalled the English Revolution, after 1775 it was mentioned only to invoke or to lay to rest the ghost of Cromwell vis-à-vis George Washington. These speeches were published, intended especially for popular consumption. See Benjamin Hichbo[u]rn, *An Oration Delivered March 5th, 1777* (Boston, 1777), 18; William Tudor, *An Oration*

Delivered March 5th, 1779 (Boston, 1779), 8–9; Jonathan Mason, *An Oration Delivered March 6th, 1780* (Boston, 1780), 15–17; Thomas Dawes, *An Oration Delivered March 5th, 1781* (Boston, 1781), 17–18; George Richards Minot, *An Oration Delivered March 5th, 1782* (Boston, 1782), 14; Thomas Welsh, *An Oration Delivered March 5th 1783* (Boston, 1783), 7, 10–11.

39. For recent scholarship, see *In Debt to Shays: The Bicentennial of an Agrarian Rebellion*, ed. Robert A. Gross (Charlottesville, Va., 1993).

40. Knox to Washington, October 23, 1786, December 17, 1786, *The Papers of George Washington, Confederation Series,* vol. 4, *April 1786–January 1787,* ed. W. W. Abbot and Dorothy Twohig (Charlottesville, Va., and London, 1995), 300, 460. His response to Knox is one of the single most passionate, indeed, turgid letters he ever wrote. See Washington to Knox, December 26, 1786, *Papers,* 481–84. Washington to Madison, November 5, 1786, *Papers,* 331.

41. "Camillus IV," March 8, 1787; "Lucius Junius Brutus II," October 19, 1786; "Lucius Junius Brutus I," October 12, 1786; *The Independent Chronicle,* in *Works of Fisher Ames, As Published by Seth Ames,* ed. W. B. Allen, 2 vols. (1854; reprint, Indianapolis, 1983), 1:85, 47, 40–41, 43–44. Charles Warren, *Jacobin and Junto: Or, Early American Politics as Viewed in the Diary of Dr. Nathaniel Ames, 1758–1822* (New York and London, 1968 [1931], 43).

42. Gary B. Nash, "The American Clergy and the French Revolution," *WMQ* 3d ser., 22 (1965): 392–412.

43. The New England clergy were mostly preoccupied with theological matters now because of the threat by deists and scoffers. Clergy like Timothy Dwight were always thorough, throwing in angry asides at the supposed Jacobin teachings that "the possession of property [i]s pronounced to be robbery," but their main concern was the dread menace of Jacobin atheism, all the more disturbing in that it seemed to infect Americans of all classes, including wealthy people like Thomas Jefferson. See Timothy Dwight, *The Duty of Americans, At the Present Crisis, Illustrated in a Discourse, Preached on the Fourth of July, 1798* (New Haven, Conn., 1798), 12. He was echoed by his brother, Theodore Dwight, in *An Oration Spoken at Hartford . . . July 4th, 1798* (Hartford, Conn., 1798), 25–26.

44. Allen, ed., *Works of Fisher Ames,* 2:196, 197. [John S. J. Gardiner], *Remarks on the Jacobiniad (Boston, 1795),* 47. Charles D. Hazen, *Contemporary American Opinion of the French Revolution* (Baltimore, 1897), 209–19; Vernon Stauffer, *New England the Bavarian Illuminati* (New York, 1918), chap. 4.

45. J. G. Randall, *Lincoln the President,* vol. 2, *Bull Run to Gettysburg* (New York, 1945), 204–5.

46. *The Papers of Andrew Johnson,* vol. 3, *1858–1860,* ed. Leroy P. Graf, Ralph W. Haskins, and Patricia P. Clark (Knoxville, Tenn., 1972), 166. See also p. 168, n. 20, for contemporary red-baiting on another issue. See also pp. 537–39.

J. Richard Olivas

PARTIAL REVIVAL: THE LIMITS OF THE GREAT AWAKENING IN BOSTON, MASSACHUSETTS, 1740–1742

 WHEN REVEREND GEORGE Whitefield preached in Boston in the fall of 1740, people from all walks of life—rich and poor, black and white, free and unfree, young and old, men and women—flocked to hear his powerful message of spiritual salvation. Respondents to the good news included not only "the Rich and Polite of our Sons and Daughters" but "young and old, middle-aged, Blacks, Papists, Episcopalians, Quakers, and very young children, with notorious sinners." Statements like these, along with a generation of scholarship, support the idea that the Great Awakening was both "great and general," that it "knew no boundaries, social or geographical, that it was both urban and rural, that it reached both lower and upper class."[1] While revivalism in 1740s New England may have known no boundaries, it eventually did encounter limits. Especially in Boston, response to the preaching of George Whitefield, Gilbert Tennent, and others was so great that people asking "What must I do to be saved?" overwhelmed revivalist ministers. Pastors from the three churches that had done the most to promote revival in Massachusetts's "[h]ead town" literally could not counsel the thousands of anxious inquirers who "repaired" to pastoral offices with soul concerns. Like triage workers sorting and treating the wounded according to the seriousness of their injuries, Boston's revivalist clerics were forced to ration spiritual help and counsel. Favored recipients of pastoral attention tended to be persons with family and kinship ties to revivalist congregations.[2]

The Great Awakening in Boston, great and general as it was, did not live up to its inclusive potential. This essay describes how a group of Boston

Table 1

Admissions to Full Communion in Congregatonal Churches,

Church Name	S/O 1740	Nov. 1740	Dec. 1740	Jan. 1741	Feb. 1741	Mar. 1741	Apr. 1741	May 1741	June 1741	July 1741	Aug. 1741
Boston, 1st (Old Church)		0	0	0	1	0	1	3	1	0	0
Boston, 2d (Old North)		1	0	1	2	0	0	0	0	1	1
Boston, 3d (Old South)		1	2	0	3	11	10	12	12	6	2
Boston, 4th (Brattle St.)		4	4	0	5	6	7	10	20	10	11
Boston, 5th (New North)		3	6	3	4	3	3	3	23	17	16
Boston, 6th (New South)		6	0	3	3	2	1	3	1	5	0
Boston, 7th (New Brick)		3	1	0	0	0	1	2	3	0	1
Boston, 8th (Hollis St.)		1	0	1	1	1	0	2	0	0	1
Boston, 9th (West Ch.)		—	—	—	—	—	—	—	—	—	—
All 3 revival churches		8	12	3	12	20	20	26	55	33	29
All Boston Churches		19	13	8	19	23	23	36	60	39	32

(S/O 1740 column labeled: Whitefield preaches in Boston, September & October 1740)

Sources: First Church (Boston), *Records: First Church Boston, 1630–1847,* pt. 3, book B, City Registrar, City Hall, Boston; Second Church (Boston), *Records: Second Church Boston, 1676–1740,* City Registrar, City Hall, Boston; idem, *Record and Index: Second Church Boston, 1741–1816,* City Registrar, City Hall, Boston; Old South Church (Boston), *An Historical Catalogue of the Old South Church (Third Church), Boston* (Boston, 1883), 40–44; idem, *Record and Index: Old South Church, Boston, 1690 to 1833,* City Registry, City Hall, Boston; Brattle Street Church (Boston), *The Manifesto Church: Records of the Church in Brattle Square, Boston, with Lists of Communicants, Baptisms, Marriages, and Funerals, 1699–1872* (Boston, 1902), 111–13, 162–70; New North Church (Boston), *Records*

pastors promoted revival in their city and how race and class circumscribed the revival's reach. Awakening pastors in Boston promoted the revival so successfully and took the gospel message to so many people that in the end they could not—or would not—extend spiritual sanctuary to all persons who desired it. Indeed, church records indicate that revivalist ministers brought only the paltriest fraction of the awakened—one in ten—to communion or full church membership.

By relying on printed sermons exclusively, most historians of Boston revivalism have analyzed the event clerically instead of congregationally. But a prorevivalist minister does not a revivalist congregation make.[3] Only three Boston churches during the years 1740–46 revived (see table 1): Third Church (Old South), Fourth Church (Brattle Street), and Fifth Church (New North).[4] These revivalist congregations were pastored by Thomas Prince and Joseph Sewall, Benjamin Colman and William Cooper, and John

Boston, Massachusetts, November 1740 to October 1742

Sept. 1741	Oct. 1741	Nov. 1741	Dec. 1741	Jan. 1742	Feb. 1742	Mar. 1742	Apr. 1742	May 1742	June 1742	July 1742	Aug. 1742	Sept. 1742	Oct. 1742
0	1	1	1	1	2	0	1	4	1	2	2	1	0
2	0	0	2	2	0	1	0	1	0	2	0	0	0
2	4	5	2	7	1	2	2	2	3	7	0	3	0
7	2	4	3	2	9	2	6	3	3	5	2	3	1
8	8	5	6	3	2	5	4	3	5	2	5	5	0
0	7	5	3	0	0	1	2	0	1	0	0	1	0
0	0	1	0	3	4	1	0	0	0	2	1	0	0
0	0	0	1	1	0	2	1	0	2	0	3	1	1
—	—	—	—	—	—	—	—	—	—	—	—	—	—
17	14	14	11	12	12	9	12	8	11	14	7	11	1
1922	21	18	19	17	14	16	13	15	20	13	14	2	

of the New North Church, Births, Deaths and Marriages, 1714 to 1797, City Registrar, City Hall, Boston; New South Church (Boston), *Records and Index: New South Church Boston, 1719–1776,* City Registrar, City Hall, Boston; "New Brick Church, Boston," *New England Historical and Genealogical Register* 18 (July 1864):237–40; 18 (October 1864):337–44; 19 (July 1865): 230–35; 19 (October 1865):320–24; Hollis Street Church (Boston), *Records and Index: Hollis St. Church Boston, 1732–1848,* City Registrar, City Hall, Boston; idem, *Records: Hollis St. Church Boston, 1733–1847,* City Registrar, City Hall, Boston. Numbers in bold indicate peak months of revival activity. Vertical lines approximate change of season. No communicants in Ninth (West) Church records. Transfers between churches not counted. Table layout by Marian McKenna Olivas.

Webb, respectively. Only churches with unified leadership revived; divided leadership spelled disaster for revival's chances in a congregation.[5]

With Boston's revivalist congregations identified, sermons, correspondence, diary entries of revivalist pastors, and records of revival churches may be used to probe more deeply into the nature of urban awakening. Cohesiveness among Boston's three revivalist churches resulted in part from their early history of united action against the town's traditional orthodoxy. Founding members of Boston's Third Church (Old South) split from First Church in 1668 when newly installed First Church pastor John Davenport vigorously rejected the Half-Way Covenant. Third Church's founding principle was latitudinarian baptism. Boston's Fourth Church (Brattle Street) was known as the "Manifesto Church" for its publication in 1699 of "a platform of practice differing from that of the other Puritan churches." Chief among Brattle Street's ecclesiastical departures was its assertion that covenants binding together church members flowed from natural law instead of the New Testament. And early in its existence, Boston's Fifth Church (New North) called and ordained a pastor over the objection of Boston's organized clergy. Thus, each revivalist church had a tradition of departing from prevailing ministerial practice and orthodoxy.[6]

Ministers like Benjamin Colman and his revivalist colleagues looked for methodical ways of promoting revival, means they were able to control and direct. Natural disasters such as the earthquake of 1727 powerfully awakened people, but as Colman himself observed, "impressions made by judgments [were] very apt to wear off."[7] Natural calamities were not only a severe and tragic means of awaking people, they were entirely unpredictable. The Connecticut River Valley revivals of Jonathan Edwards in 1735–36 intrigued revivalist clerics because they were "surprizing" and had not been prompted by natural disaster.

George Whitefield's ministry represented the best hopes of "the senior *Pastors* of the Town" to promote piety. Whitefield's ability to promote revival distinguished him from all other preachers and recommended him strongly to Boston's revivalist clergy. His dreams of revival suddenly within grasp, Benjamin Colman personally invited Whitefield to come to visit the Bay Colony's head town. On the eve of his Boston visit, Colman and Cooper defended Whitefield's "character and preaching" and prayed "that his purposed coming to us, may be with as full a Blessing of the Gospel of Christ as other Places have experienc'd, and much more abundant, by the Will and Grace of our God!" For good measure, they quoted Whitefield's own words and hoped the evangelist might "be kept humble and dependent on our dear Lord Jesus."[8]

The cause of reviving piety exceeded in importance any shortcomings in God's appointed instrument to help bring it about. Colman and Cooper remarked that South Carolina minister Josiah Smith's sermon vindicating Whitefield was "very unusual, or, perhaps, altogether new. But so is the Occasion. And the Discourse must be look'd upon to be Apologetical rather than Encomiastic. The manifest Design is to support the Cause by vindicating the Man." By distinguishing between God's cause and human agency, Boston's revivalist ministers revealed that their thinking about spiritual awakening proceeded from distinct premises. First, God's cause was paramount. Second, all private concerns must be subordinated to the divine cause. In this view, God's human instruments (like Whitefield) merited correction if they did not promote God's will.[9]

Whitefield, for his part, assured Colman that he shared the "catholick spirit" of Boston's venerable ministers: "When I come to *New England* I shall endeavour to recommend an universal charity amongst all the true members of Christ's mystical body. . . . Assist me, dear Sir, in your prayers, that my coming may be in the fulness of the gospel of peace—I shall come only with my sling and with my stone.—If the Lord shall be pleased so to direct me, that I may strike some self-righteous *Goliahs* to the heart."[10] Colman was well aware that Whitefield's "universal charity" might yield to his willingness to "strike some self-righteous Goliaths to the heart" in Boston. But Colman and others in the revivalist clique desperately wanted Whitefield to come to Boston. Moreover, they felt confident in their ability to shape and control revivalism's outcome. Because Colman and like-minded Boston ministers saw revivalism as the instrument through which Congregationalism might be permanently transformed, they welcomed Whitefield with open arms.

Most congregational churches shared in the fruits of Whitefield's Boston ministry, but not all congregations shared equally. Boston's three revivalist churches got the largest share of Whitefield's time and preaching. Analysis of Whitefield's journal entries reveals that, among Boston's congregations, he spoke most often in the Third, Fourth, and Fifth churches.[11] Boston's revivalist ministers welcomed Whitefield's visit because their vision of revived piety prepared them to take advantage of the Grand Itinerant's ministrations once he arrived.

Whitefield's spiritual power impressed Boston's revivalist ministers and encouraged them to believe that God might send the revival for which they had prayed. Midway through Whitefield's Boston ministry, Benjamin Colman wrote a London correspondent that his "raised expectations are not only answered but exceeded; . . . We pray and hope," continued Colman, "that both we and our congregations shall be quickened & enlarged by [the] Flames of piety and divine love that accompany Mr. Whitefield in his preaching and conversation; & if it please God [that] our souls catch a spark of his heavenly flame."[12] Colman and like-minded minsters, especially those from the Third, Fourth, and Fifth churches, indeed "caught a spark" from Whitefield. By the time Whitefield left Boston, Colman had seen and learned enough. Any remaining doubts he may have had about his own ability to promote a mighty revival of piety vanished. No longer cautiously optimistic, Colman exuded complete confidence.

Colman's assurance that revival was coming stemmed from a belief that he was on the verge of glimpsing God's American "Sion" in all its glory. In a sermon he preached shortly after Whitefield's departure, *Souls flying to Jesus Christ*, Colman argued that prophecies of ecclesiastical glory and Gentile ingathering were being fulfilled as he spoke. The church, he declared, "is call'd upon to *lift up her Eyes*, and *see round about*; the People gathering and *flowing* to her. And though at *first* there might be some *Fear* and *Distrust*, as *Peter* felt, when he was about to go unto the *Uncircumcised*; yet that wou'd be *soon over*, and her narrow *doubting* Heart *enlarg'd* with Joy . . . because of the *Abundance of the Sea*, and the *Forces of the Gentiles*, coming to her."[13] Colman believed that God was about to fill Boston with prosperity and piety. On the basis of this conviction, Colman activated his plan to revive Boston's churches.

Church revivalism sought to sanctify Boston's ecclesiastical order by encouraging widespread spiritual conversion to Christ. Congregational clergy for more than a century had envisioned the conversion of people from all ranks of society. What changed in the thinking of Colman and revivalist clergy was the rapidity and scope of conversion. Comparing people coming to Christ as a cloud, Colman proclaimed that "the Cloud flies irresistibly; no Act or Power of Man can stop it." The doctrine that a person was drawn irresistibly to Christ was an ancient Calvinist tenet. In a time of revival, however, many individuals came to Christ simultaneously. What Colman propounded, in effect, was a doctrine of mass conversion: "And so should the gathering to Christ be, and into his Church; more general and *universal. Not, as it is with us commonly, now and then a single soul*; but as it was in the Beginning of the Christian Church, when they came in *Thousands*." Not only would "thousands" be quickly converted, but conversion would be "universal," encompassing all ranks of people. Colman foresaw spiritual conversions of "[h]igh and low, rich and poor, Parents and Children, *Ministers* and *People* together! how good and pleasant would this Unity among us be! not for a *Party*, not for a *Distinction*, no but *Heaven*; all without Distinction." Colman then proceeded to invite to the Lord's Table the people he envisioned as belonging to this unified, distinction-free Christianity: "the Men of Merchandize and Business, of Labour and Diligence," "poorer Brethren," "Parents and Children," "Servants, and the meanest of our Household Servants, even our poor Negroes," and "Elder People."[14] Thus, the immediate, post-Whitefield period in Boston was one of tremendous optimism and millennial expectations.

In the interval between Whitefield's departure from Boston in October 1740 and Gilbert Tennent's arrival two months later, revivalist pastors continued the spiritual awakening begun by Whitefield's preaching. What they experienced during Whitefield's ministry only whetted their appetites. At the opening of a new Tuesday evening lecture, Colman expressed the determination of revivalist pastors to continue what Whitefield had begun. Among much of the populace, too, enthusiasm for spiritual things continued to increase after Whitefield's departure. According to one Boston newspaper, "Last Tuesday Evening the Rev. Dr. Sewall took the second Lecture at the Meeting-House in *Brattle Street*. Tho' the Evening was dark and wet, there was a vast Assembly. It is suppos'd four or five thousand within the Walls; and many came that could not get in. The Congregation seem'd greatly affected; and it is really surprizing to see what a Disposition there is in People now to attend upon the Ministry of the Word. So that there is great Reason to hope for a happy Revival of primitive Zeal and Godliness amongst us. *So come Lord Jesus!*"[15] Forbidding weather and the onset of one of the eighteenth century's coldest winters did not deter Bostonians from seeking the promised salvation.

An immediate problem facing the revivalist pastors was how to guide a large number of spiritually awakened persons to the next stage in the conversion process: conviction. This state of contrition, as one historian has noted, "is the moment of awareness, when a man perceives" his sinful condition before a holy God. Whitefield had awakened many but convicted few. Nathanael Appleton, a revivalist pastor from Cambridge, wondered shortly after Whitefield's departure if God was "now about to revive his Work."[16] Fervent and firm in their belief that God was about to do just that, Appleton's revivalist colleagues in Boston prepared themselves for Gilbert Tennent's arrival and the spiritual convictions they hoped his ministry would achieve.

Gilbert Tennent continued Whitefield's labors by producing a conviction of sin in those whom the Grand Itinerant had awakened. As they had done during Whitefield's visit, revivalist churches shared disproportionately in the fruits of Tennent's convicting work. Diary entries and other records indicate that Tennent had forty-one speaking engagements in Boston; thirty-two of them were in the three revivalist congregations.[17] This evidence, combined with an understanding of Tennent's use of "terrors," sheds light on the important post-Whitefield phase of Boston revivalism. Gilbert Tennent employed two primary means to bring awakened persons under spiritual conviction: the preaching of terrors and the protracted meeting. All evidence suggests that he employed both in Boston's revival churches within limits that host pastors prescribed. The preaching of terrors, designed to "wound" and "shock" hearers, was a homiletical method that involved "denouncing and describing, with the utmost vehement *pathos* and awful solemnity, the terrors of an offended *deity*, the *threats* of a broken *Law*, the miseries of a sinful *state*."[18] For maximum effect, Tennent combined "terrors" with successive, drawn-out meetings, prolonged back-to-back meetings that aided the itinerant preacher in breaking down spiritual resistance to revival in a congregation.

Tennent's tactics increasingly alarmed revivalist pastors, however, because terror preaching, if taken too far, discouraged conviction. Third Church pastors, for theological and personal reasons, tried to finesse the negative effects of Tennent's tactics upon their parishioners. Thomas Prince objected to preaching by Tennent that discouraged covenanters and others from trying to earn admission to full communion. "So far did Mr. *Tennent's* awakening Ministry shake their Hopes and hinder them," wrote

Prince, "that those whom I apprehended to be *thirsty*, and thought myself obliged to encourage, I found the impressions of his Preaching had discouraged." Careful to keep the revival from grinding to a halt by excessive introspection, Prince selectively weeded out the spiritual compunctions that Tennent had sown. "Yea, some who had been in *full Communion* were made so suspicious of themselves as to refrain partaking," wrote Prince, "and I had no small Pains to remove their Scruples." One person hindered from coming into full church membership was the Rev. Mr. Prince's own son, Thomas Prince Jr.[19]

Boston's revivalist pastors continued to support Tennent's ministry in spite of occasional misgivings and disappointments. From the beginning, revivalist pastors sought to promote and extend their own brand of middle-way revivalism that steered a course between "pious Zealots and cold, Diabolical opposers."[20] Those parts of Tennent's ministry that smacked of "pious zealotry" and boorishness, they rejected; the remainder they embraced. God's cause was greater than any single individual.

Despite gnawing doubts about terror preaching among many Boston ministers, Tennent's attempts to bring Bostonians under conviction generally succeeded. Tennent's searching sermons in Boston's three revivalist churches caused awakened parishioners to inquire seriously about their souls. Under Tennent's preaching the "happy concerns" and "excited desires" of the awakened yielded to "deep Convictions of their unconverted and lost Condition." When formerly excited hearers came "with the Enquiry, What shall we do to be saved?" Prince and his revivalist colleagues knew that their plan of church revivalism was moving in the right direction. By speaking with anxious inquirers, Prince discovered the reason that Tennent's preaching convicted so many:

[I]t was not so much the *Terror* as the *searching* Nature of his Ministry, that was the principal Means of their *Conviction*. It was not meerly, not so much his laying open the Terrors of the Law and Wrath of God, or Damnation of Hell; (for this they could pretty well bear, as long as they hoped these belonged not to them, or they could easily avoid them;) as his laying open their many vain and secret *Shifts* and *Refuges, counterfeit Resemblances* of Grace, *delusive* and *damning Hopes*, their utter *Impotence*, and impending Danger of Destruction: whereby they found all their Hopes and Refuges of Lies to fail them, and themselves exposed to eternal Ruin, unable to help themselves, and in a Lost Condition. This *searching* Preaching was both the *suitable* and principal *Means* of their *Conviction*.[21]

Awakened by Whitefield's preaching and convicted by Tennent's, large numbers of Bostonians neared the kingdom of God. Boston's revivalist clerics prepared to supply the one thing they lacked: spiritual conversion.

After Tennent preached a farewell sermon in Brattle Street Church on Monday, March 2, 1741, revivalist pastors methodically guided awakened and convicted parishioners to conversion. The pace of revivalism's third phase now quickened dramatically. Thomas Prince of Third Church said that the post-Tennent period "was such a Time as we never knew." Parishioners initiated and pastors responded. Awakened and convicted Bostonians sought conversion by visiting pastors in overwhelming numbers. Prince noted the surge of visitors seeking spiritual relief from revivalist pastors: "The Rev. Mr. *Cooper* [Fourth Church] was won't to say, that more came to him in *one Week* in deep Concern about their Souls, than in the whole *twenty-four Years* of his preceeding Ministry. I can also say the same as to the Numbers who repaired to me. . . . And Mr. *Webb* [Fifth Church] informs me, he has had in the same Space above a *Thousand*."[22]

Most Boston conversions occurred in these one-to-one sessions between pastor and individual. Few conversions took place prior to these private meetings. As table 1 shows, admissions to full communion did not commence in substantial numbers until March 1741 and then only in Prince's Third Church.[23] That Fourth and Fifth churches revived later and more strongly suggests that their pastors soon became skilled in the sort of spiritual work that Prince elaborated.

Frequent contact between parishioners and pastors stimulated popular interest in the revival. "Both People and Ministers seem'd under a divine Influence to quicken each other," wrote Prince. Bostonians also crowded evening lectures so completely that revivalist pastors were forced to begin new ones. Three new evening lectures opened—on Fridays at Boston Third and on Tuesdays and Fridays at Boston Fifth. These three new meetings, in addition to the Tuesday evening lecture at Boston Fourth, gave revivalist pastors increased opportunities to preach and counsel their parishioners. Prince also reported that at this time "private Societies for religious Exercises" formed in about thirty locations throughout Boston.[24] Meetings to promote revival now took place every night of the week. Awakening in Boston's three churches was fully underway.

In spite of the extraordinary surge of spiritual awakening, revivalism practiced by Boston's churches may have been less inclusive than contemporary reports suggest. Evidence indicates that these churches failed to take advantage of the eighteenth century's greatest opportunity to extend church membership to all sectors of Boston's populace. Revivalist pastors, overwhelmed by visits from anxious souls, turned inward, engaging in what Edmund S. Morgan, referring to the seventeenth century, identified as "Puritan tribalism."[25] The practice of caring first and foremost for souls with existing ties to the congregations, perhaps more than any single factor, limited revivalism's reach in Boston.

The brand of church awakening advocated by Boston's revivalist cadre knew, in theory, no social bounds. Preaching by Whitefield and Tennent likewise extended Christ's offer of forgiveness to all hearers without distinction. As noted earlier, after Whitefield's departure from Boston, Colman expressed his desire to see a distinctionless Christian unity that included Bostonians from all walks of life. Then to a crowded Brattle Street audience excited to hear the things of God, Colman made his intentions explicit: "Come into his Church, to full Communion, to the Lord's Table, to eat of his Bread and to drink of his Cup."[26]

First in rivulets, then in streams, and finally in rivers the people came, but their absence from contemporary church rolls has escaped the notice of Awakening historians. Thomas Prince wrote that he, William Cooper, and John Webb gave spiritual counsel to an estimated 2,200 persons over a period of three months. Awakened and for the most part convicted, these persons sought salvation and its outward emblem, admission to full communion. How many of the 2,200 earned admission to full communion? Only an educated guess is possible, but consider the following: 256 persons were admitted to full communion in Boston's three revivalist churches in the twelve months following March 1741, the month in which pastors began to counsel prospective communicants about their souls. This figure represents only 11.6 percent of the 2,200 prospective communicants. Surviving records do not indicate what happened to the rest.[27] Unless we are to believe that nearly two thousand people lost their conviction or never had it to begin with, some other explanation for the massive drop in numbers must be found.

There can be no doubt that revivalist pastors initially desired and promoted mass conversions. Colman spoke for the revivalist coterie when he urged that the gathering of New Englanders to Christ should be "as it was in the Beginning of the Christian Church, when they came in *Thousands*." Yet thousands of prospective communicants lined up to inquire about their souls, and a bottleneck formed at the pastor's office. As Prince described it, "*Boys* and *Girls*, *young Men* and *Women*, *Indians* and *Negroes*, *Heads of Families*, *aged* Persons; those who had been in *Full Communion* and going on in a Course of Religion *many Years*." How particular revivalist ministers dealt with the souls of persons from these groups no doubt differed, but small windows into this clergy-led process exist in a variety of surviving documents. Colman's response to enslaved blacks and white servants, for instance, was very otherworldly and left undisturbed their bonded positions. He preached: "O that *Masters* would take more care of your precious Souls! The *pious* Master, who is Christ's *Servant*, will be glad to see his *Negro* above a Servant, a *Brother* at the Lord's Table with him. It is in my *Sight*, I can truly say, a Beauty to our Communions, to see a Number of the poor *Blacks* with us."[28] Colman's words imply more than a mere invitation to communion. Brattle Street's minister asked the slaveholding member "to see his Negro . . . at the Lord's Table with him," that is, as a spiritual equal. But Colman left no doubt that he intended to deliver "poor Negroes" only from Satan's chains, not those of "pious Masters." Moreover, for reasons not entirely clear, his reference to "a Number of the *poor Blacks*" seems to restrict the upper limit of potential black communicants, something he did not do for any other group.

Nevertheless, Colman's offer to admit blacks to the Lord's Table threatened to disturb a long-standing church practice of denying formal church admission to the enslaved blacks of church members. Colman, in fact, had no congregational authority to broaden church membership to include enslaved converts. Admission of blacks to full communion, even if approved by a revivalist pastor, depended ultimately on the master's willingness to differ from his social peers. In Colman's Brattle Street Church only two servants were admitted to full communion in the twelve months following Whitefield's Boston ministry: "Violet, Servant to Mr. Wm. Tyler" and "Violet. Negro Servt. to Mr. Righton."[29] Since admission to full communion at Brattle Street in theory granted a person the right to vote on important church matters, some masters may have resisted formal recognition of black spiritual equality. Whether or not Righton and Tyler differed from other slaveowners on this question is not clear. In admitting two women, Brattle Streeters granted membership only to slaves who, because of their sex, were denied the vote and therefore would be unable to participate in church governance.[30] Most blacks invited to full communion by Colman never saw that invitation fulfilled. Black men and other black women were permitted only adult baptism in Brattle Street Church. In the twelve months following Whitefield's visit to Boston, eleven adult blacks were baptized, presumably because masters forbade conferral of membership and what that membership implied.[31]

What was true for enslaved blacks was almost certainly true for indentured servants. The case of Ashley Bowen illustrates the experience of one young male servant who visited John Webb of Boston's Fifth Church for spiritual advice. After being apprenticed at the age of thirteen to a Boston ship captain named Peter Hall, Bowen wrote in his journal:

> Now it was in the time of New Lights or Whitefield and Company. As my sister Molly was baptized by Mr. [Simon] Bradstreet some small time before, she then being a member at our Uncle Webb's New North Meeting House, and so she would have me baptized there. My master indulging me to spend the evening with her, she took the opportunity to take me with her to Parson Webb's and fit me to baptized &c. As we [were] preparing our ship for sea, my master allowed me to go to my sister's as often as I should desire, and in order for my being the better prepared for the business he, Mr. Webb, gave me a book of instructions, and I read it as often as I could find time. At length the day was fixed on that I was to be baptized. Note: my master was not consulted in the business, and it happened that one H. Johnson,

being at tea at his acquaintances', happened to hear this discovery that there was to be a grand christening at the New North on Sunday. He being a church-man [he] came and acquainted my master of its being me. He, my master, came home and inquired into the affair and found that I had a book, which he demand[ed]. I shew it to him. He directed me to take the book and carry [it] to Parson Webb's with his compliments and said I was his apprentice and I should not be christened in his time. So I left the book and came off well satisfied as to christening.[32]

Bowen's journal entry illuminates a number of important aspects of the counseling experienced by awakened persons. His first visit to Boston's Fifth Church stemmed more from his sister's interest than his own. John Webb's apparent familial relation to Bowen perhaps caused him to give the young man more attention than he might otherwise receive. Webb likely discerned that Bowen was awakened but not under conviction, so he gave the indentured servant "a book of instructions" to produce spiritual conviction and, in Bowen's view, "fit him for baptism." Bowen apparently paid return visits to Webb, because "at length the day was fixed on" that he should be baptized. New North had only one pastor, so it was Webb who, in a judgment of charity, considered Bowen to be a new creature in Christ and scheduled the baptism. In spite of Bowen's hopeful status and his familiarity with "Uncle Webb," Webb then acceded to Captain Peter Hall's refusal to permit Bowen's baptism "on [Hall's] time." Hall did not attend New North, and unlike "pious masters" who did attend (along with their black slaves), he did not have to fear the implications of granting formal spiritual equality to his servant who would then sit at the Lord's Table with him. Yet Hall's inquiry "into the affair" and his demand to see the book suggest hostility specifically to the new revivalist religion. Moreover, the complicity of "one H. Johnson" in tipping off Peter Hall indicates that another "churchman" saw reason to stop the proceeding before it went too far or at least to give power over Bowen's prospective membership to his master, despite the latter's unregenerate status. Was Johnson doing unto Hall what he would want Hall to do unto him? Webb evidently did not challenge Hall's reason for denying baptism to Bowen. As a result, young Bowen "left the book" Webb had given him and "came off well satisfied as to christening."[33] Although Bowen seems not to have cared about his canceled baptism, scholars are left to wonder about reasons for Hall's refusal and (more important) Webb's acquiescence in a social arrangement that prohibited him from discharging his spiritual duties to baptize new converts.

By yielding to a master's polite but firm insistence that his servant be denied baptism, Webb revealed the limits of pastoral authority in 1740s Boston. Revivalist ministers were able to redefine soteriological doctrines in order to promote the revival, and they maintained their prerogative to decide who was converted. But ministers encountered deep resistance when they sought to admit enslaved persons and servants to full communion. Slaveholding church members apparently withstood attempts by revivalist ministers to confer church membership on their slaves. In so doing they relied on attitudes and precedents that the revivalists themselves had shared in and agreed to. Historians must therefore sort out why Colman invited blacks and indentured servants into church membership in the first place despite a long-standing practice of excluding them. Colman welcomed blacks and indentured servants, but he welcomed others more.

The customary way of adding what Colman once referred to as "persons proper" to the church was to admit prospective communicants from families with existing ties to a church. Signposts in the documentary record indicate that this was the path of least resistance for revivalist churches. Revivalist minsters like Joseph Sewall believed that conviction and conversion spread most rapidly among family members because "what toucheth the one; affecteth the other. And this is in an especial manner observable in such as are near and dear to each other. When the Child is in Distress, the tender Parent is presently touched with the feeling of it's Sorrow: When the Brother crieth out in Anguish of Soul, the kind Sister can't forbear to console with him. Accordingly, When it pleaseth the holy Spirit to use these Inclinations and Affections in Men as Means, good Impression[s], by the divine Blessing, wonderfully propagate and multiply."[34] Thus, families were both the means and end of conversion. John Webb, who admitted more people to full communion than any other revivalist minister, clearly concentrated his efforts on awakened and convicted souls who belonged to established New North families. Records from Fifth Church reveal that at least six of every ten persons admitted to full communion in the fourteen months following Whitefield's departure from Boston were related to existing parishioners.[35] As long as the revival continued, Webb strengthened the piety of Boston families deeply rooted in the church. Once revivalist ministers were satisfied with their catch, they drew in their nets.

Their churches brimming with clannish communicants, revivalist ministers grew increasingly frustrated with the unconverted and indicated that Christ shared their feeling. In September 1741, as conversions in New North Church plunged toward their prerevival level, John Webb warned his hearers that Christ's wooing soon would turn into wrath: "And what art thou made of, O Sinner, that thou can'st resist all this Importunity? O, arise, and open to him immediately, least this hot Love, by thy obstinate Refusals, should quickly turn into flaming Wrath."[36] Despite the theological problems of ascribing to Christ the capricious qualities of a scorned lover, Webb's rhetoric suggests that mutual edification between pastors and people had ceased. Formation of an antirevivalist congregation by a son of the venerable Cotton Mather in December 1741 convinced revivalist ministers that positive aspects of the revival had reached the point of diminishing returns.[37] Convinced that the cause of Christ was beginning to suffer, Colman and his revivalist clerics no longer thought of enlarging the revival but instead strove to conserve the fruit of it.

Thus, in late 1741, a revival of tremendous force and vitality cooled. Whitefield's powerful ministry spiritually awakened Bostonians from all walks of life, and Tennent's searching preaching within the city's Third, Fourth, and Fifth churches convicted many of their need for spiritual salvation. In an attempt to guide awakened and convicted souls to Jesus, revivalist ministers preached both publicly and privately. Their original intention of meeting each anxious inquirer face-to-face, in the end, proved impossible. Deluged with Bostonians asking "What must I do to be saved?" revivalist clerics bestowed their spiritual labors largely on prospective communicants who had familial ties to existing church members. Once ministers admitted to church membership large numbers of clan members, they apparently concluded that their work was substantially complete.

Beyond these three churches, however, Boston revivalism retained enormous vitality by late 1741. Revivalist clerics could not put an end to the spiritual seeking of the Bostonians they had passed over in the process of spiritual rationing. Despite barriers to church membership erected by ministers, a "great Number" of non-family members and lowly Bostonians was "still seeking and striving to enter in at the strait Gate." Excluded from the Lord's Table within the church walls of Boston's revivalist congregations, they carried on the revival "out of doors" in late 1741 and 1742. This second, more radical phase of the revival provided an outlet for their religious expression, and to the extent that people found salvation, fulfilled the inclusive potential the Awakeners originally envisioned.[38]

For their part, John Webb and his revivalist colleagues no longer spoke of Boston revivalism as on ongoing process but rather as a past event. From fall 1741 on, they praised revival's spread elsewhere. Revival's focus shifted to towns in northern Essex County, the Piscataqua region of New Hampshire and modern-day Maine, and southeastern Massachusetts. Thomas Prince, William Cooper, and Webb spoke nostalgically of the "wondrous work of God" that was "making its Triumphant Progress thro' the Land. . . . [It] has already forced many Men of *clear Minds, strong Powers, considerable Knowledge*, & firmly riveted in the *Arminian* and *Socinian* Tenets, to give them all up at once & yield to the adorable *Sovereignty* & *Irresistibility* of the Divine Spirit in his saving Operations on the Souls of Men."[39] By this time, the revival had passed through Boston and gone on.

While never disavowing the revival, Benjamin Colman distanced himself from "pious zealots" who preached to Bostonians passed over in revivalism's first phase. In particular, he urged his people to avoid giving

"Countenance and Encouragement to *illiterate* and *half-learnt* Persons to go about *exhorting* and drawing *Hearers* by their *Shew of Affection* to Souls for their spiritual Profit and saving Good." Colman wrote that his testimony about the revival "is humbly given, *for* the Great and *wondrous Work of God's Grace* manifest in many Parts of the Land, and also *against* some Things which may dishonour and obstruct it." At the same time, Colman reemphasized whenever possible his well-known commitment to catholicity in order to soften public perception that he and his church had been tainted by a "party" spirit. Whether it was inviting a Presbyterian minister into his pulpit or keeping an uncharacteristically low profile during an intense debate over the extravagances of revivalism, Colman returned to his moderate and latitudinarian roots.[40]

Colman's revivalist colleagues likewise acted to contain problems connected to the revival and to prevent further commotions. Joseph Sewall urged stronger pastoral oversight of religious societies meeting in homes throughout Boston. Sewall wrote: "Let the more private Meetings of Christians be encouraged, & well regulated. Exercise yourselves in such Duties as are proper for you, and let good Hours be observed, that Family-Religion and Closet-Piety may have their due Proportion of Time. . . . And if for Want of a due Regard to these Seasons, our Families should suffer in their Spiritual or Temporal Interests, the God of Order will be displeased with us." Sewall also made clear that a barrier had been erected around the Lord's Table: "Let those of us who are invited to sit down at the Lord's Table the next Sabbath, look to it that we go to that holy Feast with earnest Desires after Christ, and the Blessings which flow from his Death."[41] Only those persons who were "invited to sit down at the Lord's Table" were allowed to partake of its spiritual nourishment. This restriction no doubt reassured parishioners that their slaves and servants would not presume full equality with them. Revivalism did not reform more than an occasional master's piety enough to think and do otherwise.

Revivalism's limitations convinced Colman that God's kingdom invaded this world much less dramatically than he had once thought. It became apparent to Colman early in 1742 that the prophesied "glory of Sion" had not, in fact, arrived. There is no evidence that Colman confessed his involvement in erroneous date setting. Rather, he seems to have concluded that God "magnified his Word in the Prophecies and Promises of it, accomplished and fulfilled to his People," not suddenly but "gradually, in wondrous Manner brought about, in Spite of all the Opposition made against it." Boston revivalism had been a miracle whereby "God maintains the Honour of his Word."[42] What Colman and his revivalist colleagues witnessed was not the dawning of the millennial age after all but a divine sign that God still loved and favored New England. The revival without limits that revivalists had once anticipated lay in the distant future, at the consummation of the age. Partial revivalism was the best one could hope for in this life, at least in 1740–41 Boston.

Notes

1. Benjamin Colman to [George Whitefield], 8 June 1741, in *The Weekly History* 22 (5 Sept. 1741), 2. [John] M[oorhea]d *to a Friend in* Glasgow, 19 June 1741, in *Weekly History* 26 (3 Oct. 1741), 3; Edwin S. Gaustad, "A Great and General Awakening," in *The Great Awakening: Event and Exegesis,* ed. Darrett B. Rutman (New York, 1970), 16. See also Gaustad, "Society and the Great Awakening in New England," *WMQ* 3d ser., 11 (1954): 566–77.

2. This essay abridges chapter 3 of my doctoral dissertation. See J. Richard Olivas, "Great Awakenings: Time, Space, and the Varieties of Religious Revivalism in Massachusetts and Northern New England, 1740–1748" (Ph.D. diss., University of California, Los Angeles, 1997).

3. For a recent attempt to categorize Boston's Awakening-era churches clerically, on the basis of the published sermons of their ministers, see Rosalind Remer, "Old Lights and New Money: A Note on Religion, Economics, and the Social Order in 1740 Boston," *WMQ* 3d ser., 47 (1990): 566–73.

4. According to the criteria used in this study, a congregation is said to have experienced revival when ten or more adults made religious professions in any one of three categories—baptism, owning the covenant, or earning admission to full communion—in a single month. The numerical threshold of ten is arbitrary but useful. While the impact of ten conversions undeniably would be greater on a smaller congregation, most of Boston's Congregational churches appear to have had rough parity in terms of size. Exceptions would be younger congregations such as Eighth and Ninth churches, founded in 1732 and 1737, respectively, both with strongly anti-revivalist pastors. In any case, Boston's other Congregational churches fell far below the minimum numerical threshold for revival. Excepting Sixth Church, not one of the city's remaining churches registered more than four admissions to full communion at any time in the seven-year period from January 1, 1740, through December 31, 1746.

5. Pastors played a disproportionate role in the revival of local congregations. They possessed something akin to a spiritual "veto" over revival in a particular church; they could not promote it single-handedly, but they could prevent its occurrence. A minister's ability to veto revival also existed in a co-pastorate, such as was common in Boston. If co-pastors divided over revival, as in the cases of First and Second churches in Boston, awakening did not occur.

6. Departures from orthodoxy by the three churches individually are well known. See Harold Field Worthley, *An Inventory of the Records of the Particular (Congregational) Churches of Massachusetts Gathered 1620–1805,* Harvard Theological Studies, no. 25 (Cambridge, Mass., 1970), 69–70; Church in Brattle Square (Boston), *Records of the Church in Brattle Square[,] Boston, with Lists of Communicants, Baptisms[,] Marriages and Funerals: 1699–1872* (Boston, 1902), 3, esp. Article XIV; Robert Middlekauff, *The Mathers: Three Generations of Puritan Intellectuals, 1596–1728* (New York, 1971), 219–20, 362–64; Charles W. Akers, "Religion and the American Revolution: Samuel Cooper and the Brattle Street Church,"

WMQ 3d ser., 35 (1978): 477–98; John Corrigan, "Catholick Congregational Clergy and Public Piety," *Church History* 60 (1991): 210–22; Anthony Gregg Roeber, "'Her Merchandize . . . Shall Be Holiness to the Lord': The Progress and Decline of Puritan Gentility at the Brattle Street Church, Boston, 1715–1745," *New England Historical and Genealogical Register* 131 (1977): 175–94. Less well known is the alignment of Third, Fourth, and Fifth churches that made possible 1740–41 revivalism in Boston.

7. Benjamin Colman, *The Danger of People's Loosing the good Impressions made by the late awful Earthquake* (Boston, 1727), 1. See also Joseph Sewall, *The Duty of a People to Stand in Awe of God* (Boston, 1727).

8. William Cooper, *The Doctrine of Predestination unto Life* (Boston, 1740), 4. Ministers from Boston's three revivalist churches had been ordained longer than other Boston clergy, with the exception of Rev. Andrew LeMercier, pastor of Boston's French Huguenot Church, and Thomas Foxcroft of First Church. On his arrival in Boston, Whitefield affirmed that it was "the Rev. Dr. Colman, who long since had sent me an invitation." See diary entry of George Whitefield, 18 September 1740, in *George Whitefield's Journals* (Guildford and London, 1960), 457. See also *Three Letters to the Reverend Mr. George Whitefield* (Philadelphia, [1739]); Josiah Smith, *The character, preaching, &c. of the Reverend Mr. George Whitefield*, with a preface by Benjamin Colman and William Cooper (Boston, 1740), vi.

9. Colman and Cooper, preface to *Character, preaching*, i. Revivalist ministers' willingness to criticize the messenger while still supporting the message would be important later, when they selectively criticized Whitefield and Tennent and, later still, the radical Awakeners more broadly. They did so because God's cause, in their opinion, was suffering.

10. George Whitefield to Benjamin Colman, 24 January 1740, in *The Works of the Reverend George Whitefield*, 3 vols. (London, 1771; reprint, with additional letters, London, 1976), 1:142.

11. Within the city limits of Boston, Whitefield preached twenty-six times: six times on the Common, one time apiece at the city's alms- and workhouses, and eighteen times in the pulpits of Boston's nine Congregational churches. Whitefield preached in Boston's revival churches as follows: Third Church (Old South), five times; Fourth Church (Brattle Street), four times; and Fifth Church (New North), three times. In Boston's nonrevival churches, Whitefield preached as follows: twice in First Church (Old Church) and Second Church (Old North) and once each in Seventh Church (New Brick) and Eighth Church (Hollis Street). In Boston's Sixth Church (New South) and Ninth Church (West Church) he did not speak. In the former a meetinghouse stampede killed five people and forced the only service there to be dismissed and reconvened on the Common. See *George Whitefield's Journal*, 456–63, 468–74.

12. Benjamin Colman to William Harris et al., 3 October 1740, Benjamin Colman Papers, Massachusetts Historical Society, Boston (microfilm).

13. Benjamin Colman, *Souls flying to Jesus Christ* (Boston, 1740), 7–8. Whitefield's ministry, Colman believed, initiated fulfillment of Isaiah 60:1–8.

14. Colman, *Souls flying*, 7, 8, 14, 23–25.

15. *The Boston Weekly News-Letter*, 30 October 1740, 2.

16. Norman Pettit, *The Heart Prepared: Grace and Conversion in Puritan Spiritual Life*, 2d ed. (Middletown, Conn., 1989), 18. Reformed Protestants did not always agree on precise stages in the *ordo salutis* (way of salvation), but awakening and conviction preceded conversion in most formulations. See Charles L. Cohen,

God's Caress: The Psychology of Puritan Religious Experience (New York, 1986), 75–77. See also Nathaniel Appleton, *God, and not minister to have the glory* (Boston, 1741), 23.

17. The primary source for reconstructing Gilbert Tennent's New England itinerary is Daniel Rogers, The Diary of Reverend Daniel Rogers, 1740–51, Daniel Rogers Papers, New York Historical Society, New York (microfilm). Other sources for confirming and augmenting details in Rogers's account include Boston's four newspapers and Nicholas Gilman, "The Diary of Nicholas Gilman," trans. and ed. William Kidder (M.A. thesis, University of New Hampshire, 1982). Totals are approximations only, since a few entries in Rogers's diary are either unaccounted for or difficult to decipher.

18. Gilbert Tennent, "A Prefatory Discourse to the following Sermons with Relations of some Memoirs of the Author's Conversion and Character," in John Tennent, *The Nature of Regeneration opened* (London, 1741), iii, quoted in Milton J. Coalter Jr., *Gilbert Tennent, Son of Thunder: A Case Study of Continental Pietism's Impact on the First Great Awakening in the Middle Colonies* (New York, 1986), 43.

19. Thomas Prince, *The Christian History, Containing Accounts of the Revival and Propagation of Religion in Great-Britain, America &c*, 2 vols. (Boston, 1744–45), 2:396; Hamilton Andrews Hill, *History of the Old South Church (Third Church) Boston, 1669–1884*, 2 vols. (Boston, 1890), 1:519 n. 1.

20. John Moorhead to John Willison, 30 July 1742, in "Glasgow-Weekly-History, 1743," *Massachusetts Historical Society Proceedings* 53 (1920): 211–13. Moorhead, pastor of Boston's First Presbyterian Church, summarized a ministerial ethos shared by Boston's revivalist pastors.

21. Prince, *Christian History*, 2:381–82, 2:381 n. 1, 2:390.

22. Ibid., 2:391–92, 2:391.

23. It may be that Third Church revived first because Prince ably distinguished between those effects caused by terrors and those caused by searching preaching. To visitors under terrors but still not convicted, Prince preached privately in a searching manner. Prince wrote that "*searching* Preaching by *our own Ministers and others*, I also observed was the most successful Means of bringing People into powerful *Convictions*." See Prince, *Christian History*, 2:390. Admissions to full communion most reliably indicate conversions, though the former never guaranteed the latter.

24. Ibid., 2:392, 395.

25. Edmund S. Morgan, *The Puritan Family: Religion and Domestic Relations in Seventeenth-Century New England* (Boston, 1944; reprint, rev. and enl., New York, 1966), 168–86.

26. Colman, *Souls flying*, 23.

27. Prince, *Christian History*, 2:391. Cooper and Prince each counseled "about *six Hundred* different Persons in *three Months* Time." Webb "had in the same Space above a *Thousand*." These numbers do not include repeat visits by the same person nor different people seen by Joseph Sewall and Benjamin Colman, co-pastors with Prince and Cooper at Third and Fourth Churches, respectively. For a different view, see John William Raimo, "Spiritual Harvest: The Anglo-American Revival in Boston, Massachusetts, and Bristol, England, 1739–1742" (Ph.D. diss., University of Wisconsin, 1974), 111. One year's time easily would have permitted revival churches to absorb into membership prospective communicants from the March–May 1741 period. From March 1741 to February 1742, revivalist pastors admitted 263 persons to full communion. Of these, Third Church contributed 74;

Fourth Church, 91; and Fifth Church, 98. Boston's five remaining Congregational churches admitted only 67 in the same twelve-month period, with 27 of those occurring in Sixth Church (New South). Communicant statistics for Ninth (West) Church do not exist. The percentage of successful communicants drops when the total number of seekers includes prospective communicants who visited the two remaining revivalist pastors. The three-month period that Prince referred to included the immediate, post-Tennent months: March, April, and May 1741. (*Christian History*, 2:391). Also, totals exclude prospective communicants who visited revivalist pastors before March and after May. Even if the remaining 67 admissions from all Boston churches are figured in, a maximum of 14.7% of prospective communicants could have been admitted. In all probability, fewer than one in ten prospective communicants from the March–May 1741 period earned admission to full communion.

28. Colman, *Souls flying*, 8, 14, 24–25; Prince, *Christian History*, 2:391. Significantly, Prince did not describe prospective communicants in the revival's early phase in terms of rich and poor. Colman may have been more apt to do this.

29. Records of the Church in Brattle Square, 111–12. Only two other "servants" were admitted to Brattle Street Church during the five-year period from 1742 through 1746. Whether or not servants had surnames of their own, Congregational church records from the eighteenth century routinely categorized blacks separately. New North Church, for example, maintained a separate listing, "Negroes & Mulattoes," in its records. See Thomas Bellows Wyman, comp., *The New North Church Boston 1714* (Baltimore, 1995), 84–86. Of the forty-five blacks who made public religious professions in New North (Fifth) Church between 1724 and 1779, only four were admitted to full communion (and none of these during the Awakening). The designation "servant" accompanied each entry. Thus servants, especially if they were black, were identified as such.

30. Female communicants were probably not permitted to vote in Brattle Street Church business meetings. See Mary Maples Dunn, "Saints and Sisters: Congregational and Quaker Women in the Early Colonial Period," *American Quarterly* 30 (1978): 589–90.

31. *Records of the Church in Brattle Square*, 163–64. The twelve-month period extends from November 1740 through October 1741. In the following five years, another eight adult black slaves were baptized.

32. After becoming a widower with nine children and being remarried to a widow with children of her own, Ashley's father and stepmother decided that Ashley and a stepbrother "would lessen their family much if they were both bound out." Thus, Ashley was bound out to sea for seven years because of familial hardship. See *The Journals of Ashley Bowen (1728–1813) of Marblehead*, 2 vols., ed. Philip Chadwick Foster Smith, *Publications of the Colonial Society of Massachusetts*, vols. 44–45 (Boston, 1973), 1:8–9, 11–12. Chapter 1 covers the years 1728–1758. Whether or not Bowen, son of Marblehead justice of the peace and almanac writer Nathan Bowen, was related to Webb is not clear.

33. Bowen's satisfaction definitely does not refer to the possibility that he got baptized at a later date. New North Church's records for the period 1714–1799 show no entry for Nathan Bowen under any category of public religious profession. See Wyman, *New North Church*, 15.

34. *Records of the Church in Brattle Square*, 21; Joseph Sewall, *The Holy Spirit convincing the world of sin* (Boston, 1741), 19.

35. In the thirteen months between November 1740 and December 1741, 109 persons were admitted to full communion in Fifth Church (New North). Of these,

67 persons (61%) belonged to families with established church ties. Among the 109 persons, three groups stand out: a core group of 47 from established church families with one or more previous communicants; a peripheral group of 20 from "less religious" church families with one or more covenanters but no previous communicants, the first in their respective families to move beyond the covenant to full communion; and a third group of 44 communicants with no apparent connection to established church families and the first in their respective families to make any kind of public religious commitment in New North. Without additional research, it is impossible to tell how long the 44 communicants sat in the pews before being admitted. The 44 communicants were not necessarily unchurched prior to the revival; they may have been attending New North services for some time. The social standing of this third group of newest communicants is the interpretive key to knowing if New North's revival converts, like those from Brattle Street, were of the "better sort." See table 1. See also New North Church (Boston), *Records of the New North Church: Births, Deaths and Marriages, 1714 to 1797* (City Registry, City Hall, Boston); and Wyman, *New North Church.* The latter work, arranged alphabetically by surname and then chronologically by date of religious commitment, helps unravel communicants' relationship to established church families.

36. John Webb, *Christ's suit to the sinner* (Boston, 1741), 29–30.

37. Chandler Robbins, *A History of the Second Church, or Old North, in Boston. To which is added a history of the New Brick Church* (Boston, 1852), 122–23; Hill, *History of the Old South Church*, 1:526.

38. William Cooper, foreword to *The distinguishing marks of a work of the Spirit of God*, by Jonathan Edwards (London, 1742), 3, cited in *Christian History*, 2:398. On the radical phase of Boston revivalism, see Patricia U. Bonomi, *Under the Cope of Heaven: Religion, Society, and Politics in Colonial America* (New York, 1986), 152–60. See also Olivas, "Great Awakenings," chap. 4.

39. Thomas Prince, John Webb, and William Cooper, preface to *The spirits of the present day tried*, by David McGregore (Boston, 1742), v.

40. Benjamin Colman, *The great God has magnified his word to the children of men* (Boston, 1742), 31, ii; Prince, Webb, and Cooper, preface, *Spirits of the present day*, i–iv. Colman left a detailed, theological defense of revivalism to his colleague William Cooper.

41. Joseph Sewall, *God's people must enquire of him to bestow the blessings promised in his word* (Boston, 1742), 28, 24. Earlier, Sewall remarked to parishioners: "And use your best Endeavours that your Servants may become the Children of God, and Heirs according to the Promise, by Faith in Jesus Christ," p. 22. Sewall pointedly said nothing about servants coming to the Lord's Table.

42. Colman, *The great God*, 12–14, 15.

Sylvia R. Frey

INEQUALITY IN THE HERE AND THE HEREAFTER: RELIGION AND THE CONSTRUCTION OF RACE AND GENDER IN THE POST-REVOLUTIONARY SOUTH

THE DECADES SURROUNDING the American Revolution represent a watershed in American history, when a series of disparate but interrelated forces transformed the economic, political, social, and cultural landscapes. For the nation as a whole the most significant consequences of the revolution were the creation of a new political order and a new national consciousness, a society distinctly different from and free of many of the old constraining values of the past, and a new political-cultural agenda based on the notion of civic virtue and Christian faith. Viewed together, these changes suggest an integrated, coherent cultural and political entity and a new community identity based on the concept of equality, which had provided the justification for revolution and served as the norm for the reordering of society.

In fact, the new emerging nation lacked a clear self-understanding. In attempting to construct an identity based on the notion of equality, Americans found meaning in difference, which involved excluding and separating groups of people and institutions one from the other. The emphasis on difference produced a second fundamentally contradictory tendency of separation: of home life from the workplace, of the public from the private, of the church from the state, of women's sphere from men's sphere, of elite culture from popular culture, of the elitist world of print from oral discourse, of rich from poor, of blacks from whites. These diametrical oppositions were part of the process by which the revolutionary generation sought to redefine and affirm itself along lines that mirrored its understanding of the meaning of equality. In the arena of religion that process had peculiar and important ramifications for the construction of race and the cultural evaluation of women.

Although historians disagree over the degree to which American Christianity was democratized by the forces of revolution, most concede the vitality of religious culture in the decades preceding and following the revolution.[1] A mass movement known as the Great Awakening swept through the colonies, beginning in the 1740s and continuing intermittently in the 1760s and 1770s. Interrupted by the social and political convulsions of the American Revolution, the movement resumed in an unprecedented burst of religious activity beginning with the Great Revival of 1800. Prerevolutionary evangelical revivalism challenged ministerial authority, orthodoxy, and church order; transformed religious *mentalité;* wrought a rhetorical revolution; devastated the old cultural landscape; and, some argue convincingly, contributed significantly to a political revolution.[2] The cycle of revivals surrounding the Great Revival of 1800 span the period when the revolutionary equality became a central and defining national value. Evangelical religious movements were central to the articulation of that value and therefore afford an opportunity to view crucial developments in the elaboration of the ideal of equality.

The evangelical Protestant gospel of the spiritual equality of all Christians, women and men, rich and poor, black and white, represented an integrating cultural system. Had it been fully realized, it would have changed society drastically. Nowhere did the logic of the doctrine of spiritual equality have more serious implications for the existing social order than in the American South. From its inception southern evangelicalism was marked by conflict and anxiety, in no small measure owing to its seeming "dedication to the ingathering of marginalized outsiders."[3] Led initially by religious outsiders proclaiming a message of Christian fellowship and the priesthood of all believers, evangelical Protestantism offered those on the social margins a place to become active participants in the spiritual community. It stirred a vigorous activism among white women and African-American men and women, some of whom came perilously close to claiming literal equality, at least in religion.

For a brief edenic moment during the first Great Awakening and again in the Virginia revivals of the 1780s, evangelical Protestantism achieved fellowship and a kind of rough equality that manifested itself structurally in the movement of churches out of doors and into open fields and in the abandonment of traditional seating by rank order in favor of undifferentiated space. The linguistic expression of these developments was modeled not on the family—a central metaphor of early modern political discourse invoked to support the notion of a divinely ordained patriarchal chain that established an order on earth and in heaven—but rather on the potentially more radical model of fraternity, which imagined a spiritual gathering of diverse groups united in love for one another through the saving experience of the new birth.[4]

Emphasis on the heart more than on the head, on "affections" more than reason, created a new dynamic in human relations. An incident described by Reverend James Meacham vividly captures the essence of what was surely one of the most radical manifestations of the evangelical moment. At a biracial meeting somewhere on the Tar River circuit in North Carolina, as Meacham preached from a biblical text in Matthew, "the blessed Lord came in power unto them[;] Some convicted[;] others who had grievously backslidden was pricked [in] the heart. Many useless prostrated on the floor because of the power of love [of?] others with convictions. . . . Some of the dear humble White Sisters went out with the dear black & God poured out his divine Spirit & love upon them."[5] The emotional experience of conversion described in this incident masked differences in gender, class, and race and made each conscious, however dimly, of the essential unity of the great human family. For that fleeting moment the perception of God's love for the individual self inspired reciprocal affection for all others.[6]

The apogee of religious experimentation with Christian fellowship before 1800 was reached in the Moravian communities of Bethabara and Salem, the congregational towns that functioned as the religious, administrative, and economic center of Moravian life in North Carolina. Drawing on New Testament teachings, Moravians established a unique model of interracial fellowship through the innovative choir system, which organized groups according to age, gender, and marital status. Although the sexes did not share equal power, widows and single women, black and white, enslaved and free, lived, worked, and worshipped together in distinctive sisterhoods that allowed talented individuals to exercise pastoral care as pastors' assistants and, for a brief period, as preachers. The Moravians' symbolic universe received its most poignant expression in congregational graveyards at Salem, Bethabara, and Hope, each of which was racially integrated. Buried side by side according to choir, the brethren achieved in death as in life a rare unity between word and action, between preaching and practice, that lasted until the late eighteenth century.[7]

Christian fellowship and the priesthood of all believers continued to be stock currency in the everyday discourse of evangelicals during the extended bursts of revival activity that began with the Great Revival of 1800. Increasingly, however, the practical meaning of those terms bore the clear imprint of Reformation tradition. Indeed, the course of early-nineteenth-century evangelical thought cannot be understood without reference to Reformation theology. Heirs of the Protestant Reformation, the native-born leadership of the post-1800 revival movement offered little that was new or innovative on the practical meaning of Christian fellowship and spiritual equality as it applied to women and to bondpeople. Although the Protestant Reformation that swept Europe beginning in the sixteenth century challenged the established order and at times the gender hierarchy, it bequeathed a deeply ambiguous legacy respecting the equality of men and women.

The Protestant rejection of chastity as an ideal in favor of early marriage to avoid the perils of unsatisfied lust enshrined marriage as the foundation of social existence. Historians of the Reformation are in profound disagreement on the implications of that development for women. One side of the argument maintains that the new importance given to the family unit actually enhanced women's roles within the family as supervisors of households, as helpmates to their husbands, and as primary caretakers of their children. The Protestant concept of assigning responsibility to mothers for the spiritual instruction of children provided a stimulus for the education of women and girls. Even the most positive evaluations of the effects of the Reformation concede that the woman's pedagogical role did not extend to public speech or to preaching. Luther's idea of the "priesthood of all believers" referred only to the need for all members of the religious community to instruct and support one another. Further, the Pauline insistence that women remain silent laid the foundation for the reformed liturgy, which allowed women to pray and to join in congregational singing but denied them the right to all ministerial functions, such as preaching or administering baptism, or to leadership within the church.[8]

The other side of the argument maintains that Protestant theology established theoretical equality between husband and wife but implemented "a vision of natural patriarchal authority and female subservience." Far from constituting a challenge to patriarchy, Protestant reformers subordinated women to the patriarchal household and subjected them to different standards of moral conduct that were in time inscribed in laws mandating state scrutiny of sexual matters and prescribing more severe punishments for female sexual offenses. The ultimate effect was a thoroughgoing transformation of sexual relations based on an elaboration of male and female natures as inherently different. The idealization of the pastors' wife as the model of domesticity provided opportunities for some women to be part of the church, if only in the role of consort, a passive model that had negative implications for what constituted socially acceptable female behavior both within and beyond the religious sphere.[9]

No less important as a pattern for American evangelicals were Reformation biblical arguments sanctioning serfdom and bondage. Pauline teaching on obedience, on defiance toward civil authority, and on freedom in the hereafter contributed to what one scholar has called a "unique separation of the world of the body from the world of the spirit." Among European Protestants, the Pauline dualism of body and soul provided a particularly convenient rationale to reconcile the doctrine of spiritual equality and the acceptance of servitude and serfdom. It provided as well the basic explanation for racial differentiation and enslavement. Although George Fox, the founder of the Society of Friends, accepted slavery as an institution justified by the ancient Pauline dualism of body and soul, some Protestant groups began to argue, if only temporarily, that Christian egalitarianism applied to the body as well as to the soul.[10] It found its most radical expression in the militant Hussite revolution, which grew out of the Czech reform movement in the fifteenth century. Under the leadership of Peter Chelcice, a rural philosopher who drew on New Testament teaching to design an egalitarian social doctrine, the first community of the Unity of Brethren established itself in Bohemia and Moravia and there briefly experimented with the creation of a new social order without classes or oppression. By the early sixteenth century the Unity, or Moravians, had abandoned the most radical social doctrines advanced by Chelcice in favor of the traditional Protestant view of the social order as divinely ordained.[11]

American Protestantism left undisturbed those assumptions of female inferiority and built on the Pauline dualism of body and soul. The potency of the new rhetoric of fellowship created by the evangelicals derived from its apparent ability to transcend all differences, which helped to ensure its appeal to those on the social margins. In practice, the notion of fellowship was inherently paradoxical. In its general usage it "affirmed and sealed" the boundaries of the new spiritual order and obscured the spiritual and social differences between men and women, rich and poor, black and white.[12] But if, as Russell Richey has cautioned, it encircled, it also divided. The term *brother*, for example, carried at least three interrelated yet distinct meanings. In a general sense it embraced the whole society—all who shared the emotional experience of the new birth. Yet African Americans were commonly identified as "black Brethren," a kind of linguistic code that suggested a separate and distinct spiritual identity and a fundamentally different order of Christians. Membership rolls that unambiguously differentiated black church members as property—"Captain Drew's Harry," "Gatewood's Aaron," "Graves's George,"—at once constituted black Christians as objects and fashioned a spiritual taxonomy based on race.

The words *brother* and *brotherhood* signified more specifically the special relationship shared by the brotherhood of preachers.[13] Above all, the ministry involved issues of spiritual identity. The male ministry sought to monopolize communication with God and to act exclusively on behalf of the community by claiming to be divinely chosen for pastoral hegemony. In defining God as male they established the legitimacy of an exclusively male ministry. Many African-American men assumed the role of preacher, and some were admitted to the itinerancy. But markers or referents of race still defined their differential access to moral authority. Although Harry Hosier traveled extensively with Francis Asbury, Thomas Coke, and Freeborn Garrettson, he was always "Black Harry," never "Brother Harry," and he never rose above the rank of exhorter. Eventually—and reluctantly— black men were admitted to the male order of preachers, the great majority of them as exhorters, deacons, and local ministers, positions whose duties were carefully defined and limited.[14] The act of denying this rhetorical badge of membership symbolically divided the brotherhood into two distinct orders in which spiritual authority was determined primarily by race.

As the notion of fellowship established the spiritual primacy of the male clerical order, it also established asymmetry between males and females. The term *sister* recognized women as members of the evangelical community, but it was not analogous to *brother*. Rather it presupposed and disclosed real distance. This development is most striking in the allocation of religious speech roles on the basis of gender. The anticlerical sentiment that characterized the prerevolutionary revivals created opportunities for women to step outside their prescribed roles as spiritual consorts and moral authority figures. In some southern churches gender ceased to be a prohibitive factor for active church membership. Following in the tradition of radical sectarian female prophets of the English civil war era, a few women attempted to rewrite Protestant liturgies by making manifest female potential referred to in Scripture. Both black and white women began to "speak" as visionaries, a form of uncontrolled enthusiasm for which women were thought to be uniquely suited by virtue of their weak, emotional, and irrational nature.[15] It was primarily as exhorters that black and white women were able to reinvent a female spiritual identity. Although exhorting had limited spiritual significance, it was, it has been argued, far more influential than preaching in creating and sustaining revival culture. A powerful form of affective prayer and personal testimony, exhorting prepared the audience to receive the gospel message and to accept conversion. More important, for all women and for African Americans, exhortation provided "an opportunity to participate fully, creatively, and as equals."[16]

In the reordered spiritual world that emerged in the quarter century after the revolution, women's rights to speak were contracted and eventually rescinded. The cultural elaboration of an extensive set of "male" and "female" oppositions are revealed in the "queries" that Baptist congregations posed to themselves.[17] When, for example, in 1787 the Waterlick Baptist Church of Shenandoah County, Virginia, was asked by its pastor "[W]hether a sister in the church is at liberty to have a vote therein," the church answered in the affirmative.[18] But the 1798 response of the Roanoke District Association to the query "What is the duty and privilege of a female member in a gospel church?" clearly signaled the closing of speech roles for women. Citing 1 Tim. 2:11–12 and 1 Cor. 14:34–36, the association declared "the females to be silent having no part or lot in the Government of the Church."[19] The fact that women constituted two thirds of the membership of South Carolina's Mechanicsville Baptist Church did not deter the church from deciding in 1804 that only "male members should have the privaledge of praying publickly," one of the "few acts of public witness permitted women in lowcountry churches."[20]

By the late eighteenth century the once radical Moravian experiment with interracial fellowship and a common gender identity had largely run its course. Racial tensions stemming from concern over a lack of deference and unauthorized interracial liaisons led the brethren to abandon their more radical positions in favor of the Pauline strictures on women and servants. Although women still functioned independently within the choir system, they were removed from positions of leadership and were no longer ordained as priests.[21] Even in all-black churches, where gender segregation was not so rigidly enforced, preaching was culturally defined as inappropriate for women. The Maryland slave Elizabeth, who believed herself divinely ordained to preach, "was looked upon as a speckled bird by the ministers to whom I looked for instruction . . . some would cry out, 'you are an enthusiast;' and others said 'the Discipline did not allow of any such division of the work.'"[22] The "final denial of female spiritual authority," as Susan Juster puts it, was the silencing of white female visionaries by characterizing them as "mad" or "delusional."[23] Black female visionaries, to whom occult powers were generally ascribed, were able to maintain roles for themselves in noninstitutionalized spiritual traditions such as supernaturalism and conjure.[24]

For all their radical discourse about making a new world, evangelicals were, at heart, committed to many of the same values and tendencies that distinguished traditional patriarchy and the customary social order. Methodists and Baptists were moving "toward the exercise of religious authority, not away from it," as Jon Butler has put it. Not coincidentally, they were simultaneously moving toward the reinstitution of the familial model of the Christian community. In postrevolutionary America the "family of God" was reconfigured along distinctly hierarchical and patriarchal lines and was institutionalized in the structure of church government.[25] Local Baptist congregations formed themselves into associations and founded theological seminaries.[26] Methodists organized themselves as the Methodist Episcopal Church and created a church hierarchy and a ministerial order that excluded women and African Americans.

As evangelical denominations centralized, they also segregated, a development that found architectural expression in Protestant churches across the South.[27] Practices differed between regions and denominations. The Anglican church had an exclusionary tradition reaching back to Reformation England, when pews were first introduced. Thereafter the placement of people within the church functioned as "the visible representation of the local hierarchy."[28] In the American South pew assignments were not held in perpetuity, but rank order was maintained and racially distinct seating was common, although neither was accomplished without a struggle.[29] Competition over seating indicates general recognition of its symbolic importance. In St. Philip's of Charleston, for example, black members of the congregation originally sat on benches in the belfry.[30] When galleries were built, around 1731–32, the more affordable pews there were taken over by poorer whites, and the black members of the congregation moved downstairs to occupy seats in the aisles of the church. By degrees, the aisles were completely taken over by black members, first by the elderly and then by those "who came for the purpose of religious worship." By the eve of the revolution, the custom had, as the vestry minutes recall, "become general and anyone who chose to do so availed himself (or herself) of the privilege."[31]

The controversy over seating in St. Michael's, built to accommodate the overflow from St. Philip's, contained elements of class as well as race. In an apparent attempt to maintain the distinction between themselves and the black members of the church, a number of poor white parishioners asked permission "to carry Chairs etc. to the Church, to be plac'd in the Aile for Seats." The vestry obliged and in 1773 ordered new benches built for "the sole use of the Poor White People who may want Seats" and instructed "that no Negroes shall be permitted to sitt on the Benches so ordered to be made." Benches belonging to black members were removed to the gallery and under the belfry, creating both the representation and the reality of greater social and racial distance. More to the point, the displacement of black members created a kind of cultural space that defined and limited the definition of spiritual equality to white members of the congregation.[32] The church in Portsmouth, Virginia, made the message explicit by painting the "negro benches" black.[33]

Methodist and Baptist churches throughout the eighteenth-century South were constructed on a biracial basis. Both had, as Russell Richey has observed of Methodism, deep ambivalence about slavery and the African Americans who made up a disproportionate share of the membership of many southern churches. This ambivalence is reflected in the transient nature of their commitment to the antislavery position and in their struggle over the inclusion/exclusion of black members.[34] The division of sacred space gave substance to that ambivalence. Methodists rejected the notion of a pewed church on the grounds that "the pew system must necessarily be extremely offensive to the Lord's poor."[35] Methodist meetinghouses were relatively integrated, owing in part to what was by now settled custom in parts of the South and in part to Bishop Francis Asbury's instructions that elderly and infirm black Methodists be permitted to use aisle pews on the ground floor. Nevertheless, the preoccupation with order and organization that were the distinguishing characteristics of the Second Awakening in the South began to manifest itself in the structural distinctions noted by Moreau de St.-Méry at a Methodist church in Norfolk, Virginia as early as 1794: "Although the minister teaches that all must suffer alike in the hereafter, everything in this church harps upon class distinction. The women sit on the right, the men on the left; there are separate sections for free colored men and for slaves, and these are again divided according to their sex."[36]

Despite the apparent chaos of the camp meetings, postrevolutionary revivals functioned as instruments of regulated behavior and therefore of social control. Revivals after Cane Ridge in 1801 combined a progressively more gendered and racialized representation of the Christian social order. Benjamin Henry Latrobe's sketch of a camp meeting in Virginia in 1809 shows spatially distinct sections labeled women's seats and men's seats and, in the space behind the preacher's stand, rows of "Negroes tents."[37] The movement of the revival indoors "fostered not only segregation . . . but the drawing of all sorts of lines," as Russell Richey has observed.[38] There was considerable variation in the congregationally organized Baptist churches, but many southern Baptist churches, like the biracial First Baptist Church of Savannah, Georgia, employed pew sales to create a communal hierarchy based on the size and location of church pews. By designating three "free" pews on the side of either aisle of the church for "strangers," the First Baptist admitted all whites to the claims of fellowship.[39] The customary practice of turning "the blacks out of their seats" to make room for whites clearly communicated conditional membership.[40] Local gatherings such as the Methodist class meeting as well as the Baptist church membership rolls were carefully segregated by race and gender.[41] Although the Moravian congregations at Salem, Bethabara, Hope, Bethania, and Friedberg remained integrated until at least 1815, integrated seating became an issue as early as 1789, when the Congregational Council directed the church sexton to "show [black non-Moravians] to a back bench." During the 1790s white congregants began to separate themselves informally from the black brethren, and in 1797 the young white members of the Older Girls Choir walked out of a meeting to protest the presence of a young black woman.[42]

The gradual encroachment of black men and women into space understood to reflect both social position and spiritual standing forced white southerners to recognize, if only unconsciously, the extent to which their authority was relational—a social construction rooted in both the material and the ideological worlds. This gathering sense of anxiety was exacerbated by the fact that order was being challenged outside as well as inside the church. Gabriel's Revolt in Virginia in 1800 and the Vesey Revolt in South Carolina in 1822 led to an intensification of racial tensions. Under these conditions, church seating became a matter of even greater social and theological importance. The struggle to contain the threat of spatial anarchy and reassert authority expressed itself in the increasing polarization of race and the hierarchy of class and gender. In 1826, Virginia's biracial Goose Creek Baptist Church thought it "proper to make some new arrangements for the Black people to enter the gallary by an outside conveyance." Some congregations, like the Coan Baptist Church of Virginia and Savannah's Independent Presbyterian Church, constructed partitions "between the white persons and persons of colour."[43]

In their hasty retreat from biracial fellowship the Brethren exceeded other Christian churches. Barely twenty years after blacks had become members of Moravian congregations in Salem, Bethabara, Bethania, and Hope, black brethren were excluded from the foot washing, or ceremonial cleansing ritual; the kiss of peace, the traditional ritual of induction into the Unity, was abandoned in favor of a handshake; the interracial system of baptismal sponsorships was made race-specific; blacks were excluded from the choir system; and segregated burials were mandated. The final break came in 1822, when a separate black congregation was organized at the Negro Quarter outside Salem, apparently with the enthusiastic support of black brethren.[44]

Those African Americans who took the presumption of spiritual equality seriously did not simply react or adapt to these developments but rather created ideologies in counterpoint to them. When the biracial Baptist Church of Charlottesville, Virginia, ordered blacks to give up their seats to whites, a black member of the church and occasional preacher "preached a sermon from a text, showing that all are of one blood." Fearful that "such preaching would raise an insurrection among the negroes," white members of the church threatened to whip the man unless he could "prove his Doctrine by Scripture." Accordingly he preached another sermon which "proved his doctrine" to the satisfaction of the white churchmen.[45] Such claims to moral and spiritual equality were common in the postrevolutionary South. Black evangelicals were understandably reluctant to relinquish seats that in certain ways reified their spiritual expectations. By claiming seats to which they had no "right," they symbolically rejected the principal of spiritual inequality. In Salem, North Carolina, Baltimore, Maryland, Wilmington, Delaware, Alexandria, Virginia, Washington, D.C., and Charleston, South Carolina, they chose to deal with their disparate understanding of the meaning of spiritual equality by withdrawing from biracial churches and forming their own autonomous black churches.[46]

Mass defections of the black membership of southern churches shattered the illusion of Christian fellowship and created rifts in conservative congregations like St. Philip's of Charleston, whose white membership divided between those who believed that even an implicit assertion of moral equality posed a threat to the social order and those who saw the arrangement of seating as a means to preserve the social order. In 1828 thirteen prominent churchmen called on the vestry to remedy the "evil" of blacks occupying the aisles of the church. Mindful of the precedent set by the walkout in 1817 of 4,376 black members of Charleston's Bethel Methodist Church,[47] the committee appointed by the vestry to look into the matter questioned whether "the inconvenience complained about could be removed without turning away from the congregation many colored persons among whom are some who have been all their lives (as well as their ancestors for one or two generations back) worshipping in this church." The committee's carefully worded reminder that during the Vesey Revolt "not one [of the 250 black members] belonging to the Episcopal church having been found in the ranks of the Insurgents—But the colored man (belonging to Mr. Prioleau) who gave information of the plot was of the association of this church," signals a shift already underway in the South toward recognition of the stabilizing potential of religion.[48]

Still the social and spatial markers that segregated the living continued into death. As Lawrence Taylor has observed, "death is not only a problem, but also an opportunity—an occasion for furthering social, cultural, and political ends."[49] Above all, the "construction of death," as cultural anthropologists refer to it, provided an opportunity to display belief in shared spiritual destiny. Protestant rhetoric acknowledged the notion of a final end from which there was no escape, regardless of wealth or social status. Although mortuary rituals and behavior during the revolutionary era varied significantly, not only by class but geographically and ethnically—differences made increasingly possible by participation in the consumer economy and growing affluence—the material culture of death and the landscape of heaven and hell constructed by black and white Protestants provide us with direct evidence of the cultural and spiritual values that connected and divided black and white Protestants. Generally speaking, cemeteries display two strikingly different conceptions of death: one called by anthropologists "hierarchical" or differentiated death, which celebrates the social hierarchy through material display, the other "egalitarian" death, which reaffirms egalitarian communal values.

The placement of the dead can be read as a collective statement on attitudes toward equality in the afterlife. Burial grounds are both vehicles for the construction of identity and "memory places," to borrow Pierre Nora's concept, where social identities are permanently enshrined.[50] As such they give spatial expression to the most deeply felt commitments—to self, to family, to community. The first step in creating social and racial distinctions was to carve up cemetery space to create and affirm the Christian community's own version of itself. A particularly telling cultural expression of the Protestant spiritual universe is the "Old" or "Brick" cemetery now known as Colonial Park Cemetery of Savannah, Georgia.

Colonial Park Cemetery was established some twenty years after the first burial ground was designated for Jews. Because the Savannah Jewish community was excluded from the parish church cemetery traditionally used by white Christians in Europe and in eighteenth-century America, Governor James Oglethorpe created the first communal cemetery by allotting land for the use of the Jewish community. (Until health concerns put a stop to it, the corpses of enslaved people were unceremoniously dumped into the nearest river or stream.) Located on the present-day median of Oglethorpe Avenue, the Jewish cemetery serves as a reminder of how cultural prejudices shaped the culture of the dead. With the growth of the city, the cemetery was eventually surrounded by residences. By 1770 the original portion was completely occupied. Jewish petitions for permission to expand met with strong opposition from Christian townspeople, some of whom were concerned for property values. A "Memorial of Freeholders" maintaining that "no Person would choose to buy or rent an House whose Windows looked into a Burial Ground of any kind particularly one belonging to a People who might be presumed from Prejudice of Education to have imbibed Principles entirely repugnant to those of our most holy Religion," indicates that the real problem was the identity of the dead as Jews.[51]

As urban populations grew and concerns for public health increased, formal space was set aside by city administrations for burials. The "Old" or "Brick" cemetery of Savannah was created in the 1750s by acts of the Provincial Council and Assembly as the parish cemetery of Christ Church. Located on a part of the town common near what is now the southeastern corner of Abercorn and South Broad Streets, it originally served as a public cemetery, but since Jews and African Americans were explicitly excluded, for all practical purposes only white Anglicans were interred there.[52]

The ordinance of 1789 represented a reshaping of the symbolic universe of the dead into one that was congruent with postrevolutionary Protestantism. In that year the City Council of Savannah, following a general trend of moving burial grounds to new sites at some distance from the parish church, formally declared the Old Cemetery a public burial ground "for the interment of all Christian people of whatever denomination."[53] The brick wall built around the cemetery formed a protected enclosure and at the same time served as a symbolic representation of the Christian community as a structured and bounded group. This idealized view of the religious landscape conveyed the belief that there were no distinctions among the dead. In reality, however, the explicit exclusion of African Americans, over three hundred of whom were members of Andrew Bryan's First African Baptist Church, and the religious and ethnic segregation of the dead communicated the idea of a separate spiritual identity for white Georgians.

Although the graves themselves display certain minimal equality, the interior space was apportioned into sections, each religion with its own section, each section roughly subdivided according to ethnicity. Anglican plots dominate, spreading out from the original burial sites along the western wall near Abercorn Street. Moravians occupy a small area on the northern boundary, their austere graves not differentiating one from another. Catholics are arrayed along the eastern line of Abercorn Street, with Irish Catholics in one compact corner and French Catholics adjacent to but separated from them, an indication, perhaps, of the crucial importance of religious affiliation and belief in the construction of spiritual and social identities.

The ordinance of 1789 assumed that all persons buried within the public cemetery would belong to a recognized Christian denomination and would in death, as in life, rest alongside co-religionists in a community of worship. The dispatching of African Americans to an isolated enclave on the common stood as a stark repudiation of the notion of Christian fellowship and a constant reminder of their exclusion from the community of the dead. The portion of the common allotted to blacks was enlarged on several occasions, generally in response to complaints about the intrusion of black burials into the space allocated to white Christians. An ordinance passed in 1813 ordered that the black burial ground be posted and railed to prevent burials outside the designated area and imposed fines for white and thirty lashes for black transgressors. Frequent complaints of black encroachment on the grounds reserved for white Christians suggests that African Americans resisted the exclusion of their members and implicitly claimed a right to burial in the communal cemetery and hence to spiritual equality.[54]

The material aspects of death provided another opportunity to display widening social distinctions, the products of a more highly differentiated social system. The careful detailing of prices for clerical services established a range of religious rituals available according to the ability to pay. St. Michael's of Charleston created an elaborate price structure that included, among other things, charges for the minister: $6 to attend the corpse from the house into the church; $4 to advance from the house to the churchyard; $3 to continue from the churchyard gate to the place of interment. There were similar charges for the clerk and the organist plus a $2 fee for the sexton for digging the grave and another $1 for "striking the bell."[55] The Methodist Conference meeting in Georgetown, South Carolina, in 1820, eschewed the more refined social differentiations implicit in the Episcopal rituals of death while upholding the principle of racial separation. The resolutions approved by the conference provided for free burial for all white members of the Methodist Episcopal Church and a modest fee of $15 for other white persons "friendly to the Methodists." The exclusion of two categories of Methodists from consecrated grounds—suicides and blacks—can be read as an expression of wishful thinking held by most whites that in death, as in life, the immortal souls of blacks and whites were intrinsically unequal.[56]

The development of permanent markers, many of which celebrated civic themes, and the emergence of differences in material displays in the early nineteenth century were visible indicators of the heightened consciousness of race, class, and gender. Obituaries were a commonly used means of fixing social identity. The obituary of Hannah Wereat, "wife of John Wereat, Esq." and descendant of "the ancient family of the Handleys by her mother's side," reflects a self-conscious insistence on the importance of domestic relationships for the social identity of elite white women.[57] The obituary of Mordecai Gist constructed an identity of the civic individual by evoking the memory of Gist's service as a brigadier general in the Revolutionary War. The reminder that Gist's sacrifices brought him "honor, credit, and applause" drew attention to heroic military service and inspired the collective consciousness of a historic event.[58]

Increasingly elaborate funeral rituals in which religious and secular themes were merged was one of the most prominent markers of the new social order. The funeral of William Drayton, District Judge for South Carolina and Grand Master of the South Carolina Ancient York Masons, who died in 1790 at age fifty-eight, was a pageant of political theater and Masonic choreography. In a display of hierarchy evocative of eighteenth-century English civic rituals, Charleston's political and social elite solemnly gathered at the home of Stephen Drayton for an elaborate foot procession to St. Michael's Episcopal Church. Responsibility for organizing the procession was assumed by officers of Charleston's Masonic lodges, who played a quasi-ecclesiastical role in carrying the body to St. Michaels. Family mourners followed immediately behind the body. Next came the Five Orders of Architecture. Behind them walked the grand secretary carrying the Bible and the "Book of Constitutions," or Masonic bylaws, on crimson cushions. A symbolic vocabulary borrowed from English Masonry, they held particular significance as a metaphor of the modern Protestant republic. After divine service at St. Michaels the parade of brothers moved to Gibbe's Wharf, where the corpse was embarked in a vessel for conveyance to the family cemetery at Drayton Hall. Officers and lodge members wore mourning for a period of six weeks.[59]

The power and significance of the street processional created a sense of identification among the mourners and an identification with the deceased Drayton, endowing him with the power to represent all the patriarchal founders and fraternal citizens. The addition of men's societies like the Masons or the Society of the Cincinnati to funeral rituals continued the process of merging religious and civic ideology and celebrating essentially civic and therefore masculine themes. The celebration of the dead with pomp furnished the community with a set of religious and political standards and symbols that served the cause of the social order and at the same time forged new "American" values, prominent among which was the family. The Middleton crypt on the Ashley River is a conspicuous example of the trend to turn individual graves into family shrines. Certain elements of the elite funeral—notably, funeral processions and permanent headstones with inscriptions, suggesting the meanings the deceased wished their lives to bear—spread down the social hierarchy.

Among the surviving examples of what anthropologists call egalitarian death is the slave burial ground at Hickory Hill Plantation in Hanover County, Virginia.[60] It is located on land originally owned by Robert Carter as piecemeal property to his Charles City County plantation, Shirley. It contains the earthly remains of slaves given by Carter as a marriage present to William Fanning Wickham and Anne Butler Carter. The cemetery is located in a heavily wooded area near the western boundary of the property. The burials are arranged randomly. Burial sites are identified by grave depressions, head markers of rough stones, crude wooden carvings, and living markers, usually a cedar tree, reflecting perhaps the West African veneration of trees or groves. Except for two markers, no mortuary monuments preserve the identity of individuals, celebrate their lives, or venerate their spiritual worth.

African-American funerals, like church seating and cemetery space, were a contested area. Early efforts by colonial authorities to quash African-influenced burial rituals failed, and slave masters were eventually forced to concede to slave demands to honor their dead with public rituals.[61] The funeral of Jacques, a South Carolina slave, illustrates the kinds of death rituals probably observed by plantation slaves at Hickory Hill and throughout the South. The rituals were a varied collection fused from an African past and a Christian present. As the word of Jacques's death circulated through the slaves' communication system, bondpeople from neighboring plantations gathered around the little hut where his body, attired in grave clothes he had collected, rested in a simple wooden coffin. At intervals during the "setting up," or wake, hymns were sung and refreshments were served. Sometime around midnight a torchlight procession led by six women dressed in white escorted the body to the burial site near the river, where it was interred along with "simple monuments of affection" offered by the mourners. A sermon by a black funeral preacher concluded the ritual. A hugh oak tree, its limbs spreading over the grave "as if protecting the dwelling of the dead," was the solitary monument to Jacques's existence.[62]

By the turn of the century, attention centered less on rituals and more on ritual responsibility. Self-proclaimed black preachers, like the one who presided over Jacques's funeral, insisted on the right to act as intermediaries to guide their dead into the world of the spirits. Aware of the cultural significance of death rituals, white preachers were concerned that their ritual responsibilities were being seriously eroded by black funeral preachers. Like many of his brother preachers, John Holt Rice, pastor of the Cub Creek Presbyterian Church in Charlotte County, Virginia, objected to the "great numbers of negro preachers" who insisted on officiating at "negro funerals." Several times Rice "proposed that I should preach the funerals of the negroes who die in the congregation. . . . But the Negro preachers think that their craft is in danger and are most vehemently opposed to the plan."[63] By insisting on their right to preside over the funerals of their own people, black funeral preachers were able to carve out an alternative cultural space to the white Christian culture of death.

In the ongoing struggle over the meaning of spiritual equality, black and white Christians developed their own distinct maps of the afterworld, along with different prescriptions for reaching it. Until the evangelical movement brought them into intimate spiritual contact with large numbers of black southerners, the theme of distinction in the afterlife had a powerful appeal for white southerners. Since they could not conceive of the possibility that Africans had souls, neither would they accept the vision of a shared postmortem destiny. The Reverend Francis Le Jau provides a good illustration of the white preference for distinguishing fates in the afterlife. "Is it possible," wondered a prominent member of Le Jau's Goose Creek congregation, "that any of my slaves could go to heaven, & must I see them there?"[64] But the physical intimacy of the revival movement and the emotional intimacy of the conversion experience made it impossible for white Christians to deny the humanity of black Christians or their capacity for salvation.

Just how far the scope of heaven had been enlarged to accommodate black Christians is manifest in the deathbed scene described by the Reverend John Bradley of Chesterfield County, Virginia. As his wife lay dying, she "exhorted us to meet her in Heaven. Then to one of the black women who came into the room, then to another, and had the others called in and exhorted, warned, entreated, advised and instructed them all, asking them if they did not want to meet her in Heaven." At the dying woman's request, Bradley called in all the black people, whereupon she continued to entreat them to "get religion and meet her in Heaven. . . . They promised to try to get religion and to meet her in Heaven."[65]

If some white Christians were more willing to make room for their black brothers and sisters in heaven, they also created space for them in hell. Hell was, as Piero Camporesi has called it, "an adjustable space" capable of being enlarged or restricted to accommodate "new inventions in the typology of sinners and the dammed."[66] As Juster has shown for New England, postrevolutionary evangelicals created a gendered version of sin.[67] They also championed a moral order that redefined sin on a racial basis. Certain categories of sin were assigned exclusively to black Christians: running away, lying and disobedience to the master, rebellion. For these transgressions, black sinners were doomed to the eternal flames of hell.

African-American beliefs about an afterlife were directly influenced by Christianity but Afro-Christians were not willing to concede to whites exclusive control over the next world. At the heart of black theology was a belief in the moral concern of God and a retributive eschatology, which found expression in racially distinct visions of the afterworld. To black Christians the notion of spiritual equality conveyed the idea that the church was the guarantor of security for all and that the standards of morality established by the church were equally incumbent on all. Divine retribution was therefore a requirement of justice. Accordingly, they insisted on moral discrimination in the afterlife.

George White's "night vision" imagined a day of retribution when the vain, the greedy, and the ambitious would confront divine justice: "I next beheld a coach, with horses richly furnished, and full of gay, modish passengers, posting to this place of torment; but when they approached the margins of the burning lake, struck with terror and dismay, their countenances changed, and awfully bespoke their surprise and fear."[68] One of the "fundamental rules" of black Christianity detailed by Charles Ball was the belief that shared space in heaven would establish death as a continuation of life's injustice. According to Ball, black Christians expected no less than that a future judgment would separate the good from the evil. The punishment imagined for the overseer: "a return . . . of the countless lashes that he has lent out so liberally here."[69]

The chaos of the revolutionary years left the evangelical universe, like other social institutions, in disarray. Although Americans rejected the state church tradition and traditional assumptions about deference and the social order in favor of religious pluralism, the evolution of a new social order in postrevolutionary America combined a progressively more gendered and racialized representation of orthodoxy. Spiritual inequality was always assumed; by the end of the first quarter of the nineteenth century it was clearly established. In prerevolutionary America evangelical Protestant churches had played a major role in lowering racial and social barriers. In the postrevolutionary period they assumed a leading part in institutionalizing the notion of racial inequality and the suppression of female religious expression. Within that newly constructed spiritual order, black Christians crafted a distinct definition of spiritual equality that helped shape a new discourse on the meaning of the word.

Notes

1. See, for example, Patricia U. Bonomi, *Under the Cope of Heaven: Religion, Society, and Politics in Colonial America* (New York, 1986); Jon Butler, *Awash in a Sea of Faith: Christianizing the American People* (Cambridge, Mass., 1990); Nathan O. Hatch, *The Democratization of American Christianity* (New Haven, Conn., 1989).

2. Representative examples include Alan Heimert, *Religion and the American Mind from the Great Awakening to the Revolution* (Cambridge, Mass., 1966), whose emphasis is on the importance of millenarian ideas; Hatch, *Democratization*, and Bonomi, *Under the Cope of Heaven*, which focus on public behavior and popular experience; David S. Lovejoy, "'Desperate Enthusiasm': Early Origins of American Radicalism," in *The Origins of Anglo-American Radicalism*, ed. Margaret Jacob and James Jacob (Boston, 1984), 231–42.

3. John Walsh, "'Methodism' and the Origins of English-Speaking Evangelicalism," in *Evangelicalism: Comparative Studies of Popular Protestantism in North America, the British Isles, and Beyond, 1700–1990*, ed. Mark A. Noll, David W. Bebbington and George A. Rawlyk (New York, 1994), 31. For a discussion of religious conflict in Virginia, see Rhys Isaac, *The Transformation of Virginia, 1740–1790* (New York, 1982).

4. Susan Juster, *Disorderly Women: Sexual Politics and Evangelicalism in Revolutionary New England* (Ithaca, N.Y., 1994), 38.

5. James Meacham Papers [Journals 1788–1797], February 15–May 29, 1790, Perkins Library, Duke University, Durham, N.C.

6. For an important discussion of the psychological effects of the conversion experience, see Charles Lloyd Cohen, *God's Caress: The Psychology of Puritan Religious Experience* (New York, 1986), 160–61.

7. See Jon F. Sensbach, "Interracial Sects: Religions, Race, and Gender among Early Moravians," in *The Devil's Lane: Sex and Race in the Early South*, ed. Catherine Clinton and Michele Gillespie (New York, 1997), 154–67; Sensbach, "A Separate Canaan: The Making of an Afro-Moravian World in North Carolina, 1763–1856" (Ph.D. diss., Duke University, 1991), 438–41.

8. This line of argument is generally contained in the following essays: Charmarie Jenkins Blaisdell, "The Matrix of Reform: Women in the Lutheran and Calvinist

Movements," 13–44, esp. 15, 21, 25, 29, 33; Keith L. Sprunger, "God's Powerful Army of the Weak: Anabaptist Women of the Radical Reformation," 45–74, esp. 54; Richard L. Greaves, "Foundation Builders: The Role of Women in Early English Nonconformity," 92; and Dorothy P. Ludlow, "Shaking Patriarchy's Foundations: Sectarian Women in England, 1641–1700," 93–123, all of which appear in Richard L. Greaves, ed., *Triumph over Silence: Women in Protestant History* (Westport, Conn., 1985).

9. This paragraph summarizes recent views of the Reformation from Lyndal Roper, *The Holy Household: Women and Morals in Reformation Augsburg* (Oxford, 1989), 165; and the following in *Women in Reformation and Counter-Reformation Europe*, ed. Sherrin Marshall (Bloomington, Ind., 1989): Merry E. Wiesner, "Nuns, Wives, and Mothers: Women and the Reformation in Germany," 8–28; Susan C. Karant-Nunn, "The Women of the Saxon Silver Mines," 29–46; Diane Willen, "Women and Religion in Early Modern England," 140–65; Sherrin Marshall, "Protestant, Catholic, and Jewish Women in the Early Modern Netherlands," 120–39. Even radical sectarians accepted the sexual hierarchy as divinely ordained. English Quakers and the radical Anabaptists granted women a greater role than they customarily enjoyed in contemporary society. Anabaptist and Quaker women enjoyed unparalleled prominence as prophetesses, visionaries, and lay witnesses of the gospel but they were denied the right to preach and to teach; neither could they be elected as leaders nor vote for church leaders. See Claus-Peter Clasen, *Anabaptism: A Social History, 1525–1618* (Ithaca, N.Y., 1972), 205–7.

10. Forrest G. Wood, *The Arrogance of Faith: Christianity and Race in America from the Colonial Era to the Twentieth Century* (New York, 1990), 74–75.

11. Sensbach, "Separate Canaan," 47–48.

12. Russell E. Richey, *Early American Methodism* (Bloomington, Ind., 1991), 6.

13. Ibid., 6–8.

14. For examples of the obstacles black men faced, see *Black Itinerants of the Gospel: The Narratives of John Jea and George White*, ed. Graham Russell Hodges (Madison, Wis., 1993), 14–15, 56–64, 66, 68–70.

15. Although there were over two hundred female prophets in England during the Interregnum (1649–60), they spoke not in their capacity as individuals but by claiming that it was the voice of God speaking through them. See Phyllis Mack, "Women as Prophets during the English Civil War," in Jacob and Jacob, eds., *Origins of Anglo-American Radicalism*, 217–18.

16. G. A. Rawlyk, *Ravished by the Spirit: Religious Revivals, Baptists, and Henry Alline* (Montreal, 1984), 111–12.

17. Rhys Isaac suggests that the Baptist inquiries concerning rules of conduct reveal the willingness of popular evangelicals to test "commonplace assumptions," "a process Isaac refers to as "cognitive reappraisal." "Radicalized Religion and Changing Lifestyles: Virginia in the Period of the American Revolution," in Jacob and Jacob, eds., *Origins of Anglo-American Radicalism*, 258.

18. Quoted in William L. Lumpkin, "The Role of Women in 18th-Century Virginia Baptist Life," *Baptist History and Heritage* 8 (1973): 161.

19. Minutes of the Roanoke District Association (May, 1798), 162, 168–69, 178, Virginia Baptist Historical Society, Richmond, Va.

20. Quoted in Stephanie McCurry, *Masters of Small Worlds: Yeoman Households, Gender Relations, and the Political Culture of the Antebellum South Carolina Low Country* (New York, 1995), 141, 181.

21. Sensbach, "Interracial Sects," 161–62.

22. "Elizabeth," in *Black Women in Nineteenth-Century American Life*, ed. Bert James Loewenberg and Ruth Bogin (University Park, Pa., 1976), 132.

23. Susan Juster, "To Slay the Beast: Visionary Women in the Early Republic," in *A Mighty Baptism: Race, Gender, and the Creation of American Protestantism*, ed. Susan Juster and Lisa MacFarlane (Ithaca, N.Y., 1996), 33; Lynn Lyerly, "Enthusiasm, Possession, and Madness: Gender and the Opposition to Methodism in the South, 1770–1810" (paper presented at the Southern Association for Women Historians, Houston, June 1994).

24. Yvonne Chireau, "The Uses of the Supernatural: Toward a History of Black Women's Magical Practices," in Juster and MacFarlane, eds., *A Mighty Baptism*, 171–88. See also Juster, "To Slay the Beast," 34.

25. Butler, *Awash in a Sea of Faith*, 128. The reinstitution of the family model is convincingly argued by McCurry, *Masters of Small Worlds*, 158, 179.

26. Paul K. Conkin, *The Uneasy Center: Reformed Christianity in Antebellum America* (Chapel Hill, N.C., 1995), 130–39.

27. Richey, *Early American Methodism*, 20.

28. Richard Gough, *The History of Myddle* (London, 1988), 77–272; Susan Dwyer Amussen, *An Ordered Society: Gender and Class in Early Modern England* (Oxford, 1988), 137–40, 144. I owe thanks to my colleague Linda Pollock for calling my attention to these sources.

29. For a discussion of American Anglicanism's "middle-range ethos," see Butler, *Awash in a Sea of Faith*, 168–69.

30. For a discussion of the importance of race and class in Low Country churches in antebellum South Carolina, see McCurry, *Masters of Small Worlds*, 158–66, 171–205.

31. St. Philips Episcopal Church, Charleston, August 22, 1828, Vestry Minutes, 1823–1831, South Carolina Historical Society, [50-315B-7], Charleston, S.C.

32. *The Minutes of St. Michael's Church of Charleston, S.C. from 1758–1797*, comp. Anne King Gregoire (Charleston, S.C., 1948), 54, 61, 108.

33. *Moreau de Saint-Méry's American Journal [1793–1798]*, trans. and ed. Kenneth Roberts and Anna M. Roberts (Garden City, N.Y., 1947), 64; François-Alexandre-Frédéric, duc de la Rochefoucauld-Laincourt et D'Estissac, *Travels through the United States of North America in the Years 1795, 1796, and 1797*, 2 vols. (London, 1799), 2:6; *Travels in Virginia in Revolutionary Times*, ed. Alfred J. Morrison (Lynchburg, Va., 1922), 88.

34. Richey, *Early American Methodism*, 55, 58.

35. Peter Cartwright, *Autobiography of Peter Cartwright: The Backwoods Preacher* (1856; reprint, Salem, N.H., 1985), 480–82.

36. *Moreau de St. Méry's American Journal*, 48.

37. *The Journals of Benjamin Henry Latrobe, 1770–1820: From Philadelphia to New Orleans*, 3 vols., ed. Edward C. Carter, John C. Van Horne, and Lee W. Formwalt (New Haven, Conn., 1980), 3:109.

38. Richey, *Early American Methodism*, 108 n. 25.

39. First Baptist Church Savannah, Georgia [Reel 250A], 20 December 1812, Mercer University Library, Special Collections Department. McCurry notes that the observation of racial, gender, and other distinctions was prevalent in predominantly yeoman congregations as well as in churches frequented by planter families. *Masters of Small Worlds*, 141.

40. *Narrative of James Williams: An American Slave* (New York, 1838), 27.

41. Richey, *Early American Methodism*, 108 n. 25.

42. Sensbach, "Separate Canaan," 452–56, 487–88.

43. Goose Creek Baptist Church, August 2, 1812, April 3, 1826, April 24, 1813, 2d Saturday June, 1813; Coan Baptist Church, January 23, 1808, Virginia State Library, Richmond, Va. Trustees Minutes Book 15 [1807–1822], Independent Presbyterian Church Records #2182, Georgia Historical Society, Savannah, Ga. My thanks to Tim Lockley for sharing this note.

44. Sensbach, "Separate Canaan," 441–42, 489–90, 492, 512–13, 514.

45. *Narrative of James Williams*, 25.

46. Sylvia Frey and Betty Wood, *Come Shouting to Zion: African-American Protestant Christianity in the American South and British Caribbean to 1830* (Chapel Hill, N.C., 1998), chap. 6.

47. Vincent Harding, "Religion and Resistance among Antebellum Negroes, 1800–1860," in *The Making of Black America: Essays in Negro Life and History*, ed. August Meier and Elliott Rudwick (New York, 1969), 184–85.

48. St. Philips Episcopal Church, Charleston, Vestry Minutes, 24 August 1828.

49. Lawrence J. Taylor, "Introduction: The Uses of Death," *Anthropological Quarterly* 62 (1989): 149.

50. Quoted in Thomas A. Kselman, *Death and the Afterlife in Modern France* (Princeton, N.J., 1993), 353 n. 57.

51. *The Colonial Records of the State of Georgia* (1732–1782), comp. Allen D. Candler, 27 vols. (Atlanta, 1904), 17:571–72.

52. African Americans were explicitly excluded by an act of 1763.

53. An Ordinance for enlarging the cemetery or public burial ground and for laying off a burial ground for Negroes, July 29, 1789, Ordinances 1787–1817, U-13-1, Clerk of Council's Office, City Hall, Savannah, Ga.

54. See the ordinances of 1789, 1810, 1813, in Ordinances 1787–1817, U-13-1, Clerk of Council, City of Savannah. My thanks to Connie Lewis for locating these ordinances for me.

55. Minutes of St. Michael's Church, Charleston, 170–71.

56. Records of the Georgetown Methodist Church [SCHS][50–65]. Originals in the collections of the Historical Society of the South Carolina Conference, Wofford College, Spartansburg, S.C. My thanks to Tim Lockley for this note.

57. *Georgia Gazette*, February 4, 1790.

58. *Georgia Gazette*, September 13, 1992.

59. *Georgia Gazette*, May 27, 1790. According to Stephen Bullock, the Masonic funeral procession was especially popular in the South beginning at midcentury. The procession drew upon "a familiar vocabulary of hierarchy," the roots of which reach back to Reformation England and the rise of a urban oligarchy. *Revolutionary Brotherhood: Freemasonry and the Transformation of the American Social Order, 1730–1840* (Chapel Hill, N.C., 1996), 55, 78–79.

60. Many African-American urban cemeteries have disappeared. Those that have survived are located in rural areas and were formerly plantation cemeteries. A number of these are threatened by development. Several late-eighteenth and early-nineteenth-century sites destined for development have been the sites of archaeological excavation: the Clifts in Westmoreland County, Virginia, a prosperous tobacco farm occupied from roughly 1670 to 1730; College Landing, a port town and point of supply for Williamsburg; and Cactoctin Furnace, the site of an iron complex located in Frederick County, Maryland, beginning around 1776. The ideology of these early burial sites is difficult to determine. Although physical anthropology of the burials at College Landing and Catoctin Furnace suggest that they were

first- or second-generation Africans, the distinctive burial practices found at later sites in the lower South are not present. All were interred in coffins in individual graves. Most were buried in the traditional Christian posture, the majority on an east-west axis. Grave goods and decorations are largely absent. This may indicate either the systematic repression of African practices or the assimilation of Christian practices; alternatively goods or decorations may have been used initially but subsequently destroyed. See Sharon Ann Burnston, "The Cemetery at Catoctin Furnace, Md.: The Invisible People," *Maryland Archaeology* 17 (1981): 19–13; Carter L. Hudgins, "Historical Archaeology and Salvage Archaeological Excavations at College Landing. An Interim Report," unpublished report supplied to the author by Carter L. Hudgins. In a telephone conversation September 26, 1988, Professor Neiman informed me that one individual was facing west rather than east.

61. See David R. Roediger, "And Die in Dixie: Funerals, Death, and Heaven in the Slave Community, 1700–1865," *Massachusetts Review* 22 (1981): 163–83; and Sylvia R. Frey, *Water from the Rock: Black Resistance in a Revolutionary Age* (Princeton, N.J., 1991), 40–41, 301–4.

62. Carolina Howard Gilman, *Recollections of a South Carolina Matron* (New York, 1838), 81–82. Compare this to the funeral of Shadrach described by Francis A. Kemble, *Journal of a Residence on a Georgian Plantation in 1838–39* (New York, 1863), 12–13.

63. Report of John Holt Rice to the General Assembly's Committee of Missions, *Evangelical Intelligencer* (1809), 309, 391–92. For the competition among black funeral preachers themselves, see "Query from the Brewington Church," *Dover (Virginia) Association Minutes* (1826): 9, 10.

64. Le Jau to the Secretary, 5 September 1711, in *Carolina Chronicle, 1706–1717*, ed. Frank J. Klingberg (Berkeley, Calif., 1956), 102.

65. Rev. John R. Bradley to William Spencer, July 11, 1811, Writings of William Spencer (typescript copy transcribed by Annie L. Winstead), United Methodist Historical Society of the Baltimore Annual Conference Library and Museum, Lovely Lane, Baltimore, Md.

66. Piero Camporesi, *The Fear of Hell: Images of Damnation and Salvation in Early Modern Europe* (University Park, Pa., 1991), 5.

67. Juster, *Disorderly Women*, 146, points to a crucial shift in church discipline in postrevolutionary America—"from community to character." Sin was increasingly understood more as "a breach of morality than a lapse in charity." McCurry, *Masters of Small Worlds*, 182, 183–84, notes that congregational discipline in low-country churches "focused inordinately on sexual transgressions" and held women accountable for breaches of family relations and spousal duties.

68. Hodges, *Black Itinerants*, 56.

69. Charles Ball, *Slavery in the United States: A Narrative of the Life and Adventures of Charles Ball, a black man who lived forty years in Maryland, South Carolina, and Georgia as a slave* (1837: reprint, New York, 1969), 170.

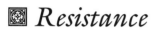 *Resistance*

Neal Salisbury

"I LOVED THE PLACE OF MY DWELLING": PURITAN MISSIONARIES AND NATIVE AMERICANS IN SEVENTEENTH-CENTURY SOUTHERN NEW ENGLAND[1]

> [I]t was not inevitable that the confrontation of European colonizers and Native Americans should lead to mortal combat. Inevitability is not a satisfactory explanation for any human event because it implies that man's destiny is beyond human control and thus relieves individuals and societies of responsibility for their actions.
>
> — GARY B. NASH[2]

 IN MARCH 1676, New England was consumed by war. Many of the region's Native Americans had resorted to armed struggle nine months earlier in an effort to halt the colonists' relentless encroachments on their land and sovereignty. Amid the carnage an improbable scene unfolded at Mount Wachusett in central Massachusetts; two people were having an animated discussion of the meaning of a particular verse in the Bible. Of course, such discussions were common in the homes, churches, and synods of seventeenth-century New England; this one was unusual because Mount Wachusett was the central encampment of the *anti*-English Indians, and the discussants were one of those Indians and Mary Rowlandson, an English woman and minister's wife who had been captured by them. Rowlandson was ridiculing the Indian's claim that 2 Kings 6:25 provided a Christian rationale legitimizing the eating of horse-meat by Christians during times of famine.[3] The substance and merits of their respective arguments need not detain us, but the fact that the discussion was taking place at all should. Thirty years earlier, Puritan missionaries had begun preaching to Indians in southeastern New England, confidently expecting to turn them into not only good Christians but "civilized" English men and women. That some of their "converts" would turn against the English while continuing to profess Christianity makes clear that the program had deviated far from the missionaries' intentions. How did this happen and why?

The activities of Puritan missionaries in the colonies of Martha's Vineyard, Massachusetts Bay, and Plymouth represent the most sustained Protestant effort to convert Native Americans in the seventeenth century. For three centuries thereafter, most commentators described this effort in the missionaries' terms, as an attempt by benevolent "apostles" to introduce ignorant "savages" to the virtues of Christianity and English "civilization." Like the missionaries themselves, many exaggerated the program's successes and emphasized the neophytes' innocent piety. Others followed the missionaries' seventeenth-century detractors in concluding that Indians' savagery was simply impervious to any civilizing influences.[4] Since 1970 the scholarship has grown more complex and sophisticated but has tended to diverge. Some revisionists have reassessed the missionary enterprise as simply one dimension of the colonial project in which the English conquered and subjugated Indians and their lands, going on to suggest that Natives were forced against their will to convert and/or that they had internalized English Puritan values as part of the conversion process.[5] In contrast, others have emphasized the role of Native agency, asserting that Indians turned to Christianity as a means of surviving and rebuilding their society in the face of the enormous disparity between their own power and that of the English.[6]

By now scholars should be prepared to accept that each of these two scholarly strands contain elements of both fundamental truth and gross oversimplification. Certainly, to deny, downplay, or overlook the imperial context within which Indians and missionaries encountered one another is to adopt a historical myopia that can most charitably be described as willful ignorance. To come fully to terms with that context means recognizing that however Natives came to Christianity, they did not freely "choose" it as if they were modern-day shoppers thoughtfully perusing the offerings in some spiritual supermarket. At the same time, as overwhelming as was the power of the English compared to that of the communities from which the earliest Indian converts were drawn, scholars should not jump to the conclusion that such converts were either brainwashed or forced to pretend they were Christians. Indians struggled as best they could to define and control their lives and destinies in the face of what Osage/Cherokee theologian George E. Tinker terms cultural genocide.[7] Scholars must find ways to reconcile the realities of imperial power and of Native agency before they can comprehend the totality of Indian experiences with Puritan Christianity.

This essay takes one step toward such a comprehension by examining Native conversions in light of the histories of Native communities and Native individuals; for conversions to Calvinism, whether from non-Western traditions or from the Church of England, were at once individual and social in their underlying motives and in their long-term implications. It argues that, on a human landscape utterly devastated and transformed by English colonization, some Indians found in Christianity a basis for reordering their lives materially, politically, and spiritually. Rather than entailing a loss of Native cultural identity, Christianity—especially as practiced beyond the purview of the missionaries—may actually have served to sustain and reinforce that identity for some Indians, and to have strengthened rather than weakened their resistance to cultural genocide.[8]

At the beginning of the seventeenth century, southern New England—roughly comprising the present states of Massachusetts, Connecticut, and Rhode Island—was inhabited by about one hundred thousand Natives, who practiced a seasonally calibrated combination of farming, hunting, gathering, and fishing.[9] Closely linked to this way of life was a set of spiritual beliefs and ceremonies. The most important ceremonies honored Cautantowwit, the spiritual figure credited with being the source of agricultural fertility. A more menacing spirit, Hobbomock, caused physical or mental illness and could be warded off only with the assistance of a *powwow*, or shaman. In all their rituals and other practices, Indians sought above all to maintain reciprocity in their relations with the supernatural forces inhabiting their environments.

Reciprocity likewise constituted the norm for New England Indians' social and political relationships. Games and rituals were means by which communities redistributed wealth among members, thereby reaffirming the communities' general egalitarianism as well as the special status of sachems (political leaders), who depended on popular support rather than coercion in order to remain in power. Diplomatic and other intercommunal gatherings placed great emphasis on the ceremonial exchange of gifts as a means of cementing intercommunal ties. Though much of the material exchanged by Indian communities served utilitarian purposes, certain objects valued for their *manitou*, or spiritual power, were exchanged over long distances in New England and elsewhere in North America for thousands of years before Europeans arrived.

Although there were earlier contacts, European adventurers and fishermen began to frequent the New England coasts regularly at the outset of the seventeenth century. In the late 1610s one expedition left behind a catastrophic epidemic that struck the coastal villages of New England, reducing their population by about 90 percent. Meanwhile, in England, the social-economic unrest of the period was exacerbated for many Puritans by the efforts of Archbishop William Laud to enforce religious conformity. In 1620 a few dozen Separatist Puritans founded Plymouth colony among the disease-ravaged Wampanoags. Their modest success inspired the far larger "Great Migration" to New England between 1629 and 1642. During that period a second epidemic, this time of smallpox, swept through the region. By the time the Great Migration abruptly ended with the outbreak of civil war in England, the more than fifteen thousand colonists on the coast of Massachusetts Bay and Plymouth easily outnumbered the one to two thousand surviving Pawtucket, Massachusett and Wampanoag Indians there (see fig. 1).

The vast majority of immigrants to southern New England arrived as members of independent, "middling" farm families, most of whom adhered at least nominally to the radical, voluntaristic Puritanism that defined the colonies' very purposes. Ministers and other leaders enjoined the colonists to create a godly society. Puritan leaders expected that the region's Indians would embrace Christianity, not through the exhortations of missionaries but through the example of ordinary, pious immigrants. The Massachusetts Bay Colony seal depicted an Indian pleading, "come over and help us," and its charter expressed the hope that the immigrants' "good life and orderlie conversation maie wynn and incite the natives of [the] country to" Christianity. New England would be a society in which the primary social and political distinction was religion, and this distinction would now cut across and supersede even the ethnic boundary separating the colonists from the Native inhabitants.[10]

To Native people, the English—with their overwhelming numbers, their technological achievements, and their remarkable system of written communication, as well as the destructive force of their diseases and weapons—appeared to possess great resources of manitou.[11] Their awe quickened English expectations that wholesale Native conversions were imminent. But the Indians' recognition of manitou in the English, far from representing a move away from their spiritual traditions, appears rather to have confirmed those traditions. Such confirmation is evident in the archaeological evidence of Indian–European contact. Prior to the early seventeenth century, southern New England Indians were buried in small

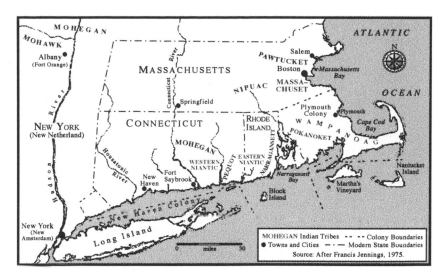

Fig. 1. Indian tribal areas of southern New England. Courtesy Chris Langevin.

plots with a few prized possessions to take with them to Cautantowwit's house, as they termed the spiritual afterlife, where they expected to dwell forever. As epidemics and other factors arising from the English invasion brought catastrophic losses of population, Native communities established large cemeteries, and the quantity of goods that each took to Cautantowwit's house rose markedly. Alongside ceramic pots and shell beads were European-made brass arrowheads, copper kettles, iron hoes, glass beads, textiles, and other manitou-bearing goods.[12] Most of these objects had been obtained from European traders in exchange for furs, wampum, land, and labor, or from other Indians. [13] Not only did the Natives become enmeshed in the world of European commerce, but they incorporated the English into their own networks of reciprocal exchange. Two conclusions seem evident from these patterns. First, from very early in the colonial period—prior to the beginning of formal missionary efforts—what the English regarded as strictly commercial transactions, with diplomatic overtones, were understood by Indians in spiritual terms as well. Second, exchanges with the English and with other Indians were part of the process by which Natives reordered social and political relationships in their rapidly changing environment.

From the early 1640s to the late 1660s most Indian–English exchanges involved members of strong, politically cohesive Native alliances and nearby colonists—the Mohegans with Connecticut, the Narragansetts with Rhode Island, and the mainland Wampanoags, whose center of power was at Pokanoket, with Plymouth. Excluded from these relationships were those Indian communities farthest removed from the centers of Indian-English trade and of Indian power—on the geographically isolated island of Nope (Martha's Vineyard) and in eastern Massachusetts Bay, where the epidemics had been most destructive and English settlement was most concentrated. While other, stronger Indian polities in the early 1640s were cementing ties with colonists through commerce and diplomacy, the Nope Wampanoags submitted to the authority and protection of the nascent colony of Martha's Vineyard (a separate jurisdiction from Massachusetts Bay until 1692); the Pawtuckets and the Massachusetts likewise placed themselves under Massachusetts Bay. In the process, the latter groups of Natives agreed to renounce tributary links with more powerful Indian polities.[14] These agreements were profoundly ambiguous, representing at once the subjugation of powerless Natives to colonial authority and a variation on the more equitable Anglo-Indian alliances that were rooted in trade.[15]

The submissions by certain Indians to English authority were also significant because they coincided with the recognition by some Puritans that the example of their fellow colonists was failing to produce significant numbers of Indian converts. Indeed, most settlers regarded Indians not as potential fellow Christians but as impediments to the land they sought for themselves. Moreover, detractors of the colonists in England were calling attention in Parliament and the press to the lack of converts. In these circumstances the United Colonies of New England—a newly formed confederation that included Massachusetts Bay, Plymouth, Connecticut, and New Haven—authorized a missionary program to be directed at those Indians who had submitted to English political authority but not at stronger allies with whom relations were more genuinely reciprocal and on whom the colonies depended.[16] On Martha's Vineyard, Thomas Mayhew Jr., son of the proprietor to whom the Nope Wampanoags had submitted the year before, began preaching to them in 1643.[17] And in the following year, the Massachusetts Bay Colony enacted legislation requiring all subject Indians to undergo religious instruction, opening the way for missionary John Eliot to begin his work among the Massachusett and Pawtucket Indians.[18]

The close association between missionaries and civil authorities indicates that Mayhew and Eliot were able to command the Natives' attention in ways that individuals acting independently of state authority never could have. Nevertheless, the two missionaries began slowly, each focusing on likely individual prospects rather than on whole communities.[19] This initial strategy reflected both a Protestant emphasis on saving individual souls and a recognition that communal ties among Indians remained strong. But Mayhew and Eliot also recognized that many Natives' confidence in their traditional beliefs, customs, and institutions had been shaken by the cumulative impact of catastrophic epidemics, massive English immigration, and isolation from other Indians.

One particularly vulnerable area of traditional belief and practice was medical healing. Over time the credibility of the powwows, feared by most Indians for the terrible supernatural power they yielded, had been undermined by waves of plague, smallpox, and other unfamiliar diseases to which Natives lacked immunity. Many Wampanoags had interpreted the initial epidemic of the late 1610s as punishment for failure to honor Cautantowwit fully and properly.[20] For two more decades, few Indians doubted that diseases impervious to the powwows' ministrations were retribution for departing from traditional ritual practices. But during the smallpox epidemic of 1633–34, some Massachusett and Pawtucket Indians concluded that the disease arose instead from their failure to honor the Christian God and converted before succumbing themselves.[21]

From the outset of their preaching a decade later, Mayhew and Eliot were unremitting in their hostility to the powwows. Mayhew called them "the strongest cord that binds [Natives] to their own way."[22] The missionaries vividly described the powwows' healing procedures as, simultaneously, silly superstition and satanic darkness. Viewing the medicine men as agents of Satan himself, the English prohibited them from practicing within their colonies. Nevertheless, the powwows continued to attract partisans, and even many Christian converts hesitated to forsake them altogether.[23]

Disease provided the direct opening through which Mayhew began converting Nope Wampanoags. He had made only one convert, a man named Hiacoomes, when an epidemic erupted on Martha's Vineyard in 1643. Whereas most Wampanoags interpreted the outbreak as punishment for departing from tradition as far as they already had, Hiacoomes saw his immunity as a sign that the Christian God was protecting him. After a sachem who had warned Hiacoomes against forsaking the powwows was struck by lightning, Hiacoomes gained a few followers. Two years later another epidemic struck a number of Wampanoags but spared the Christians, leading many more to break ranks with the powwows. Meanwhile, Mayhew used combinations of bleeding and prayer to restore the health of several sick persons on whom the powwows had given up. That the Wampanoags considered Mayhew a substitute for the powwows was made explicit by Towanquatticks, a sachem and father of one of those healed. "A long time agon," he told the missionary after his son recovered, the Indians "had wise men, which in a grave manner taught the people knowledge, but they are dead, and their wisedome is buried with them." The wise men of the present, he concluded, were the English preachers.[24]

Mortal illness was also a factor in the conversion of Massachusett Indians. Eliot found cause to rejoice over both deathbed conversions and converts who survived epidemics during which unconverted Indians perished.[25] His first convert, Waban, testified that he was first drawn to the English religion "after the great sikness."[26] The experience of approaching and then drawing back from the brink of death was instrumental in the conversions of several Indians. Nookau saw his renewed life as a confirmation of God's power, whereas Antony thought his illness and an accident, in which "God brake my head," were expressions of divine anger.[27] The deaths of loved ones drove other Indians to reconsider their own spiritual state. Robin Speen, a former powwow, interpreted the deaths of his three children as punishment for his sinful transgressions, and Monoquasson attributed the deaths of his wife and child to a similar cause. The deaths of a brother and friend were milestones on Antony's road to conversion.[28]

By the 1640s, deaths from unfamiliar causes had been common in coastal Indian communities for three decades. But it took that long before significant numbers began to conclude that the old assurances that life would be followed by a carefree existence in Cautantowwit's house had lost their meaning. Separated from their traditions by the deaths of most people they knew, by their distance from other Indians, and by a wall of English people and power, they looked to the English god, a god whose followers were largely immune to the maladies that devastated their own communities.[29]

It is tempting to conclude that the Indians' fears simply played into the Calvinist formula, whereby sinners confront the terror of an existence without God's grace and thereupon succumb to his will and power. Yet there was another side to Natives' resorting to Christianity in order to combat epidemic diseases. In all the cases noted above, Indians confronted a vengeful God whose anger could be placated only with the aid of extraordinary individuals—the missionaries—who wielded unusual spiritual powers. As such their experiences paralleled almost precisely their earlier encounters with the malevolence of Hobbomock, which they had countered by calling on the powwows and their extraordinary manitou. Less than an abandonment of tradition, Christianity represented for its earliest Indian adherents a means of survival and of countering the new, more lethal malevolent powers inhabiting the colonial environment.

But survival and spiritual power were not the only factors to figure in Natives' decisions to adopt Christianity. The fragmentation of Indian families and communities in the face of epidemics and English settlement reinforced interest in the newcomers' religion, especially among the Massachusetts and Pawtuckets. It is hardly surprising that several of the earliest converts among these peoples reported that they first heard of Christianity while "going to English houses."[30] Although Totherswamp loved God primarily for giving humankind Jesus Christ, he was also thankful for "all outward blessings, as food, clothing, children, gifts of strength, . . . especially that he giveth a Minister to teach us, and giveth us Government."[31] And Waban reported how, "after the great sikness, I considered what the English do; and I had some desire to do as they do; and after that I began to work as they work; and then I wondered how the English come to be so strong to labor."[32]

The very ubiquity of the English, then, rendered their religious teachings and way of life attractive to many Indians. For that very reason, however, others clung all the more closely to family and friends in the face of pressures to abandon them. Totherswamp initially feared that turning to Christianity would cause him to lose "many friends who loved me," while Magus held back at first because "none of our Rulers beleeve or pray to God."[33] Yet the same impulse could lead other Indians toward conversion. John Speen, for example, confessed that initially he "did not pray for my soul, but only I did as my friends did, because I loved them," whereas Nataous, known as William of Sudbury, resisted praying until hearing that his sachem was doing so. As others in his village began praying, Monoquassen considered "running away because I loved sin" but he decided to stay and overcome his aversion to Christianity because "I loved the place of my dwelling."[34]

At this point it is appropriate to pause and interrogate the reliability of these conversion accounts as historical evidence as well as the validity of this essay's reading of them. For while purporting to represent the voices of Natives themselves, the accounts of their conversions quoted in the foregoing paragraphs were, as Eliot himself acknowledged, interpreted and recorded by him and in some cases by other English. One could reasonably argue, then, that these are not the words and feelings of Native people but rather Eliot's representation of those words and feelings. There can be no doubt that Eliot frequently exaggerated his own accomplishments to attract financial support. Moreover, everything he wrote about Indians was framed within the categories of "savage" and "pagan," categories having nothing to do with Native culture and everything to do with the cultural constructions being developed by Europeans in the course of their imperial expansion.[35] Nevertheless, in spite of the likelihood that Eliot distorted aspects of Indians' conversion experiences, a case for the general plausibility of the above readings can be made on the grounds that the readings are consistent with what scholars know, independently of Eliot, about the history to which the accounts refer.

Assuming the general validity of Eliot's accounts, there remains the even thornier problem of determining how Natives and missionaries understood one another. Once missionary distortion and ideological representations have been accounted for, how can scholars assess the actual communication between two peoples of such disparate cultures and experiences? There is no absolutely certain answer to this question, just as there is none for most critical historical questions, leaving scholars to make the best educated guess they can. George E. Tinker offers one useful guideline for reading the Indian confessions interpreted and reported by Eliot. Drawing on Noam Chomsky, he posits that while praying Indians and missionaries understood one another's "surface structure" meanings, each missed the more substantive "deep structure images" that were basic to the consciousness of the other. A close reading of the Indians' own accounts of their religious conversions shows, Tinker maintains, the simultaneity of surface-structure understandings and deep-structure mistranslations. Tinker's distinction makes clear how Eliot could read his converts' pain while misunderstanding its origin and meaning and how, as Charles L. Cohen has pointed out, Indians could hear Eliot's message of salvation but miss the Puritan idea of divine love and grace that underlay it.[36]

In particular, Indians' longings for what Eliot translated as "love" in fact express their desires and efforts to revitalize kinship and community and particularly to restore bonds of unquestioning loyalty and trust of the kind that had become elusive with the onset of English colonization. Praying Indians prefaced virtually all their conversion accounts with expressions of loneliness and their alienation from traditional culture. Feeling alone and spiritually malnourished, converts repudiated their past behavior and beliefs for a message that seemed at once to explain the success of the English and to offer them the possibility of spiritual and social renewal.

The needs of Christian Indians seemed to mesh easily with the missionaries' goal of spreading the gospel and saving souls in the "wilderness" of America. But in keeping with their view of America as wilderness, the missionaries also concluded that the conversion of Natives could not proceed independently of their cultural transformation. To put it in their parlance, the savages had to be civilized before they could become truly Christian. The differences between conditions in Martha's Vineyard and in Massachusetts Bay led Eliot to pursue this project more ardently than Mayhew did. On the island, where Indians outnumbered settlers, Mayhew and his father, Thomas Mayhew Sr. (who, though not a minister, assumed missionary duties after his son died at sea in 1657), employed little overt pressure on Wampanoags to "civilize," concentrating on spiritual matters and urging rather than requiring their converts to adopt English institutions.[37]

Eliot, on the mainland, was a forceful proponent of civilization and worked among a steadily diminishing minority of Indians in a colony dominated by land-hungry settlers. He set out to civilize the Massachusetts and Pawtuckets by organizing "praying towns," wherein they would be isolated from both settlers and other Indians. Each town was to be administered by rulers of tens, fifties, and hundreds, as outlined in Exodus 18, with the supreme leader serving as magistrate; and each had a legal code devised by Eliot and consented to by the residents. The codes prohibited, on pain of fine, Native customs and behavior that allegedly conflicted with the Bible or with English values. Thus, residents of Natick, Eliot's first praying town, were enjoined from idleness and from moving from one house to another. Women could not cut their hair short nor men let theirs grow long. Concord's Indians had to forgo traditional games as well as lying. Eliot and his co-workers urged all praying Indian men to abandon hunting and concentrate on farming individual plots and learning crafts, while women were to give up gathering, turn farming over to their husbands, and learn the domestic arts of English housewifery. Toward this end the missionaries distributed farming tools to men and sewing implements to women. Finally, they undertook an ambitious program to teach the Indians to read and to write in Roman script, not in English but in their native Massachusett language.[38]

Although the towns constituted the communal core of praying Indians' transformation, that transformation did not entirely conform to the kind of civilization envisioned by Eliot. Several factors worked to steer the towns in a somewhat different direction. One was the Indians' own discovery that, without compromising their Christianity, they could be far more selective in their adoption of civilization than Eliot demanded. For example, while utilizing many of the tools and other goods distributed by the missionaries, the praying Indians also took some of these items to their graves and exchanged others with non-Christian Indians. Items recovered from the seventeenth-century cemetery at Natick, for example, include glass beads, metal utensils, and a sleigh bell, as well as a clay pipe, wampum beads and shells, and other indigenous objects.[39] The range of American and European provenances represented in such an array indicates that praying Indians valued European goods not because they believed or hoped that the goods would enable them to become more like the English (who, believing that their material goods had value only in this world, bequeathed them to earthly descendants). Rather, they recognized the new objects as possessing manitou, that is attributes valued in indigenous tradition rather than in the "new tradition" being advocated by the missionaries. The burial goods makes clear that praying Indians drew a less pronounced distinction between Cautantowwit's house and the Christian heaven than did their missionary teachers.

A second factor shaping Indian Christianity in New England was the internal autonomy of the praying towns. The first such town, Natick, was an entirely new community created under Eliot's auspices, but those that followed were simply traditional towns in which the sachems and a considerable number of inhabitants (by no means all) identified themselves as Christians. In electing their rulers, praying Indians generally chose men from the sachem's lineage and the sachem himself as their magistrate, thereby maintaining continuity in their communities and reconciling traditional and colonial political-legal systems.[40] The towns also had Native religious teachers who were appointed by Eliot and Daniel Gookin, Massachusetts Bay's superintendent of Christian Indians. But the fact that religious teaching, discussion, and even reading and writing were in Massachusett, rather than in translated English, meant that there was ample space for Native understandings to shape the content of received Christianity.[41]

Yet another factor undermining the goal of civilization was the praying towns' very success. With Eliot's guidance and patronage, many praying Indians found niches in the colonial market economy as producers of meat, dairy products, produce, and baskets and brooms, or as construction workers, unskilled laborers, and domestics.[42] In this respect, too, they used the missions to secure a place for themselves in the new economic environment. The inexorable spread of market relations meant that those Natives who continued to hold out against Christianity would eventually pay a price for their resistance. By a decade or so after Eliot began his work, Christianity was attracting at least some Indians for its economic and political rather than its spiritual attributes. The most notable such opportunistic conversion was that of the Massachusett sachem, Cutshamekin, who resisted Christianity for several years until realizing that it was his only means of retaining the support of his Christian followers, now in the majority, as well the patronage of the English.[43]

Finally, the civilization of Indians was made all the more difficult by the anti-Indian hostility of most colonists, a hostility that amounted to racism because it was directed at all Indians without regard for the Christianity of some. Although praying Indians ceded much of their land to the colony, many of their English neighbors resented *any* lands being set aside for them. English families resisted missionaries' efforts to apprentice Christian Indian children in their households. Eliot's own Roxbury congregation only reluctantly allowed eight Natick Christians to join them for a season so they might experience Christian fellowship before beginning New England's first Indian congregation. That congregation had to endure ten years of repeated rejections of its public confessions as well as other trials before it finally was certified by a board of elders. The behavior of English Christians, frequently deplored by the missionaries, further served to deter praying Indians from identifying too closely with the English at the expense of their own communities and traditions.[44]

For a generation after their founding, the missions consolidated their hold on the allegiances of the Nope Wampanoags and of the Pawtuckets and Massachusetts. Meanwhile, the expansion of English settlement, particularly as a second generation of colonists came of age in the 1660s, intensified pressures on other Indian groups to part with their lands. It was then that two of these groups—the mainland Wampanoags in Plymouth colony and the Nipmucs of central Massachusetts—confronted missionaries intent on reaching new converts.

The mainland Wampanoags, whose principal sachem resided in the western Plymouth town of Pokanoket, had been steadfast allies of Plymouth since 1621, when they rescued the struggling survivors of the colony's first winter.[45] Since then, they had lost their tributaries at Nope to the Mayhews in 1643 and had ceded thousands of acres to Plymouth. Wampanoag resistance to English encroachments stiffened after 1660, when the colony began demanding land that was not only economically essential to the Natives but enabled them to move freely between their villages.[46] At the same time, Puritan missionaries began preaching to some mainland tributaries of Pokanoket. A layman, Richard Bourne, established a new praying town, eventually known as Mashpee, among the Nauset Wampanoags of Cape Cod, and John Cotton Jr., the minister at Plymouth, preached at some Wampanoag towns nearer the colony capital.[47] As part of their conversion, many Wampanoags ceased paying tribute to Pokanoket and its sachem, Metacom (known to the English as King Philip), undermining his once formidable polity. Metacom and his councilors later provided a Native perspective on these changes when they told a Rhode Island peace delegation how English cheating, discrimination, and pressures to sell land, submit to Plymouth colony's authority, convert to Christianity, and consume alcohol had undermined a half century of friendship and driven him and his non-Christian followers to the point of war. They placed particular emphasis on the role of missionaries in dividing the Wampanoags, saying that "they had a great fear to have any of their Indians called or forced to be Christian Indians. They said that such [Indians] were in everything more mischievous, only dissemblers, and then the English made them not subject to their kings and, by their lying, to wrong their kings."[48]

The event that finally triggered open war in 1675 pointed up how Christian conversion and conflicting cultural identities were dividing New England Natives. John Sassamon was a Christian Massachusett Indian who had lived in Natick, Eliot's first praying town, where he learned to read and write English, and had attended Harvard College. But at some point he left his life among the English to become an interpreter, English-language scribe, and counselor for the Pokanoket Wampanoags and their sachem, Metacom. Sassamon served Metacom for more than a decade, even as Plymouth–Wampanoag relations grew increasingly bitter. But in March 1675, with tensions at fever pitch, Sassamon informed Plymouth's governor,

Josiah Winslow, that Metacom was conspiring with other Indians to launch an all-out war against the English. Whether Sassamon was telling the truth or had invented his tale in order to ingratiate himself once again with the English was never determined, for a week later he was dead. Three associates of Metacom were accused by a Christian Indian who testified that he had witnessed them beat Sassamon to death and throw his body in a pond. Plymouth selected a jury of twelve Englishmen plus six Christian Indians, especially appointed to give the trial an appearance of even-handedness. The jury found the three guilty, and on June 8 they were hanged. The trial confirmed the worst fears of Metacom and his follow-ers—the English sought to destroy them. They were not impressed by the English effort to legitimize the trial in Indian eyes, complaining to the Rhode Islanders that "if 20 of their honest Indians testified that a English-man had done them wrong, it was as nothing, and if but one of their worst Indians testified against any Indian or their king when it pleased the Eng-lish that was sufficient" to find him guilty. Indeed, Metacom and his fol-lowers were mobilizing for war even as the trial progressed.[49]

Of special concern to the Massachusetts Bay Colony as tensions rose were the Nipmucs, who occupied the southern New England heartland linking the colonies' potential Indian enemies. Anxious to ensure their loy-alty, Gookin toured the Nipmucs' villages in July 1673. As John Eliot had done three decades earlier among the Massachusett Indians to the east, Gookin hastily sought to organize eight Nipmuc villages into praying towns by appointing "praying Indians" as ministers and magistrates to gov-ern them. While successful at seven of his eight stops, Gookin failed to per-suade the inhabitants of Nashaway to "abstain from drunkenness, whore-dom, and powwowing, and all other evils" in order to be assured of "eternal and temporal happiness."[50] But Nashaway had already experienced an unusual amount of English interference in its internal affairs and, in re-jecting Gookin's overture, made clear that its sympathies would lie with Metacom and the other anti-Christian Indians.[51]

The mounting intercultural tensions burst into what became known as King Philip's War in 1675. On one side were all the English plus the Mohe-gans and Pequots of Connecticut and Christian Wampanoag, Nipmuc, and Massachusett Indians of Plymouth and Massachusetts Bay. On the other was a loose coalition of Wampanoags, Nipmucs, Narragansetts of Rhode Island, and Pocumtucks and other Natives of the Connecticut River Valley. When war first broke out, pro-English Natives volunteered their services in all the colonies, where they proved highly effective, not only as warriors but as scouts, advisers, and spies. But authorities in Massachusetts and Ply-mouth encountered such formidable popular hostility toward the Native allies that they finally discharged this most valuable asset to their cause.

Upon learning that some anti-English Nipmucs were converts, many English immediately concluded that all Native Americans were traitors and that "praying Indians" were the most deceitful and treacherous of all. Praying Indians were frequently harassed, jailed without cause, and, in several notorious instances, killed by vigilantes. When missionaries and others, such as Eliot and Gookin, sought to defend Native Christians, their lives too were threatened. Indeed, the issue of whether to consider praying Indians friends or foes precipitated a political crisis in Massachusetts that, like Bacon's Rebellion, which was raging at that very moment in Virginia, threatened to become a civil war as well as an Indian war. To avert that outcome in their own colony, Massachusetts authorities reached a consensus on the problem of the praying Indians. They ordered all loyal Massachusett and Nipmuc families moved to Deer Island in Boston harbor, ostensibly to protect them from both hostile colonists and anti-English Indians. Although indeed separated from all outsiders, friendly or hostile, the Indian captives on Deer Island lacked means of obtaining adequate food and shelter; therefore, many died as prisoners of their supposed allies. Meanwhile, without Indian assistance, Massachusetts troops proved utterly unable to locate their enemies and prevent the ambushes and surprise attacks that devastated the colony from the fall of 1675 to the following spring.[52]

The growing harassment and atrocities suffered by praying Indians, culminating in the order to move to Deer Island, presented many Christian Nipmucs and Wampanoags with a profound crisis of cultural loyalty and identity. They had embraced the religion of the English as well as much of the civilization offered by the colonists and had reason to assume that their becoming Christians would guarantee them, at the very least, the goodwill of English Christians. At the same time, while identifying themselves as distinct from the traditional, non-Christian segments of their communities, they had nevertheless maintained contact with people in these segments, many of whom were kin and longtime neighbors. In short, they had forged new identities for themselves by straddling a line between two cultures and ways of life. In 1675 they discovered that nearly all English, as well as many Indians, did not recognize the legitimacy of their syncretic identities.

Confronted with this crisis, praying Indians pursued various solutions. The several hundred taken to Deer Island had few choices, although some, upon reaching the island and seeing its prospects, managed to escape. Others avoided the roundups, joining the anti-English Indians and participating actively in opposing the colonists. Still others were captured by anti-English Indians before the English could get to them; many of these thereafter changed their minds and joined in fighting the English. Probably typical was the case of James Printer, a Nipmuc known among Indians as Wowaus. Printer derived his English name from having worked for New

England's leading printer for sixteen years before returning to his home and family in the praying town of Hassanamesit at the outbreak of war. Among other works, he had printed numerous Puritan missionary tracts publicizing his and other Christian Indians' piety. Falsely accused, along with ten other Christian Nipmucs, of participating in the August 1675 raid on Lancaster, he narrowly escaped death at the hands of an English lynch mob. Three months later anti-English Indians attacked Printer's town of Hassanamesit and gave the outnumbered inhabitants the choice of accompanying the raiders to their encampment or remaining in their town and having their corn stores burned. Knowing that if they left their village in search of food they would almost certainly be captured by the English and sent to Deer Island, Printer and the other Hassanamesit Nipmucs chose to join forces with their captors.[53]

Some of the best documented evidence of praying Indians among the anti-English forces comes from Mary Rowlandson, the English woman who discussed biblical exegesis with one of her captors at Mount Wachusett. In her account of her captivity, Rowlandson offers ample evidence of Christian Indians mocking, fighting against, and killing colonists. What is most striking about her evidence is that the Indians she describes had not renounced their Christianity, including one Nipmuc who led a decidedly unchristian ceremony before a battle as well as the one with whom she discussed horsemeat. Some of these anti-English Christians were never detected by the colonial authorities. Rowlandson saw one of her cruelest tormentors after the war ended, she writes, "walking up and down Boston, under the appearance of a Friend-Indian, and severall others of the like cut."[54]

By early 1676, English military leaders recognized that without friendly Indian assistance, they would never understand their enemies' fighting ways as well as their enemies understood theirs. Accordingly, in the spring of 1676 they began allowing Christian Indian men to leave their island confinement to serve as scouts, guides, and soldiers, contributing substantially to the upturn in English military fortunes that followed. By the summer of 1676, the anti-English Indians had been decisively vanquished, ending all vestiges of Indian political autonomy and military prowess in southern New England.[55]

In the meantime, Christian Indians on the two sides served another vital role by facilitating the release of English captives among the anti-English Indians. From the beginning it was clear that pro-English Nipmucs held the key to the release of the English captives. They had relatives and friends among the anti-English forces, and they alone could approach the anti-English encampments without being harmed. The obvious place to find someone to undertake such a mission was Deer Island. In late

March, English intermediaries secured the services of Tom Dublet, a Nipmuc otherwise known as Nepanet, and Peter Conway, whose Indian name was Tatatiqunea, to carry a message to the central Indian encampment at Mount Wachusett. On the anti-English side, none of the sachems could write their own letters. But they were able to call on others in their ranks to write replies for them in English. These scribes were Nipmucs, among them James Printer, who had become literate in English while attending mission schools in the praying towns.[56] The war ended with the anti-English Indians completely routed. English justice was, not surprisingly, swift, unforgiving, and thorough. Indian men who were considered leaders of the uprising or guilty of killing English were publicly hanged with great fanfare.[57] Several of these were Christians, and one, known to the English as Captain Tom, was vigorously defended by Christian Indians loyal to the English and somewhat less vigorously by Gookin.[58] The colonies sold most other Indian male captives to slave traders who took them to the West Indies, Bermuda, Virginia, the Iberian peninsula, and in at least one instance, North Africa. There are no figures on the number of Indians shipped out as slaves except in tiny Plymouth colony, where the official count was 188. The wives, children, and other family members of Native American captives were generally retained as slaves within the colonies.[59] Given the colony's record during the war, there can be little doubt that there were loyal Christian Indians among those enslaved thereafter.[60]

Other southern New England Natives, particularly those who had opposed the English, fled the region and found refuge among Mahicans and other Algonquian-speaking Indians in the colony of New York or among Abenakis, both in upper New England and in Catholic praying towns established by French missionaries in Canada.[61] At least some of these were Christians. When England and France went to war in 1689, southern New England refugees in and near Canada found ample motivation to enlist in the French cause and raid English villages to the south.[62] One Nipmuc, having captured several women and children in a raid on Haverhill, Massachusetts, in 1689, told one of his captives "that when he prayed the English way, he thought that was good; but now he found the French way was better."[63]

In the meantime, those praying Indians who had remained in southern New England returned to villages destroyed by war and further depopulated and to English neighbors who continued to suspect their loyalty and covet their land. Whether or not they were Christians, most Natives who remained in Massachusetts Bay were confined to Natick, Wamesit, Punkapoag, and Hassanamesit, just four of what had been fourteen praying towns to be reopened. The praying towns had been transformed into government reservations, which were in reality little more than enclaves within which were confined members of a subjugated, ethnically distinct minority.[64] Nevertheless, these enclaves served to sustain Natives, both Christian and non-Christian, and their cultural identities in the decades and, in many cases, centuries to come. Those who had been displaced did not give up on the prospects of returning to their original homelands, and in later years asserted their ownership through lawsuits or simple reoccupation. Thus it was that Nipmucs and other Native peoples persisted in eastern and central Massachusetts into the eighteenth and later centuries.[65]

Throughout his career, John Eliot, the most forceful proponent of Puritan missions, understood Indians' embracing of Christianity as "conversion" and assumed that such conversions entailed an embrace of civilization as well. Most scholars since then have proceeded from Eliot's assumptions when evaluating the evangelical enterprise in New England. Indians' responses to Christianity cannot be measured in terms of their civilization and departure from traditional ways. The Indians who initially accepted Christianity were those who were most devastated by epidemics and cut off physically from the social and political world of Native reciprocity. In the missionaries' spiritual message, as well as in the political and material rewards of conversion, they found the key to revitalizing themselves, their families, and their communities in a new, bicultural environment. But in spite of their Christianity and their adoption of many English goods and customs, the converts' new lives represented a selective blend of Indian and English ways.

The Christian Indians' cultural transformation was a variation on, rather than a departure from, that of their non-Christian counterparts. Both groups sought to participate in the political, social, and economic life of their now-colonized homeland. At first, the non-Christians, with their traditional polities and land bases intact, had the advantage over the isolated, depopulated Indians of the coast. But after pressures to expand the areas of English settlement and the scope of English authority culminated in King Philip's War, the non-Christians lost their remaining political and legal autonomy. Thereafter, praying Indians were distinguished from other Natives largely by their religious orientation and by their literacy in their native tongue. Religion had given way to race and ethnicity as the primary social distinction in New England.

Notes

1. This essay represents a return to and reconsideration of themes explored in "Red Puritans: The 'Praying Indians' of Massachusetts Bay and John Eliot," *WMQ* 3d ser., 31 (1974): 27–54. Portions have appeared previously in that article, in *The*

Sovereignty and Goodness of God, by Mary Rowlandson, with Related Documents, ed. Neal Salisbury (Boston, 1997), Introduction; and in Pontificio di Scienze Stroiche, *Il Cristianesimo nel Mondo Atlantico nel Secolo XVII: Atteggiamenti dei Cristiani nei confronti dei popoli e delle culture indigeni* , Atti e documenti, 6 (Vatican City, 1997), 233–41. I wish to thank arrangers and audience participants where I presented earlier versions: the roundtable, "Christianity in the 17th Century Atlantic World, with Particular Reference to Christian Attitudes towards Native Peoples and Cultures," 18th Congress of Historical Sciences, Montreal, August, 1995; Institüt für Historische Ethnologie, J. W. Goethe University, Frankfurt, June 1996, especially Christian Feest and Sylvia Kasprycki; the Joint Neale and Commonwealth Fund Conference, "British Encounters with Indigenous Peoples," University College, London, February 1997; and the Harvard University Native American Program, May 1997. I wish also to acknowledge the enormously valuable research assistance of Kim Kosakowski.

2. Gary B. Nash, *Red, White, and Black: The Peoples of Early North America*, 3d ed. (Englewood Cliffs, N.J., 1992), 27.

3. Salisbury, ed., *Sovereignty*, 99.

4. Most such conclusions were drawn by denominational historians and others whose interests in Native Americans were at best peripheral. The major exception was Alden T. Vaughan, *New England Frontier: Puritans and Indians, 1620–1675* (Boston, 1965).

5. Salisbury, "Red Puritans"; Francis Jennings, *The Invasion of America: Indians, Colonialism, and the Cant of Conquest* (Chapel Hill, N.C., 1975); Henry W. Bowden, *American Indians and Christian Missions* (Chicago, 1981), chap. 4.

6. The most compelling works with this emphasis are William S. Simmons, "Conversion from Indian to Puritan," *NEQ* 52 (1979): 197–218; James Axtell, *The Invasion Within: The Contest of Cultures in Colonial North America* (New York, 1985); Harold W. Van Lonkhuyzen, "A Reappraisal of the Praying Indians: Acculturation, Conversion, and Identity at Natick, Massachusetts," *NEQ* 63 (1990): 396–428; Charles L. Cohen, "Conversion among Puritans and Amerindians: A Theological and Cultural Perspective," in *Puritanism: Transatlantic Perspectives on a Seventeenth-Century Anglo-American Faith*, ed. Francis J. Bremer (Boston, 1993), 233–56; Jean M. O'Brien, *Dispossession by Degrees: Indian Land and Identity in Natick, Massachusetts, 1650–1790* (New York, 1997). Axtell's odd polemic, "Were Indian Conversions *Bona Fide?*" in *After Columbus: Essays in the Ethnohistory of Colonial North America* (New York, 1988), 100–121, esp. 120, harks back to the pre-1970 era, when the assumption of a monolithic Christianity with universal appeal went virtually unchallenged in the scholarly literature.

7. For George E. Tinker, "[c]ultural genocide can be defined as the effective destruction of a people by systematically or systemically (intentionally or unintentionally in order to achieve other goals) destroying, eroding, or undermining the integrity of the culture and system of values that defines a people and gives them life." *Missionary Conquest: The Gospel and Native American Cultural Genocide* (Minneapolis, 1993), 6.

8. For a Native-authored history that recognizes the critical role played by Christianity in maintaining one community's Indian identity, see Russell M. Peters, *The Wampanoags of Mashpee: An Indian Perspective on American History* (n.p., 1987), esp. 16–28, 32–35.

9. This paragraph and the four that follow are drawn from my *Manitou and Providence: Indians, Europeans and the Making of New England, 1500–1643*

(New York, 1982). For a recent, comprehensive overview of Native life and culture in this period, see Kathleen J. Bragdon, *Native People of Southern New England, 1500–1650* (Norman, Okla., 1996).

10. For a reproduction of the seal, see Salisbury, ed., *Sovereignty*, 20. For the charter, see *Records of the Governor and Company of the Massachusetts Bay in New England*, ed. Nathaniel B. Shurtleff (5 vols. in 6; Boston, 1853–54), 1:17. For other citations, see Salisbury, "Red Puritans," 29 n. 5.

11. Salisbury, *Manitou and Providence*, 37–39.

12. Bert Salwen, "European Trade Goods and the Chronology of the Ft. Shantok Site," *Bulletin of the Massachusetts Archaeological Society* 34 (1966), whole issue; Lorraine E. Williams, "Ft. Shantok and Ft. Corchaug: A Comparative Study of Seventeenth-Century Culture Contact in the Long Island Sound Area" (Ph.D. diss., New York University, 1972); William Scranton Simmons, *Cautantowwit's House: An Indian Burial Ground on the Island of Conanicut in Narragansett Bay* (Providence, 1970); Bert Salwen and Susan N. Meyer, "Indian Archaeology and Rhode Island," *Archaeology* 31 (6):57–58; *Burr's Hill: A Seventeenth-Century Wampanoag Burial Ground in Warren, Rhode Island*, ed. Susan G. Gibson, Haffenreffer Museum of Anthropology, Brown University, Studies in Anthropology and Material Culture, 2 ([Providence, R.I.], 1980); Paul A. Robinson, Marc A. Kelley, and Patricia E. Rubertone, "Preliminary Biocultural Interpretations from a Seventeenth-Century Narragansett Indian Cemetery in Rhode Island," in *Cultures in Contact: The Impact of European Contacts on Native American Cultural Institutions, A.D. 1000–1800*, ed. William W. Fitzhugh (Washington, D.C., 1985), 107–30; Peter A. Thomas, "Cultural Change on the Southern New England Frontier, 1630–65," in *Cultures in Contact*, 131–61; Elise M. Brenner, "Sociopolitical Implications of Mortuary Ritual Remains in 17th-Century Native Southern New England," in *The Recovery of Meaning: Historical Archaeology in the Eastern United States*, ed. Mark P. Leone and Parker B. Potter (Washington, D.C., 1988), 147–81; Constance A. Crosby, "From Myth to History, or Why King Philip's Ghost Walks Abroad," in *Recovery of Meaning*, 183–209.

13. Neal Salisbury, "Indians and Colonists in Southern New England after the Pequot War," in *The Pequots in Southern New England: The Fall and Rise of an American Indian Nation*, ed. Laurence M. Hauptman and James D. Wherry (Norman, Okla., 1990), 81–95, esp. 82–90.

14. William S. Simmons, "Conversion from Indian to Puritan," *NEQ* 52 (1979): 202–3; *Records of Massachusetts Bay*, 2:55–56.

15. Salisbury, "Indians and Colonists," 82–85.

16. The colonies' strongest Indian allies, the Pokanoket Wampanoags and Mohegans, repeatedly rebuffed efforts to convert them. Salisbury, "Red Puritans," 30–31, 38.

17. Simmons, "Conversion from Indian to Puritan," 203–4.

18. *Records of Massachusetts Bay*, 2:166, 176–79.

19. Simmons, "Conversion from Indian to Puritan," 204–5; Jennings, *Invasion of America*, 230–31, 239–41; Daniel Mandell, "'Standing by His Father': Thomas Waban of Natick, circa 1630–1722," in *Northeastern Indian Lives, 1632–1816*, ed. Robert S. Grumet (Amherst, Mass., 1996), 167–69.

20. Edward Winslow, "Good Newes from New England" (1624), in *Chronicles of the Pilgrim Fathers*, ed. Alexander Young (1841; reprint, New York, 1971), 358–59.

21. Salisbury, *Manitou and Providence*, 191.

22. Henry Whitfield, *The Light Appearing More and More Towards the Perfect Day* (London, 1651) reprinted *CMHS* 3d ser., 4 (1834): 113.

23. John Eliot and Thomas Mayhew Jr., *Tears of Repentance: Or, A Further Narrative of the Gospel amongst the Indians in New-England* (London, 1653) reprinted *CMHS* 3d ser., 4 (1834): 204; Daniel Gookin, *Historical Collections of the Indians in New England* (1674; reprint, n.p., 1970), 21–23, 154.

24. Henry Whitfield, *Strength out of Weaknesse; Or a Glorious Manifestation of the further Progresse of the Gospel among the Indians in New-England* (London, 1652), reprinted in *CMHS* 3d ser., 4 (1834): 109–12; quote on p. 112.

25. Whitfield, *Strength out of Weaknesse*, 133–34, 165–66; Eliot and Mayhew, *Tears of Repentance*, 259–60.

26. Eliot and Mayhew, *Tears of Repentance*, 234.

27. Ibid., 254, 256–57.

28. Ibid., 248, 239, 256–57.

29. Although life expectancies of white seventeenth-century New Englanders have been scaled somewhat downward from the extraordinarily high figures estimated by historians in the 1970s, it is clear that they remained markedly higher than those of Native people and that the colonial population rose steadily upward while that of the Natives declined precipitously. Compare Sherburne F. Cook, "The Significance of Disease in the Extinction of the New England Indians," *Human Biology* 45 (1973): 485–508, and Richard Archer, "New England Mosaic: A Demographic Analysis for the Seventeenth Century," *WMQ* 3d ser., 47 (1990): 477–502.

30. Eliot and Mayhew, *Tears of Repentance*, 229, 231, 232, 256.

31. Ibid., 230.

32. Ibid., 231.

33. Ibid., 229, 252.

34. Ibid., 246, 247, 233, 237.

35. Neal Emerson Salisbury, "Conquest of the 'Savage': Puritans, Puritan Missionaries, and Indians, 1620–1680" (Ph.D. diss., University of California, Los Angeles, 1972), chaps. 4–5.

36. Tinker, *Missionary Conquest*, 34–36; Cohen, "Conversion among Puritans and Amerindians," esp. 255.

37. Simmons, "Conversion from Indian to Puritan," 214–17.

38. Salisbury, "Red Puritans," 32–34.

39. Elise Melanie Brenner, "Strategies for Autonomy: An Analysis of Ethnic Mobilization in Seventeenth Century Southern New England" (Ph.D. diss., University of Massachusetts, Amherst, 1984), 229–31.

40. Susan L. MacCulloch, "A Tripartite Political System among Christian Indians in Early Massachusetts," *Kroeber Anthropological Society Papers* 34 (spring 1966): 63–73.

41. Compare Kathleen J. Bragdon, "Vernacular Literacy and Massachusett World View, 1650–1750," in *Algonkians of New England: Past and Present*, ed. Peter Benes (Boston, 1993), 26–34.

42. See, for example, Thomas Shepard, *The Clear Sun-shine of the Gospel Breaking Forth upon the Indians in New-England* (London, 1648), reprinted *CMHS*, 3d ser., 4 (1834): 59; John Josselyn, *An Account of Two Voyages to New-England, Made during the years 1638, 1663* (1675; 2nd ed., Boston, 1865), 115; "New England's First Fruits" (1643), in Samuel Eliot Morison, *The Founding of Harvard College* (Cambridge, Mass., 1935), 423; S. F. Smith, *History of Newton, Massachusetts* (Boston, 1880), 45; Josiah H. Temple, *History of Framingham, Massachusetts* (Framingham, Mass., 1887), 51, 79; Frank G. Speck, *Eastern Algonkian Block-Stamp Decoration: A New World Original or an Acculturated Art* (Trenton, N.J., 1947), 30–32; Virginia

DeJohn Anderson, "King Philip's Herds: Indians, Colonists, and the Problem of Livestock in Early New England," *WMQ* 3d ser., 51 (1994): 605–6.

43. Salisbury, "Red Puritans," 35–36.

44. Ibid., 40–41, 46, 51–52.

45. Neal Salisbury, "Squanto: Last of the Patuxets," in *Struggle and Survival in Colonial America*, ed. David G. Sweet and Gary B. Nash (Berkeley, Calif., 1981), 228–46; Salisbury, *Manitou and Providence*, 114.

46. Douglas Edward Leach, *Flintlock and Tomahawk: New England in King Philip's War* (New York, 1958), 14–16; Jennings, *Invasion of America*, 288–97.

47. Gookin, *Historical Collections*, 89–96.

48. John Easton, "A Relacion of the Indyan Warre, . . . , 1675," in *Narratives of the Indian Wars, 1675–1699*, ed. Charles H. Lincoln (New York, 1913), 10.

49. Jill Lepore, "Dead Men Tell No Tales: John Sassamon and the Fatal Consequences of Literacy," *American Quarterly* 46 (1994): 479–512; Jill Lepore, *The Name of War: King Philip's War and the Origins of American Identity* (New York, 1998), 21–47; Leach, *Flintlock and Tomahawk*, 14–29; Easton, "Relacion," 11.

50. Gookin, *Historical Collections*, 79–88, quote on pp. 86–87.

51. Neal Salisbury, "Introduction," in *Sovereignty*, 13–15, 19–20.

52. Daniel Gookin, "An Historical Account of the Doings and Sufferings of the Christian Indians in New England," *Archaeologia Americana, Transactions and Collections of the American Antiquarian Society* 2 (1836): 423–523; Leach, *Flintlock and Tomahawk*, 145–54; Patrick M. Malone, *The Skulking Way of War: Technology and Tactics among the New England Indians* (Lanham, Md., 1991), 84–88; Jenny Hale Pulsipher, "Massacre at Hurtleberry Hill: Christian Indians and English Authority in Metacom's War," *WMQ* 3d ser., 53 (1996): 459–86. On Bacon's Rebellion, see Wilcomb E. Washburn, *The Governor and the Rebel: A History of Bacon's Rebellion in Virginia* (Chapel Hill, N.C., 1957); Edmund S. Morgan, *American Slavery, American Freedom: The Ordeal of Colonial Virginia* (New York, 1975), 250–70.

53. Gookin, "Historical Account," 507–8; Samuel G. Drake, *Biography History of the Indians of North America*, 11th ed. (Boston, 1851), 240–41.

54. Salisbury, ed., *Sovereignty*, quote on p. 87, also see pp. 99–101.

55. Leach, *Flintlock and Tomahawk*, 153–54.

56. Gookin, "Historical Account," 475–76; Drake, *Biography and History*, 114–15, 265; Salisbury, "Introduction," in *Sovereignty*, 33–34.

57. *Diary by Increase Mather, March, 1675–December, 1676*, ed. Samuel A. Green (Cambridge, Mass., 1900), 47; *The Diary of Samuel Sewall, 1674–1729*, ed. M. Halsey Thomas, 2 vols. (New York, 1973), 1:23; Drake, *Biography and History*, 241, 267,

58. Gookin, "Historical Account," 527–29. A few Indians, most notably James Printer, took advantage of a pardon extended briefly in July 1676 to any anti-English Indians not accused of murder and pledging loyalty to the colony. Within weeks, Printer returned to his employer and resumed printing books and tracts for the New England reading public. Drake, *Biography and History*, 115; Robert K. Diebold, "A Critical Edition of Mrs. Mary Rowlandson's Captivity Narrative" (Ph.D. diss., Yale Univeristy, 1972), clxxii.

59. Almon Wheeler Lauber, *Indian Slavery in Colonial Times within the Present limits of the United States* (1913; reprint, Williamstown, Mass., 1970), 109–111, 125–31, 137–53.

60. Compare Lauber, *Indian Slavery*, 144.

61. Neal Salisbury, "Toward the Covenant Chain: Iroquois and Southern New

England Algonquians, 1637–1684," in *Beyond the Covenant Chain: The Iroquois and Their Neighbors in Indian North America, 1600–1800*, ed. Daniel K. Richter and James M. Merrell (Syracuse, N.Y., 1987), 71; Evan Haefli and Kevin Sweeney, "Revisiting *The Redeemed Captive*: New Perspectives on the 1704 Attack on Deerfield," *WMQ* 3d ser., 52 (1995): 14, 20–26.

62. Haefli and Sweeney, "Revisiting *The Redeemed Captive*," 9–26, 45.

63. *Diary of Samuel Sewall*, 1:372–73.

64. Drake, *Biography and History*, 273; Lauber, *Indian Slavery*, 144; Leach, *Flintlock and Tomahawk*, 245.

65. O'Brien, *Dispossession by Degrees*; Thomas L. Doughton, "Unseen Neighbors: Native Americans of Central Massachusetts, A People Who Had 'Vanished,'" in Colin G. Calloway, ed., *After King Philip's War: Presence and Persistence in Indian New England* (Hanover, N.H., 1997), 207–30; Barry O'Connell, ed., *On Our Own Ground: The Complete Writings of William Apess, A Pequot* (Amherst, Mass., 1992); Donna Keith Baron et al., "They Were Here All Along: The Native American Presence in Lower Central New England in the Eighteenth and Nineteenth Centuries," *WMQ* 3d ser., 53 (1996): 435–86.

Billy G. Smith

BLACK WOMEN WHO STOLE THEMSELVES IN EIGHTEENTH-CENTURY AMERICA

ONE SUMMER DAY in 1799, Amy Reckless decided she would no longer be a slave to Robert Johnston. Along with her young daughter she boarded the morning stage from Salem, New Jersey, to Philadelphia. By her account, she simply "got into it as other passengers—used no means to prevent being seen, and was not molested by any one." Reckless had told Johnston a few days earlier that she would not remain with his family any longer because his wife had treated her cruelly, "having knocked two of her front teeth out with [a] brush handle and on other occasions pulled handfulls of hair from her head." In addition, Robert's mother had promised to liberate Amy, but Robert failed to keep that pledge when his mother died. After living in Philadelphia for several weeks, Amy received word from Robert that if she "would return to his house and give him her child, he would set [Amy] free." Rather than relinquish her daughter, Amy sought help from the Pennsylvania Abolition Society. The results of her bold quest for freedom unfortunately are not known.[1]

Thousands of female slaves stole themselves in early America. Only a handful, like Amy, provided brief accounts of their own flight, while masters and mistresses described the escape of numerous others in newspaper advertisements offering rewards for their apprehension. Most runaways appear in the historical record only fleetingly. The owner of another Amy, who lived in Philadelphia in 1793, dispatched her to the workhouse for "absconding from him eight times in the course of [a single] week."[2] In 1785 four generations of women ran away together from their South Carolina owner. He described them as "Jenny, an elderly short wench; Dido her daughter about 35 years of age, middle stature; and Tissey, her grand-daughter, with a young child at her breast." They hoped to use Jenny's pass, allowing her to search for a new master in Charleston, to facilitate their escape.[3]

These vignettes provide glimpses into the world of slave women who fled racial bondage in eighteenth-century America. They are a summons to research the attempts by black women to run away. This essay analyzes the circumstances in which such women made their decisions about whether and when to flee and their objectives in taking flight, as well as the signifi-cance of thousands of black women resolving to abscond. Slave families and work, the early antislavery movement, and the nature of the historical sources are all important to evaluating women's escape attempts. The essay then considers the regional and gender variations in runaway attempts, the manner in which reproductive and productive labor shaped the options available to slave women, and the strategies and goals of female fugitives. The importance of escape, especially during and after the American Revo-lution, is the focus of the essay's final section.

Approximately one of every six people in eighteenth-century America lived in perpetual bondage. Slaves accounted for about 60 percent of the inhabitants of the lower South, roughly 30 percent of Virginians and Ma-rylanders, and close to 5 percent of residents in the North. The vast major-ity of bondpeople, both women and men, engaged in agricultural tasks, raising rice and indigo on large plantations in the lower South, tobacco and wheat on smaller plantations in the Chesapeake, and grains and livestock on small farms in the mid-Atlantic region. High population density and the concentration of slaves on large farms and plantations enabled slaves in the Chesapeake and to a lesser extent in the lower South to reproduce and to fashion lasting families and communities, especially after the eighteenth century's initial decades. Because their numbers were small and sometimes widely dispersed, mid-Atlantic bondpeople experienced considerably greater difficulties forming enduring kinship and community ties with other slaves. These distinctions are important for evaluating regional dif-ferences in escape attempts.[4]

The abolitionist movement was another important ingredient in slave decisions to take flight. During the second half of the eighteenth century the antislavery movement enjoyed notable successes, which affected the lives of blacks and provided some with new opportunities to escape or to es-tablish their freedom by other means. Influenced by religious, revolution-ary, and economic arguments against slavery, many whites in the North and the upper South manumitted their human property. In 1780, Pennsylvania became the first state to legislate the gradual emancipation of slaves, and by 1804 all of the states north of Pennsylvania had passed similar legislation.[5]

The nature of the historical record limits our ability to understand female fugitives. Eighteenth-century female slaves left virtually no firsthand accounts. Historians consequently have relied primarily on sources produced by slave owners and the political and legal institutions of their dominant white culture. These records, written by the oppressors of slaves, contain significant biases, and they must be handled with care. Even a sympathetic reading of the sources cannot eliminate all the distortions, and interpretations based on them must be offered tentatively.

This essay draws heavily on information contained in approximately 4,500 advertisements for runaway slaves printed in newspapers from New York City to South Carolina during the eighteenth century. The notices, most of which were composed by masters offering rewards for the apprehension and return of their property, chronicle the stories (as related by owners) of thousands of fugitives and permit a systematic examination of many of their characteristics. Nearly all the advertisements delineate a host of details about the runaways, including their physical traits—age, sex, height, and color—and the type of clothing they wore. Various features of their daily lives, from the kind of work they performed to the type of chains in which some were shackled, often are reported, along with their place of birth, musical and linguistic talents, number of previous owners, and frequency of escape attempts. The advertisements also indicate the fugitives' names and occasionally their language, ritualistic African markings, religion, literacy, and connections to friends and family, as well as the owners' assessment of their motivations, goals, and escape strategies.[6]

These advertisements, like all historical records, exhibit a peculiar set of limitations. Most important, they reflect the perspective of the owners rather than the slaves being described. Still, many whites, especially those who worked side by side with blacks on small farms or in shops and who sometimes shared living quarters with them, knew their slaves well; that knowledge often was reflected in the meticulously detailed descriptions included in many of the notices. Masters also had a strong incentive to provide accurate descriptions of fugitives because reliability would enhance the chances of their recapture. Many owners received information about the whereabouts of a runaway slave before paying for a newspaper advertisement, thus increasing the trustworthiness of their judgment about the goals of an escapee.[7]

The portrayal in the notices of physical traits of fugitives, such as their sex, height, and bodily markings, is more reliable than the owners' subjective assessments of their bondpeople. For the purposes of this essay, patriarchal notions of male owners introduce the most significant potential bias in ads about women. Many masters may have believed that slave women— as women—could not easily act independently and that they therefore sought the aid of relatives and friends more often than actually was the case. Yet the attitudes of most eighteenth-century owners about female slaves are far from clear. White males obviously did not see all women, both black and white, through one lens. Masters apparently did not hesitate, for example, to assign field work to female slaves, tasks that they usually believed were not appropriate for white women.[8]

The subjective beliefs of owners shaped the advertisments in important ways, but the notices still reveal various material characteristics of female escapees. Even though masters had gendered preconceptions, they could still accurately ascertain that female fugitives fled more often in groups, less frequently left their children behind, ran away at earlier ages, and took refuge in cities more often than did males. While the paucity of firsthand accounts by female slaves makes it difficult to recapture the feelings and motivations of individual escapees, it is nonetheless possible, based on information in the advertisements, to delineate the conditions under which most slave women made their choices.

Running away was primarily a male activity. Although they comprised slightly less than half of the North American slave population during the eighteenth century, women accounted for only about one of every nine advertised fugitives (see table 2). This disparity in advertised runaways skews the actual sex ratio of escapees somewhat, because masters often hesitated longer before advertising for females than for males, meaning that more women than men were apprehended before being advertised.[9] Owners were more reluctant to pay for notices and to offer rewards for women, partly because their monetary value was lower than that of men.[10] Moreover, masters believed that females fled temporarily to relatives and friends more frequently than did males. Expecting that women likely would return voluntarily after a few days or weeks of "visiting," owners often delayed offering rewards for their apprehension.[11] A better estimate of the actual sex ratio of escapees is that females accounted for one of every five or six fugitives.[12]

The data in table 2 raise questions about the ways in which gender influenced the decisions of slaves to take flight. Most important, why did women flee less frequently than men? The conventional wisdom, offered by both contemporaries and scholars, is that the successful formation of slave families discouraged African Americans in general and women in particular from taking flight. As one New Jersey indentured servant commented, "Masters make [slaves] some amends by suffering them to marry, which makes them easier and often prevents their running away."[13] But these familial duties affected men and women differently. The responsibility of parenting fell disproportionately to women, since slave children usually lived with their mothers. Those duties restricted women's escape options because absconding with children was problematic, and very few

Table 2
Gender of Runaway Slaves

Region	Female %	Male %	N
Delaware Valley: 1719–96	12	88	1777
1719–75	9	91	886
1776–84	16	84	442
1785–96	14	86	449
New York and New Jersey: 1716–83	14	86	753
1716–75	9	91	439
1776–83	20	80	314
Southern Maryland: 1745–79	9	91	NA
Virginia: 1730–87	12	88	1262
1730–74	11	89	742
1775–87	12	88	520
North Carolina: 1748–75	11	89	128
South Carolina: 1732–90	22	78	2468
1732–75	21	79	1941
1779, 1781–83	31	69	292
1783–90	29	71	235
1790–1799	33	67	808[a]
Georgia: 1763–75, 1783–95	19	81	981
1763–75	13	87	453
1783–95	24	76	528

NA: The number of runaways is not available.

[a]This number of fugitives is not comparable to earlier South Carolina data because it is derived from a different data set.

Source: All of the data are based on counts of runaways advertised in newspapers, as indicated in the following.

Delaware Valley (includes Pennsylvania, northern Delaware and Maryland, and southern New Jersey): My count from 28 newspapers published in Pennsylvania, New Jersey, and Delaware.

New York and New Jersey: "Pretends to Be Free": Runaway Slave Advertisements from Colonial and Revolutionary New York and New Jersey, ed. Graham Russell Hodges and Alan Edward Brown (New York, 1994), 307.

Southern Maryland: Allan Kulikoff, Tobacco and Slaves: The Development of Southern Cultures in the Chesapeake, 1680–1800 (Chapel Hill, N.C., 1986), 374.

Virginia: Lathan Algerna Windley, "A Profile of Runaway Slaves in Virginia and South Carolina from 1730 through 1787" (Ph.D. diss. University of Iowa, 1974), 65. Gerald Mullin counted 1,279 black fugitives, 11% of them female, in Virginia newspapers between 1736 and 1801; Flight and Rebellion: Slave Resistance in Eighteenth-Century Virginia (London, 1972), 89, 103. Philip D. Morgan and Michael Nicholls found that approximately 10% of the 1,764 slaves advertised in Virginia newspapers between the 1730s and 1789 were female; "Runaway Slaves in Eighteenth-Century Virginia" (paper presented at the annual meeting of the Organization of American Historians, 1990) p. 7 and table 2.

North Carolina: Marvin L. Michael Kay and Lorin Lee Cary, "Slave Runaways in Colonial North Carolina, 1748–1775," The North Carolina Historical Review 63 (1986): 11.

South Carolina: The data from 1732 to 1790 is from my count of five Charleston newspapers. The data for the 1790s is from Philip D. Morgan, "Black Society in the Lowcountry 1760–1810," *Slavery and Freedom in the Age of the American Revolution*, ed. Ira Berlin and Ronald Hoffman (Charlottesville, Va., 1983), 100. Morgan also reported that 19% of 7,650 slaves advertised in South Carolina newspapers between 1732 and 1806 were willingly left their offspring behind.[14] As various historians have concluded, "marital and familial obligations limited the number of female slaves who ran away." Conversely, single men enjoyed greater freedom to flee, while married men who lived separately from their families had a strong incentive to run away to visit their wives and children.[15]

Parenting commitments and kinship bonds undoubtedly shackled some women more tightly than most men within racial bondage. But for several reasons, slave families did not play the sole or even the most significant role in curtailing the number of women (compared to the number of men) who fled slavery. Significantly, family obligations fail to explain the regional variations in the sex ratio of escapees. If maternal responsibilities generally deterred women from taking flight, then in the Delaware Valley, where bondpeople were least successful in creating long-lasting families, the proportion of female fugitives should have been greater than in the southern states and colonies, where enduring families were more common. Instead, the percentage of female escapees was nearly twice as high in the lower South as in either the mid-Atlantic or the Chesapeake (see table 2). The high proportion of female fugitives in South Carolina and Georgia is especially impressive because the gender imbalance in favor of males in the slave population was greater there than in any other region.[16]

Instead of deterring women from taking flight, ties with children, family, and friends often encouraged and enabled them to flee. Rather than being discouraged from escape by their children, some mothers fled primarily for their children's sake. As Harriet Jacobs, a nineteenth-century slave, observed, "I could have made my escape alone; but it was more for my helpless children than for myself that I longed for freedom. Though the boon would have been precious to me, above all price, I would not have taken it at the expense of leaving them in slavery." Although difficult, it was not impossible for women to abscond with their offspring, as the escape of Amy Reckless (recounted at the beginning of this essay) illustrates. Likewise, Kate departed with her thirteen-year-old son and five-year-old daughter even though she herself was seven months pregnant. She seized a propitious time when her master and his family were sick, causing him to rage at

---

female. Other studies found similar proportions of females among runaways in South Carolina. Lathan Algerna Windley discovered that 23% of runaways in South Carolina between 1732 and 1787 were female; "Profile of Runaway Slaves," 65. Daniel E. Meaders calculated that 25% of runaways advertised between 1732 and 1801 were female; Meaders, "South Carolina Fugitives as Viewed through Local Colonial Newspapers with Emphasis on runaway Notices, 1732–1810," Journal of Negro History, 40, (1975): 292 Daniel C. Littlefield discovered that 18% of runaways between 1732 and 1775 were female; Rice and Slaves: Ethnicity and the Slave Trade in Colonial South Carolina (Baton Rouge, La., 1981), 144.

Georgia: The data are calculated from Betty Wood's count from notices in The Georgia Gazette; "Some Aspects of Female Resistance to Chattel Slavery in Low Country Georgia, 1763–1815," The Historical Journal 30 (1987): 613.

"this inhuman creature [who], when she went away, left myself extreme[ly] ill in one bed, her mistress in another and two of my children, not one able to help the other." Sixteen percent of female fugitives in both the Delaware Valley and South Carolina fled with at least one child.[17]

Many women departed to preserve the unity of their families, taking to their heels when their household was liable to be torn asunder by sale, by their master's decision to relocate, or by the dispersal of the human property after their owner's death. "Having a husband, children, and other connexion" in Maryland, Phebe bolted "for fear her master had not sold her, and would take her to Kentuckey with him." Berry fled with her husband and three children, and Sue escaped with her spouse and child when they were auctioned as part of their master's estate. That these and many other families ran together when in peril of separation is poignant evidence of the strength of kinship ties and the actions that slaves would take to preserve them.[18]

The comparatively rapid turnover in slave ownership in the lower South also threatened African-American kinship and community bonds and induced women to take flight more frequently than in the Delaware Valley. Advertisements for runaways indicate that at least 34 percent of South Carolina's female fugitives had a previous owner, and many fled shortly after being sold. In the Delaware Valley, however, only 12 percent of female fugitives had been owned formerly. In this area, where African Americans were less enmeshed in a web of family and friends, their transfer from one master to another less frequently broke up families and was therefore not as likely to precipitate escape attempts.[19]

Female slaves sometimes absconded in an effort to protect themselves and their daughters from sexual abuse. Both the age distribution of escapees and the disproportionate number of daughters taken with them are suggestive in this regard. Most men who absconded were between twenty and thirty-five years of age. By contrast, women tended to flee more often during their late teens, before most of them acquired maternal responsibilities and at a time when masters may have begun to harass them sexually.[20] In addition, slave parents, perhaps prompted by the fear that their daughters might become the future rape victims of their owners, spirited away three times more girls than boys. As Harriet Jacobs lamented, "Slavery is terrible for men but it is far more terrible for women" since many of them were liable to sexual abuse. Like Jacobs, many slaves must have been concerned about the mistreatment their daughters might have to endure. "My heart was heavier than it had ever been before," she moaned, "when they told me my newborn babe was a girl." [21]

Slave families and communities provided not only motivation for flight but also support systems of people with whom and to whom women could run. Women fled collectively much more often than men did (see

Table 3
Characteristics and Objectives of Runaways

Characteristics and Objectives	South Carolina 1732–1790 Females (%)	Delaware Valley 1719–1796	
		Females (%)	Males (%)
Characteristics			
Ran individually	53	59	81
Ran with a relative	28	32	4
Ran with a nonrelation	19	9	15
Objectives			
Freedom	58	62	86
To relatives	30	19	7
To friends	12	19	4

Sources: Advertisements in twenty-eight newspapers published in Pennsylvania, New Jersey, and Delaware and five newspapers published in Charleston, S.C.

table 3). Roughly 45 percent of South Carolina and Delaware Valley females departed with at least one other person, whereas just 19 percent of Delaware Valley males joined forces with another slave. Even more striking, about 30 percent of females in both areas but only 4 percent of males in the Delaware Valley coordinated their escape with a family member.

Women also took refuge with family and friends more often than did men. In South Carolina, 42 percent of female fugitives sought the aid of other blacks; in the Delaware Valley 38 percent of women but only 11 percent of men solicited help from others (see table 2).[22] Many female fugitives attempted to reunite with their loved ones, either for a temporary visit or as a brief stop on the road to freedom. Free Poll went first to Baltimore and then to Philadelphia to be with her husband; Nancy left the Quaker city vowing "to see her mother" in the country; and Sophy tried to make her way from South Carolina to Bermuda to join her mother. Even though they lived far away, relatives often offered sanctuary, as illustrated by the case of Catharina. Her master was perplexed about whether she and her young daughter would take asylum with her father on a South Carolina plantation, her mother in Charleston, or her sisters and "other Relations" in Georgia. This behavior of female fugitives suggests that slave women were more oriented than men to kin and community.[23]

Bearing and caring for children and the successful creation of long-lasting families and communities could thus encourage as well as discourage slave women from taking flight. Because these reasons only partly explain, at best, why fewer women than men decided to take flight, what other factors were at work in shaping women's decisions? The most convincing explanations center around the work roles defined for black women and men and the options available to potential runaways.

Eighteenth-century slave women generally led circumscribed lives that made it exceedingly difficult from them to escape.[24] Although a few carried and sold produce to nearby town markets and some served as domestics, the great majority of black women labored in the fields during the day, then spun, sewed, cooked, and cared for their families during the evening. Most were physically confined to the area around their master's farm or plantation, which curtailed their geographic knowledge, escape opportunities, linguistic skills, literacy, and overall confidence in coping with whites. These limitations likely intensified the fears of many women about their ability to engage in a successful escape. Although the majority of slave men also performed agricultural labor, more men than women were assigned skilled and semiskilled tasks, especially in the Chesapeake and mid-Atlantic regions. Many of them drove carts and wagons, operated canoes and flatboats, and delivered messages and goods, all of which expanded their awareness of and opportunities for escape as well as their ability to interact with white strangers.[25] Indeed, an African-American woman on the road was an oddity that would arouse suspicion, and thus some female runaways disguised themselves as men. It is telling that while a few slave men escaped on horses, virtually no women chose that means to flee; they rarely possessed horse-riding skills, and they would have been so obviously out of place.[26]

If the nature of their work narrowed women's prospects for escape, the availability of places to which they could run also shaped their decisions about taking flight. Once having absconded, women encountered greater obstacles to earning a living and avoiding recapture than did men. The presence or absence of nearby urban centers thus was critical to the calculations of black women about their chances for a successful escape. Cities afforded them the chance to use their domestic skills to bake and peddle food items or to find work washing and ironing clothes or as house servants, seamstresses, or prostitutes.

New York City and Philadelphia in the mid-Atlantic area and Charleston and Savannah in the lower South were magnets that attracted female escapees hoping to find employment, refuge, friends, and anonymity in a crowd of black faces. Blacks accounted for nearly half the inhabitants of eighteenth-century Charleston, and slave women dominated its markets. Many southern fugitive females calculated that their best opportunity to elude recapture and to live as free persons was to head for the South Carolina capitol. Thus, Nancy "has been in Charleston the greatest part of her time since her absence, passes for a free wench, and it is said washes and irons for a livelihood"; Amy "[h]as been seen in Charles-Town, selling

Things about the Streets, pretending to be a free Woman"; and Jenny "absented herself last Summer, passed for a free Wench, and both workt out and took in Neddle-work, Washing and Ironing, in and near Charles-Town." The urban demand for the skills women possessed is further evident in the fact that early North American cities nearly always contained more black women than men.[27]

The Chesapeake, however, remained decidedly rural throughout most of the eighteenth century. This lack of urbanization accounts in large part for the lower proportion of female fugitives in Virginia and Maryland than in the lower South. The lure of cities also helps explain why the proportion of all slaves who attempted to escape was greater in the lower South and the mid-Atlantic than in the Chesapeake.[28]

Given the many challenges to executing a successful escape, the decision to flee was an extraordinarily difficult one; it held, literally, grave consequences for failure. If unsuccessful, runaways faced punishments ranging from being whipped, shackled, or sold to being maimed, branded, or killed. The master of Dorinda, for example, offered a reward for her "dead or alive," and the owner of Ruth exhorted would-be captors to "give her 50 good Lashes" for having escaped.[29] In some cases, even fugitives who succeeded in passing as free people must have traded friends, family, and a measure of stability for a frightening future fraught with uncertainty. Under these circumstances, only a minority of bondpeople chose to elope, although their numbers at various times, especially during the revolutionary decades, were still substantial.

Most fugitives, both female and male, accepted incredible risks in daring attempts to gain their freedom. Liberty was their ultimate goal. Masters and mistresses presumed that 62 percent of fugitive women in the Delaware Valley and 58 percent of those in South Carolina were attempting to escape bondage permanently (see table 3). Thus, Charlotte absconded "with an Intent never to return to [her] Owner"; Phebe fled to Philadelphia, where she "pretends to be free"; Moll "changed her name to Judah, and says she is free"; and Kate, along with her husband and three children, "passed for free Negroes" for eighteen months in the backcountry of South Carolina. As discussed below, the enormous increase in the number of female fugitives when escape opportunities expanded during and after the revolutionary war is testimony to their commitment to freedom.[30]

Even though fugitives hungered for liberty, some used flight principally as a means to achieve other goals. While not desiring to remain unfree, some runaways recognized that the chances of establishing their permanent freedom were highly improbable. Before the revolution, for instance, relatively few runaways of either sex likely believed that they could establish and preserve their liberty, since virtually no place on the continent afforded them the prospect of achieving that goal. Complete desperation with the horrors of slavery or a crisis event like a whipping or the selling of their loved ones precipitated some women to run, even though their primary goal may not have been to gain their permanent freedom. Other women absconded to gain immediate relief from the stress of bondage or to visit their kin and friends temporarily.

Some slaves employed escape as a bargaining tactic, a strategy that has received scant attention from historians, partly because the evidence for such activity would have been recorded only rarely. Flight and the threat of flight was a tool that slaves occasionally used in negotiations with their masters for privileges. In the complicated interchange between slaves and owners, masters wielded most but not all of the physical and psychological authority. As scholars have amply demonstrated, slaves used various forms of resistance, from work slowdowns to feigning sickness, to pressure their masters into making concessions. Similarly, fugitives sometimes ran away as a means to assert control over their lives and, in the process, to curtail the power of their masters and mistresses.

This is most clearly apparent in the ways in which slaves used escape to change masters. The right to locate another owner was a perquisite claimed by many blacks and apparently acknowledged even by some whites in early America, especially in the mid-Atlantic region. Silvia Dubois, an eighteenth-century New Jersey slave, insisted that "when the slave thought the master too severe, and the slave and the master did not get along harmoniously, the slave had a right to hunt a new master." Thus, Philadelphian John Meredith wrote a note for Loretta granting her "my permission to seek a master. She is a good Ironer and washer and plain cook," Meredith proclaimed, and "is strictly honest and sober." And James McHenry, another Philadelphian, scrawled a similar certificate authorizing his slave "to look out for a master." The slave's price, McHenry stipulated, "is two hundred Dollars." When masters provided such permits, slaves sometimes took advantage of the freedom of movement thereby conferred to escape. Mary, for instance, absconded when her owner furnished her with "a pass for three days to look for a master."[31]

All of the above instances of owners allowing slaves to seek new masters occurred in the mid-Atlantic area, and this prerogative was most commonly enjoyed by slaves in the North, in urban centers, and in parts of the upper South, where bondpeople frequently were hired out by their masters or found their own employment and returned a share of their wages to their owners. Yet examples of such concessions by masters occurred in the lower South as well. Sukey fled bondage in South Carolina with "a ticket of leave to find a [new] master." As previously recounted, a comparable tactic helped Jenny, her daughter, granddaughter, and great-granddaughter to escape.[32]

Slaves sometimes used flight to compel their owners to sell them, if possible to a more lenient master or perhaps to one located nearer to the slave's loved ones. Rose, a mulatto slave belonging to Eleanor Moore in Lancaster, Pennsylvania, adopted this bold strategy in an unambiguous fashion. In 1792, Rose asked a friend to contact the Pennsylvania Abolition Society to inquire "whether she cannot get a new master[,] for her master that bought her is dead and her mistress is married again and they use her very ill and beats [her] severely so that she is not able to endure the severity she is put to." The society's response is unknown. However, Rose took matters into her own hands two years later by taking flight. In the notice offering a reward for her capture, Eleanor Moore noted that "[s]aid Wench has been dissatisfied with her place for some time past, [and] if she returns, she shall have the liberty to choose a master."[33]

Masters used newspaper advertisements to convey comparable concessions to runaways throughout early America. When she fled her South Carolina owner at the end of the revolution, Phoebe took her baby daughter Belinda and returned to the plantation from which her new master had purchased her, either to visit or to take refuge with relatives and friends. In the subsequent advertisement, her new master complied with her ostensible demand: "If they will return of their own accord," he offered, "they shall have a ticket to choose their own master." Another South Carolina owner promised that if Jemmy and Athy return, "they will be pardoned, and have tickets given them to look for a new master." That owners expected runaways, few of whom could read, to learn about the offers contained in the advertisements suggest that such information was expected to circulate within the black community.[34]

That slaves absconded as a means to induce owners to sell them is likewise evident in the routine practice of masters offering runaways for sale while they were fugitives. On occasion, slaves must have struck deals with whites to purchase them cheaply once they ran away. Francis Goddard "supposed" that Sarah, who had been "branded on the right cheek and right shoulder with FG" (presumably her master's initials), "is kept by some person that has a mind to purchase her." Kate and her son Billy apparently took refuge with "some white people who have received wages of her, and others who have a desire to purchase her."[35]

Common complaints by owners that other whites "seduced," "harboured," sold, reenslaved, indentured, and hired their runaways indicate that a considerable number of escapees successfully found new masters or, if more fortunate, became employees rather than property. The owner of Banaba had "a strong Suspicion of her being Harboured by some evil disposed white persons" since Banaba was "a remarkable fine Seamstress, and easily kept at her Work, without Discovery." Her master offered £50 for the conviction of "any white Person harbouring her." William Williamson was willing to pay £10 for the return of his slave, Betty, but ten times that amount for the conviction of any white who concealed her. Sophia Maybury fumed that she was "certain there are people that encourage her Negroes [to escape] . . . and as she hath forewarned them of such underhand dealings by advertisement, published in Dutch and English some time ago: She hereby now offers a reasonable reward to any one who will make information . . . [about] such persons . . . that she may prosecute them according to law." All of these negotiating strategies, of course, were extremely risky and at times even foolhardy, as slaves could hardly trust masters to keep their end of the deal. Yet, operating from a position of weakness rather than strength, slaves utilized whatever leverage was available. At times, it apparently succeeded.[36]

Escape always was a forceful act of personal and political rebellion, but the implications of flight changed during the course of the eighteenth century. During and after the American Revolution, running away assumed considerably greater importance as a direct challenge to the institution of racial bondage. In the Delaware Valley, a host of individual runaways helped bring slavery to a relatively quick conclusion. In the lower South, flight and resistance by both individuals and groups disrupted the labor system and defied the authority of masters. Moreover, slave women and men, inspired by the ideology and opportunities of the American Revolution and the slave revolt in Saint Domingue, grew increasingly bold in their resistance during the century's final decades.

The revolution provided the first realistic opportunity for many slaves to achieve and maintain their liberty. With the exception of the Civil War, the revolutionary conflict involved the largest successful slave rebellion in American history, as blacks fought and fled for their freedom. When Lord Dunmore invited slaves to join his forces in 1775 and when Sir Henry Clinton extended that invitation more broadly four years later, tens of thousands of bondpeople responded. One result, as Henry Muhlenberg, a Pennsylvania minister observed, was that blacks "secretly wished that the British army might win, for then all Negro slaves will gain their freedom. It is said that this sentiment is almost universal among the *Negroes* in America." The manpower requirements of revolutionary armies and militias likewise forced them to offer black recruits freedom, and the general turmoil of the war provided additional opportunities for slaves to escape.[37]

In the Delaware Valley, black women took advantage of the confusion and upheaval of the war to flee in record numbers. The British occupation of New York City throughout the war and of Philadelphia in 1777 and 1778 was a godsend for escape-minded slaves, many of whom seized the opportunity. More women fled their owners in New York and New Jersey during the seven years of the revolutionary war than in all of the previous six

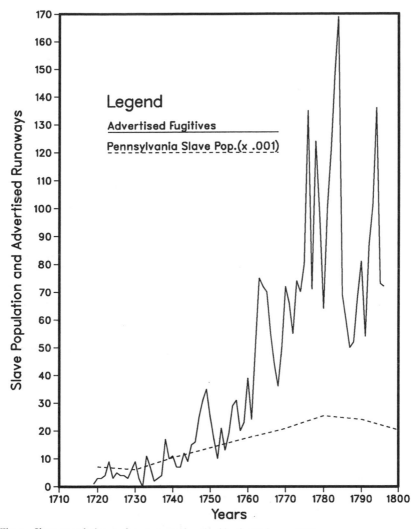

Fig. 2. Slave population and runaways advertised in the Delaware Valley.

decades combined. The number of fugitives advertised in newspapers published in the Delaware Valley skyrocketed from 43 annually between 1750 and 1775 to 108 each year during the revolutionary war (see fig. 2). The Black Guides and Pioneers (which included at least fifteen women) belonged to the British military forces in Philadelphia, and this company of African Americans undoubtedly strengthened the resolve of nearby slaves to declare their freedom.[38]

African-American women seized the moment. Peg "went into Philadelphia, whilst the British troops were there," where she may have encountered Phyllis, Poll, and Jude, who had fled to the city previously. Rachel departed New Jersey early in the war and spent two years following her husband in the First Maryland Regiment, during which time she "passed herself as a free woman." Shortly after being apprehended and returned to her master, she ran again, even though pregnant and slowed by a six-year-old son. Although "big with child," Sue "went to camp with a white woman commonly called Captain Molly, who has a husband in the 4th regiment of Light Dragoons." Two other slave women left their owner in New York City in 1776, headed for "the army." Not to miss her chance, Dinah "[r]an Away with the last of the British troops from the city of Philadelphia."[39]

Black women responded even more enthusiastically than black men to the opportunities provided by the war and its aftermath. The proportion of advertised runaways who were female increased dramatically in the northern states when the fighting broke out. Women accounted for 9 percent of fugitives in the mid-Atlantic region before the revolution and between 16 and 20 percent during the war (see table 2). Their proportion grew correspondingly in the lower South as well. Women constituted as many as one third of the Virginia slaves who absconded during the war and nearly one-half of the blacks evacuated when the British left Savannah. New opportunities to gain their liberty while taking their children with them also shaped the strength of the response by slave women. The proportion of female fugitives remained high during the century's final decades as women found refuge in a rapidly growing population of slaves and free blacks in American cities.[40]

Slaves in the Delaware Valley absconded in even larger numbers during the early 1780s (see fig. 2), in part because Pennsylvania's 1780 gradual emancipation law inadvertently encouraged blacks to take leave of their masters. The number of escape attempts declined in 1779 and 1780, as many bondpeople apparently decided to wait for the final outcome of the state legislature's heated debates about abolishing human bondage. But the 1780 statute specified that the children of slaves born after March 1 would be free after they had served as bound servants for twenty-one years if they were female or for twenty-eight years if they were male. When they discovered that the law failed to liberate any living slaves, scores of disappointed bondpeople took to their heels in the early 1780s, and Delaware Valley blacks continued to flee in substantial numbers, many gravitating to Philadelphia. During the 1780s, slaves who liberated themselves through flight probably outnumbered those who were manumitted by their masters.[41]

Slaves grew more openly defiant in the Delaware Valley during the postrevolutionary decades as the coercive power of owners declined. By Pennsylvania law, masters could no longer sell bondpeople out of state, which reduced the ability of owners to inflict psychological anguish on slaves by moving them far away from family and friends. By custom, corporal punishment for convicts, servants, and slaves became less acceptable. Imprisonment in Philadelphia's workhouse therefore increased in popularity as one of the few means available to discipline recalcitrant bondpeople. Consequently, slaves enjoyed a stronger position in negotiating with their masters. As Gary B. Nash and Jean R. Soderlund have demonstrated, one result was that many slaves were able to strike bargains to gain their freedom. Others simply liberated themselves by taking flight and maintaining their independence.[42]

In the Delaware Valley, many female runaways played on stronger anti-slavery feelings and gradual emancipation laws to force their owners to negotiate for their freedom. One example illustrates this process. Mrs. Chambre belonged to a group of French migrants who fled the slave revolt in Saint Domingue. She settled with her two slaves, Magdalen and Zaire, in Philadelphia in 1793. After "five calendar months and three weeks"—one week shy of the six months required by Pennsylvania law to make her bondwomen free—Chambre took them to Burlington, New Jersey, where they would still be slaves. Magdalen and Zaire immediately fled back to Philadelphia and contacted the Pennsylvania Abolition Society, which sued for their freedom, arguing that their owner's residence in the state actually exceeded the necessary "six lunar months [calculated by the 28-day cycle of the moon] in computation of time." Magdalen and Zaire lost the lawsuit, but both ran away again several months later. They were apprehended, but they were able to use this leverage to persuade their mistress to sell them and, in the process, to change their status from perpetual slaves to servants bound for only a few more years. (Both servants, incidentally, absconded from their new masters as well).[43]

Scores of slaves forced owners to recognize their de facto freedom by running away repeatedly. Poll fled so frequently that her discouraged Philadelphia master, Christopher Marshall, gradually spent less time, effort, and money and eventually gave up completely on her recapture. Like many other Delaware Valley slave owners, Stephen Girard, one of the nation's wealthiest merchants, decided it was easier to switch to European indentured servants after three of his slaves, including Rosette, ran away regularly.[44]

As slavery became more vulnerable in the Delaware Valley, losing much of its legal and moral foundation during the postrevolutionary decades, many black women issued an additional challenge: they simply refused to do their masters' bidding. Their names and the charges against them tumble off Philadelphia's workhouse and prison dockets for the 1790s. After serving a month in the workhouse for absconding, Laurencine refused "to return to the Service of her Master" and was incarcerated in prison. Fortune and Zemire landed in jail for "refusing to serve" their masters, while Eve and Clarissa were charged with physically assaulting their owners. The problem masters faced was widespread: between 1793 and 1797, they confined nearly seven hundred blacks to Philadelphia's workhouse at a time when the city contained fewer than two hundred and the entire state fewer than two thousand slaves. A great many of the most recalcitrant slaves jailed after 1793 arrived in the city with their French masters, who were themselves fleeing the slave revolt in Saint Domingue. As Gary B. Nash has argued, the militancy of the West Indian slaves inspired new black immigrants and Philadelphia's creoles to intensify their own resistance.[45]

By fleeing, threatening escape, and refusing to obey, slave women and men thus helped bring slavery to a relatively rapid end in the North. In Pennsylvania, slavery died a much quicker death than was mandated by the gradual emancipation legislation of the 1780s. Slaves either physically liberated themselves or forced their masters to agree to their manumission in return for a pledge of a few more years of faithful service as a bound servants. Northern slave women thereby played active roles in their own emancipation.[46]

The problems created by rebellious and fugitive slaves were even more critical during and after the revolution in the South, even though slavery obviously did not end there. The intractability of slave women during the war distressed many whites. South Carolinian Thomas Pinckney grumbled that female slaves on his plantation "pay no attention" to the overseer; his mother, residing on another estate, complained that "they all do now as they please everywhere." Pall, a North Carolina slave, "became intolerable in neglect and contempt of any order or command of her Mistress" and was so "ungrateful, insolent, disobedient, and lazy" that she was "no profit but an expense" to her owner, who consequently made arrangements to send her to the Pennsylvania Abolition Society. One Baltimore master advised his overseer not to perturb his slave Ruth or "she will run off, for she is an arch bitch."[47]

A great many African-American women fulfilled their masters' nightmares of the black "arch bitch" by taking flight when the opportunity arose. A group of thirteen slaves, four of them women, absconded from Virginia in the summer of 1780, attempting, their master believed, to sail up the Chesapeake Bay to Baltimore or farther north, where they intended to "pass as free people." Among them was at least one family, consisting of the parents and their two children. Terra and Virginia fled their Maryland master to join "the French troops when they halted at Baltimore, passing for free Negroes"; Nanny "absented herself from [her master's] service" and "went with the British from Savanna to St. Augustine"; and six fugitive women were "harboured in the Quartermaster-General's different Departments" while the British occupied Charleston. The tide of black refugees in the lower South nearly drowned the British military and threatened to destroy completely the institution of racial bondage. Since their intent was to cripple their enemy but not to demolish slavery, alarmed British officers often returned slaves to their masters, even if their owners were revolutionaries.[48]

Scholars have often underestimated the significance of unmanageable and fugitive slaves. But the importance of runaways is reflected by the actions taken by southern slave owners and politicians during and after the revolution. Between 55,000 and 100,000 bondpeople (or 9 to 17 percent of slaves) eloped or otherwise eluded their masters during the war. Their "disappearance" temporarily shattered the southern labor system, and during the postrevolutionary decades, whites in the lower South imported Africans in record numbers to replace bondpeople lost during the war. Fugitives also presented a significant psychological dilemma for southern masters since their hegemony was brought into serious question. If masters were unable to restrain blacks, especially slave women, then the vulnerability of the supposedly total system of slavery that regulated all aspects of African-American life would be exposed, thereby weakening racial bondage itself.[49]

The preoccupation of southern leaders with the issue of escapees after the revolution demonstrates their deep concern with runaways and their need to reassert their authority over bondpeople. Southern delegates to the United States Constitutional Convention were so worried about maintaining the slave trade and the rights of owners to pursue fugitives into northern states that they engaged in what might best be called the "dirty compromise" with northern representatives. In return for the constitutional protection of the slave trade for twenty more years and for the inclusion of a fugitive slave clause in the Constitution, southern representatives bargained away one of the South's vital commercial interests, an issue that had earlier created a great deal of hostility toward Great Britain. Moreover, southern congressmen continued to advocate additional and ever more restrictive fugitive slave laws from 1793 through the Compromise of 1850. Finally, Great Britain's refusal to return runaways after the revolutionary war or to reimburse their owners persuaded many southern politicians to oppose normalizing relations.[50]

Eighteenth-century slave women struggled to make decisions within a system of economic, racial, and sexual inequality and oppression that afforded them minimal latitude. The dual burden of reproductive and productive work limited black women's alternatives when they considered the possibility of escape. Parental responsibilities bound some securely within slavery, although others fled precisely because their families were threatened.

More crucial were the ways in which the tasks assigned to slave women by masters curtailed their ability to take flight. The availability of destinations and opportunities also were important. Women were most apt to abscond when they resided near a city that provided refuge or when cataclysmic events like the American Revolution expanded the possibilities of engaging in successful flight.

The majority of female fugitives sought to escape the horrors of slavery and to establish their liberty. But some women, like some men, used flight to achieve different goals. Many undoubtedly despaired at the improbability of achieving irrevocable freedom, especially during the colonial era, when no area of British America had renounced slavery. Instead, some women employed escape and other forms of resistance as bargaining devices to assert some control over their own lives and to curtail the power of their owners. This strategy might not gain their freedom, but it could improve the lives of slaves who desired a different master or wanted to live closer to kin and friends.

Slaves who absconded and disobeyed their masters not only risked their lives for personal gain, but they also challenged the system of racial bondage, especially during the revolutionary and postrevolutionary decades. Many liberated themselves and thereby accelerated the demise of slavery in the North. Runaways also severely disrupted the South's labor system and threatened their owners' authority during the revolutionary war. Anxious white southerners responded with extraordinary steps to reassert their hegemony over their human property.

Runaways in early America established an enduring legacy of solidarity and resistance that linked their struggle with that of nineteenth-century black abolitionists and rebellious slaves who were inspired by their defiance. Successful escapees joined with other free blacks to construct vibrant African-American communities in northern cities, and they thereby provided way stations, destinations, and hope for succeeding generations of slaves who would resist inequality and steal themselves to freedom.

Notes

For their helpful comments on this essay, I thank Graham Hodges, Susan E. Klepp, Mary Beth Norton, Marylynn Salmon, Jean R. Soderlund, Shane White, Michael Zuckerman, and the editors of this volume.

1. Box 4A: Manumissions, Indentures and Other Legal Papers, 1799, The Papers of the Pennsylvania Abolition Society, Historical Society of Pennsylvania, Philadelphia.

2. Vagrancy Dockets, February 9, 1793, Volume: 1790–1797, 36 volumes, Philadelphia City Archives.

3. *Gazette of the State of South-Carolina*, August 11, 1785.

4. On slave family and community formation in early America, see Ira Berlin, "Time, Space, and the Evolution of Afro-American Society on British Mainland North America," *AHR* 85 (1980): 44–78; and Mary Beth Norton, Herbert G. Gutman, and Ira Berlin, "The Afro-American Family in the Age of Revolution," in *Slavery and Freedom in the Age of the American Revolution*, ed. Ira Berlin and Ronald Hoffman (Charlottesville, Va., 1983). On the mid-Atlantic, see Billy G. Smith, "Black Family Life in Philadelphia from Slavery to Freedom," in *Shaping a National Culture: The Philadelphia Experience, 1750–1800*, ed. Catherine E. Hutchins (Winterthur, Del., 1994), 77–98; Jean R. Soderlund, *Quakers and Slavery: A Divided Spirit* (Princeton, N.J., 1985), 79–80; and Susan E. Klepp, "Seasoning and Society: Racial Differences in Mortality in Eighteenth-Century Philadelphia," *WMQ* 3d ser., 51 (1994): 473–506. The Chesapeake region is considered in Allan Kulikoff, *Tobacco and Slaves: The Development of Southern Cultures in the Chesapeake, 1690–1800* (Chapel Hill, N.C., 1986); and the lower South in Peter Wood, *Black Majority: Negroes in Colonial South Carolina from 1670 through the Stono Rebellion* (New York, 1974); and Philip D. Morgan, "Black Society in the Lowcountry, 1760–1810," in *Slavery and Freedom in the Age of the American Revolution*, ed. Ira Berlin and Ronald Hoffman (Charlottesville, Va., 1983), 83–141.

5. The antislavery movement is discussed in Arthur Zilversmit, *The First Emancipation: The Abolition of Slavery in the North* (Chicago, 1967); Soderlund, *Quakers and Slavery*; and Gary B. Nash and Jean R. Soderlund, *Freedom by Degrees: Emancipation in Pennsylvania and Its Aftermath* (New York, 1991).

6. I read and coded information from advertisements for runaway slaves in twenty-eight newspapers published in Pennsylvania, New Jersey, and Delaware between 1719 and 1796 and in five newspapers published in Charleston, South Carolina, between 1732 and 1790. These advertisements describe 219 runaway women in the Mid-Atlantic and 550 fugitive females in South Carolina. I also read notices reproduced in *"Pretends to Be Free": Runaway Slave Advertisements from Colonial and Revolutionary New York and New Jersey*, ed. Graham Russell Hodges and Alan Edward Brown (New York, 1994), and in *Runaway Slave Advertisements: A Documentary History from the 1730s to 1790*, comp. Lathan Algerna Windley, 4 vols. (Westport, Conn., 1983). The sources for table 2 indicate some of the studies that used newspaper notices.

7. For two of the dozens of masters who learned of the whereabouts of their runaways slaves and included that information in their advertisements, see the notices for Violet in the *Pennsylvania Gazette*, July 4, 1771, and for Franke in the *South Carolina Gazette*, May 11, 1734.

8. On masters' attitudes toward slave women in the nineteenth century, see Deborah Gray White, *Ar'n't I a Woman? Female Slaves in the Plantation South* (New York, 1985). The strengths and weaknesses of these advertisements as historical records are further considered in Billy G. Smith and Richard Wojtowicz, *Blacks Who Stole Themselves: Advertisements for Runaways in the Pennsylvania Gazette, 1728–1790* (Philadelphia, 1989), 4–5; and in Hodges and Brown, eds., *"Pretends to Be Free,"* xiv–xvi. It is important to note that the published notices by no means indicate *all* of the escape attempts by blacks in North America since fugitives often were not advertised. As Peter Wood observed, advertised runaways probably represent "little more than the top of an ill-defined iceberg" (*Black Majority*, 240). Philip D. Morgan and Michael Nicholls counted 2,300 advertised runaways in Virginia from the 1730s through the 1780s, but they found a minimum of 6,700 additional

runaways in other records; "Slave Runaways in Eighteenth-Century Virginia" (paper presented at the annual meeting of the Organization of American Historians, Washington, D.C., 1990), 3–4. See also Betty Wood, *Slavery in Colonial Georgia 1730–1775* (Athens, Ga., 1984), 170–72; and Philip D. Morgan, "Colonial South Carolina Runaways: Their Significance for Slave Culture," *Slavery and Abolition* 6 (1985): 57–58.

9. Half of the owners of female runaways in South Carolina, for instance, waited at least seventeen days to advertise; this is based on my count from five Charleston newspapers. Also see Morgan, "Colonial South Carolina Runaways," 58, 75 n.7.

10. The median reward offered by mid-Atlantic owners was £2 for women and £3 for men. Masters also believed that female fugitives would be apprehended more quickly than males. As one Pennsylvania master wrote about Phoebe, "she has been advertised even since she went off, with only Eight Dollars Reward, imagining that she would have been secured in a few days." *Pennsylvania Ledger*, November 9, 1782.

11. For example, Hagar Jones, characterized as "an artful jade," obtained "a pass for 8 days, in order to visit a child of her's in the city of Philadelphia," but when she failed to reappear, her owner waited several months before placing a notice in the newspaper; *Pennsylvania Gazette*, February 20, 1772.

12. While admittedly speculative, this figure has some basis in scattered evidence. First, among advertised runaways in the mid-Atlantic area, 3% of women and 5% of men were described in the notices as having fled previously, suggesting that the disparity in the sex ratio of runaways was not as great as the notices indicate. Second, of the 694 slaves committed by their masters to Philadelphia's workhouse during the 1790s for attempting to escape or for misbehaving, 20% were females; Vagrancy Dockets, Volume: 1790–1797, 36 volumes, Philadelphia City Archives. During the same years, only 14% of advertised fugitives in the region were females. Third, in Virginia during the 1780s, females accounted for only one of every seven advertised escapees, but lists of slaves who left with the British military indicate that one of every three evacuees was female; Morgan and Nicholls, "Slave Runaways," tables 1 and 2.

13. *The Infortunate: The Voyage and Adventures of William Moraley, an Indentured Servant*, ed. Susan E. Klepp and Billy G. Smith (University Park, Pa., 1992), 94.

14. The advertisements indicate that only a handful of women left their children. During the revolutionary war, for example, Maria "left behind her three young children . . . and is going towards New-York after a married white man, who is a soldier in the Continental service there." *Pennsylvania Gazette*, August 7, 1776. For a description of an extraordinary display of dedication to her children, see the nineteenth-century slave narrative by Linda Brent (alias for Harriet Jacobs) in *Incidents in the Life of a Slave Girl*, ed. Maria Child (San Diego, 1973).

15. Marvin L. Michael Kay and Lorin Lee Cary, *Slavery in North Carolina 1748–1775* (Chapel Hill, N.C., 1995), 125. See also B. Wood, "Some Aspects of Female Resistance to Chattel Slavery in Low Country Georgia, 1763–1815," *The Historical Journal* 30 (1987): 614–17; and Morgan and Nicholls, "Slave Runaways," 7–8.

16. On the sex ratio of slaves in the various regions, see Marvin L. Michael Kay and Lorin Lee Cary, "Slave Runaways in Colonial North Carolina, 1748–1775," *The North Carolina Historical Review* 63 (1986): 12; and B. Wood, "Some Aspects of Female Resistance," 606–7. Because of the way in which historians compiled information about runaways, it is necessary in this essay to define the Delaware Valley as

inclusive of Pennsylvania, northern Delaware and Maryland, and southern New Jersey. The mid-Atlantic encompasses that area as well as New York and northern New Jersey.

17. Child, ed., *Incidents in the Life of a Slave Girl*, 91–92. The advertisement for Kate appeared in the *South Carolina Gazette*, October 13, 1757. Other pregnant fugitives who took children with them appear in advertisements in the same newspaper in the following issues: January 11, 1739; April 18, 1748; August 15, 1748; April 10, 1749; and October 20, 1758.

18. The description of Phebe is in the *Delaware Gazette*, March 19, 1790; Berry is described in the *South Carolina Gazette*, March 19, 1750; April 4, 1754. For other women who fled after being sold, see the following *South Carolina Gazette* issues: September 24, 1753; March 15, 1760; and June 6, 1761.

19. The statistics in this paragraph are based on advertisements in twenty-eight newspapers published in Pennsylvania, New Jersey, and Delaware and five newspapers published in Charleston, South Carolina.

20. While 17% of South Carolina advertised fugitive women between twenty and forty years old took a child with them, none of the young women between sixteen and twenty ran with a child. In the mid-Atlantic, 17% of the former and 9% of the latter fled with their offspring. Based on advertisements in twenty-eight newspapers published in Pennsylvania, New Jersey, and Delaware and five newspapers published in Charleston, South Carolina, the age structure of runways was as follows:

Ages of Advertised Runaways

Age	South Carolina 1732–1790 Females ($N=550$)	Delaware Valley 1719–1796 Females ($N=219$)	Males ($N=1558$)
Younger than 15	23%	13%	4%
16–19	19	17	12
20–29	32	38	56
30–39	18	23	21
40+	9	9	8

21. Child, *Incidents in the Life of a Slave Girl*, 79. Jacobs's fifteenth birthday began "a sad epoch in the life of a slave girl" when her "master began to whisper foul words in my ear" (p. 26). On the sexual abuse of slave women, see White, *Ar'n't I a Woman?*, 95–96, 152–53; Darlene Clark Hine, "Rape and the Inner Lives of Southern Black Women: Thoughts on the Culture of Dissemblance," in *Southern Women: Histories and Identities*, ed. Virginia Bernhard, Betty Brandon, Elizabeth Fox Genovese, and Theda Perdue (Columbia, Mo., 1992), 177–89; Thelma Jennings, "'Us Colored Women Had to Go through a Plenty': Sexual Exploitation of African-American Slave Women," *Journal of Women's History* 1 (1990): 45–74; and Helene Lecaudey, "Behind the Mask: Ex-Slave Women and Interracial Sexual Relations," in *Discovering the Women in Slavery: Emancipating Perspectives on the American Past*, ed. Patricia Morton (Athens, Ga., 1996), 260–77.

22. Since these figures are based on the assessment of masters, they are, or course, liable to error. But the disparity in the statistics for women and men is sufficiently large to suggest that female and male fugitives pursued significantly different escape strategies. The case of eighteen-year-old Hannah illustrates how mid-Atlantic

slaves sometimes fled to their family shortly after being separated by their master. In August 1765, Michael Hulings, who lived near the city's wharves, offered Hannah for sale, advertising her as a "hearty Negroe Girl . . . this Country born, has had the Small-Pox and Measles, is either fit for Town or Country Business; sold for no Fault but for want of Employ." Moreover, she had been "bred in Michael Huling's family." A tavernkeeper a few miles from Philadelphia purchased Hannah in October. Two months later, she fled either to her family in Philadelphia, her new master believed, or to her brother and sister in Wilmington, where Hulings had hired them out. *Pennsylvania Gazette,* August 29, 1765, and December 12, 1765.

23. The notice for Free Poll is in the *Pennsylvania Gazette,* May 16, 1781; an advertisement for Sophy appears in the *South-Carolina Gazette and General Advertiser,* February 24, 1784; and a notice for Catharina is in the *South Carolina Gazette,* December 17, 1772.

24. On the circumscribed lives of black and white colonial southern women, see Mary Beth Norton, "'What an Alarming Crisis Is This': Southern Women and the American Revolution," in *The Southern Experience in the American Revolution,* ed. Jeffrey J. Crow and Larry E. Tise (Chapel Hill, N.C., 1978), 210–11, 230. On slave women's work, see Jacqueline Jones, "Race, Sex, and Self-Evident Truths: The Status of Slave Women during the Era of the American Revolution," in *Women in the Age of the American Revolution,* ed. Ronald Hoffman and Peter J. Albert (Charlottesville, Va., 1989), 301; and Carol Berkin, *First Generations: Women in Colonial America* (New York, 1996), 111–12.

25. In the advertisements for 219 runaway women in the mid-Atlantic, masters described 3 as housekeepers and 2 as washerwomen. Few owners designated an occupation for the 550 fugitive females in South Carolina: 12 were described as housekeepers, 4 as seamstresses, 1 as a milk woman, and 5 as washerwomen. Male fugitives had a much wider variety of skills. Of the 1,558 men who were advertised in the mid-Atlantic, 113 were craftsmen, 57 were laborers or watermen, 27 were personal servants, 36 had a service skill, and 67 were agricultural workers.

26. Their owners believed that Molly and Mary both disguised themselves as men; *South Carolina Gazette,* December 24, 1763, and November 29, 1773. While 2.7% of fugitive men stole horses in the mid-Atlantic, 1.8% of fugitive women in the mid-Atlantic and 0.4% of them in South Carolina took a horse. In advertisements in Virginia newspapers, 55 men but not a single woman rode off on horses; Morgan and Nicholls, "Slave Runaways," 8. Further evidence of the circumscribed lives of slave women compared to slave men is contained in the advertisements. While 4.4% of fugitive males in the mid-Atlantic could read, only 0.5% of escaped females in the mid-Atlantic and none of the 550 females advertised in five Charleston newspapers were literate. Fugitive males in the mid-Atlantic likewise were twice as likely as females to be multilingual.

27. At least 21% of mid-Atlantic female fugitives fled to Philadelphia, 49% of those in South Carolina ran to Charleston, and 38% of Georgia female escapees headed to Savannah. On black women in urban centers, see Robert Olwell, "'Loose, Idle and Disorderly': Slave Women in the Eighteenth-Century Charleston Marketplace," in *More Than Chattel: Black Women and Slavery in the Americas,* ed. David Barry Gaspar and Darlene Clark Hines (Bloomington, Ind., 1996), 97–110; Philip D. Morgan, "Black Life in Eighteenth-Century Charleston," *Perspectives in American History,* new ser., 1 (1984): 187–232; B. Wood, "Some Aspects of Female Resistance," 614–15; and Gary B. Nash, *Forging Freedom: The Formation of Philadelphia's Black Community 1720–1840* (Cambridge, Mass., 1988). Advertisements

for Nancy and Jenny appear in the December 6, 1784, and June 16, 1777, issues of the *Gazette of the State of South-Carolina;* the notice for Amy is in the December 5, 1771, issue of the *South-Carolina Gazette and General Advertiser.*

28. On rates of escape in the Chesapeake, see Morgan and Nichols, "Slave Runaways," 6.

29. *South Carolina Gazette,* February 1, 1759, February 1, 1739.

30. *South Carolina Gazette,* May 16, 1771; *Pennsylvania Gazette,* September 1, 1763; *Gazette of the State of South-Carolina,* August 15, 1785; *South Carolina Gazette,* March 13, 1775. Owners believed that 80% of all fugitives—men and women—were attempting to establish their permanent freedom in the mid-Atlantic and that 40% in Virginia were involved in a similar quest. The first figure is based on my count from twenty-eight newspapers published in Pennsylvania, New Jersey, and Delaware; the Virginia statistic is from Gerald W. Mullin, *Flight and Rebellion: Slave Resistance in Eighteenth-Century Virginia* (London, 1972), 108. Based on five South Carolina newspapers, I calculated that masters perceived that 58% of women runaways tried to escape bondage permanently.

31. C. W. Larison, *Silvia Dubois, A Biografy of the Slav Who Whipt Her Mistres and Gand Her Fredom,* ed. and trans. Jared C. Lobdell (New York, 1988), 54. The August 8, 1801, pass for Loretta and the July 7, 1801, certificate for James McHenry's slave are in Box 3A, Series 4, Papers of the Pennsylvania Abolition Society. The advertisement for Mary is in the *Pennsylvania Packet,* September 29, 1778.

32. Sukey, *Royal Gazette,* Sept. 19, 1781; Jenny and her progeny, *Gazette of the State of South-Carolina,* August 11, 1785.

33. Box 4B, Series 4, Papers of the Pennsylvania Abolition Society; and *Pennsylvania Gazette,* December 3, 1794.

34. Phoebe and Belinda, *South-Carolina Gazette and General Advertiser, February* 23, 1784; Jemmy and Athy, ibid., October 31, 1761.

35. Sarah, *South-Carolina Gazette and General Advertiser,* February 26, 1737; Kate and Billy, ibid., May 21, 1750.

36. Banaba, *South Carolina Gazette,* August 30, 1773; Betty, ibid., November 22, 1760; Sophia Maybury, *Pennsylvania Gazette,* July 28, 1748.

37. Quote from *The Journals of Henry Melchoir Muhlenberg,* ed. Theodore G. Tappert and John H. Doerstein, 3 vols. (Muhlenberg, Pa., 1958), 3:78. On the activities of African Americans during the American Revolution, see Sylvia R. Frey, *Water From the Rock: Black Resistance in a Revolutionary Age* (Princeton, N.J., 1991); and Benjamin Quarles, *Black Mosaic: Essays in Afro-American History and Historiography* (Amherst, Mass., 1988). On female fugitives during the war, see Jones, "Race, Sex, and Self-Evident Truths," 325–28; and Norton, "'What an Alarming Crisis Is This,'" 213–14.

38. The source of fig. 2 is my count of advertisements for runaway slaves included in twenty-eight newspapers published in Pennsylvania, New Jersey, and Delaware.

39. The notice for Peg was in the *Pennsylvania Gazette,* July 7, 1779. Advertisements for Phyllis and Poll appeared in the *Pennsylvania Ledger,* May 6, 1778. Notices for Rachel, Jude, Dinah, and Sue appeared, respectively, in the *Pennsylvania Packet,* October 15, November 3, July 16, 1778, and July 6, 1779. The two slave women were advertised in the *New-York Gazette; and the Weekly Mercury,* December 2, 1776, as reproduced in *"Pretends to Be Free,"* ed. Hodges and Brown, 194–95. Jacqueline Jones notes that black women were part of the Black Pioneers; "Race, Sex, and Self-Evident Truths," 328.

40. On Virginia fugitives, see Morgan and Nicholls, "Slave Runaways," 7, table 2. Mary Beth Norton also noted that women ran in greater numbers during the war, and she indicated the sex ratio of blacks evacuated with the British from Savannah in "'What an Alarming Crisis Is This,'" 213. Jacqueline Jones estimated that one-third of wartime refugees was female; "Race, Sex, and Self-Evident Truths," 327. On the explosion of Philadelphia's black population after the war, see Nash, *Forging Freedom*.

41. The 1780 law is discussed in Nash and Soderlund, *Freedom by Degrees*, 100–14. During the 1780s the number of runaways advertised in Philadelphia newspapers was three fourths of the number of slaves manumitted in the city. Since many more slaves escaped than were advertised, it is probable that more slaves gained their freedom by absconding than by manumission (pp. 140–41).

42. Ibid., 4, passim. On the difficulty of escaped slaves maintaining their freedom, see Billy G. Smith and Richard Wojtowicz, "The Precarious Freedom of Blacks: Excerpts from the *Pennsylvania Gazette*, 1728–1776," *Pennsylvania Magazine of History and Biography* 113 (1989): 237–64.

43. The case of Magdalen and Zaire is in *Judicial Cases concerning American Slavery and the Negro*, ed. Helen T. Catterall, 5 vols. (New York, 1926; reprint, 1968), 4:17. These two slaves also appear in the following entries of the Vagrancy Dockets, Volume: 1790–1797, 36 volumes, July 14, 1794; February 9, 1796; and October 12, 1796. In the last two entries, the status of the two women changed from slaves to bound servants.

44. *Extracts from the Diary of Christopher Marshall, 1774–1781*, ed. William Duane (New York, 1969); and Harry Emerson Wildes, *Lonely Midas: The Story of Stephen Girard* (New York, 1943), 99–102.

45. Vagrancy Dockets, Volume: 1790–1797, entries for Laurencine on January 20 and February 22, 1797; entries for Fortune on November 4 and December 4, 1797; entry for Zemire on December 4, 1797; entry for Eve on October 18, 1790; and entry for Clarissa on November 16, 1797. The number of slaves in Philadelphia and Pennsylvania between 1793 and 1797 is estimated from the tabulations of the 1790 and 1800 federal censuses. Gary B. Nash, "Reverberations of Haiti in the American North: Black Santo Dominguans in Philadelphia," *Pennsylvania History, Supplement* 65 (1998): 44–73.

46. The demise of slavery and various ways that slaves obtained their freedom are discussed in Nash and Soderlund, *Freedom by Degrees*, 4–7, and chap. 5.

47. Pinckney is quoted in Norton, "'What an Alarming Crisis Is This,'" 214. Pall's description is from the Committee of Correspondence Letterbook: 1794–1809 (AMS081), pp. 74–75, December 15, 1800, Papers of the Pennsylvania Abolition Society. The Baltimore master is quoted in Benjamin Quarles, *The Negro in the American Revolution* (Chapel Hill, N.C., 1961), 126.

48. The group of thirteen slaves was described in the *Maryland Journal and Baltimore Advertiser*, June 27, 1780. Ads for Terra and Virginia appear in the *Maryland Journal and Baltimore Advertiser*, September 17, 1782; the notice for Nanny is in the *South-Carolina Gazetter and General Advertiser*, April 22, 1784; and the six women are advertised in the *Royal Gazette*, July 11, 1781. See also Jones, "Race, Sex, and Self-Evident Truths," 326; Norton, "'What an Alarming Crisis Is This,'" 223; Frey, "Between Slavery and Freedom: Virginia Blacks in the American Revolution," *Journal of Southern History* 49 (1983): 383.

49. Sylvia Frey estimates that 55,000 slaves were "missing" during the war, whereas Benjamin Quarles puts the number at 100,000 of 600,000 slaves. Frey,

Water from the Rock; Quarles, *Negro in the American Revolution*. Many southern slave owners believed they were "ruined" when their slaves fled during the war, as explained by Daniel Meaders, *Dead or Alive: Fugitive Slaves and White Indentured Servants before 1830* (New York, 1993), chap. 10.

50. The compromise empowered the federal government to levy export as well as import duties, and it permitted those decisions to be made by simple majorities of Congress rather than by a two-thirds vote. This ran directly contrary to southern interests since tobacco, rice, and indigo planters did not want the export of their products controlled by a central government. On the "dirty compromise," see Paul Finkelman, "Slavery and the Constitutional Convention: Making a Covenant with Death," in *Beyond Confederation: Origins of the Constitution and American National Identity*, ed. Richard Beeman, Stephen Botein, and Edward C. Carter II (Chapel Hill, N.C., 1987), 188–225; and Staughton Lynd, *Class Conflict, Slavery and the United States Constitution: Ten Essays* (Indianapolis, Ind., 1967). Several fugitive slave laws were passed by the U.S. Congress during the 1790s, and a fugitive slave law was a key part of the Compromise of 1850. Southern opposition to the Jay treaty and to normalizing relations with Great Britain is described in Meaders, *Dead or Alive*, 255–56.

Sterling Stuckey

AFRICAN SPIRITUALITY AND CULTURAL PRACTICE IN COLONIAL NEW YORK, 1700–1770

> The most important fact about the West African funeral use of earthenware fragments is that the pieces are not actually interred but are carefully placed on the surface of the grave.
>
> —ROBERT FARRIS THOMPSON

IN WEST AFRICA, singing while working seemed natural prior to the Atlantic slave trade. In fact, work without song was considered very peculiar indeed by Africans, whose attitude toward the two did not change appreciably with American slavery. "From the beginning," writes Alan Lomax, "it was the white man standing in the shade, shouting orders with a club or whip or gun in his hand—while out in the sun the blacks sweated with the raw stuff of wealth, cursing under their breath, but singing at the tops of their voices."[1] If work songs flowered more in the South than the North, the intensity of labor accounts for the difference. Singing was used to ease the burden of labor while recording its physical and spiritual toll. For the African, the conditions of life, increasingly harsh under slavery, were more likely to fertilize the ground of creation, which ultimately contributed to the spread of the African aesthetic in America. That they created under such circumstances makes it more ironic that American leaders, having enslaved close to a million Africans by 1800, argued that there was too much work to be done for whites to be concerned with artistic creation.

Indeed, there was the belief, perhaps best articulated by Benjamin

Franklin, "that nothing is good or beautiful but in the measure that it is useful"; and he added: "Thus, poetry, painting, music, (and the stage as their embodiment) are all necessary and proper gratifications of a refined state of society but objectionable at an earlier period, since their cultivation would make a taste for their enjoyment precede its means." John Adams thought the genius of the country scientific rather than imaginative, "that the arts sprang from luxury, that riches created despotisms, that the arts had been prostituted to the service of despotism and superstition from the dawn of history, and so should be avoided in the young nation."[2] The notion of art as a liberating force or a supple armor that might protect one's inner being was not considered. And it was ironic, considering Adams's coupling of art with luxury, that creativity in music and dance was occurring largely among blacks at the bottom of society.

Cultural historian Neil Harris draws attention to the low esteem in which art was held in colonial America, noting that this attitude did not change until industrialization, nationalism, and urbanization "helped dissociate art from its craft-like connotations and granted it dignity and honor among civilized men." Further, he points out that "nationalism, industrialism and urbanization were all lacking in Colonial America, and with them the need for art."[3] This early American attitude toward art helps explain why African music and dance were viewed as somehow strange. Yet they became preferred arts for whites at large festivals before attracting the attention of large numbers of theatergoers in antebellum America.[4]

African sculpture was among the finest in the world, it would later be learned, at the time Thomas Jefferson claimed that he had never seen "even an elementary trace" of such artistic inclination. African dance in due course would be similarly regarded by students of the subject, both forms serving as sources for modernist movements in the West.[5] African sculpture and dance were not merely useful or beautiful but both and usually were rooted in religion. Still, it hardly mattered to Americans that African sculpture was a vehicle of religious expression because few knew that such an art form existed in Africa. Indeed, it took the lapse of well over a century after Jefferson's *Notes on the State of Virginia* for Americans to begin to appreciate African ability in that realm.

The failure of white Americans to understand the African aesthetic and how it relates to African religion has persisted in the historiographic perception of African art and religion. Historian Jon Butler finds a "distinctive paternalism" in colonial and antebellum slavery and argues that traditional "African religious systems" were brought to North America and destroyed, leaving slaves "remarkably bereft of collective religious practices before 1760." In fact, he has written that "those who molded and imbibed slavery also produced the most important religious transformation to occur in the

American colonies before 1776: an African spiritual holocaust."[6] On the contrary, the molding of crucial aspects of slavery had more to do with slave creativity and vitality than with the parasitical nature of masters, which helps explain why the master class was as much a spectator class when observing slaves cultivate crops as when attending festivals.

Given the organic link of the religious leader to the African polity and the mingling in slavery of ethnic peoples from different religious backgrounds, the very idea that African religious systems existed in this country strains credulity. It should be pointed out, however, that the absence of systems should not imply the absence of religion or communal religious expression. In North America drastically different political conditions favored the sharing of spirituality across ethnic lines, with the slave priest and artist (the two were often the same) leading in the process.

Actually, Butler presents no anatomy of the alleged transformation. Nor does he define "religious systems," though he uses the phrase over and over. The closest thing to a definition is a reference to "*qua* systems,"and that is hardly a refinement. In short, the identification of African religious values does not concern Butler, which raises questions about the means, within the context of his argument, by which slaveholders determined what needed to be transformed.[7] No evidence of an African spiritual holocaust, North or South, is presented in *Awash in a Sea of Faith*, for there is no demonstration of the means by which the denuding of African spirituality occurred. At a minimum such would be required before persuading us—an even larger task—that it was in the interest of the slave system that Africans be hopelessly disoriented when their labor was desperately needed. It defies reason to argue that Africans suffered more after reaching North America, where primary interest in them was as slave laborers, than during the Atlantic voyage. It stands to reason that the cruel siftings of the trade meant that only the strongest survived to perpetuate needed qualities of their cultures.

The failings of early colonial observers to understand African art stemmed from misconceptions about the purpose of that art. While dance was the principal means by which African sacred values were brought to North America, slave dance was thought by whites to be frivolous and, like the sex they thought it suggested, dirty. To be sure, pelvic movement while dancing seems to have been interpreted quite differently by blacks and whites. Dance influenced them differently, precisely because Africans so often danced. Their dance was thought by many whites to suggest a certain physical license.[8] Such presumption on the part of white observers inhibited their ability to perceive the depths of meaning that dance expressions held for blacks. A related overlay of ignorance that led to a "cover" of concealment resulted from the fact that whites, overwhelmingly, considered dance a secular art. Africans came from cultures in which dance was often a form of prayer, hence the challenge of dance to slaveholders attempting to control them was no small thing. Moreover, since African dance was observed in settings thought inappropriate for worship, the sacred was thereby disguised and found expanded space for expression in slavery. This was paralleled by the way Africans extended the sacred over time, its practice occurring through the week.

In cultures in which dance is vital it takes on a life of its own, and those who begin dancing when young remain dancers. Not only are the forms and rhythms of dance maintained for life, more than any other art form dance is an art of the subconscious, of reflex action, the body at times seeming to have cognitive powers.[9] Dance is also preeminently an art of visual cues that, working through group memory, can immediately lead to recall and the restoration of motor habits in all their fullness. This is so because dance is the most effective means of representing rhythm visibly, and consequently, seeing others dance enables one to recall movements appropriate to a particular dance. In part because of such qualities of renewal, dance is the most durable of all cultural forms, which among people for whom dance is integral only physical death can end. Moreover, a single dancer can project a vital cultural symbol. The influence of such a performer can be as important as that of thousands of nonartists because a single artist—the dancer, for example—can make the flame of art flare as needed.

Unlike the European tradition—in which dance and music were often in competition, with music supreme—dance in America, as in Africa, was nearly unthinkable without music or music without dance. Moreover, in the African tradition dance has often served as midwife to music, ushering it into being. Consequently, dance was not considered inferior to music. In fact, in the African aesthetic there is no higher art than dance, and it is anything but elitist. A democratic art form, in its proper setting it is indistinguishable from music; it is the soul of music made manifest.[10]

In light of Neil Harris's observations regarding art and industrialization, one should bear in mind that jazz dance and music, both rooted in slave culture, are emblems of technological life in much of the world today.[11] Jazz's development depended greatly on the work songs of slavery. Such was the creative richness of these songs that something of their rhythm and timbre—and pain—eventually got into jazz and the blues. "Indeed, from the further development of the work song" together with ring dance, writes Robert Farris Thompson, "have arisen the basic cafe musics of the world in the twentieth century." The perspective of time enables us to appreciate what the founders could not, the musical genius of slaves working under the blazing sun and singing: "I know my robe's gonna fit me well / I tried it on at the gates of hell."[12]

Examples of authentic African and African-American dance were never hard to find. Two of the nineteenth century's greatest observers of American society and culture witnessed such performances and were affected by them. In his days as a newspaper editor, Walt Whitman acknowledged the prevalence of such art forms. In a Brooklyn market, Whitman noticed that butchers, it seemed, were particularly affected by black music and dance. "The capacities of the 'market roarers' in all the mysteries of the double shuffle," he wrote, "it needs not our word to endorse. And the whistling! whose ears have not drunk in the full, rich melody thereof?" Elsewhere he worked these moments into his poetic art: "The butcher-boy puts off his killing clothes, or sharpens his knife at the stall in the market / I loiter enjoying his repartees and his shuffle and breakdown."[13]

Herman Melville was exposed to black dance and music early in life in Albany and in New York City. By the time his family moved to Albany in 1829, that city's reputation as a center of African dance and music, dating from the eighteenth century, had long been established. Over the ten years that the Melville family lived there, blacks regularly provided performances of dance to whistling in summer months on Albany corners a block from the Melville residence. A keen student of dance and a dancer himself in youth, Melville detected similarities in dance styles between Albany and New York City blacks: the circle dance, double-shuffle, and breakdown were all pivotal to black dance in both places.

There is, moreover, reason to believe that Melville's voracious reading of travel accounts as a teenager led to the discovery of African dance on the decks of ships, a subject that engages his attention in *Benito Cereno*, one of his masterpieces. Considering his interest in the slave trade and slavery and his command of so much of that history, it is likely that such reading led him to the accounts of captains of slave ships in which there is mention of circle dance not unlike what he was observing around him at the time.[14]

Indeed, circle dance was so pervasive in Africa that captains of slave ships, while ashore, saw variants of it performed, possibly by captives-to-be. In the early 1700s, Captain Canot saw a "whirling circle of half-stripped girls" engaged in dance to the beat of tom-toms. And Captain Drake commented on dance on the deck of his ship: "We had tambourines on board, which some of the younger darkies fought for regularly, and every evening we enjoyed the novelty of African . . . ring dances."[15] Thus, even aboard slave ships, Africans were known to dance to the sound of the tambourine, an African instrument whose influence gained in power over time. Slaves who fought for the tambourine during the Middle Passage and played it to the ring dance of others practiced elements of African religions before the very eyes of slavers no more conversant with them than slave masters awaiting their arrival in colonial North America. As horrible as it was, the

Atlantic voyage did not strip Africans of such practices or the values they represented.

Millions of Africans perished during forced marches to coastal factories and during the Middle Passage, a tragedy of vast proportions that has been crucial to arguments that the retention of African culture was virtually impossible under such circumstances. But the argument that African culture was destroyed, without reference to the values of African people, fails to persuade. The fact that slave trade studies in this country have been blind to the cultural dimension of the trade, however, helped prepare the ground for such arguments. The trade has until now been the province mainly of the historian, who counts the number of Africans involved from particular regions of Africa, with some attention to economics and the death toll but virtually none to the spiritual consequences of its prosecution.

Yet nowhere has the emotional impact of the trade been treated more convincingly than by artist Tom Feelings in his magisterial yet terrible *Middle Passage*, an arresting display of drawings that recall, as art historian Suzanne Blier has suggested, Michelangelo.[16] Feelings makes as fine an argument as any artist for the personal being universal, for the agony and response of a single soul expressing that of a people. Just as the plight of a lone individual might reflect that of the group, so too might the individual artist, male or female, represent the values of a community of slaves, and that clear inference might be drawn from a number of Feelings's drawings. He shows us, by revealing the inner pain of the enslaved, that horror was a routine occurrence, that nothing to follow could conceivably be more shocking or cruel. With poetic insight that mounts to a similar conclusion, W. E. B. DuBois probed the lives of those ensnared by the trade: "Raphael painted, Luther preached, Corneille wrote, and Milton sang; and through it all, for four hundred years, the dark captives wound to the sea amid the bleaching bones of the dead; for four hundred years the sharks followed the scurrying ships; for four hundred years America was strewn with the living and dying millions of a transplanted race; for four hundred years Ethiopia stretched forth her hands unto God."[17]

Our best channel to the interior lives of those shackled men, women, and children remains the Ibo tale, for through it they speak directly to us. The storyteller Gullah Joe, in a tale that bears his name, survived the Atlantic voyage to recount the experience. He tells us that during the Middle Passage, as Africans were lured onto boats, some jumped off and were drowned. Others were overpowered, thrown into the bottom of the ship, and chained, "packed in dere wuss dan hog in a car when dey shippin' 'em." Joe continues:

An' every day dem white folks would come in dere an' if a nigger just twist his self or move, dey'd cut the hide off him wid a rawhide whip. An' niggers died in de bottom er dat ship wuss dan hogs wid cholera. Dem white folks ain' hab no mercy. Look like dey ain' know wha' mercy mean. Dey drag dem dead niggers out an' throw 'em overboard. An' dat ain' all. Dey tho'wed a heap of live ones wha' dey thought ain' guh live into de sea. . . . An' it look like we been two or three months in de bottom er dat ship. . . . It seems to me I would be satisfied ef I jes could see my tribe one more time. . . . I is a ole man now an' de folks here been good to me. Anything good atter dat vessel. . . . I has a longin' to walk in de feenda. I has a wife an' chillun here, but when I thinks er my tribe an' my friend an' my daddy an' my mammy an' de great feenda, a feelin' rises up in my th'oat an' my eye well up wid tear.[18]

The kikongo word *feenda* establishes that "Gullah Joe" is a Bakongo tale. Kikongo is the language of people of Kongo-Angola, who made up almost one third of all Africans caught in the slave trade and forcibly brought to North America. Through it all the power of African culture was such that well into the twentieth century African ethnic forms were still being kept alive by storytellers despite the mistaken notion that African ethnicity could not be identified in American slavery after 1800. That ethnic cultural forms are found in collections of tales that cover the eighteenth and nineteenth centuries means that slave culture in America was more powerful — to say nothing of being more subtle — than suspected.[19]

"The King Buzzard" is about tragedy "way back in slavery times — way back in Af'ica." A giant buzzard, horrid to the eye and poisonous in smell from eating the dead and vomiting them up, causes the protagonist to seek refuge in a canebrake. The storyteller tell us, however, that what the protagonist thought he had witnessed was not an actual buzzard but an African chief who betrayed thousands of his people into slavery before he is himself knocked down, chained, and made to undergo the Atlantic voyage:

An' when he dead, dere were no place in heaven for him an' he were not desired in hell. An' de great master decide dat he were lower dan all the other mens or beasts; he punishment were to wander for eternal time over de face er de earth. Dat as he had kilt de sperrits of mens an' womens as well as dere bodies, he must wander on an' on. Dat his sperrit should always travel in de form of a great buzzard. . . . An' sometimes he appears to mens, but he doom is settled. . . . An' dey say he are known to all de sperrit world as de King Buzzard, an' dat forever he must travel alone.[20]

"The King Buzzard" is an Ibo tale the meaning of which transcends time and place. The Ibo fear of endless restlessness of the spirit was widely shared in Africa and by Africans in North America. Through the anguished creation of the slave, we have in "The King Buzzard" the classic example of the tale as timeless myth. "Gullah Joe" and "The King Buzzard" were recounted and transcribed in English, and each contains African spiritual values. To recall the *feenda*, the sacred forest or sacred body of water, is to evoke the Bakongo cross and, below its horizontal bar, the world of the ancestors, all of which the Bakongo inscribed through ring dance, rotating counterclockwise like the sun as observed in the Southern Hemisphere.[21] Owing to such symbolism, thousands of Africans who threw themselves overboard might have thought they were joining the ancestors.

A linguistic finding, together with the research of African anthropologists and the work of historians of African art, help us to discern the relationship of "Gullah Joe" to dance, which was at the heart of the African aesthetic. Such disciplines enable us to demonstrate, contrary to the conventional scholarly wisdom, the presence of African ethnic forms in antebellum slavery— some Ibo, others Bakongo, and still others according to the African background proper to them.[22] More powerful and richly textured than anthropologists and historians have thought, African values have been influential in North America since the seventeenth century.

Warming themselves at the fires of culture, most who survived the Middle Passage underwent a remarkable spiritual and physical rebound to lay the foundations of the American national economy. As the revolution approached, slaves were doing the work of tobacco and rice cultivation in Virginia, Maryland, and the Carolinas. Who was dependent on whom for the profits from that labor? Is there doubt that black labor was the fulcrum on which the freedom of whites rested?[23] The dependence of the master on the slave cannot be separated from the continuing need for African slave imports in colonial North America.

Early in the eighteenth century, some think in the first decade, an African boy was sold into slavery in Albany, New York. It is unclear where he had been before that time, but it is said that in infancy he had "been brought from Angola in the Guinea Gulf; and when but a boy . . . became the purchased slave of one of the most ancient and respectable merchant princes" of Albany. What the boy, later named Charley, knew of African cultures before arriving in Albany cannot be known with certitude; but Joel Munsell, an authority on Albany history, remarks of African cultural influences to which Charles and other blacks in Albany were exposed: "The dances were the original Congo [Bakongo] dances, as danced in their native Africa. . . . The old settlers said Charley was a prince in his own country and was supposed to have been one hundred and twenty-five years old at the time of his death!"[24] The fact that he resided in a town relatively thinly populated with blacks—they were a distinct minority—should be noted, for almost universally it has been contended that, under such circumstances, there can be no significant African culture or fertile ground in which an African aesthetic might flower.

From an early age, Charley was exposed to African dance and drumming and to songs and tales in African languages. His generation was one of the most African in the history of American slavery. But Phillip Curtin, an authority on the African slave trade, argues that since only 930 slaves were

African-born imports to New York colony "over the whole period 1715–67," the course of safety "is simply to disregard the slave imports to the northern colonies." Yet the continuing impact of African culture in the colony cannot be ignored. Related is Curtin's finding that most slave imports into New York were from the West Indies, a point usually broached to argue a significant reduction in African influences. Such an inference presupposes that formative values can easily be erased or reversed, an unstated assumption of historians of African slavery in North America; hence, in Curtin's opinion, the need to focus exclusively on the slave trade to the South.[25] But if Curtin's conservative figures are accurate, the evidence of African cultural expression of various types in Albany is the more astonishing, indicating a greater need than ever to study slave culture everywhere, regardless of the volume of the slave trade into a particular region.

The principal artistic forms of Albany were those of the black community. Charley combined music and dance to become a master drummer as well as a great dancer, all skills perfected in the first half of the eighteenth century when, it is argued, so very few Africans from the continent were brought into New York colony. And in that time, Albany blacks became a dominant cultural force, with African dance and music central to their art. In fact, the mounting cultural strength of blacks and their being positioned to dominate Albany's principal festival, Pinkster, coincides with Butler's period of spiritual holocaust, from 1700 to the 1760s.

Celebrated in many areas of New York, Pinkster, as Gabriel Furman notes, was "considerable of a festival among the Dutch," who rode "in parties about the country making visits." He adds, interestingly, "Considering its origins, this festival, from its singular mode of observance, was one of the strangest of the American customs. From a very early period, probably from the first settlement of the country, until the commencement of the present century, *Pinckster* was a holiday among our Dutch inhabitants. It was celebrated as the day of *Pentecost*, the day upon which occurred the miraculous descent of the Holy Spirit upon the apostles."[26]

Apparently, Pinkster as an African festival was just getting underway when Charley was brought to Albany. At that time there were only two hundred Africans living there out of a total of two thousand people, just 10 percent of the population. These relatively small numbers did not prevent the shift of Pinkster toward an expression of African spirituality. In this regard, it is worth repeating that most Africans were dancers who responded to music, that both dance and song in black Africa tended to be more collective than in the West, contributing to a sense of community in spiritual and recreational matters, the audience scarcely existing since African "observers" were participants.[27] Charley's career must be viewed in light of such aesthetic principles.

In 1737, there were 1,630 Africans in Albany, or slightly more than 15 percent of the total population, and by that time Charley had achieved prominence within the slave community. By 1771, there were close to 4,000 Africans in an Albany population of close to 40,000 whites. Such demographics, in Albany and elsewhere, must be kept in mind when considering the alleged destruction of African spirituality. With the importation of slaves into Albany from the West Indies, where many slaves were African born, imported to replace those who had been worked to death, the Albany slave community grew over the first half of the eighteenth century, peopled largely by those who survived the horrors of the Middle Passage.[28] Africa, then, was not as far removed from Albany blacks as one might think. In fact, those importations meant that Charley moved among those who knew a great deal about African values.

Charley not only learned the language of the drum but also that of African song: "As a general thing the music consisted of a sort of drum, or instrument constructed out of a box with sheep skin heads upon which . . . Charley did most of the drumming, accompanied by singing some strange African air." To sing African songs, a practice more widespread in the North than assumed, meant that slaves were communicating with each other, not with whites, and communicating what they pleased, for whites seldom took enough interest in Africans, over centuries of slave trading, to learn African languages.[29] So Charley sang as he drummed, his sense of timing strengthening his dancing. With black participation in the Pinkster festival or carnival disproportionate to their numbers and status, no performer in the festival was more prized than the drummer, except possibly the dancer—and Charley was both and a singer as well.

Alice Morse Earle, who wrote on festivals, observed that nowhere was Pinkster "a more glorious festival than at Albany, among the sheltered, the cherished slave population in that town and vicinity."[30] Evidence of slave disaffection in eighteenth-century Albany and elsewhere in the colony raises questions as to whether blacks were "sheltered" and "cherished." Indeed, Munsell takes a different view from Earle, asserting that Albany slaves were "much feared" by their masters, which occasioned restrictions on the number of slaves allowed to travel together and prohibitions against slaves having access to certain implements and tools, tactics thought to have fostered "race hysteria."[31] Much greater hysteria was caused in New York City at the time Charley was about ten years of age and capable of understanding why slaves might revolt against their masters. On the morning of 7 January 1712, between twenty-five and thirty slaves and two Indians torched a building in New York and, armed with guns, knives, and clubs, attacked whites who rushed to the scene, killing eight and seriously wounding five or six. The ritual carried out by the slave rebels prior to the outbreak was especially disturbing in its suggestion of the depths of slave commitment to African values that might protect the conspiracy. The conspirators had welcomed the New Year "by tying themselves to secrecy . . . Sucking ye blood of each Others hand," and to reassure themselves, they accepted a charm offered by a free Negro. It was reported by one correspondent that "we have about seventy Negro's in Custody, and 'tis fear'd that most of the Negro's here (who are very numerous) knew of the late conspiracy to murder the Christians."[32]

Though there is no overt evidence of slave disaffection at Pinkster in New York colony, slave resistance anywhere in the colony became a part of the consciousness of slaveholders and of whites generally in attendance at Pinkster, especially when executions occurred in May, the month of Pinkster. Thomas J. Davis writes of another instance of slave resistance in New York City: "Thirteen black men burned at the stake. Seventeen black men hanged. Two white men and two white women also hanged. All thirty-four were executed in New York City between May 11 and August 29, 1741, as part of the episode early New Yorkers called the 'Great Negro Plot' or the 'New York Conspiracy.'"[33] Since slaves in New York City constituted the second largest urban slave population in North America, amounting to 20 percent of the total population and second only to that of Charleston, slave numbers alone caused concern among whites—all the more since the conspiracy, according to Davis, "revealed a range of animosities and patterns of everyday personal relations and interactions among blacks and whites." Though the events of that spring and summer underscored "prevailing racial attitudes" and "the troublesome slave presence" in New York City, whites were also accused of deep involvement in the plot, indeed of having led it. Be that as it may, when "hearing talk and seeing evidence of arson, theft and illicit meetings, the authorities followed public opinion to draw a most threatening picture of the blacks' intentions and the motives of their white companions." The brutality of the punishment indicates something of white concern about maintaining control, and the news of the event and punishment must have spread far and wide, reaching Charley, who was then in his thirties or turning forty, and other blacks in Albany.

But quieter times were more the order of the day in New York; tensions were just beneath the surface but did not often explode into violence. Such was the nature of slavery, however, that in the most unlikely settings, even Pinkster, the consciousness of either slave or master might be clouded with a certain unease. Still, Pinkster at Albany and elsewhere continued to be very much welcomed by slaves. Such was the case for Albany whites as well, and with increasing interest they began gathering to fix their gaze on the winding procession that made its way to Pinkster grounds. Led by Charley— hailed as "King of the Blacks"—a grand assemblage of slaves, lengthening itself and "covered with Pinkster *blummies*—the wild azalea," moved "from young massa's house . . . up State street to Bleecker Street to Bleecker Hill, on the crown of which was the . . . Burying-ground" and the Pinkster field. During Pinkster, the Negroes engaged in games and feasting and, to most whites, appeared to have few if any cares, making merry and "paying homage to the [Pinkster] king, who was held in awe and reverence as an African prince."[34]

By the time blacks began dominating Pinkster, whites no longer held it to religious standards. Their perception of the festival as not particularly religious accounts in part for their willingness to be spectators as blacks, largely untouched by Christianity, took their place at the center of Pinkster performance. The drama with which blacks invested religious activity, the prominence of dance and music in their ceremonies, meant that what was for them, in significant measure, a form of spiritual solace was perceived by whites as mere entertainment.[35] Thus, dance served to conceal religious activity, there being no clear line between sacred and secular dance in the African aesthetic.

Charley's Pinkster king attire "was that of a British brigadier—ample broadcloth scarlet coat, with wide flaps, almost reaching to his heels, and gayly ornamented everywhere with broad tracings of bright gold-lace," a "strange and fantastical costume" considered amusing to most whites, the "dances and antics of the darkies" affording "great amusement for the ancient burghers." Munsell remembered gatherings when Charley, of "charcoal blackness, dressed in his gold laced scarlet coat and yellow britches, used to amuse all the people."[36] While Mikhail Bakhtin reminds us that the election of a king at European carnivals was for laughter's sake, as at Pinkster, references to slaves as "darkies" and "Sambos" and "niggers" polarized the humor in ugly ways and helped set a pattern that would last deep into the twentieth century.[37] But thanks to the interaction between Africans of different ages, African artistic and spiritual values were no less strong. Charley represented a link between generations: he reigned when the much younger Jackey Quackenboss, to whose drum rhythms he danced, was at the height of his powers and possibly the greatest drummer in the slave population, North or South. Quackenboss earned laurels for drumming just as younger slaves around Charley carried them for dance, extending the Albany dance tradition well into the nineteenth century.[38]

A certain joy was no stranger to blacks at Pinkster. As a holiday, Pinkster was, within limits, an occasion for release from the restraints of slavery and a vehicle for lightening spirits made heavy from the weight of the past and present. There was, to be sure, some protection from spiritual pain—the presence of one's own king whose will at Albany was "law among all the negroes."[39] Moreover, so talented a king as Charley invested the office with special dignity that helped enhance slave artistic and spiritual values. Approval of his work in such realms served in some degree to balance the indirect rule of slaves affected through him. Being king cut both ways: There were no extremes of oppression or freedom for blacks at Pinkster. However, the fact that most matters of discord among slaves during Pinkster were considered internal to the slave community and left to Charley to settle—"he had only to decide, and the matter was settled, and his fiat, whatever it might be, was quickly submitted to"—indicates that the artistic and spiritual realms were left largely under his control.[40]

Charley's prime years as an artist were from roughly 1730 to 1755, but by the time James Eights, a native of Albany, saw him in 1770, Charley must have been close to seventy. Eights described him as "tall, thin and athletic; and although the frost of nearly seventy winters had settled on his brow, its chilling influence had not yet extended to his bosom, and he still retained all the vigor and agility of his younger years."[41] Eights thought Pinkster had its "peculiarities" and called African dance and music "singular in the extreme." Indeed, he writes that "everything else connected with this august celebration . . . had its peculiarities." The dance consisted mainly of couples "joining in the performances at varying times, and continuing it with their utmost energy until extreme fatigue or weariness compelled them to give space to a less exhausted set."[42] The vigor and sustained character of the dance to the complex rhythms of the drum convey the African character of the performance. The description of the drum to which the dancers and those in rhythm with them responded and the cries of the drummer in an African tongue provide further insight into the distinctive nature of the ceremony and the aesthetic from which it drew. Eights writes:

The music made use of on this occasion was likewise singular in the extreme. The principal instrument selected to furnish this important portion of the ceremony was a symmetrically formed wooden article usually denominated an *eel-pot,* with a cleanly dressed skin drawn tightly over its wide and open extremity—no doubt obtained expressly for the occasion. . . . Astride this rude utensil sat Jackey Quackenboss, then in his prime of life and well known energy, beating lustily with his naked hands upon its loudly sounding head, successively repeating the ever wild, though euphonic cry of *Hi-a-bomba, bomba, bomba,* in full harmony with the thumping sounds. These vocal sounds were readily taken up and as oft repeated by the female portion of the spectators not otherwise engaged in the exercises of the scene, accompanied by the beating of time with their ungloved hands, in strict accordance with the *eel-pot* melody. . . . Merrily now the dance moved on . . . rapid and furious became their motions . . . copiously flowed the perspiration, in frequent streams, from brow to heel, and still the dance went on in all its energy and might.[43]

The drum was freshly made for the festival, which of itself enhanced the genuineness of Quackenboss's performance. As the performance unfolded, Eights "would oft times turn" and "seek relief by searching for the king . . .

and there enclosed, within their midst, was his stately form beheld, moving along with all the simple grace and elastic action of his youthful days, now with a partner here, and then with another there."[44] Absalom Aimwell observed African women in ring dance at Pinkster:

> Afric's daughters full of glee,
> Join the jolly jubilee.
> Up the green and round the ring,
> They will throng about their king;
> Dancing true in gentle metre,
> Moving every limb and feature.

And again:

> Every colour revels there,
> From Ebon black to lilly fair.
> Ah! How much happiness they see,
> In one short day of Liberty!
> And now they move about the ring,
> To see again the jovial king.
> Charles rejoices at the sight
> And dances, bowing most polite.[45]

Dance, for the African, was a visible sign of complex rhythms related to the gods' or ancestors' use of the body as a temporary abode during religious observances before decamping with the end of spiritual transport. Slaveholders had not the slightest understanding of its being such a vehicle. The frenzied dancing at Pinkster, much of which was not dissimilar to dance on the plantations of the South during ring ceremonies, means that possession was almost certainly a feature of the "performance." In such circular movement one finds a language as familiar to Africans as written script to their European contemporaries, one that reached across the continent symbolically, antedating by a century its presence across the American South as the primary means by which multiethnic union would occur among slaves in the antebellum era.[46]

African ring dance left its impact on white performers trying to imitate blacks. According to Constance Rourke, "The climax of the minstrel performance, the walkaround, with its competitive dances in the maze of a circle, was clearly patterned on Negro dances in the compounds of the great plantations, which in turn went back to the communal dancing of the African." But Rourke does not stop there. She gives us further reason to connect slave culture in the South with slave culture in the North: "The ancestry was hardly remote. Many who saw the minstrels in the Gulf States or along the Mississippi must have remembered those great holidays in New Orleans early in the century when hundreds of Negroes followed through the streets a king chosen for his youth, strength, and blackness."[47] Albany and New Orleans holiday ceremonies shared much in common, including much of the music and dance that slaves brought to the festivals. Challenging competitive dance to Quackenboss's drumming occurred in a "wild and intricate maze," and competitive dance, according to Rourke, occurred in the "maze of a circle" on plantations. Sacred symbolism was even more likely to be called to consciousness when dancing took place on ground used as the slave cemetery, the principal ground for ring dance in North America.[48]

But the Pinkster slave cemetery could cause psychic and spiritual pain that could never be forgiven by some slaves who visited Pinkster grounds:

> Now if you take a farther round
> You'll reach the Africs' burying ground.
> There *as* I *rambled* years ago,
> To pass an hour of love-lorn woe;
> I found a stone at Dinah's grave,
> On which was carv'd the following stave

>> Here lie Dinah, Sambo wife
>> Sambo lub her like he life;
>> Dinah die 'bout sik week go,
>> Sambo massa tell him so.[49]

Such was the importance of funerals to the African that one doubts that cruelty of that sort could have been widespread in slavery without the institution's best interest being seriously at risk.

For the African, the cemetery mirrored the other world and was a grim reminder of the losses of life on this side of the divide, especially at Pinkster, for the Pinkster burying ground was where Albany blacks were executed. Such was the case in 1793, when two black women and one black man, accused of having set the downtown area of Albany on fire, devastating a wide swath of dwellings and businesses, were hanged, then buried on Pinkster ground. Into the cemetery setting, terror was once more introduced.[50] What possessed the city fathers to have executions on the ground of the dead is not fully understood, but mere convenience is not the complete answer. The placement and the use of gallows on such ground was yet another assault on the spirits of blacks that failed to shatter them. Still, Albany slaves regarded the funeral as the most sacred of all ceremonies and whenever possible would have brought to it African practices proper to the ceremony, for evidence abounds elsewhere in the colony that African burial practices were, whenever possible, followed.

In fact, perhaps in no sphere were slaves more successful than in providing a proper burial for their deceased. Pivotal to that process was the belief, widely shared in Africa, that a proper burial fosters the serenity of the spirit when it passes to the other side; otherwise, bad luck is likely to befall the living. A proper burial hinges on careful command of certain West African practices, "the deliberate decoration of graves in the African manner with surface deposits of broken earthenware and possessions," writes art historian Robert Farris Thompson. Regarding possessions, one of Thompson's informants observed: "They used to put the things a person used last on the grave. This was supposed to satisfy the spirit." And another: "Everybody there threw a handful of dirt on the grave and when the gravediggers fixed the mound we put some of Catherine's things on the top. There was a little flower vase with the bottom knocked out, and the pitcher she made ice water in." Thompson notes: "The last detail is impressive. An intimate act characteristic of the deceased is recalled forever on the surface of the grave by means of the particular object selected. What appears to be a random accumulation is in fact the distillation of a life."[51]

During a recent construction project in New York City, workers rediscovered the African Burial Ground, a cemetery in which twenty thousand slaves were buried before the cemetery was closed in the 1790s. Earthenware, broken glass, and toys were found by archaeologists, which establish the presence of West African funeral rites in the colonial North. Indeed, the toys found at grave sites have great spiritual meaning since half the black population of New York City, over generations, is thought to have died at birth or in early childhood. The placement of the toys on the burial mounds of children represented the distillation of their lives and attempts to satisfy their spirits. Another fascinating find was a "British marine officer's" uniform apparently worn by a slave "of high status," which calls to mind King Charley in his British brigadier's coat.[52] Though some men, women, and children were buried in wooden coffins and sometimes had headstones above them, the evidence from these graves indicates clearly that slaves in New York City adhered to certain unmistakable African practices.[53] Such principles and practices did not come suddenly into being, like Athena from the head of Zeus. Their presence has been noted over centuries in West Africa.

Despite restrictions on slave burial rites following the New York Conspiracy of 1741—no more than twelve slaves were permitted to attend funerals because it was thought resistance might occur, and palls could not be used to cover coffins for fear that weapons might be secreted beneath them—it is reported that "heathenish rites" were performed over the deceased.[54] One such rite involved the placing of food on top of the grave to nourish the spirit of the deceased, and we know that shells, when they could be found, were placed on top of graves and, at least in one instance, in the grave next to the head of the deceased. The shell probably represented the Bakongo four moments of the sun principle. According to Thompson, "Shells thus become visual synonyms for persistence and the immortal spiral in the sky, the journey of the sun, emphasizing that traditional Kongo time is circular." The souls of the deceased are thought to be "second suns, moving through time and space, following the circle of the sun from east to north to west," counterclockwise as in ring dance.[55] With such practices occurring despite restrictions on burial rites and in the shadow of gallows on the Common nearby, burial rites in the black burial ground were African to a surprising degree and practiced throughout much of the seventeenth century. While relatively little is known about the Albany Pinkster cemetery, that site almost certainly contains African artifacts.

Recalling old and recent deaths of family members and friends at Pinkster brought sorrow, as did the eventual appropriation by whites of forms of cultural expression brought to the Albany festival by slaves. Interest in black music and dance at Pinkster drew the attention of white performers, especially that of John Diamond, the greatest white dancer in America in the 1830s and 1840s.[56] Thought to have been influenced by King Charley's dance style, Diamond was perhaps the most gifted of white minstrels. Considering Albany's reputation as a center of black music and dance, it is possible that he and other minstrels visited Albany to study black dance and music as whites are thought to have visited plantations to copy black performance styles, for Munsell writes: "Charley generally led off the dance, when the Samboes and Philises, juvenile and antiquated, would put in the double-shuffle-heel-and-toe-breakdown, in a manner that would have thrown Master Diamond and other modern *cork*-onions somewhat in the *shade*." In a formulation that seems, at least in part, to base white minstrelsy on the performances of blacks at Pinkster, Munsell, writing in 1871, adds: "Negro minstrelsy has held its own down to the present day, it now being in full feather, and is likely to continue for years to come."[57]

Minstrelsy was an encrustation of distortions that disfigured and concealed what was authentic about slave and free black music and dance, to say nothing of religion. Thus, the conception of black music, and especially dance, as frivolous was deepened by minstrelsy as some white performers launched commercially rewarding careers. Still, slave celebrations and festivals in Albany and elsewhere in New York led to the affirmation of aspects of the African aesthetic by growing numbers of whites. White performers listened to black music and watched blacks dance, with some, in time, patterning their art after that of blacks. As the black aesthetic spread, dance and music were increasingly united, the emotive and intuitive were drawn on in greater measure, and the techniques of African art avidly studied by aspiring performers. The process began before the replacement of whites at the center of Pinkster performance by blacks, certainly by the time Charley was recognized as an exemplary practitioner of African music and dance.

It was nearly three quarters of a century later that young Herman Melville began hearing of Charley the legendary dancer and king of the blacks. Since his school, the Albany Academy, almost shared Pinkster grounds, what Pinkster Hill represented in its earlier days was often a matter of interest for him. In later years, certainly by the time he was well into his teens, Melville made the association between the Pinkster Hill cemetery in Albany and New York City's "Negroes Burial Ground" and the Common, which were but a ten-minute walk from where the Melvilles at one time lived before moving to Albany. The importance of the cemetery to blacks and its close association with artistic expression were known to Melville, who could contrast this with the tendency of white Americans, even into the early nineteenth century, to keep cemeteries at a distance. The spirit of artistic expression at Pinkster—the Common was an important locus of Pinkster activity in New York City—was not divorced from the dead, as Melville was aware. People of African ancestry revered the ground of the dead as a place from which art finds expression and the symbolic nurturing of the dead occurs. In remarkable degree, Melville, by the time he began writing, was exposed to African cultural values, thanks to experiences mainly in Albany and New York City.

The supreme proof of Melville's command of such values is found in his presentation of them in *Moby-Dick*.[58] His is no romanticized depiction of African culture; rather, the negative attitudes toward blacks at Pinkster and elsewhere are found in the novel even as African spirituality is universalized: sailors from around the globe do a ring dance to the music of the tambourine that recalls dance to that instrument on the decks of slave ships. But this time the authorial context is radically different, for the dance in "Midnight, Forecastle" of *Moby-Dick* is the one most prized by slaves in North America, the sacred Ring Shout, dating back to Quackenboss, Charley, and thousands more at Pinkster. In the novel the double-shuffle for which Charley was known follows the ring dance so evident when he held forth. Melville linked the two, one growing out of the other, and he refers to the former, the ring portion, as "Indian-file," the Ring Shout so dreaded by missionaries in Melville's time attempting to convert slaves to Christianity. Largely through his sense of dance in New York, in one of the finest and most subtle treatments of that art in American literature, Melville immortalized African spirituality.[59]

Notes

1. Alan Lomax, *The Folk Songs of North America* (Garden City, N.Y., 1960), 514.
2. Constance Rourke, *The Roots of American Culture* (New York, 1942), 3, 5.

3. Neil Harris, *The Artist in American Society* (New York, 1966), vii.

4. Injunctions against artistic performance did not undermine the desire of whites to be entertained by artists, which helped clear the way for them to become spectators at performances by black artists before imitating them, a pattern that we see taking shape at least as early as the mid-eighteenth century. For the best discussion of minstrelsy, see David Roediger, *The Wages of Whiteness* (New York, 1991), chap. 4.

5. Thomas Jefferson, *Notes on the State of Virginia* (1787; reprint, New York, 1982), 140; André Malraux, "Behind the Mask of Africa," *New York Times Magazine*, May 5, 1966, 30.

6. Jon Butler, *Awash in a Sea of Faith: Christianizing the American People* (Cambridge, Mass., 1990), 129–30.

7. Butler, *Awash in a Sea of Faith*, 130. The neglect of dance in studies of slavery is rife. Even less observable are treatments of dance that incorporate music and treatments of music that incorporate dance, as in Africa and in American slavery. Thus, the power of slave dance to regulate Christianity has been missed by nearly all historians. This is as curious a development as can be found in the study of slavery, for it is rare to encounter a primary source that treats slave religion on plantations in which dance is not prominent.

8. A fine discussion of this is found in McKinley Helm's biography of singer Roland Hayes, in which Hayes asserts: "To native Africans, sexual intercourse is creative and holy, allusions to it in their songs are respectful, not obscene; and the bodily movement which accompanies the performance of songs of love is not vulgar to African eyes. On the contrary, it is an artistic symbol of exalted experience." McKinley Helm, *Angel Mo' and Her Son, Roland Hayes* (Boston, 1942), 29.

9. The resilience of dance, African and African-American, has nowhere been better demonstrated than in the writing of novelist Richard Wright, who once thought slaves in America, almost from the beginning, were bereft of African values. Wright correctly sees the survival of African dance forms in America for a period extending over centuries. See Richard Wright, *Black Power* (New York, 1954), 56, 57.

10. The most striking example of dance being midwife to music is found in the Ring Shout, a sacred dance of Africans in slavery that contributed greatly to the birth of jazz. See Marshall W. Stearns, *The Story of Jazz* (New York, 1956), 12–15. I am led to the formulation regarding music's relationship to dance by a remark of Paul Robeson, who once referred to the spiritual as "the soul of the race made manifest." *New York Times*, April 5, 1931.

11. André Malraux writes that "Africa has transformed dancing throughout the world—this is its first contribution to the art of dancing." Malraux, "Behind the Mask," 30. A fine example of that influence in America is the Charleston, which surfaced out of slavery to have a profound effect on American popular culture following World War I. For a detailed consideration of the impact of black dance on the larger society, see Lynne Emery, *Black Dance* (Princeton, N.J., 1972), and Jean and Marshall Stearns, *Jazz Dance* (1964; reprint, New York, 1968), esp. pts. 4–6.

12. Robert Farris Thompson, "African Influence on the Art of the United States," in *Black Studies in the University*, ed. Armstead L. Robinson (New Haven, Conn., 1969), 126; Paul Robeson, "By 'n' By," *The Power and the Glory*, Columbia Records 47337.

13. See Joseph J. Rubin and Charles H. Brown, *Walt Whitman of the New York Aurora* (State College, Pa., 1950), 21; Walt Whitman, "Song of Myself" (1855), in *Walt Whitman: Complete Poetry and Collected Prose* (New York, 1982), 36.

14. Sterling Stuckey, "The Tambourine in Glory: African Culture and Melville's Art," in *The Cambridge Companion to Melville*, ed. Robert Levine (New York, 1998), 37–64.

15. Theodore Canot, *Adventures of an African Slaver* (New York, 1928), 73; Richard Drake, *Revelations of a Slave Smuggler* (New York, 1860), 44.

16. Tom Feelings, *Middle Passage: White Ships, Black Cargo* (New York, 1995). Blier, who had seen Feelings's workbook of drawings, made the comment during a break at "The Herskovits Legacy," a symposium at the Schomberg Center for Research in Black Culture of the New York Public Library, May 27 and 28, 1988.

17. W. E. B. DuBois, *Black Folk Then and Now* (1939; reprint, Millwood, N.Y., 1975), 144.

18. E. C. L. Adams, *Tales of the Congaree* (Chapel Hill, N.C., 1987), 277–78.

19. See Lorenzo Turner, *Africanisms in the Gullah Dialect* (Chicago, 1949), 193. I would like to thank linguist John Rickford of Stanford for bringing the Kikongo word *mfinda* to my attention years ago (interview with author, spring 1981). In addition to the tales collected by Adams, there is Reverend William John Faulkner's marvelous *The Days When the Animals Talked* (Chicago, 1977).

20. Adams, *Tales*, 121.

21. The best study of Bakongo faith and art is Robert Farris Thompson, *The Four Moments of the Sun* (Washington, D.C., 1981), 27–54.

22. For an extended discussion of African ethnicity in antebellum America, see Sterling Stuckey, *Slave Culture: Nationalist Theory and the Foundation of Black America* (New York, 1987), chap. 1.

23. Edmund S. Morgan, *American Slavery, American Freedom: The Ordeal of Colonial Virginia* (New York, 1975), 1–6; Curtis P. Nettles, *The Emergence of a National Economy: The Economic History of the United States*, 2 vols. (New York, 1962), 2:49. As Peter Wood has demonstrated, nowhere was the master class more dependent on slave labor than in colonial South Carolina. Peter Wood, *Black Majority: Negroes in Colonial South Carolina from 1670 through the Stono Rebellion* (New York, 1974), chaps. 2, 4. See also Robert McColley, *Slavery and Jeffersonian Virginia* (Urbana, Ill., 1964), chap. 1.

24. Joel Munsell, *Collections of Albany* (Albany, N.Y., 1865), 56.

25. Phillip D. Curtin, *The Atlantic Slave Trade* (Madison, Wisc., 1969), 143. To Curtin's credit, he does identify ethnic people affected by the trade but without discussion of cultural consequences in the Americas.

26. Gabriel Furman, *Antiquities of Long Island*, ed. Frank Moore (New York, 1874), 265–66 (emphasis in original).

27. Edgar McManus, *A History of Negro Slavery in New York* (Syracuse, N.Y., 1966), 197. For a superb discussion of the collective nature of African song, including work songs, see Alan Lomax, *Folk Songs of North America*, part 4.

28. McManus, *History of Negro Slavery in New York*, 197–98, 198–99.

29. Munsell, *Collections of Albany*, 56. The continuing strength of African languages in the North in the eighteenth century and later is another indication of the power of African culture in America. John Fanning Watson writes of a ceremony in a Philadelphia cemetery circa 1800, in which Africans from various ethnic groups participated, that recalls the concerted yet distinctive activity of ethnic Africans in the Vesey conspiracy in Charleston, South Carolina, in 1822. Watson has this to say about the burial field: "In that field could be seen at once more than one thousand of both sexes, divided into numerous little squads, dancing, and singing, 'each in their own tongue,' after the customs of their several nations in Africa." Watson,

Annals of Philadelphia (Philadelphia, 1856–57), 2:265. In Rhode Island, during Election Day ceremonies in the last half of the eighteenth century, the announcement of the "governor" of blacks was known to bring on "a general shout . . . every voice upon its highest key, in all the various languages of Africa." See Orville Platt, "Negro Governors," *Papers of the New Haven Colony Historical Society* 6 (1900): 319; also see Hubert H. S. Aimes, "African Institutions in America," *Journal of American Folklore* 18 (Jan.–March 1905):15. For discussion of African languages and slaves elsewhere in America, North and South, see Stuckey, *Slave Culture*, chap. 1. The importance of the fact that whites did not learn African languages can scarcely be exaggerated when studying the means by which Africans were able to retain important features of their value system. For a pioneering study of Africans bearing the burden of languages, see David Dalby, *Black through White: Patterns of Communication* (Bloomington, Ind., 1970).

30. Alice Morse Earle, *Colonial Days in Old New York* (New York, 1896), 196.

31. See E. A. A., "Sassafras and Swinglingtow: or, Pinkster Was a Holiday," *American Notes and Queries* (June 1946): 38.

32. Herbert Aptheker, *American Negro Slave Revolts*, rev. ed. (New York, 1974), 172. Twenty-seven slaves were condemned for their part in the conspiracy, although six, including a pregnant woman, were pardoned. The form of punishment meted out to the other twenty-one was defined by the whim of the governor, hence "some were burnt others hanged, one broke on the wheele, and one hung a live in chains in the town, so that there has been the most exemplary punishment inflicted that could be possibly thought of" (p. 173).

33. Thomas J. Davis, *A Rumor of Revolt* (New York, 1985), ix.

34. "A Glimpse of an Old Dutch Town," *Harper's New Monthly Magazine* 62 (March 1881): 525–26.

35. For a pathfinding discussion of the drama of black religion, of the reproduction in the church "in microcosm" of "the great world from which the Negro is cut off by color-prejudice and social condition," see W. E. B. DuBois, *The Souls of Black Folk* (1903; reprint, New York, 1989), 133–37.

36. "A Glimpse of an Old Dutch Town," 526; Munsell, *Collections of Albany*, 56. Also see E. A. A., "Sassafras and Swinglingtow," 38.

37. Mikhail Bakhtin, *Rabelais and His World*, trans. Hélène Iswolsky (Bloomington, Ind., 1984), 7. A description of Pinkster in New York City that typifies this type of ugly humor can be found in James Fenimore Cooper's, *Satanstoe* (1845; reprint, New York [c. 1937]), 58, 73, 74.

38. James Eights, "Pinkster Festivities in Albany," in *Readings in Black American Music*, comp. and ed. Eileen Southern (New York, 1971), 41.

39. Furman, *Antiquities*, 268.

40. Ibid., 269.

41. Eights, "Pinkster Festivities," 44. Eileen Southern believes the "event described by Eights took place in the 1770's" (*Readings in Black American Music* [New York, 1971], 41). The original edition of Eights's description of Pinkster was published in Albany in 1867.

42. Eights, "Pinkster Festivities," 45–46.

43. Ibid., 46.

44. Ibid.

45. Absalom Aimwell, "Pinkster Ode, Albany, 1803," *New York Folklore Quarterly* 8 (spring 1952): 36, 42.

46. See Zora Neale Hurston, *The Sanctified Church* (Berkeley, Calif., 1981), 103.

For the uses of dance to effect unity across cultures, see Stuckey, *Slave Culture*, chap. 1.

47. Constance Rourke, *American Humor* (1931; reprint, Tallahassee, Fla., 1986), 88, 89.

48. The phrase "wild and intricate maze" is taken from Eights, "Pinkster Festivities," 46. For numerous examples of Ring Dance in cemeteries, see Georgia Writers' Project, *Drums and Shadows* (1940; reprint, Athens, Ga., 1986). Here is one such example out of Georgia: "Ain so long sence dey stop makin drums. Wen I wuz a young man, we use to make em. . . . Dey wuz bout fo feet high. At duh fewnul wen we beat duh drum we mahch roun duh grabe in a ring" (*Drums and Shadows*, 107).

49. Aimwell, "Ode," 42, 43.

50. Joel Munsell, *Collections: History of Albany* (Albany, N.Y., 1867), 378–83.

51. Thompson, "African Influence on the Art of the United States," 150–51.

52. Is this the grave of Charley's counterpart at New York's Pinkster? That is a possibility. Since Charley lived to such a great age in Albany, it would seem unlikely that he would have been taken to New York City and to have died there, but we cannot at this stage be certain. What *is* certain is that not just any slave could have worn such a uniform and that such a person would have attracted attention at any festival in New York City.

53. "Black Cemetery Yields Wealth of History," *New York Times*, August 9, 1992.

54. "A Black Cemetery Takes Its Place in History," *New York Times*, Sunday, February 28, 1993, sec. 4-1. In 1865 one David T. Valentine, a nineteenth-century local historian, wrote concerning Africans and the Negroes Burial Ground: "Many of them were native Africans, imported hither in slave ships, and retaining their native superstitions and burial customs, among which was that of burying by night, with various mumuries and outcries. This custom was finally prohibited by the authorities from its dangerous and exciting tendencies among the blacks." "Dig Unearths Early Black Burial Ground," *New York Times*, October 9, 1991.

55. Thompson, *Four Moments*, 43–44. A related interpretation of the meaning of the shell has been offered by the current archaeologist of New York City, Daniel N. Pagano, who thinks the shell "ties into one of the traditional sayings, 'By the sea we came, by the sea we shall go' and was perhaps symbolic of spiritual freedom" ("Black Cemetery Yields Wealth of History").

56. Stearns and Stearns, *Jazz Dance*, 46

57. Munsell, *Collections of Albany*, 56.

58. Herman Melville, *Moby-Dick* (1851; reprint, New York, 1950), chap. 40.

59. Stuckey, "Tambourine in Glory"; Ezra Stiles Ely, review of "Methodist Error" [by John Fanning Watson], *Quarterly Theological Review* 2 (April 1819): 226, 228–29.

Laurel Thatcher Ulrich

SHEEP IN THE PARLOR, WHEELS ON THE COMMON: PASTORALISM AND POVERTY IN EIGHTEENTH-CENTURY BOSTON

 ON AUGUST 13, 1753, three hundred spinners, some children as young as seven or eight, carried their wheels to Boston Common, where they demonstrated their skill for the assembled crowd. This remarkable demonstration was the culminating event in a day-long celebration sponsored by the Boston Society for Encouraging Industry and Employing the Poor. Already supported by subscriptions from local merchants and by a healthy subsidy from the town, the society hoped to raise additional funds to support a large spinning factory it was building on Tremont Street. The crowd on the Common in the afternoon was almost as large as at one of George Whitefield's revivals, but there was no sign of the disorder some contemporaries associated with religious enthusiasm. The spinners sat in three neat rows, their wheels at attention, as their benefactors walked by, reviewing them almost as if they had been a company of militia.[1]

Meanwhile, another group of girls was busy at Abigail Hiller's school on Cambridge Street and at Elizabeth Murray's shop near the upper end of King Street, producing sheep for the parlor. Woolly with French knots or sleek as satin, these embroidered creatures pranced across the valances of bed curtains or grazed in pictorial pastures framed in walnut and gold. The young embroiderers were the daughters of New England's most prominent families—Mary Pickering and Sally Derby came from Salem; Sarah Warren, Hannah Otis, and Eunice Bourne from Barnstable; Priscilla Allen from Cape Elizabeth in what is now Maine; and Faith Trumbull from Connecticut. Their brothers at Harvard, the girls entered less well-known but equally elite institutions, learning dancing, penmanship, and fine stitchery.[2]

Sheep in the parlor, wheels on the Common: at first glance the two phenomena seem related to each other ironically, if at all. Yet the very distance between them is instructive. The spinning factory and the embroidery schools were dual manifestations of growing inequality in colonial Boston and of the Anglicization that apparently accompanied it. As Gary Nash long ago explained, the spinning factory developed during a period of economic and social distress. Faced with an escalating poor rate and a surplus of dependent widows and children, Massachusetts authorities "reached out in their frustration at mid-century to grasp at a straw that had floated across the Atlantic"—the notion of building a factory to employ the poor.[3] Decorative arts scholars argue that out of this same "urban crucible" emerged a vibrant new consumer economy that sustained silversmiths, cabinetmakers, clockmakers, engravers, printers, wigmakers, jappaners, mantua makers, upholsterers, and a host of proprietory schools and shops that sold expensive fabrics and threads, sheet music and instruments, and taught young ladies to dance, draw, speak fashionable French, and embroider pastoral images on canvas and linen. Pastoralism was so much a part of the Anglicized culture of mid-eighteenth-century Boston that when the young John Singleton Copley began his career in the 1750s, he painted a young Boston woman as a shepherdess.[4]

That pastoralism and poverty appeared together in colonial Boston is hardly surprising. Literary scholars have observed the same conjunction of idealized landscapes and economic distress in seventeenth- and early-eighteenth-century England. Following Raymond Williams, they argue that pastoral poetry served the needs of a landed gentry and nobility that wished to naturalize their own appropriation of common lands. As legalism supplanted moral economy and as notions of agricultural improvement eroded customary rights and obligations, country house poems and pastoral lyrics obscured the struggles of the poor "beneath predominantly celebratory images of a countryside bursting with produce and nurturing values of rural community." During the same decades, merchant clothiers reorganized textile production, putting out raw materials to poor cottagers for spinning.[5]

There is more logic than may at first appear, then, in combining a study of schemes for employing the poor with an analysis of pastoral embroidery. Both topics become more interesting, however, when seen in the light of rural manufacturing. This essay offers a three-part look at "women's work" in the region. It begins with a reassessment of the factory, moves to a broader discussion of textile manufacturing, and concludes with some observations on pastoral embroidery. It argues that beneath the seeming differences, elite women, rural women, and poor widows and their children shared common assumptions about the relationship between work and marriage. The dependence of poor women exposed the constraints facing all women, while the textile work of rural women parodied the artistic productions of elite women. Looked at together, the three groups help us to see the intersections of class and gender in eighteenth-century New England.

The Boston Factory

I still remember the excitement I felt when I first read Gary Nash's "The Failure of Female Factory Labor in Colonial Boston." Deep in research for the dissertation that eventually became my first book, I was reassured to know that one of the best of the new social historians believed it possible to reconstruct the working lives of women. Although Boston was not part of my own study, I was inspired by Nash's ability to tease out evidence from fragmentary sources. Building on essays by Patricia Branca, Olwen Hufton, Theresa McBride, and others, he demonstrated that Boston women, like laboring-class women in other settings, were working women, though much of their work took place beyond the sight of conventional records. Wives "contributed to the family economy by helping in their husbands' shops, taking in washing, serving as seamstresses for middle- and upper-class families, and doing daytime domestic labor in the houses of the well-to-do." Since Boston received few of the immigrants and slaves that supplied labor needs elsewhere, much of the demand for household workers "must have been filled by young, unmarried women and by the wives of lower-class men." Anomalies in Boston census records suggested that Boston widows were renting rooms and furnishing board to transients and unmarried mariners.[6]

The imperial wars of the 1740s took a disproportionate toll on Boston's economy. "While in Philadelphia and New York the legislatures avoided war taxes by authorizing only a few companies of provincial troops, Massachusetts sent large numbers of its men off to die of starvation and disease." War and the depression in shipping that followed devastated the city's maritime economy, filling the port with widows and their children. Unwilling to send respectable families to the almshouse or the workhouse, Boston leaders hit upon the idea of manufacturing linen. Opening free spinning schools, they advertised abroad for skilled weavers, eventually opening a factory where poor but willing workers would spin yarn under their protective care. The factory failed, not only because of technical difficulties in producing cloth as cheaply as it could be done in Britain but because "many poor women refused to submit to a work routine that disrupted their way of life and split dual functions of laboring-class women—work and family

—into separate spheres." Although ministers decried "the Swarms of Children of both Sexes, that are continually strolling and playing about the Streets of our Metropolis, cloathed in Rags and brought up in Idelness and Ignorance," the town fathers were ultimately unwilling "to deny aid to women who would not submit to factory work for meager wages."[7]

Nash implied that the experiment might actually have succeeded if Boston officials had been willing to adopt a kind of "workfare," cutting off relief to those who refused to come into the factory. "It was this lack of coercion by elected officials that allowed most of Boston's widows and children to remain in their homes, spinning as time allowed within their familial routines." Nash admitted that the evidence of women's resistance was "mostly indirect," but it was consistent with scattered references that showed far more cloth being produced for "Private persons" than in the factory. In an argument inspired as much by E. P. Thompson as by the new feminist history, Nash concluded that the spinning factory failed not because it was attempting to make the wrong product in the wrong time and place but because the values of entrepreneurial capitalism had not yet banished moral economy. Because town officials were unwilling to force poor women and their children into the unfamiliar routines of industrial labor, the factory could not turn a profit. "Boston's leaders had found a way of making work for the poor and unemployed but had not discovered how to adapt the work to the needs and values of those who were to do it."[8]

As an exercise in historical detection, "The Failure of Female Factory Labor in Colonial Boston" was impressive. It rescued an intriguing episode in colonial history from antiquarian marginality and in the process gave the poor women of Boston a small place in history. Twenty years later it is difficult to fault the broader argument that the spinning factory collapsed because the model of manufacturing it borrowed from England was ill-suited to local circumstances. That the major problem was the resistance of poor women seems less certain, however. The same set of documents suggests another explanation, that it was not the "needs and values" of working women that doomed the Boston spinning factory but faulty economics. Attempting to replicate patterns of production borrowed from commercial cloth-making districts of Ireland, the society channeled far more of its resources into the hands of male weavers, suppliers, overseers, and construction workers than ever reached the poor.

If the purpose of the factory was to bring down the cost of poor relief, the town fathers picked an expensive way to do so. In order to employ a few hundred spinners, they had to organize and sustain a complex operation that required both a large capital investment at the outset and continuous and careful management throughout. The public pronouncements of the Society for Encouraging Industry and Employing the Poor made the project seem easy. All they had to do was open the factory and the poor would flock to its doors, transforming indigence into industry, unused time into cloth. Their own records reveal the frustrating realities behind that dream. The managers had to recruit and train spinners, purchase raw materials far beyond what they could initially process, buy tools and implements, and pay able-bodied men (not poor women and children) to perform essential tasks in production such as hatcheling, bleaching, dying, and weaving, all the while generating enough income to pay for fundraising, rent, fuel, and housing.

An anonymous correspondent to a Boston newspaper argued that the spinning factory would contribute to the good of society "by taking away all pretence from a Number of idle Beggars, who are a Scandal to every Community, pointing out the Way in which they have it in their Power to get an honest Livelihood for themselves and their Families, and obliging them to enter upon it." This could only be accomplished, of course, "by witholding that injudicious Relief, which is distributed at our Doors, and which by a very mistaken Apellation, is usually term'd *Charity*."[9] Yet the factory itself was an even more conspicuous recipient of charity. Although detailed accounts of income and manufacturing costs do not survive, a summary of auxiliary credits and debits for the period 1751–1759 is revealing. "Coating, hankerchiefs, Linning & other Manufactures" yielded profits of only £165.13.6, or 2 percent of the recorded income during that period. Contributions from subscribers totaled more than £1,200. Other gifts, including a "Ladies Donation" of £87.16.4, brought the total on the credit side to £1845.17, barely enough to match debits for wood, rent, printer's bills, clerical fees, wages for a school mistress, and payments to the master weaver, Elisha Brown. These totals do not include the £1,800 the society spent on its handsome brick building, an enterprise financed by government loans and subsidies.[10]

The society was able to raise all this money because for a time it convinced underwriters that the project would soon be self-sustaining. In February 1753, a Boston newspaper reported that in the past three months, the factory had made "four hundred eighty nine Yards of Cloth, on Account of the Company, and three hundred and forty Yards on Account of private People." Even in the aftermath of a smallpox epidemic, there seems to have been no shortage of workers. "The Spinners are now so increased, that there is paid to them by the Company and private Persons, Fifty Pounds and upwards, old Tenor, weekly, and there will be considerable more paid weekly, as the Days grow longer." The spinning school had already supplied "a great many excellent Spinners" and there were hopes of many more. Surely, Boston was about to solve its poor relief problem. Poor children would no longer go hungry or be clothed in rags. Poor laborers would be relieved of part of their burden of supporting their families. Even the fishery would be assisted "as the Women and Children might get a Living for themselves, while the Men were upon their Voyages." The province as a whole would also be blessed. Farmers in Massachusetts would be encouraged to raise more flax and the factory would no longer have to import "the greatest Part of what we use from the neighboring Governments."[11]

This was an amazing projection since the output the newspaper reported could only have provided work over the three months for a single weaver and about ten spinners working full time. Production no doubt accelerated. "Mr Brown says he can gett 100 Spinners this Winter," an unsigned document in the company papers asserts, adding that "21 Looms have been Employed for a year or two & no want of spinners." But that level of production was never sustained. By 1759 the company was so deeply in debt that the General Court ordered their building sold at auction. Over the ten years it was in operation, the factory produced 17,221 yards of cloth "on account of the Company" and another 35,441 for "Private persons," barely enough cloth to keep one loom working full-time. It is hardly surprising that the society (and its public benefactors) eventually gave up trying to keep it going.[12]

The ratio of company production to private production led Gary Nash to conclude that poor women withdrew their labor from the factory; "they preferred to stay at home, working at their wheels in their free time, selling their yarn to independent weavers, and counting on private and public relief to supplement their meager income."[13] Poor women may have disdained factory labor. Nothing in the sources, however, suggests that work for private persons in any way undermined the activities of the factory which existed not so much for spinning as for producing finished cloth. In its first advertisement, the company informed the public that "sundry Looms for weaving of Linen of all Sorts, are set up at the Linen Manufactory-House in the Common, below the Seat of Thomas Hancock, Esq; where all Persons may have their Yarn wove in the best and cheapest Manner." Although the company distinguished beween cloth made on its own account and that woven for private persons, it relied for its success on both. The 1753 report, for example, used payments to spinners "by the Company and private Persons" as evidence that the enterprise was accomplishing its objective of providing employment to the poor.[14]

The secondary sources on which Nash relied may have led him to draw too sharp a distinction between factory work and work performed at home. In the nineteenth century, mechanized spinning required centralized production. That was not the case in the eighteenth century. There is no reason to believe that widows with very young children could not have spun at home. The factory may not have been designed primarily for adult workers, however, but for children. The specter of unsupervised children, begging or playing in the streets, enters all the arguments in favor of the factory. For indigent families, factory work may have been an attractive alternative to having their offspring bound out by the overseers of the poor. Certainly, the spinning schools offered poor girls opportunities they could get nowhere else. Sharon Braslaw's study of public indentures in Boston has shown that while poor boys were usually apprenticed to craftsmen with the promise that they be offered some kind of vocational training, girls were bound out to upper-class families as household servants. Private indentures discriminated against girls in the same way, the words *art, trade, and mystery* being crossed out when the child being apprenticed was a female.[15]

Training and managing a troop of very young workers (or conversely, placing bundles of flax in individual households) cannot have been easy. According to the 1767 report, the 23,757 pounds of flax the society purchased "should have made at least as many yards of cloth, whereas only 17,221 yards were made."[16] That is, 25 percent of the company's projected output simply disappeared. Yarn produced by inexperienced spinners may have been too coarse or weak to be used, or workers in or out of the factory may have stolen materials. Just as likely, the flax may have been of poor quality to begin with and the projections themselves flawed, being based on maximum rather than probable yields. Whatever the reason for the slippage, it exposes the complexity of hand production. Spinning alone guaranteed neither the success nor the failure of clothmaking.

A set of "schedules" compiled by the society or its successors of 1767 shows the relationship of spinning to other tasks. "Mr. James Traits scheme for making Linnen Cloth," for example, gives detailed costs for producing plain linen in eleven grades, ranging from 800 to 1,800 threads "in the Reed." (The higher the reed count, the finer the fabric.) In addition to spinning, there were costs for winding, washing, dressing, warping, weaving, and bleaching, and for ashes used in processing yarn. A second table offers relative costs of raw materials, spinning, and weaving for nineteen different kinds of plain cloth. Spinning ranged from 30 percent of the cost of coarser fabrics to 47 percent in the highest grades. Since the Boston factory operated at the lower end, we may presume that costs of raw materials, warping, weaving, and bleaching always outweighed spinning.[17]

From a purely economic point of view, then, Boston offered only one advantage to a would-be manufacturer—an apparent supply of poor spinners. Since raw materials had to be brought in from "neighboring provinces" or abroad, prices and supplies were never certain.[18] Weavers, like the production schedules they worked with, also were imported: Irishmen who brought with them clear ideas about the rights and prerogatives of their craft. Since they were paid by the yard rather than the hour, they wanted compensation for the extra time and trouble required to warp and weave poorly spun yarn, and they insisted on receiving an extra day's pay for every piece of linen under twenty yards. Since the costs for spinning almost exactly matched the costs for weaving most fabrics, the company's records inadvertently reveal that wages for weavers were as much as ten times those for spinners. Over and over again, records note that "1 Loom will Employ 10 Spinners" (a ratio typical of commercial cloth-producing enterprises everywhere in this period).[19]

The full significance of the Boston spinning factory can be grasped, therefore, only when we consider all the costs of production. Comparing the Boston factory with contemporary rural manufacturing reinforces the point. Crucial to an understanding of preindustrial production is the distinction between spinning and weaving. Understanding a gender division of labor that brought apprentice-trained males from Ireland is essential to understanding the differences between urban and rural production.

Rural Production

In a report to the Boston town meeting on December 2, 1767, a committee appointed to consider reopening the factory offered a clear-eyed assessment of the difficulties of urban manufacturing. Having "made a full enquiry into the steps taken by the late society for carrying on the Linnen Manufacturer, and the method they pursued for establishing the same, Examined all their Books and Accompts, and procured from several of the Gentlemen concerned all the information relative to their proceedings in that Business they were able to give," they concluded that linen manufacturing could be undertaken once again "if the Government would give encouragement," that is, if the old game of subsidies and subscriptions could be renewed. They added that "the carrying on this Business in a Factory will be attended with greater Expence than in private Families (as by experience has been found in Scotland & Ireland as well as among ourselves) where the Spinning and Weaving are done when they have no other Employ, whereas in a Factory they must be wholly supported by the Manufacture therefore cannot afford their work so cheap."[20] The committee did not propose abandoning the factory. Instead they suggested switching to a new product.

Learning that "from the surest advices they have obtained from many parts of this Province, that the Woolen & Linnen Manufactures are carried on to so great a degree, as that a very great part of the Inhabitants in most Towns supply themselves with their own Cloathing," the Boston committee suggested that instead of trying to make fabrics for clothing and household use, they focus on sailcloth or duck for outfitting ships. They noted that "Mr. John Brown who now lives in the Factory, did make a proposal that he would engage on certain Conditions to manufacture and deliver them Linnens at the same price they are imported from London," but after careful examination they concluded that it was not "practicable for him to comply with the proposals he had made." Sailcloth was a more reliable enterprise because it was "less liable to so many accidents as the Linnen, nor so great an Expence to establish it." Furthermore, it could be made from either flax or hemp; and since hemp could, if necessary, be gotten from Russia, the manufactury would not be so "liable to fail by reason of a drought."[21]

Ample evidence sustains the committee's assertions that families in towns outside Boston were engaged in household manufacturing, but the circumstances of manufacture were quite different there from those of textile-producing areas of Ireland, Scotland, England, and the Continent. In Europe, men still did the weaving, some working as independent producers, many as rural outworkers. In New England, sometime in the second quarter of the eighteenth century, families abandoned the gender division of labor that had long prevailed elsewhere (and that the Boston Society had attempted to replicate). At all levels of the social spectrum, cloth making became a female enterprise. Although few women wove for pay, most produced for household use, producing simple fabrics used for work shirts, grain bags, handkerchiefs, aprons, rough blankets, and, as their skill improved, sheets, towels, and tablecloths. In Boston, poor women and children worked for wages a tenth of those paid male artisans. In the countryside, wives and daughters typically worked for free.

The feminization of weaving can be traced through changes in the ratios of wheels and looms in probate inventories. In seventeenth-century New England spinning was done at home, but because weaving was part of a male occupational system in which tools and skills, like land, were passed on from father to son or transmitted through formal apprenticeship, most towns had only a few skilled weavers. In Essex County, Massachusetts, for example, nearly half of household inventories listed spinning wheels by 1700, but only 6 percent had looms. In the early decades of the eighteenth century, however, a surprising new pattern developed, not only in Essex County but nearly everywhere else in New England. Rural families began to acquire looms, and women began to weave part-time as other household duties allowed. In rural Suffolk County, Massachusetts, the area just outside Boston, there was one household with a loom for every two or three owning wheels by 1750. By the time of the revolution, 69 percent of Suffolk County probate inventories listed wheels and 24 percent had looms.[22]

The contrast with Boston is stark. Only two of fifty-one Boston inventories for the 1750s listed wheels. None had a loom. Shopkeeper John Osborne kept his wheels upstairs in the "Negro's Chamber." Widow Mary Downing owned two spinning wheels as well as a few yards of homespun, though most of the fabrics in her shop were imported. In the rural Suffolk sample, on the other hand, twenty-five of forty-five inventories had wheels, and seven had looms. Wheel owners were scattered across the social spectrum. Daniel Smith of Walpole, husbandman, owned thirteen sheep and lambs and coarse woolen cloth as well as wheels. Jacob Beal of Hingham, yeoman, also claimed unprocessed flax and "a loom and tackling." Abel Cushing of Hingham, gentleman, owned a fulling mill, spinning wheels, eighty sheep and thirty lambs, and an eighth interest in a sloop.[23]

The records of those "neighboring provinces" that presumably supplied flax to the Boston factory in the 1750s show even more evidence of household manufacturing. In New Hampshire in the period 1749–1753, 73 percent of inventories listed wheels and 23 percent looms. In Warwick, Rhode Island, 64 percent had wheels and 16 percent had looms. Percentages in Connecticut were similar. It is important to recognize that the intensification of household manufacuring long predated the boycotts of the 1760s. There is little difference between the distribution of cloth-making equipment at midcentury and in the 1770s. In rural Suffolk County, however, the boycotts may have had some effect. Whereas in 1750 only 39 percent of inventories listed wheels, the number soared to 62 percent in 1774. The ratio of looms to wheels remained about the same; 15 percent of households had looms in 1750 and 24 percent in 1774.

In Boston, however, old patterns persisted. In Alice Hanson Jones's 1774 inventories, only that of William Molineux, merchant, included equipment for manufacturing. This is not surprising. In 1769 the Boston town meeting had voted to give "Mr. Mullineux" £200 "to enable him to purchase Spinning Wheels, Cards, and to procure convenient place and Appartments for carrying on the Spinning Business, and a sufficient number of Spinning Mistresses well skilled and experience in the Art and Mistery of spinning Wool into good Yarn," all for the relief of the poor. [24] To the end of the eighteenth century, textile manufacturing in Boston remained a heirarchical (and unsuccessful) enterprise organized by gentlemen for the employment of the poor.

Textile production thrived in the countryside, just as the Boston committee suggested, because it allowed families to make use of bits and pieces of time. No person could sustain herself, let alone support a family, on spinning and weaving alone; but with raw materials produced on their own farms, wives and daughters could make fabrics that might otherwise drain a family's credit at the store. Families with marriageable daughters made the most cloth. Manufacturing fabrics for sheets, towels, tablecloths, pillow cases, blankets, and coverlets, young women between the ages of fifteen and twenty-five relieved their fathers of some of the expense of oufitting them for marriage. The link between household production and marriage was symbolized in wool breaking, flax scutching, spinning, and quilting "frolics" that, like husking bees and communal house raisings, brought men and women together for work and play.

Spinning frolics took on patriotic significance during the revolution. In 1769–1770 hundreds of rural women gathered at their ministers' houses to demonstrate patriotism, charity, and their skill at spinning. Some of these spinning demonstrations imitated elements of the Boston affair of 1753. In Dorchester and Brookfield, spinners gathered with their wheels on the green; in Braintree and Bridgewater there were parades; and in Gloucester, Chebacco, Linebrook, Newburyport, Braintree, and Rowley, Massachusetts, spinning matches were preceded by sermons. The Society for Encouraging Industry and Employing the Poor had exported little cloth to the countryside in the ten years of its operation, but in the realm of public relations it had passed along a few good ideas.[25]

The contrast between country and town is amplified in private papers. Mary Palmer Tyler, who grew up in Boston in a prosperous merchant family, had no experience with textile manufacturing until her father's business failure forced the family to relocate in Framingham, Massachusetts. "We learned to spin," she wrote, "borrowing wheels of our good-natured neighbors, who seemed pleased to teach the city ladies their craft."[26] Ruth Belknap responded differently. When her husband became pastor of the Congregational Church in Dover, New Hampshire, she discovered that it was more difficult in the country than in town to appropriate other women's labor. In a mock pastoral poem titled "The Pleasures of a Country Life," she complained about the vicissitudes of life without a maid. Addressing her verses to "starch'd up folks that live in town," she satirized the pastoral images that her own generation of girls had stitched so patiently into the borders of their petticoats and samplers.

> . . . my spouse can get no cloaths
> Unless I much offend my nose.
> For all that try it know it's true
> is no smell like colouring blue.
> Then round the parish I must ride
> And make enquiry far and wide
> To find some girl that is a spinner,
> Then hurry home to get my dinner.[27]

In both accounts, pastoral dreams dissipated when real wool and flax appeared.

New England Pastoral

At first glance the pastoral embroideries of colonial Boston seem insubstantial, derivative, worthy of parody. When they are examined in their immediate context, however, they too have a great deal to tell us about the intersection of class, gender, and textiles. Made from imported materials, they connected New England's aspiring families to the imagery and habits of the English gentry. They were not unrelated to the values that sent young girls into spinning schools in the 1750s, however, or that kept rural women bent over looms. As artifacts of female socialization, they celebrated private property, companionate marriage, and female industry.

Colonial Boston had dozens of schools at midcentury, not just town schools, spinning schools, and the famous Latin school but entrepreneurial schools run by ambitious craftsmen and tradespeople. When John Singleton Copley's mother married the engraver Peter Pelham in 1753, she moved from Long Wharf into a neighborhood filled with such enterprises. Not far from where the new Mistress Pelham kept her tobacco shop ("in Lindel's Row, against the Quaker's Meeting House, near the upper End of King Street, Boston"), Elizabeth Murray offered both the latest imported English goods and instruction in needlework. Copley's stepbrother, Charles Pelham, offered lessons in "English manners, reading, writing, arithmetic, needlework, dancing, painting on glass, and French."[28] There were also notable schools in the North End, such as that of Susanna Condy, wife of Boston's writing master. When Mistress Condy died, her sister-in-law, Abigail Hiller, opened a school in Fish Street near the Baptist Meeting House where she taught "Dresden and Embroidery on Gauze, tenth Stitch and all sorts of coloured Work." She also took "young Ladies to board or half board, at a very reasonable Rate; likewise sells Gold and Silver Gymp, Plate, Twist and Thread, Shades of Naples."[29]

Pictorial embroideries were almost always created in such schools—the teacher or a hired assistant drawing the designs, the young ladies working them with various degrees of success. The most elaborate works, called "chimney pieces" by contemporaries, were meant to be hung on the wood paneling above a fireplace. A panel worked by Eunice Bourne of Barnstable exemplifies a cluster of closely related embroideries, usually referred to as the "fishing woman" pictures because of the frequent use of an identical image of a woman with a suitor at her side dangling her fishing pole into a tiny pond. (The prototype may have been an illustration on a contemporary playing card.) To the right of the fishing couple in Eunice's picture is a country maiden with her swain, to the left a woman spinning with an old-fashioned distaff and drop spindle. Three lambs cavort nearby. Whoever drew Eunice's picture had a repertoire of pastoral images borrowed from prints or from

English schools that could appear alone or together in various combinations. Traced onto canvas in simple outlines, they could be embellished according to the whim of the embroiderer and the direction of the teacher.

These scenes are charming in part because they have no grounding in time or space. Although some of the clothing in Eunice's picture vaguely alludes to the early eighteenth century, the activities and accessories are stylized. No one in colonial New England was spinning with a drop spindle. As Alexander Pope, the most prominent eighteenth-century theorist wrote: "[P]astoral is an image of what they call the Golden age. So that we are not to describe our shepherds as shepherds at this day really are, but as they may be conceiv'd then to have been; when the best of men follow'd the employment." It is exactly this element of the genre that has attracted the ire of twentieth-century scholars. At a time when rural workers were being forced off their land or into low-paid outwork, it was useful for landlords to revel in a nostalgic vision of a once golden age.[30] In New England, however, it was not landlords who promoted pastoral but an aspiring elite of merchants, ministers, ship captains, artisans, and farmers who in other parts of the world would have been considered middle-class.

In getting at the significance of these pictures, it helps to think about what they do *not* do. Although they focus on rural life, they do not acknowledge the hard labor of planting or reaping. Nor do they represent family life. There are no babes in arms or descending ranks of children, as in much folk art from early nineteenth-century New England. Our eighteenth-century embroideries submerge gender inequalities in an idealized vision of heterosexual love. In doing so, they build on European motifs. As one renaissance theorist explained, love and art come together most naturally in pastoral settings. "The playing of music was invented during herding—either as a natural impulse, or in imitation of the birds and the rustling of the trees. For leisure is the source of pleasure and wantonness." The shepherd, having leisure and "being well-fed with milk and meat, encouraged by the clement season and solitude, and having no experience of sorrow, fear, or hate, very easily enters upon sexual intercourse."[31]

Although New England schoolmistresses would no doubt have been horrified to read of such connections, the embroideries they created were ultimately derived from such materials.[32] Men and women in these pictures are situated in a middle space between the realm of streets, wharfs, and counting houses and the interior world of families. Courting couples are as essential a part of the imagery as sheep. In this natural landscape (as perhaps nowhere else) they join in a relation of equality and complementarity. It is the equality of idealized love.

In the poems of Boston's Mercy Otis Warren such images take on political significance as well. Writing in 1766 to her husband, James, who was then in Boston, she invoked the world of pastoral:

> Come leave the noisy smoky town
> Where vice and folly reign,
> The vain pursuits of busy men
> We wisely will disdain
> . . . .
> The solemn shades, the sylvan scene
> All nature bright array
> Secure and guard the wandering mind
> From errors baneful way.[33]

At one level, the poem voices an artful plea from a lonely lover. At another, it is a statement about the centrality of private happiness in the political vocabulary of revolutionary America. Vice and folly belong to the town; sylvan scenes restore virtue.[34]

This same contrast between city and town persists in Warren's plays. Although her political satire typically employs a male voice, in the epilogue to her play *The Group*, pastoral enters in a short poem "spoken by a Lady."

> What painful scenes are hovering o'er the morn,
> When spring again invigorates the lawn!
> Instead of the gay landscape's beauteous dies,
> Must the stained field salute our weeping eyes.[35]

This is pastoral mutating into mourning (as in dozens of silk embroideries of the late eighteenth century). The message is clear: Bad politics and rapacious commerce destroy the sylvan scene. Good politics preserves it. Although ladies had no direct role in politics, they were central to the production of political imagery, as mistresses of country houses, mates of public officials, celebrants of private virtues, and guardians of sylvan scenes.

Although pastoral imagery transformed rural labor into artful leisure,[36] the production of pastoral embroideries was itself a kind of work, as any eighteenth-century schoolgirl could attest. As a popular sampler verse put it, "This needle work of mine can tell / When I was young I learned well / And by my elders I was taught / Not to spend my time for naught." Precisely placed stitches trained a hand for future work—for seaming and hemming sheets, constructing baby clothing and men's shirts, and marking linens with fine cross-stitch. Stitchery also trained the mind and spirit. A sampler of 1747 spoke to viewers then and now:

> Behold the labour of my tender age
> And view this work which did my hours engage
> With anxious care I did these colours place
> A smile to gain from my dear parents face
> Whose care for me I ever will regard
> And hope that heaven will give a kind reward.[37]

Little girls from prosperous families began their education in stitchery at about the same time Boston's poor children began to spin—at about seven or eight. Large pastoral embroideries like those of Eunice Bourne were made by more experienced embroiderers, often young women in the years just before marriage.

The artificiality of eighteenth-century pastoral should not confuse us. Embroidered landscapes celebrate private property, companionate marriage, and female industry—the pursuit of happiness, American style. In a few works the connection between pastoral scenes and gentrified New England become more explicit. In these pieces, upholstered chairs, serving trays, and backgammon tables show up in grassy landscapes, and houses begin to look less like mythical English cottages than the Georgian mansions inhabited by New England elites. One of the most striking examples of this move toward specificity is a chimney piece completed about 1750 by Mercy Otis Warren's sister, Hannah. At first glance the picture appears to be a typical rural landscape with oversized birds, strawberries, a courting couple, and a prancing horseman like those in the fishing lady embroideries. Indeed, it may have been stitched in the same Boston school where Hannah's Barnstable neighbor, Eunice Bourne, completed her embroidery. Unmistakably planted at right center, however, is Thomas Hancock's Boston mansion. Although a miniature sailboat on the tiny pond nearby offers only the faintest allusion to the maritime source of Hancock's fortune, the representation of the house, with Beacon Hill and Old North Church steeple in the background, is unmistakable. (The beacon on the hill is complete with tripod and flarepot.)[38] Yet except for the steeple, nothing in Hannah's picture indicates its urban setting, certainly no glimpse of the crowded streets that brought three hundred spinners onto Boston Common on August 8, 1753, a few hundred feet from Hancock's house.

In the sermon he preached before the Society for Encouraging Industry and Employing the Poor that day, Samuel Cooper shifted back and forth between Puritan condemnations of idleness, Whiggish celebrations of commercial wealth, and pastoralized visions of New England. Charitable Bostonians should surely continue to "visit *helpless* poverty, in her retired Abodes," he insisted, yet they must "take Care, that these Bounties do not become the Wages of Idleness." Only full employment can "make Plenty and happiness circulate thro' a whole Community." In the most poetic part of the sermon, Cooper imagined a world in which a specter called "Idleness" would succumb to a hero called "Industry": "When we mention this Vertue, we cannot but immediately reflect upon the Blessings, which under the Smiles of Providence, it has procured to Mankind;—the Fields it has planted and reaped;—the Flocks and Herds it has raised;—the Cities it has founded and supported:—the Navies it has built; and the

Commerce it has sustained. Industry, turns even the Wilderness into a fruitful Field, and the barren Rock into a luxurious Soil."[39] It was not men and women who planted and reaped those fields, but an abstraction called "industry."

Industry flourishes, he continued, only where liberty prevails. In some countries, tyranny robbed men of "the Fruits of honest Diligence," but in a place where "every Man may *sit under his own Vine, and under his own Fig-Tree;* and enjoy with Security, what he has earned with the Sweat of his Face," there was no excuse for failing to encourage industry. It seems not to have occurred to Cooper that Boston's poor widows neither sat under their own vines and fig trees nor participated in the political liberties of the Boston town meeting. They were dependents, a problem for the Overseers of the Poor. Had Boston's poor been predominately male, Cooper's arguments about the fruits of political and economic liberty would have been more difficult to make. Because his poor laborers were women and children, he could offer moral rather than material rewards for their labor. "Spinning is a Work, peculiarly adapted to prevent Idleness," he continued, noting that since "it may be laid aside and resumed many Times in a Day, without Disadvantage," it might "fill up those little Vacancies of Time, that necessarily intervene between other Kinds of Business." Furthermore, spinning would inculcate good habits in "the Children of the Town, and especially those of the lower Sort." Industry, he continued, "adds something, even to the innocent Gaiety and Sprightliness of Childhood."[40] *Gaiety* and *Sprightliness* are words one could more easily apply to the cheerful embroiderers of the proprietary schools. Filling their tightly stretched canvases with frolicking lambs, oversized birds, and happy couples, these young ladies gave visual form to the vines and fig trees of Cooper's sermon. But the children of the spinning school were important too. If property-owning households were the foundation of the state, then women and children without husbands and fathers required the sustenance and the direction of civil authorities. Carrying their wheels onto the common, Cooper's diminutive spinners contributed a little something to their families and a great deal to the social vision of an emerging America. Meanwhile, in the unheated chambers of rural New England, ordinary girls acted out a different form of pastoral. Wrapped in rough blankets of their own manufacture, they dreamed of their country swains, pledging their hearts and hands to household industry.

In different settings and with different resources, daughters of the urban poor, the provincial gentry, and the rural yeomanry created exemplary textiles. Sheep in the parlor, like wheels on the Common, celebrated industry, private property, and a sex/gender system that grounded women's work in the household.

Notes

1. *Boston Evening-Post*, quoted in Samuel Barber, *Boston Common* (Boston, 1914), 69. The same story appears in the *Boston Gazette*, August 14, 1753.

2. *The Boston Evening-Post*, March 26, April 9, 1753; Betty Ring, *Girlhood Embroidery: American Samplers and Pictorial Needlework, 1650–1850*, 2 vols. (New York, 1993), 1:44–59 and figs. 40, 43, 44, 56, 57.

3. Gary B. Nash, "The Failure of Female Factory Labor in Colonial Boston," *Labor History* 20 (1970): 165–88, 187.

4. Paul Staiti, "Accounting for Copley," in *John Singleton Copley in America*, ed. Carrie Rebora and Paul Staiti et al. (New York, 1995), 26–28, 176–77. Copley may have been imitating the English painter Joseph Blackburn who painted Mary Sylvester as a shepherdess in Boston in 1754.

5. Andrew McRae, *God Speed the Plough: The Representation of Agrarian England, 1500–1660* (Cambridge, 1996), 262, 263. Also see Raymond Williams, *The Country and the City* (New York, 1973); Louis Adrian Montrose, "Of Gentlemen and Shepherds: The Politics of Elizabethan Pastoral Form," *English Literary History* 50 (1983): 416; Don E. Wayne, *Penshurst: The Semiotics of Place and the Poetics of History* (London, 1984), 263. The literature on English pastoral is complex and contradictory. Obviously, a genre that has survived for so many centuries has many manifestations. Useful studies include James Turner, *The Politics of Landscape: Rural Scenery and Society in English Poetry 1630–1660* (Oxford, 1979); Andrew V. Ettin, *Literature and the Pastoral* (New Haven, Conn., and London, 1984); E. Kegel-Brinkgreve, *The Echoing Woods: Bucolic and Pastoral from Theocritus to Wordsworth* (Amsterdam, 1990), and Roger Sales, *English Literature in History, 1780–1830: Pastoral and Politics* (London, 1983).

6. Nash, "The Failure of Female Factory Labor," 181–83.

7. Ibid., 180, 187, 188, 183–84.

8. Ibid., 188.

9. "The present State of the Linen Manufacture in Boston represented, and its Support recommended. In a Letter to a Friend," *The Boston Evening-Post*, February 26, 1753.

10. Ezekiel Price Papers, Massachusetts Historical Society, Boston, 311–14 (hereafter cited as Price Papers).

11. *Boston Evening-Post*, 19 February 1753.

12. A note in the company records says that "a good Workman may make 12 or 16 yds a day of 3/4 wide or 10 or 12 of 7/8 or 8 or 10 yd wd"; 522,662 yards in 10 years amounts to 5,266 yards per year. At an average of 10 yards per day, that is 526 days' weaving. Price Papers, 318, 361.

13. Nash, "The Failure of Female Factory Labor," 184–85.

14. Price Papers, 329. A note in the company's records suggests that Hancock himself took advantage of the operation, having cloth made on his own account that yielded a profit of "15 to 20 p Cent."

15. In 1757, for example, Lucy Camp, the daughter of widow Sarah How, was bound out "to Saml Wethered of Boston, Innholder, as a menial servant." The lines on the printed form requiring instruction were crossed out. For this and other indentures, see Bourn Family Papers, Houghton Library, Harvard University, Cambridge, Mass., Ms Am 579, 580, 589, and vol. 5, p. 165.

16. Price Papers, 318.

17. Ibid., 359–62.

18. A report to the Boston town meeting suggested that the Boston factory hurt badly when drought in the region reduced its supply of flax. *A Report of the Record Commissioners of the City of Boston, Containing the Boston Town Records, 1758 to 1769* (Boston, 1886), 231. On the need to purchase large quantities of flax in advance, see Price Papers, 319–22.

19. *Boston Evening-Post*, July 9, 1750, December 10, 1750; Price Papers, 359. Also see Price Papers, 364–69, for proposed plans for importing weavers and bleachers in 1768.

20. *Report of the Record Commissioners*, 227.

21. Ibid., 236. A draft of the committee's proposal in Ezekiel Goldthwait's handwriting is in Price Papers, 301.

22. Laurel Thatcher Ulrich, "Wheels, Looms, and the Gender Division of Labor in Eighteenth-Century New England," *WMQ* 3d ser., 55 (1998): 3–38. All data from probate inventories given below is from this source unless otherwise indicated.

23. Suffolk County Probate Records, Massachusetts State Archives, Boston, 44:517, 45:190, 44:142; 44:351, 44:260 .

24. "Inventory of the Goods and Estate of William Molineux," in Alice Hanson Jones, *American Colonial Wealth: Documents and Methods* (New York, 1977), 958–60; *Report of the Record Commissioners*, 274–77. All other numbers are from Ulrich, "Wheels, Looms," 37–38.

25. On revolutionary-era spinning bees, see Mary Beth Norton, *Liberty's Daughters: The Revolutionary Experience of American Women, 1750–1800* (Boston, 1980); Laurel Thatcher Ulrich, "Daughters of Liberty: Religious Women in Revolutionary New England," in *Women in the Age of the American Revolution*, ed. Ronald Hoffman and Peter J. Albert (Charlottesville, Va., 1989), 211–28; and Alfred Young "The Women of Boston: 'Persons of Consequence' in the Making of the American Revolution, 1765–76," in *Women and Politics in the Age of the Democratic Revolution*, ed. Harriet B. Applewhite and Darline G. Levy (Ann Arbor, Mich., 1990), 181–226.

26. *Grandmother Tyler's Book: The Recollections of Mary Palmer Tyler, 1775–1866*, ed. Frederick Tupper and Helen Tyler Brown (New York, 1925), 141.

27. *CHMS*, 6th. ser., 4:228–29. The poem was included in a letter written by Ruth Belknap's husband, Jeremy, who was then pastor of the Congregational Church in Dover, New Hampshire.

28. Lawrence A. Cremin, *American Education: The Colonial Experience, 1607–1783* (New York, 1970), 400–401; Paul Staiti, "Accounting for Copley," 28, 29; Ring, *Girlhood Embroidery*, 1:55 n. 4.

29. Staiti, "Accounting for Copley," 26–28; Ring, *Girlhood Embroidery*, 1:40, 42, and front endpapers; also see *Boston Evening-Post*, February 1 and 8, 1748.

30. Quoted in Ettin, *Literature and the Pastoral*, 6.

31. Kegel-Brinkgreve, *Echoing Woods*, 42.

32. This conforms with Richard Bushman's larger argument about the origins of American gentility in *The Refinement of America* (New York, 1992).

33. Rosemarie Zagarri, *A Woman's Dilemma: Mercy Otis Warren and the American Revolution* (Wheeling, Ill., 1995), 45.

34. Compare a typical sampler verse of the early republic: "Here in this green and shady bower / Delicious fruits and fragrant flowers / Virtue shall dwell with this seat / Virtue alone can make it sweet." Betty Ring, *American Needlework Treasures*

(New York, 1987), 18. On the multiple and changing meanings of virtue in this period, see Ruth H. Bloch, "The Gendered Meanings of Virtue in Revolutionary America," *Signs* 13 (1987): 37–59.

35. Mercy Otis Warren, "The Group," in *Plays by Early American Women, 1775–1850*, ed. Amelia Howe Kritzer (Ann Arbor. Mich., 1995), 52–53.

36. See, for example, Jeanne Boydston, *Home and Work: Housework, Wages, and the Ideology of Labor in the Early Republic* (New York, 1990), 142–63.

37, Ethel Stanwood Bolton and Eva Johnston Coe, *American Samplers* (Boston, 1921), 271, 272.

38. Ring, *Girlhood Embroidery*, 1:49, fig. 47.

39. Samuel Cooper, *A Sermon Preached in Boston, New-England, before the Society for Encouraging Industry and Employing the Poor: August 8, 1753* (Boston, 1753), 7, 27–28.

40. Ibid., 32.

■ *Conceptualizing Inequality*

Ronald Schultz

A CLASS SOCIETY? THE NATURE OF INEQUALITY IN EARLY AMERICA

INEQUALITY PERVADED THE early modern Atlantic world. From the centralizing monarchies of northwestern Europe, through the caliphates of northern and western Africa to the indigenous empires of Central and South America, the Atlantic world presented a vast and complex panorama of domination and subordination. Taking a variety of forms, complex systems of inequality divided people throughout the Atlantic world and placed them in hierarchical relations of wealth, power, and social prestige.

Of these systems of inequality, class is perhaps the least well understood. This claim may at first appear absurd, for historians have employed class for as long as they have written history. Ruling classes, working classes, and most ubiquitously, middle classes have populated much of modern historical writing. But while many historians have employed the term, few have dealt with class as an inherently historical phenomenon. Whether they seek to define the class nature of early modern society or, alternatively, attempt to show the irrelevance of class in this formative era, the concept of class they employ often derives from understandings current in the middle to late nineteenth century. Created to explain the phenomenon of industrial capitalist society, these explanations of class are at once historically specific and limited in their range. Yet despite some recent attempts to abandon the concept of class, it remains an essential concept in understanding past societies because economic inequality was an intrinsic and vital part of those societies. We need, then, an alternative way of approaching class, one that takes into account both the classical analyses of industrial capitalist society and the postmodern criticisms of class. This essay suggests a different view of class, one that can help to explain its role in American societies before the development of full-scale industrial capitalism in the late nineteenth century. It begins with a critical review of the most salient theories of class and social division, suggests an alternative way of conceiving class, and concludes with an examination of early American society in light of this alternative formulation.[1]

Ironically, the person most closely associated with the concept of class in modern times never wrote about class and class formation in any systematic way.[2] Karl Marx's project lay elsewhere. His fundamentally Hegelian aim was to chart the historical transformation of human productive systems, leading ultimately from humankind's bondage to nature to its emancipation from natural restraints and the eventual creation of a world of true freedom. For Marx, history was a passage from exploitation to freedom, and his foremost contribution to understanding this process was his analysis of mid-nineteenth-century industrial capitalism. For Marx, all previous productive systems had been exploitative and had created highly visible classes of exploiters and exploited. Greek and Roman slave owners, for example, had openly exploited the labor of their bondspeople just as medieval lords had blatantly exploited the labor of their serfs. Exploitation and class relationships were palpable and transparent in these early productive systems, and physical force was nakedly and brutally expressed. Capitalism, however, was different. The employer-employee relationship that was the signal expression of capitalism was the result of legal contract, not the exercise of brute force. Exploitation under capitalism was hidden, so much so that many nineteenth- and twentieth-century writers have denied that it existed at all. For his part, Marx was sure it did, and he traced the origins of exploitation to the twin facts that workers, who had no access to the means of production, could survive only through the sale of their labor and that employers could only survive by paying their workers wages that were less than the value of the products they produced.[3] Class, for Marx, was thus always a social relationship of exploitation, a relationship of production that rested on the extraction of surplus labor.

Another founder of modern social thought, Max Weber, wrote more than his predecessor about class, and he too placed it at the center of his analysis of modern society.[4] Weber wrote from the perspective of liberal individualism, and for him class was but one way in which people related to one another in society. Like Marx, Weber located class in the realm of productive relations, although for him class was less involved with exploitation than with the differential control that disparate groups possessed over a society's resources. But while Marx and Weber might have disagreed about this point, they agreed that class was a central feature of all recorded societies. Indeed, for Weber, class was one of the prime determinants of an individual's "life chances."

Marx and Weber parted intellectual company over the issue of the centrality of class in explaining modern (and future) societies. For Weber, class was important but no more so than status or party. Bureaucratic organizations and party politics were equally significant determinants of social position and life chances, and they did not always correlate with class. Bureaucrats and politicians, he pointed out, controlled powerful social resources even though they came mostly from the middle rather than the upper classes. Status, too, possessed its own social value and could elevate a charismatic figure well above his or her economic position in society. Power within society, Weber suggested, was not only rooted in the control of productive resources but of other social resources as well. None of these variables alone dictated a person's social position and life chances.

The conception of class has resonated with one or the other of these two views for much of the twentieth century, and clearly defined Marxist and Weberian schools have characterized the development of sociology and political science as well as the social sciences in general. Historians, however, have been slower to adopt these theoretical orientations, although some historians have written from a Marxist perspective since the late nineteenth century. Generally holding to older traditions of empiricism, historians have only recently made explicitly *theoretical* contributions to an understanding of class relations.[5] One of the most important of these historians was Edward Thompson. Dissatisfied with a Marxist scholarship that rehearsed theoretical concepts more than it probed the ambiguities of human history, Thompson set forth a concept of class that was both theoretically rigorous and distinctly historical.[6] Although he worked within a generally Marxist paradigm, Thompson rejected the determinism that had come to define much mid-twentieth-century Marxist writing. Class, he wrote, was not about "so many people in this or that relation to the means of production." It was instead about historical relationships: "class . . . is a *historical* category," he argued, and "we know about class because people have repeatedly behaved in class ways."[7]

For Thompson, most Marxist and social scientific writers had reified class, making what was relational into something concrete and immobile, an object possessing a life and logic of its own. Against this concept of class, Thompson counterposed a world of agency, experience, and pressures. He accepted the fundamental Marxist notion that class ws ultimately rooted in productive relationships. But rather than deriving notions of action, ideology, or political consciousness from these relationships, as traditional Marxists had done, Thompson made class formation historically contingent. People felt the effects of their class position in the experiences of their everyday work and domestic lives and consequently found themselves pushed in the direction of class awareness. But, Thompson went on to argue, the reality of class experience could do little more than exert personal and collective pressures; it could not create class consciousness or institutions. In Thompson's mind, class was a process of discovery whereby everyday experiences of exploitation and social and political subordination brought subordinate people to realize their position and to act individually and collectively to liberate themselves.

Thompson's writings have been enormously influential among social historians in general and labor historians in particular. By making ordinary people into actors rather than passive bearers of their class position, Thompson both historicized the concept of class and introduced a measure of indeterminacy into the process of class formation. Class, for him, was something that "happened" because people used their native intellects and their indigenous cultures to claim control over their own lives. Thompson thus attempted to position himself midway between Marx and Weber, accepting the productive emphasis of the one and the multidimensionality of social experience of the other. Although subtle and sensitive to other realms of experience, however, Thompson's position was ultimately that of Marx, for the power of productive relations always won out in the end.[8] The pressures exerted by class relations, rooted in the social relations of production and the economy, ultimately determined the outcome of historically contingent situations. Thompson emphasized individual and collective agency, but in the end, people responded to their experiences in ways that were already structured and given. The dead hand of the Marxist past lay heavily on Thompson's project; still, Thompson was instrumental in moving the debate about class onto specifically historical terrain and in so doing made a return to essentialism and determinism untenable.[9]

If class could not helpfully be derived from productive relations either directly or indirectly, was class a concept that could explain human action? By the late 1970s one answer was that it could not. Influenced by the intellectual preoccupation of postwar French intellectuals with linguistics and structuralism, a growing number of thinkers reacted to the poverty of essentialist social theories and proposed alternative concepts of social organization.[10] The most important of these writers for historians was Michel Foucault.[11] Proceeding from Nietzsche's *Genealogy of Morals* rather than Marx's *Capital*, Foucault located power, exploitation, and domination not in any specific social relationship but within all relationships in modern society. For Foucault, power and hence domination and exploitation had no center but pervaded Western society from the early modern era onward. Class was thus not an objective social "fact" but a subjective creation. What Marxists have called class, Foucault would view as cultural constructions of social division and power that have been historically developed and "deployed" throughout society.[12]

Given his highly abstract notions of power and domination, Foucault's conception of society has often been portrayed as antihistorical and even as anticlass. Yet Foucault has much to offer historians. First, by rejecting Durkheimian notions of social "facts" in favor of constructed relationships, Foucault makes all social theory intrinsically historical. Since ideologies and institutions are historically contingent in Foucault's view, any account of society must be historically specific. Second, and most important, by shifting the locus of power away from transhistorical, essentialist categories, Foucault permits us to understand better the personal and psychologically internalized notion of power that has been the hallmark of early modern and modern societies. In many respects, Foucault's social universe parallels that of Thompson: the indeterminacy of social relations, the historically specific construction of relations of inequality and domination, the deconstruction of received patterns of political legitimation. Where they differ is in Foucault's denial of any determining pressure exerted by productive (or any other) relations that would guarantee the eventual construction of class relationships. Although Foucault was notoriously slippery on the question of causation, he rejected entirely the idea of indirect determinacy espoused by Thompson.

What then is class? Is it merely a transient historical construction, or is it something fundamental to the makeup of society? At its most abstract, asymmetrical control of resources has been a characteristic of all surplus-producing societies, and that asymmetry is the most basic definition of class. Beginning with the Neolithic agricultural revolutions of Europe, Asia, and the Americas, the ability of human societies to produce surpluses has led to the development of groups who labor and those who live from the labor of others. Over time, this fundamental asymmetry has led to the institutionalization of power, often transmitted via kinship systems. In this respect, Marx was correct: the history of all previous societies had been a history of class. But it is one thing to claim that class existed in all historical societies and quite another to argue that all societies have been organized around a central social relationship. Here Weber and Foucault provide a useful alternative to a notion of class as the central principle of social organization.

Class can best be understood by employing a modified Marxian definition. At the heart of this view lies the idea that human societies support two sorts of productive relationships: one connects people with nature (whence they obtain food and raw materials) and the other connects people with one another (in which they transform nature into usable and salable products). Class exists when one group of people controls access to work and nature, either through direct force or the ownership of property, and forces those who lack this access to relinquish some portion of their labor to them. Class is, by definition, an exploitative relationship, whether the relationship is direct—as in the case of feudal serfs—or indirect, as in the case of industrial workers.

Relationships of exploitation are, however, not the only forms of power and control in society, as Weber and, most importantly, Foucault remind us. Class is only one among many forms of social asymmetry in wealth, power, and prestige. In this way, class coexists with other forms of power—kinship, gender, religion, politics, and the like. In any particular society one of these relationships may dominate and structure the others, or alternatively, none may exercise hegemonic power. The relationship between the different forms of power in any society is thus a profoundly *historical* question, one that cannot be derived from any set of theoretical propositions. Kinship may dominate some societies because of the military force and prestige deployed by kings and may dominate other societies that lack centralized authority. But equally, kinship may dominate a society through the use of force—for example, among the tribal clans of seventh-century Arabia—and religious groups such as the Society of Friends may dominate wealth, trade, and politics through relationships with their co-religionists, as in colonial Pennsylvania. The particular constellation of social divisions and power in a society is never predetermined but is always the result of historical relationships between people.

If we accept this notion of class as a social phenomenon embedded in a shifting constellation of forces, we are then in a position to consider the nature of class from a different perspective. If class relations have existed in one form or another in all historical societies, then our inquiries ought to be about the relationship between class and other forces in society and its relative importance to other forms of social division and inequality. In short, while class is always present in society, it is not necessarily a society's organizing concept. Class may be either a centered or decentered aspect of a particular historical society.

An analogy might prove helpful at this point. Imagine a small pond into which some small stones of equal size are thrown from points around the pond's perimeter. The resulting waves will radiate outward from the point of the stones' entries and will eventually interact in increasingly complex ways. Equal-size stones guarantee that no one wave pattern from any particular stone will dominate the wave patterns in the pond. If, however, we substitute a very large rock for one of the original stones, the resulting wave patterns will be entirely different. The greater energy stored in the rock will create one large and powerful wave that will structure and dominate the smaller waves.

Societies with decentered sources of power and inequality act very much like the pond in the first example: all forces operate, but none dominates. But in some societies, one source of power will become dominant, and as a result, power in that society will flow very much like the large wave in the second example. In the American context, much of pre-nineteenth-century society resembled the initial example, with multiple, decentered sources of power. Only at the beginning of the nineteenth century did one of these forces—capitalism and its associated class structure—begin to dominate the others and threaten to become the central organizing principle of society.

In early America a variety of inequalities structured society. Their constellation is best described by a series of broad and overlapping arcs, each delineating the geographical limits of a productive system. The first of these arcs ran west to east across New Spain and the lands bordering the Gulf of Mexico, terminating at the mouth of the Mississippi River. This region encompassed the societies of the Spanish conquest and were decisively shaped by the Spanish quest for gold and souls beginning in the sixteenth century. The second arc begins at the far end of the Lesser Antilles near Barbados and swings northwestward through the Caribbean, Florida, and coastal North America, terminating in the upper Chesapeake Bay. These societies were formed around the European plantation complex.[13] A third arc extends from the mouth of Delaware Bay northeasterly through Lake Champlain before touching the Atlantic again at the mouth of the Penobscot River. Within this arc existed the most diverse societies to be found in early America, societies that were defined primarily by the widespread numerical and social dominance of small producing farmers and artisans. The final arc originates at Louisbourg and swings in a shallow curve westward across the Saint Lawrence River to the Great Lakes. These were the societies of the French trading complex. In time, a fifth arc rose to importance and by the early nineteenth century became a center of social development and inequality. It ran southeastward from the Great Lakes to the Gulf of Mexico and encompassed the frontier, or marchland, societies of early North America.

Together, these arcs comprised the variety of New World societies created by European interaction with Africans and Native Americans. In the early years of settlement, these societies bore the heavy imprint of cultural and social dislocation, flux, and recomposition, as the first generations of conquerors and settlers attempted to impose their native European conceptions of social order on a protean world of multicultural interchange.[14] Before the seventeenth century in Spanish America and the eighteenth century in the other Euro-American colonies, they seldom succeeded. The sheer complexity of establishing footholds in the New World, of treating with the indigenous inhabitants, and of establishing viable economic connections with the home countries made for a cluster of colonial societies in which social hierarchies were attenuated. As hard as they may have tried to reconstruct the Old World in the New, Euro-Americans perforce created unique social systems that were, for a time, remarkably fluid and open. Only after several generations did Creole societies begin to resemble their transatlantic counterparts.

We can observe this fluidity most clearly in the two regions of English settlement. In the northeastern arc of English settlements, small family farms predominated.[15] Within these units of agrarian production, male household heads exercised putative legal and public power over family members, although in practice power in families flowed from many sources: men made decisions about fields and livestock; women made decisions about the household and its gardens, about the farmyard, and about the family orchard; older children directed the upbringing and tasks of younger siblings; adults directed the lives of servants and sometimes slaves.[16] Family farm communities lacked a center of power. Composed, for the most part, of economically equal members, family farm communities formed one-class societies of small producers that provided no basis for focused, centralized power. Consensual politics, even though often engineered, generally obtained in these communities, and age, more than any other factor, formed the locus of power.[17] This was especially true of New England communities, where several studies have demonstrated the persistence of "town fathers"—older men who guided community decision making—in positions of local authority.[18] These decentralized communities realized a degree of centralization only when the outside world of colonial magistrates and contending armies intruded in their affairs.[19]

In the Connecticut and Hudson River valleys and the countryside surrounding New York City and Philadelphia, agriculture took on a larger-scale, commercial quality.[20] In these areas, clientage and asymmetrical class relationships made power much more centralized. Wealthy landholders claimed economic, social, and political power throughout these commercial regions by lending money, renting and leasing land, hiring temporary labor, and helping in hard times. More often than not, these landowners turned their economic power as a rentier class into political power, manipulating the votes of their clients and lessees as a condition of their paternalism.

If power was more centralized around class relationships in commercial farming areas, they were most centralized of all in the northern seaport cities. As Gary B. Nash has shown, Boston, New York City, and Philadelphia were the most unequal places in the Northeast.[21] Dominated economically by a class of wealthy import/export merchants, the northern seaport cities supported a diverse society made up of independent artisans, retail merchants, laborers, mariners, indentured and hired servants, and slaves. In these, the most stratified locales in northern society, a rudimentary class system linked merchant to retailer, retailer to artisan, artisan to journeyman and apprentice, and everyone to the cities' bound laborers and mariners. The nature of this class system is often distorted, misunderstood, and indeed occasionally denied by those who see class existing only in its centralized, industrial form. For although centralized in comparison with its rural counterparts, the commercial economy of the seaport cities supported class relations that were remarkably decentralized compared with those that would exist in the nineteenth century. These seaport societies revolved around trade, placing merchants at the center of urban society. Merchants employed mariners for their vessels, bought the time of indentured servants, and purchased slaves as personal and household servants. But at the same time, they also contracted with independent artisans for goods and independent farmers for produce. For their part, master artisans hired journeymen and trained apprentices, but they also bought the time and persons of indentured servants and slaves as the supply of dependent labor and the size of their purses dictated. Even the position of laborers and mariners (together composing the largest group of working people in the seaport cities) was ambiguous.[22] Servants typically hired themselves out on an annual basis; mariners, for the duration of a voyage. This brought them under the direct personal supervision of their temporary owners, who controlled not only their working lives but their personal lives as well. Although they possessed some legal rights and protections, the positions of servants and mariners were closer to that of slaves than of free wage laborers, at least during the terms of their respective contracts. The overlapping diversity of these class relations was typical of mercantile communities throughout the New World and indeed characteristic of similar communities in Europe, Asia, and Africa. Class relations remained diffuse in these communities, and while in some respects they might prefigure the world of industrial capitalism, they mostly represented a semicentralized world of independence and dependence, of clientage and custom, of freedom and bondage.

When we turn to the English plantation complex, we encounter the only well-articulated and centralized class system in early America. From their inception, the English Caribbean and southern mainland settlements were designed as colonies of exploitation. Unlike the Spanish, English colonizers were unable to find significant mineral wealth or to exploit Native American labor in mainland North America, but they were able to follow their Iberian counterparts in establishing lucrative staple-producing societies.[23] Relying first on English indentured servants, these colonies quickly evolved into societies in which class was the dominant form of inequality. Developing from the English institution of yearlong contracts struck between landlords and agricultural servants, the indenture system quickly became a system of quasi-slavery.[24] Servants could be bought and sold or their persons and labor gambled away. For those found guilty of increasingly minor infractions, their time in "service" could be extended as punishment and as a means of enhancing the wealth and power of the region's planter class. The lines of class were thus clear: the bulk of the work of planting was performed by indentured servants, who labored for an increasingly wealthy class of plantation owners.[25] But if the indenture system represented the most class-centered form of inequality in seventeenth-century British American society, the slave system that superseded it was even more so.[26]

Slavery in the Anglo-Caribbean and Chesapeake colonies was in many respects a direct result of the indenture system. After 1640, slave prices fell as servant prices rose, making the purchase of slaves increasingly the norm throughout the English plantation complex.[27] By the turn of the eighteenth century the basic pattern of class relations that would come to dominate the plantation complex was in place in the island and mainland colonies. A small class of very wealthy and powerful planters, whose wealth derived from the exploitation of a subaltern class of African and African-American slaves, dominated plantation society. Interspersed throughout the plantation complex were other whites, most of whom were family farmers much like their northern counterparts, although they competed directly with large planters by growing small quantities of the local staple in addition to producing their own food and fodder.[28] The financial power of the plantation grandees, coupled with the virtual control they exercised over colonial legislatures and county court systems made the class system of the plantation regions the most centralized class system in pre-nineteenth-century North America.

Early America was thus a concatenation of systems of power and inequality. Working outward from colonial families to local communities and on to colonial society as a whole, inequalities of power in all of its aspects took on many forms. Despite the existence of rudimentary forms of capitalism and several forms of class, outside the plantation complex, class was never the central organizing institution of early American society. In fact, within the northeastern arc of the British mainland colonies, it is difficult to find any stable centers of power at all. That started to change as rapid population growth in the eighteenth and early nineteenth centuries, repudiation of colonial status, the creation of independent nationhood, and the infusion of capital into productive relationships began to transform early America into an industrial nation. But although the impact of commercial expansion and early industrial capitalism on the structure of power and inequality in the new nation was profound, the question of class in early-nineteenth-century American society admitted no unequivocal answer.

The most curious feature of inequality in America between the mid-eighteenth century and the mid-nineteenth century was how little of that inequality was due to capitalism. This may seem a surprising statement considering the considerable recent literature that views the two generations after 1780 as the age of capitalist transformation.[29] Yet capitalism remained peripheral to vast sections of late-eighteenth-century and early-nineteenth-century America, and class as a form of power was only slightly more centralized in 1830 than it was in 1780 or, for that matter, in 1730. Capitalism advanced during these years, to be sure, but only in several relatively isolated sections of the early national United States did class become the dominant form of power, inequality, and social organization.

In the southern states, the plantation complex continued to operate in ways that were little changed from the early eighteenth century.[30] A planter class remained in power from the mid-eighteenth century to the Civil War, and that power continued to rest on the labor of a class of African and African-American slaves. The introduction of the cotton gin in 1793 rescued the plantation complex from its postrevolutionary economic doldrums and opened a new era of staple-crop production, in this case producing raw cotton that fed English and later American textile mills. But the region's newfound prosperity did little to alter existing class relations, because the power of the planter class served to direct the flow of new profits into the pockets of younger members of planter families and largely kept it out of the hands of the broader white population. After 1810 the scions of eastern planter families migrated in large numbers to the Gulf States, taking capital and slaves with them.[31] They purchased the best bottomlands and effectively marginalized smaller planters and farmers. By 1820 the class system of the plantation complex had solidly transplanted itself throughout the Deep South, from Alabama to East Texas and Arkansas.

Like the world of the plantation complex, continuity marked the class structure of much of the rural Northeast. The period from 1750 to 1830 witnessed many important changes in this region of family farms, but these changes amounted to adaptations more than transformations. The agrarian history of the northeastern states has been the subject of heated debate for nearly two decades.[32] Focused especially on New England agriculture, this debate has revolved around the question of whether a capitalist transformation of the economy and class structure took place in the early United States. One school, led by the agrarian economist Winifred Rothenberg, claims that New England was essentially protocapitalist in the years before 1780 and became decisively so in the following decades, as dense networks of trade linked rural Massachusetts with Boston and the region's outports.[33] The other school, represented most ably by James Henretta, Michael Merrill, and Christopher Clark, claims instead that rural America was essentially noncapitalist before 1780 and was characterized by family-based production and a small-producer way of life.[34] But after 1780, these writers agree, changes in trade, credit, and productive strategies led gradually but inexorably to the creation of capitalist agriculture and class relations in the antebellum Northeast.

It is not necessary to take sides in this debate to access the impact that post-1780 developments had on the agrarian class structure of the northern states. In one respect, the extension of trade and credit networks into rural New England, so ably demonstrated by Rothenberg, represents less a measure of incipient capitalism than the demarginalization of Massachusetts's rural economy. New England farms, never very prosperous in the seventeenth century, were, by the eighteenth century, placed outside the mainstream of colonial agricultural production by a combination of marginal land, poor climate, and an endlessly expanding rural population.[35] After 1780, however, the movement of large numbers of young Massachusetts men and women to the frontiers of Maine, New Hampshire, Vermont, New York, and later Ohio relieved some of the pressure on land, and increasing penetration of rural areas by peddlers and country storekeepers placed goods within the reach of nearly everyone.[36] As a result, Massachusetts farmers engaged in trade more vigorously than in the past. But what implications did this commercialization of the countryside have for the region's class structure? The evidence from all sides suggests not very much. Whenever we look—in 1700, 1800, or even 1830—the maintenance of landed competency and family continuity in agriculture dominated the outlook and operation of the majority of New England farms.[37] Fathers might engage in distant credit transactions, sons might work on someone else's land until their mid-twenties, and daughters might labor temporarily in the recently established mills, but these were strategies of adjustment and accommodation that brought few dramatic changes to the rural class structure. Most New England farmers were small producers in 1700, and most remained so in 1830. Indeed, in his study of the Connecticut River Valley of Massachusetts, Clark concludes that even in this long-commercialized region of rural New England, agriculture remained only partially capitalist until after the Civil War.[38] A growing body of studies dealing with the nation's mid-Atlantic and western regions suggests much the same conclusion: the agrarian class structure of the northeastern arc was basically stable from the seventeenth century to the middle of the nineteenth.[39]

Capitalism and the employer-employee relationship that is its defining characteristic structured inequality relatively little in the agrarian North; the new nation experienced its most profound change in class structure in rural mill towns and urban production centers. In the course of the revolutionary war the agrarian colonies began to develop significant and portentous manufacturing capacity, a process that would continue to accelerate in the decades following independence.[40] Textile mills began to develop quickly in the new nation, beginning with Samuel Slater's mills in Paw-tucket, Rhode Island, and later in Dudley and Oxford, Massachusetts.[41] Nestled in existing rural communities where fast-flowing streams provided power, these mills as well as their owner and his workers fit uneasily into the social life of agrarian New England. Welcomed for the extra income they generated for the farming community, Slater's mills also represented the antithesis of rural competency and independence. Employer-employee relationships dominated life in the mills, which were populated by a grow-ing body of young men and women who had been "strolling" throughout the late-eighteenth- and early-nineteenth-century New England country-side in search of work. For some young men, work in the mills was tempo-rary, a means of earning money that could be used later to purchase land and establish a competency. For others, mill work was the beginning of lifelong dependence. The majority of Slater's employees, however, were women who, as operatives, worked the spinning and weaving machinery in long days of labor. Their future lay in eventual marriage (for which their earnings provided a dowry) or, like their male counterparts, in extended years of monotonous and underpaid wage labor.[42] As residents of the rural communities surrounding the mills came to realize that Slater's mill work-ers were not people seeking a competency like themselves but permanent wage workers, local attitudes toward Slater and his mills soured. The more that capitalist social relations regulated local mill life, the less independent farmers tolerated the demands of their increasingly quarrelsome mill owner and his suspect employees. In the end, Slater was forced to incorpo-rate his Massachusetts mill complex as the separate town of Webster, thus creating an island of modern class relations in a sea of rural competency. Despite Slater's wealth, power, and reputation, capitalist class relationships proved too weak to structure life among independent landowners; and wage labor and capitalist class relations were successfully isolated in these southern New England communities. Capitalism existed within the mills but failed to alter traditional ways of life in the communities around them.

The same cannot be said about the nation's urban production centers, where in cities such as New York City and Philadelphia a society structured by the central importance of capitalist class relations first took shape. America's urban centers had always been venues for class relationships, but they turned principally on the axis of capitalism and class only when urban production began to function on the basis of wage rather than craft labor. That transformation, which began in the years following the American Revolution, was uneven and incomplete as late as 1830, but by that year the capitalist transformation of craft production was well under way and pointed clearly toward the capitalist class relations that would dominate urban social relations for the remainder of the nineteenth century.

Detached from direct food production and dependent on the market for raw materials, family provisions, and the vending of their products, artisans were always sensitive to shifts in the market. When new and lucrative markets opened in the South and West after 1800, many merchants and master artisans began to alter their way of doing business and, in the process, created a system of manufactories (central shops employing hired labor) and outwork shops that drew growing numbers of semiskilled craftsmen and poor women into capitalist class relations.[43] The lower production costs and economies of scale enjoyed by these manufactories and outworking establishments created a situation of intense competition between these new ventures and traditional craft producers. As increasing numbers of artisans found themselves unable to produce their goods at market prices set by manufacturing and outwork production, they were forced into luxury production for wealthy clients or, more often, wage labor. Over the course of the early nineteenth century the dissolution of the craft system created an increasingly powerful and ubiquitous set of capitalist class relations that would, in time, come to dominate all other social relations in America's production centers.

Class was thus no stranger to early America, but neither was Anglo-American society thoroughly class-dominated. Class served as the central armature of society within the plantation complex, to be sure, but north of the Pennsylvania–Maryland border, class achieved dominance only in limited, relatively isolated areas. Not until the 1880s would the United States become a true class society, one in which class, more than any other form of inequality, determined the exercise of economic, social, and political power. Even then, class was never completely dominant, and inequalities that continued into the twentieth century owed their origin to race, gender, and ethnicity. The centrality of class shaped American life in decisive ways after 1880, losing its coherence and dominance only in the post–World War II era, when advertising, credit, mass merchandising, education, and consumerism brought the majority of Americans into the amorphous "middle class." But if class has indeed receded from its central role in American society, as postmodernist analysts have claimed, it continues to shape American social life as one of many forms of inequality, just as it did in the early American past.

Notes

1. An essay of this length cannot explore fully the many issues involved in a study of class in early America. What follows is meant to be exploratory, provisional, and, in the broadest sense, heuristic.

2. Marx deals with class most fully in his political writings, especially *The Communist Manifesto, The 18th Brumaire of Napoleon Bonaparte and The Class Struggle in France.* See Karl Marx, *Political Writings,* 3 vols., Vintage Marx Library (New York, 1974).

3. This is the import of Marx's *Capital.* The first volume contains a theoretical exposition of capitalism as a socioeconomic system, the second volume deals with a series of technical issues, and the final volume applies the theory contained in the first two volumes to human historical experience. *Theories of Surplus Value* completes Marx's theoretical enterprise by surveying the work of previous political economists. Karl Marx, *Capital: A Critique of Political Economy,* 3 vols., Vintage Marx Library (New York, 1974); *Theories of Surplus Value,* 3 vols. (New York: 1971).

4. Weber's increasingly refined notion of class can be followed in his essay "Class, Status, and Party," in *From Max Weber: Essays in Sociology,* ed. H. H. Gerth and C. Wright Mills (New York, 1946) and more fully in Max Weber, *General Economic History* (New York, 1927) and *Economy and Society,* ed. Guenther Roth and Claus Wittich (Berkeley, Calif., 1979).

5. Lynn Hunt, *Politics, Culture, and Class in the French Revolution* (Berkeley, Calif., 1984) and *The New Cultural History* (Berkeley, Calif., 1989); William M. Reddy, *Money and Liberty in Modern Europe: A Critique of Historical Understanding* (New York, 1987); Joan Wallach Scott, *Gender and the Politics of History* (New York, 1988); Gareth Stedman Jones, *Languages of Class: Studies in English Working-Class History, 1832–1982* (New York, 1983); Patrick Joyce, *Visions of the People: Industrial England and the Question of Class, 1840–1914* (New York, 1991); Jacques Rancière, *The Nights of Labor: The Workers' Dream in Nineteenth-Century France,* trans. John Drury (Philadelphia, 1989); William H. Sewell Jr., "Towards a Post-Materialist Rhetoric for Labor History," in *Rethinking Labor History: Essays on Class and Discourse Analysis,* ed. Lenard R. Berlanstein (Urbana, Ill., 1993), 16–23.

6. Thompson's developing ideas about class can be followed in E. P. Thompson, *The Making of the English Working Class* (New York, 1963); "Eighteenth-Century English Society: Class Struggle Without Class?" *Social History* 3 (1978): 133–65; and *Customs in Common* (New York, 1991).

7. "Eighteenth-Century English Society," 146, 147. Emphasis in original.

8. For informative and critical discussions of Thompson's work, see *E. P. Thompson: Critical Perspectives,* ed. Harvey J. Kaye and Keith McClelland (Philadelphia, 1990); *Protest and Survival: The Historical Experience. Essays for E. P. Thompson,* ed. John Rule and Robert Malcomson (London, 1993); Bryan D. Palmer, *Objections and Oppositions* (London, 1994); Scott, *Gender and Politics of History;* and Peter King, "Edward Thompson's Contribution to Eighteenth-Century Studies: The Patrician-Plebeian Model Re-Examined," *Social History* 21 (1996): 215–28.

9. Thompson's ideas about class were always in the process of revision. Compare his earlier writings with his most mature formulations in "The Politics of Theory," in *People's History and Socialist Theory,* ed. Raphael Samuel (Boston, 1981), 396–408, and *Customs in Common.*

10. In addition to the works cited in note 5 above, see Leonore Davidoff and Catherine Hall, *Family Fortunes: Men and Women of the English Middle Class, 1780–1850* (Chicago, 1987); Dror Wahrman, *Imagining the Middle Class: The Political Representation of Class in Britain, c. 1780–1840* (New York, 1995). The work of Jürgen Habermas has recently become increasingly influential in discussions of

social ontology. See "The Public Sphere," *New German Critique* 3 (1974); *Strukturwandel der Öffenlichkeit* (Neuweid, 1962), trans. with revisions as *The Structural Transformation of the Public Sphere: An Inquiry into a Category of Bourgeois Society* (Cambridge, 1989). For the better part of a generation, Stuart Hall and his students and colleagues at Birmingham U.K. University's Center for Contemporary Culture Studies have been developing alternative constructions of class and other social categories. A good sampling of this work can be found in *The Cultural Studies Reader*, ed. Simon During (New York, 1993). For a thoughtful critique of the "linguistic turn," see Bryan D. Palmer, *Descent into Discourse: The Reification of Language and the Writing of Social History* (Philadelphia, 1990).

11. Foucault's most relevant works are *Madness and Civilization: A History of Insanity in the Age of Reason* (New York, 1967); *Discipline and Punish: The Birth of the Prison* (New York, 1977); *The History of Sexuality*, vol. 1 (New York, 1980); and *Power/Knowledge: Selected Interviews and Other Writings, 1972–1977* (New York, 1981). The literature on Foucault and the structuralist/poststructuralist turn of thought is vast and growing. The most important works include Jean Baudrillard, *The Mirror of Production* (St. Louis, 1975), and Jean Baudrillard, *In the Shadow of the Silent Majorities, or The End of the Social and Other Essays* (New York, 1983); Pierre Bordieu, *Outline of a Theory of Practice* (New York, 1977); Cornelius Castoriadis, *The Imaginary Institution of Society* (Cambridge, 1987).

12. For a recent elaboration of this point from the perspective of deconstruction, see Jacques Derrida, *Politics of Friendship* (New York, 1997).

13. For the idea of an Atlantic plantation complex, see Philip D. Curtin, *The Rise and Fall of the Plantation Complex: Essays in Atlantic History* (New York, 1990).

14. Already substantial, the literature on multicultural exchange between Europeans and Native Americans continues to grow at a prodigious rate. Among the most useful studies are Neal Salisbury, *Manitou and Providence: Indians, Europeans, and the Making of New England, 1500–1643* (New York, 1982); William Cronon, *Changes in the Land: Indians, Colonists, and the Ecology of New England* (New York, 1983); James H. Merrell, *The Indians' New World: Catawbas and Their Neighbors from European Contact through the Era of Removal* (Chapel Hill, N.C., 1989); Daniel H. Usner Jr., *Indians, Settlers, and Slaves in a Frontier Exchange Economy: The Lower Mississippi Valley before 1783* (Chapel Hill, N.C., 1992); Karen Spalding, *Huarochirí: An Andean Society Under Inca and Spanish Rule* (Stanford, Calif., 1984); Inga Clendinnen, *Ambivalent Conquests: Maya and Spaniard in Yucatan, 1517–1570* (New York, 1987). A worthy guide to recent literature is James Axtell, "Beyond 1992," in *Beyond 1492: Encounters in Colonial North America* (New York, 1992), 267–316; more comprehensive is *The Cambridge History of the Native Peoples of the Americas, vol. 1: North America*, ed. Bruce G. Trigger and Wilcomb E. Washburn (New York, 1996).

15. The history of English settlement in the northeastern arc is recounted in Kenneth A. Lockridge, *A New England Town: The First Hundred Years* (New York, 1970); Philip J. Greven Jr., *Four Generations: Population, Land, and Family in Colonial Andover, Massachusetts* (Ithaca, N.Y., 1970); Virginia DeJohn Anderson, *New England's Generation: The Great Migration and the Formation of Society and Culture in the Seventeenth Century* (New York, 1991); Daniel Vickers, *Farmers and Fishermen: Two Centuries of Work in Essex County, Massachusetts, 1630–1830* (Chapel Hill, N.C., 1994); James T. Lemon, *The Best Poor Man's Country: A Geographical Study of Early Southeastern Pennsylvania* (Baltimore, 1972); and

Stephanie Grauman Wolf, *Urban Village: Population, Community, and Family Structure in Germantown, Pennsylvania, 1683–1800* (Princeton, N.J., 1976).

16. Family life in the rural Northeast is discussed in the works cited in note 15 above and in Laurel Thatcher Ulrich, *Good Wives: Image and Reality in the Lives of Women in Northern New England, 1650–1750* (New York, 1982); John Demos, *A Little Commonwealth: Family Life in Plymouth Colony* (New York, 1970); Philip Greven, *The Protestant Temperament: Patterns of Child-Rearing, Religious Experience, and the Self in Early America* (New York, 1977); and Barry Levy, *Quakers and the American Family: British Settlement in the Delaware Valley* (New York, 1988).

17. Michael Zukerman, *Peaceable Kingdoms: New England Towns in the Eighteenth Century* (New York, 1970).

18. Edward M. Cook, *The Fathers of the Towns: Leadership and Community Structure in Eighteenth-Century New England* (Baltimore, 1976); Robert A. Gross, *The Minutemen and Their World* (New York, 1976).

19. Gross, *Minutemen and Their World*.

20. Stephen Innes, *Labor in a New Land: Economy and Society in Seventeenth-Century Springfield* (Princeton, N.J., 1983); *Work and Labor in Early America*, ed. Stephen Innes (Chapel Hill, N.C., 1988); Sung Bok Kim, *Landlord and Tenant in Colonial New York: Manorial Society, 1664–1775* (Chapel Hill, N.C., 1978); Lemon, *Best Poor Man's Country*.

21. Gary B. Nash, *The Urban Crucible: Social Change, Political Consciousness, and the Origins of the American Revolution* (Cambridge, Mass., 1979).

22. Marcus Redikcr, *Between the Devil and the Deep Blue Sea: Merchant Seamen, Pirates, and the Anglo-American Maritime World, 1700–1750* (New York, 1987); Sharon V. Salinger, *"To Serve Well and Faithfully": Labor and Indentured Servants in Pennsylvania, 1682–1800* (New York, 1987); David W. Galenson, *White Servitude in Colonial America: An Economic Analysis* (New York, 1981).

23. The early history of the English plantation complex is told in Edmund S. Morgan, *American Slavery, American Freedom: The Ordeal of Colonial Virginia* (New York 1975); James Horn, *Adapting to a New World: English Society in the Seventeenth-Century Chesapeake* (Chapel Hill, N.C., 1995); Kathleen M. Brown, *Good Wives, Nasty Wenches, and Anxious Patriarchs: Gender, Race, and Power in Colonial Virginia* (Chapel Hill, N.C., 1996); Peter H. Wood, *Black Majority: Negroes in Colonial South Carolina from 1670 through the Stono Rebellion* (New York, 1974); and Richard S. Dunn, *Sugar and Slaves: The Rise of the Planter Class in the English West Indies, 1624–1713* (Chapel Hill, N.C., 1972).

24. Ann Kussmaul, *Servants in Husbandry in Early Modern England* (New York, 1981); Morgan, *American Slavery*.

25. Morgan, *American Slavery; The Chesapeake in the Seventeenth Century: Essays in Anglo-American Society*, ed. Thad W. Tate and David L. Ammerman (Chapel Hill, N.C., 1979); and *Colonial Chesapeake Society*, ed. Lois Green Carr, Philip D. Morgan, and Jean B. Russo (Chapel Hill, N.C., 1988).

26. The origins of slavery in the English plantation complex is expertly recounted in Betty Wood, *The Origins of American Slavery: Freedom and Bondage in the English Colonies* (New York, 1997); and Robin Blackburn, *The Making of New World Slavery: From the Baroque to the Modern, 1492–1800* (New York, 1997).

27. The timing of the transformation from servant to slave labor in the Chesapeake is discussed in Russell R. Menard, "From Servant to Slave: The Transformation of the Chesapeake's Labor System," *Southern Studies* 16 (1977): 355–90. For the English Caribbean, see Dunn, *Sugar and Slaves,* 71–74.

28. The history of southern white family farmers before the antebellum era is only now being told. See Timothy J. Lockley, "African Americans and Non-Slaveholding Whites in Lowcountry Georgia, 1750-1830" (Ph.D. diss., Cambridge University, 1996); Harry L. Watson, "'The Common Rights of Mankind': Subsistence, Shad, and Commerce in the Early Republican South," *JAH* 83 (1996): 13–43. The early chapters of several antebellum studies touch on the early nineteenth century. See Steven Hahn, *The Roots of Southern Populism: Yeoman Farmers and the Transformation of the Georgia Upcountry, 1850–1890* (New York, 1983); Bill Cecil-Fronsman, *Common Whites: Class and Culture in Antebellum North Carolina* (Lexington, Ky., 1992); Charles C. Bolton, *Poor Whites of the Antebellum South: Tenants and Laborers in Central North Carolina and Northeast Mississippi* (Durham, N.C., 1994); Stephanie McCurry, *Masters of Small Worlds: Yeoman Households, Gender Relations, and the Political Culture of the Antebellum South Carolina Low Country* (New York, 1995); J. William Harris, *Plain Folk and Gentry in a Slave Society: White Liberty and Black Slavery in Augusta's Hinterlands* (Middletown, Conn., 1985).

29. The prodigious literature on the capitalist transformation of postrevolutionary America is ably summarized in Allan Kulikoff, "The Transition to Capitalism in Rural America," *WMQ* 3d ser., 46 (1989): 120–44; Christopher Clark, "Economics and Culture: Opening Up the Rural History of the Early American Northeast," *American Quarterly* 43 (1991): 279–301; and Michael Merrill, "Putting 'Capitalism' in Its Place: A Review of Recent Literature," *WMQ* 3d ser., 52 (1995): 315–26.

30. The postrevolutionary development of the South is the subject of a vast literature. Among the most important studies are Lewis C. Gray, *History of Agriculture in the Southern United States to 1860*, 2 vols. (Washington, D.C., 1933); Kenneth M. Stampp, *The Peculiar Institution: Slavery in the Antebellum South* (New York, 1956); Eugene D. Genovese, *The Political Economy of Slavery: Studies in the Economy and Society of the Slave South* (New York, 1965), and *Roll, Jordan, Roll: The World the Slaves Made* (New York, 1974); Gavin Wright, *The Political Economy of the Cotton South: Households, Markets, and Wealth in the Nineteenth Century* (New York, 1978); Richard R. Beeman, *The Evolution of the Southern Backcountry: A Case Study of Lunenburg County, Virginia, 1746–1832* (Philadelphia, 1984); Allan Kulikoff, *Tobacco and Slaves: The Development of Southern Cultures in the Chesapeake, 1680–1800* (Chapel Hill, N.C., 1986); Rachel N. Klein, *Unification of a Slave State: The Lives of the Planters in the South Carolina Backcountry, 1760–1808* (Chapel Hill, N.C., 1990); James Oakes, *Slavery and Freedom: An Interpretation of the Old South* (New York, 1990); Jean B. Lee, *The Price of Nationhood: The American Revolution in Charles County* (New York, 1994).

31. Joan E. Cashin, *A Family Venture: Men and Women on the Southern Frontier* (New York, 1991).

32. See n. 29 above.

33. Winifred B. Rothenberg, *From Market Places to a Market Economy: The Transformation of Rural Massachusetts, 1750–1850* (Chicago, 1992).

34. James A. Henretta, "Families and Farms: *Mentalité* in Pre-Industrial America," *WMQ* 3d ser., 35 (1978): 3–32; Christopher Clark, *The Roots of Rural Capitalism: Western Massachusetts, 1780–1860* (Ithaca, N.Y., 1990), and introduction to *The Key of Liberty: The Life and Democratic Writings of William Manning, "A Laborer," 1747–1814*, ed. Michael Merrill and Sean Wilentz (Cambridge, Mass., 1993).

35. In addition to the works cited in nn. 15 and 16, above, see Paul Boyer and Stephen Nissenbaum, *Salem Possessed: The Social Origins of Witchcraft* (Cambridge, Mass., 1974).

36. Alan Taylor, *Liberty Men and Great Proprietors: The Revolutionary Setlement on the Maine Frontier* (Chapel Hill, N.C., 1990), and *William Cooper's Town: Power and Persuasion on the Frontier of the Early American Republic* (New York, 1995); Michael A. Bellesiles, *Revolutionary Outlaws: Ethan Allen and the Struggle for Independence on the Early American Frontier* (Charlottesville, Va., 1993); Stephen Aron, *How the West Was Lost: The Transformation of Kentucky from Daniel Boone to Henry Clay* (Baltimore, 1996); R. Douglas Hurt, *The Ohio Frontier: Crucible of the Old Northwest, 1720–1830* (Bloomington, Ind., 1996): Andrew R. L. Cayton, *Frontier Indiana* (Bloomington, Ind., 1996); Charles E. Brooks, *Frontier Settlement and Market Revolution: The Holland Land Purchase* (Ithaca, N.Y., 1996). For a larger synthesis of the early national frontier, see Gregory H. Nobles, *American Frontiers: Cultural Encounters and Continental Conquest* (New York, 1997), and Gregory H. Nobles, "Breaking into the Backcountry: New Approaches to the Early American Frontier, 1750–800," *WMQ* 3d ser., 46 (1989): 641–70.

37. Clark, *Roots of Rural Capitalism*; Vickers, *Farmers and Fishermen*.

38. Clark, *Roots of Rural Capitalism*, chap. 9.

39. In addition to the works cited above, see John Mack Faragher, *Sugar Creek: Life on the Illinois Prairie* (New Haven, Conn., 1986); Hal S. Barron, *Those Who Stayed Behind: Rural Society in Nineteenth-Century New England* (New York, 1984); and Thomas Sylvester Wermuth, "'To Market, To Market': Yeoman Farmers, Merchant Capitalists, and the Transition to Capitalism in the Hudson River Valley, Ulster County, 1760–1840" (Ph.D. diss., State University of New York, Binghamton, 1991).

40. James A. Henretta, "The War for Independence and American Economic Development," in Henretta, *The Origins of American Capitalism: Collected Essays* (Boston, 1991), 203–55.

41. Jonathan Prude, *The Coming of Industrial Order: Town and Factory Life in Rural Massachusetts, 1810–1860* (New York, 1983).

42. Prude, *Coming of Industrial Order*; Thomas Dublin, *Women at Work: The Transformation of Work and Community in Lowell, Massachusetts, 1826–1860* (New York, 1979).

43. Alan Dawley, *Class and Community: The Industrial Revolution in Lynn* (Cambridge, Mass., 1976); Sean Wilentz, *Chants Democratic: City and the Rise of the American Working Class, 1788–1850* (New York, 1984); Christine Stansell, *City of Women: Sex and Class in New York, 1789–1860* (Urbana, Ill., 1986); Ronald Schultz, *The Republic of Labor: Philadelphia Artisans and the Politics of Class, 1720–1830* (New York, 1993).

Peter H. Wood

SLAVE LABOR CAMPS IN EARLY AMERICA: OVERCOMING DENIAL AND DISCOVERING THE GULAG

> There, sir, stop:
>
> Let us not burden our remembrances with
>
> A heaviness that's gone.
>
> —PROSPERO, IN *The Tempest*[1]
>
> If you suppress any part of the story, it comes back
>
> later, with force and violence.
>
> —ELIE WIESEL[2]

 WE LIVE IN a nation in denial. For all our openness to controversy and our fascination with violence, we Americans are still unable to grasp the full depth of the huge collective wound that predated the country's founding and that haunted its infant and adolescent years. In the past decade our society has slowly become more sensitive to child abuse within families and to the lasting effects that prolonged and arbitrary mistreatment can have on all concerned. But this growing sensitivity to individual abuse and to its impact on later generations has not yet been matched by an increased awareness of the collective long-term trauma represented by race slavery. Why would we expect the nation's power structure even to acknowledge, much less come to terms with, such a dark and formative chapter in our collective family history? After all, as several eminent academics have recently reminded us, "nations need to control national memory, because nations keep their shape by shaping their citizens' understanding of the past." But as these scholars go on to point out, in

actual practice this process, for better or worse, depends heavily on individual historians. For "it is the historians who do research on the past, write
the histories, and teach the nation's youth. It is they who lock up and un-
lock memory. . . . Whether democratic leaders like it or not, historians fashion the nation's collective self-understanding."[3]

In the United States this complicated interplay between political leaders
and professional historians has existed in some form since at least the second quarter of the nineteenth century, when American history first came
into its own as a full-time vocation. In an era when political leaders were
imposing "gag laws" and allowing censorship of the U.S. mail in order to
prevent open discussion of the volatile slavery issue, many historians followed the same course, emphasizing God's "manifest destiny" for Europeans in America and ignoring slavery altogether.[4] For example, in John
Frost's popular book, *A History of the United States*, published in 1837, the
controversial subject went virtually unmentioned.[5] After 1850 some writers
would follow the lead of Harriet Beecher Stowe in criticizing the institution, but many others would imitate the example of South Carolina's John
C. Calhoun in praising slavery as a positive American institution endorsed
by George Washington himself.[6]

When the dust from a prolonged Civil War and a hopeful but unrealized
Reconstruction had finally settled, slavery times—too repugnant for most
black Americans to dwell on—became a source of nostalgia for much of
the society. "Jefferson's slaves thought that no one could be better than
their master," mused a popular elementary history text in 1902. "He was always kind to them, and they were ready to do anything for him."[7] Colonial
Williamsburg, reconstructed by John D. Rockefeller Jr., in the 1920s, marketed the gentility of planters and the satisfaction of their unpaid workers
in the Old South,[8] as did Margaret Mitchell's *Gone with the Wind* a decade
later. The publication and "docudramatization" of Alex Haley's *Roots* in
the mid-1970s surprised a generation of Americans raised on *Gone with the
Wind*, just as the films *Glory!* in 1989 and *Amistad* in 1997 have surprised a
generation that felt *Roots* had shown them all that they needed to know
about enslavement.

Still, for historians during the past thirty years to speak of "inequality in
early America" has commonly been criticized as an act of exaggeration,
presentism, or alarmist hyperbole. Mainstream writers have preferred to
emphasize the significant fact that most European immigrants sooner or
later found themselves better off in the New World than in the Old
World.[9] So long as nearly half a million Africans could be factored out of
the equation entirely, then all of England's Atlantic settlements, even the
Chesapeake colonies, could appear models of equity and harmony where,
according to one scholar, "conspicuous social issues were nonexistent"

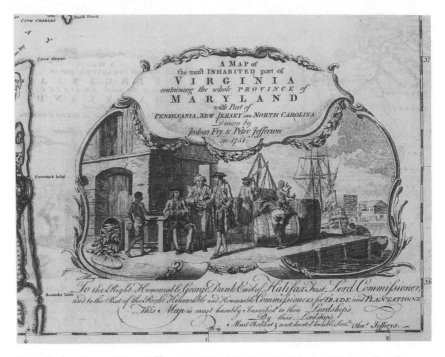

Fig. 3. Joshua Fry and Peter Jefferson, *A Map of the Inhabited Part of Virginia* (London, 1751), Cartouche. Courtesy of the Henry E. Huntington Library and Art Gallery, San Marino, California.

and where "conscious divisions, within the society" or "any obvious . . . class antagonism" proved difficult to discern. "Of all the colonies in the mid-eighteenth century," Gordon Wood wrote in the *William and Mary Quarterly* in 1966, "Virginia seems the most settled, the most lacking in obvious social tensions."[10]

"Obvious to whom?" one might ask, for the available evidence often appears ambiguous. Consider a document from that very time and place: the often-reprinted cartouche from a mid-eighteenth-century map of the Chesapeake region (fig. 3). It depicts eight men in a dockside scene where casks of tobacco are being loaded aboard a British ship. Four well-dressed individuals, obviously white, count the year's cargo, tally its value, negotiate its shipment, and consume a symbolic pipeful of tobacco. The other four persons in the picture are clearly black and enslaved. Three of them pack the tobacco they have grown into the hogsheads they have made, roll these huge barrels to the dock to be weighed, and then row them to the waiting ship, while a fourth individual serves spirits to the planter, the factor, and the captain, so that the three entrepreneurs can drink to their mutual success.

The picture is a virtual metaphor for the fundamental divisions within Virginia society, and any of the four black men could certainly have offered testimony that "conspicuous social issues" were far from "nonexistent" in the Tidewater. But if class antagonism existed on Chesapeake docks, it is not easy to discern in this traditional depiction. The artists have done everything in their power to obscure it. The map was made in the 1750s by Joshua Fry, professor of mathematics at William and Mary College, and Peter Jefferson, Virginia burgess, surveyor, and planter.[11] Needless to say, we know a tremendous amount concerning the Virginia gentry at the center of this picture (and increasingly about their spouses as well).[12] They are the people who drafted the colonial map, so to speak, who are featured on it, and who used it for their gain. We know far less about the workers on the edges of the picture, though thanks to a generation of scholarship we certainly grasp more than we once did.

After decades of concerted scholarship, however, the heart of the enslavement experience and its deepest moral and social implications still seem to elude us. This is especially true in the classroom, where even our best books and articles, lectures, and films too often fall short of the mark. (Some readers will resist the view that, despite all our efforts, we have so far failed rather significantly in conveying the deep realities of hereditary enslavement.) What follows is a brief speculation on the dilemmas of teaching about the most extreme long-term inequities of early America. The word *inequality,* when applied to our colonial past, is far from an exaggeration; it is actually a euphemism, which continues to understate and disguise shocking conditions that even now most Americans do not seem fully able to acknowledge.

If racism has proved more tenacious in modern America than many anticipated, this is due in part to the fact that racial enslavement was far worse than most Americans have understood. We have remained in denial, despite the best efforts of singular writers across several centuries to convey the full degradation of this "peculiar institution" and its links to pervasive racism. David Walker, the African American born in North Carolina who published *An Appeal to the Colored Citizens of the World* in 1829, was one such individual. "Treat us like men, and there is no danger but we will all live in peace and happiness together," he told the white readers of his fiery pamphlet. But to continue the forced incarceration of several million people would prove futile and dangerous. "We must and shall be free I say, in spite of you," he warned. "You may do your best to keep us in wretchedness and misery, to enrich you and your children; but God will deliver us from under you. And wo, wo, will be to you if we have to obtain our freedom by fighting." Historian Peter Hinks, in a fascinating recent study, makes clear that Walker repeatedly "returned to the theme that whites were simply incapable of facing honestly and fully the horror of their actions against blacks."[13]

Angelina Grimké, a white contemporary of Walker's who grew up in Charleston, South Carolina, also tried to overcome denial, by confronting northerners with the phenomenon of people being "chained and driven like criminals, and incarcerated in the great prison-house of the South." "Slavery exerts a most deadly influence over the morals of our country," she wrote, "not only over that portion of it where it actually exists as 'a domestic institution,' but like the miasma of some pestilential pool, it spreads its desolating influence far beyond its own boundaries." She was outraged at the society's willingness to continue "drinking the waters of that river of pollution," oblivious to its dire consequences for all Americans. "But this is not all," she told a northern audience in the 1830s, protesting the way in which legalized enslavement fed the nation's racial prejudices:

. . .our people have erected a false standard by which to judge men's character. Because in the slaveholding States colored men are plundered and kept in abject ignorance, are treated with disdain and scorn, so here, too, in profound deference to the South, we refuse to eat, to ride, or walk, or associate, or open our institutions of learning or even our zoological institutions to people of color, unless they visit in the capacity of *servants*, of menials in humble attendance upon the Anglo-American. Who ever heard of a more wicked absurdity in a Republican country?[14]

A few historians have been equally frank in each succeeding generation, but not until the 1960s did the effort to challenge America's persistent denial regarding enslavement take on renewed force. In 1959, Stanley Elkins had drawn upon early studies of Nazi concentration camps to suggest that American slavery constituted a similarly arbitrary and irrational institution. But this effort to compare the brutal Middle Passage and enslavement with the horrors perpetrated during World War II backfired in unfortunate ways; his discussion of how brutal treatment can traumatize and infantilize whole groups seemed to reinforce a stereotype of African Americans as hapless and helpless victims.[15] Following Elkins's assessment of slavery as a dehumanizing "total institution," fellow historians penned assertions that emphasized this dubious stance. For example, Richard Hofstadter (in a volume on early America published posthumously in 1971) summarized the arrival of slaves in the New World:

To Africans, stunned by the long ordeal of the Middle Passage, the auctions could only have marked a decrescendo in fright and depression. . . . But as one tries to imagine the mental state of the newly arrived Africans, one must think of people still sick, depleted, and depressed by the ordeal of the voyage, the terror of the unknown, the sight of deaths and suicides, and the experience of total helplessness in the hands of others. What they had been and known receded rapidly, and the course of their experience tended to reduce their African identity to the withered husks of dead memories.[16]

After rediscovering the harshness of Atlantic slavery, some liberal historians of the 1960s seemed to end up precisely where their racist predecessors had stood when they had written about Africa itself. To the earlier scholars, Africa had been an unknown dark continent with no culture worth remembering, and its exiles had been docile by nature. To the later contingent, Africa, although a viable world, had been blotted out for slaves by the trauma of the Middle Passage. Though avowedly "sympathetic" to the black experience, certain writers from the civil rights era agreed that enslaved newcomers, their "African identity" reduced to a withered husk, could only have fallen into a passive acceptance of their fate.[17] Approaching the problem of enslavement from almost opposite directions, these two groups of writers ended up in the same tobacco field.

An outcry of dismay was certainly in order, and we have spent much of the past twenty-five years examining continuities with Africa, reassessing "the weapons of the weak," cataloging acts of resistance, searching out signs of unbroken cultural strength, and applauding forms of family life that endured through enslavement. Such work is far from over, especially given the overwhelming ignorance of Africa with which most Americans, black and white, began the reassessment. But having exposed the shortcomings in various arguments that stressed total discontinuity from Africa and passivity in the face of oppression, we may have freed ourselves to revisit, with more openness, the deep and troubling question of the high human costs of long-term, hereditary racial enslavement.

Inevitably, the resistance to such a reexamination is strong, especially if the reassessment proceeds from the premise that the central story is more harrowing than all but a few have dared to portray it. What will become of the fragile and ultimately untenable "balance" that now exists in most U.S. history texts between the best insights of the new black history and the most tenacious clichés of the earlier southern history? What will become of the expanding new industry of "heritage tourism" now taking hold in the South, a business premised on the idea of balancing and reconciling inherently contradictory images of the region's past? During the 1996 Olympics, for example, the world was repeatedly invited to "come see Atlanta, birthplace of Margaret Mitchell and Martin Luther King!"

It is important to note that resistance to reexamining slavery comes from all quarters. Many, perhaps most, African Americans shy away from revisiting a chapter in our history so filled with pain and so frequently misconstrued by mainstream scholars. Conversely, many European Americans rightly suspect that further study might move the guilt away from a small category of "bad planters" personified by Simon Legree and implicate generations of Christian believers, North and South, rich and poor.[18] If African and European descendants have their reasons for ongoing denial, numerous modern migrants from Asia, Latin America, and the Middle East feel skeptical about revisiting remote chapters of Atlantic history in which they have only an indirect and uncertain stake. Finally and most important, all these groups and their leaders retain in different ways a deep commitment to the national mythology of freedom and opportunity; a long clear look at our much-denied secret could shake or even shatter that commitment. Perhaps more than anything else, "this tying of national identity to the achievement of equality and liberty has prevented the custodians of national history from publicly coming to terms with the import of slavery and its legacy of racial prejudices."[19]

If slavery seemed too close for many people to discuss clearly in the 1870s (much as the Holocaust remained too close for most persons in the 1950s), in recent times enslavement sometimes feels excessively far away. These days my students, both black and white, often peg their primary sense of racial injustice in America on the fact that buses, schools, lunch counters, and rest rooms were once segregated. When activist Dick Gregory spoke on the Duke University campus recently, I was struck by his answer to a question about progress in race relations. "People say what a bad time it is to be black in America," Gregory replied. "Trust me—try Biloxi, Mississippi in 1942."[20] In other words, the far worse situation of African Americans in 1842 or 1742 is less frequently invoked these days. For many Americans, though certainly not for Gregory, slavery remains some distant and brief aberration, unworthy of concern and therefore long forgotten.

All over the world—in Russia and Bosnia, Rwanda and South Africa, Argentina and Guatemala, Japan and Cambodia, Germany and Switzerland—people are facing similar decisions about when and whether and how closely to examine the darkest chapters of their national past. But each of these countries must wrestle with some unique twentieth-century chapter of "family abuse" writ large, whereas America's midnight of legalized hereditary bondage is a seventeenth-, eighteenth-, and nineteenth-century chapter. If our own long nightmare of "soul-murder" (to use historian Nell Painter's powerful term) seems relatively remote in time, does that make it any easier to examine? Still, the topic seems painfully hard to raise and confront at both the local and the national level, since we cling so tenaciously to a myth that the United States is exceptional in every way, unblemished by the deep scars that afflict other, more obviously dysfunctional national families.

Would a tougher reexamination of enslavement resonate with those members of our dysfunctional national family who currently refuse to acknowledge that slavery has any enduring significance? The character played by Sean Penn in the film *Dead Man Walking* comes to mind: the rough, slightly likable racist on death row who is caught up in hating and dismissing blacks, people whom he categorizes as "sitting on the porch whining about slavery." One need not visit prison cells or Hollywood sound lots to find these smoldering antagonisms; mutual resentments pervade our schools and places of work. If Americans were able to review slavery in a prolonged and sustained manner, such a renewed effort might well stem from and then help to alleviate the deep racial malaise of the United States in the 1990s. For societies, as for individuals, the act of re-membering, acknowledging, and reliving the pain of terrible experiences can lead to awareness and empathy. Only then can grieving, reconciliation, and rebirth follow.

When I first presented a draft of this essay to a conference at the Hunt-ington Library in early 1997, President Clinton had just delivered his sec-ond inaugural address, speaking on the Martin Luther King holiday and urging the improvement of race relations in America. I could still hear the voice of one young African American, interviewed at the Million Man March in Washington in 1996, who had commented wistfully, "I just wish they would say they were sorry." So I began to ruminate on themes of atonement and apology. Can public or official apologies also be heartfelt and cathartic? Can it ever be too late to apologize? Must useful apologies be asked for and accepted, or can they simply be given? My speculations about how these complex social interactions work are as personal and anecdotal as the next person's, especially since we live in a society that lacks forms of meaningful public contrition. I always watch with great interest and a good deal of cultural envy when prominent figures in Japanese business or poli-tics make public and personalized apologies regarding misdeeds for which they or their predecessors are somehow responsible. Wondering if such things could ever happen here, and marveling at the groundswell of fasci-nation with the newly opened Holocaust Museum, I was prompted to in-clude the following paragraph in my remarks about the reconsideration of slavery:

Forthright public leadership from the top in such matters would make a tremen-dous difference, of course, though the thought of such initiative seems an idle pipe dream in the current age. Imagine if the southern-born president and vice president declared a National Day of Atonement for Slavery, as some of their earliest prede-cessors used to do with serious social matters. . . . Imagine if the federal Congress . . . could undertake to put a Slavery Museum on the Mall, not far from the tremen-dously popular and undoubtedly healing Holocaust Museum. I for one would sup-port either gesture and many others besides, but I am not holding my breath.

After my talk, several fellow historians took issue with such proposals, characterizing them as impractical or diversionary and asserting that they would only cause rancorous cultural divisions. Perhaps they were correct. Several months later, emboldened by the success of his apology for the U.S. government's role in the notorious syphilis experiments at Tuskegee, Presi-dent Clinton floated the idea of an official apology for generations of government-sanctioned racial enslavement. Immediately (as my colleagues had predicted), a barrage of criticism rained down on this modest proposal. Pundits suggested that such an action was too large or too little, too early or too late, too broad or too narrow, too crudely symbolic or not symbolic enough. Made cautious by these initial outbursts, the president soon retreated from the idea, saying through his press secretary that such an apology might be considered by his Presidential Commission on Racism.

A subsequent resolution in the Congress did not fare much better during the summer of 1997. Democrat Tony Hall of Ohio and Republican Dave Weldon of Florida introduced House Concurrent Resolution 96, which consisted of a single sentence: "Resolved by the House of Representatives (the Senate concurring), That the Congress apologizes to African Americans whose ancestors suffered as slaves under the Constitution and laws of the United States until 1865." House Speaker Newt Gingrich, perhaps because his Georgia district might feel implicated in any such apology, was swift to distance himself from the proposal: "Any American, I hope, feels badly about slavery," he observed. "I also feel badly about genocide in Rwanda."[21] Clearly, even such a simple resolution remains highly controversial, and at one level I had to concede to my skeptical friends that their intuitions of trouble had been well founded. In the next breath, however, I had to ask whether the shrill tone and contradictory elements of the flare-up might not in fact confirm my suspicion of a society in lingering denial regarding a deep trauma that has been repressed rather than healed.

Whatever steps, symbolic or otherwise, elected officials may choose to take, the creative task of reconciliation and understanding ultimately falls back on concerned sectors of the public, and one such sector is professors of American history with an interest in—I shall use the euphemism—inequality. As a member of that community, let me offer two related suggestions for ways by which teachers of enslavement might revitalize the discussion of what William Dusinberre, in the title of his excellent recent book, has called *Them Dark Days*.[22] The first proposal concerns terminology, since, as Shakespeare pointed out nearly four centuries ago, how we name things has a major hold over how we understand them. "You taught me language, and my profit on't / Is, I know how to curse," Caliban, the New World slave, exclaims to his European master, Prospero, in act 1 of *The Tempest*. "The red plague rid you / For learning me your language!"[23]

I have no doubt that Caliban would support and Prospero would vigorously oppose the suggestion, intimated in my title, to substitute the term *slave labor camp* for the word *plantation*. I am sick of seeing glossy magazine ads for "plantation tours" that will introduce us to the elegant living of olden times. Examples abound. A recent issue of the southeastern regional periodical called the *Carologue* contains a full-page color ad for a numbered edition of a "coffee table" historical atlas of Carolina's tidal rice plantations.

The cost is $100, some of which will benefit Ducks Unlimited. "They harnessed the moon and turned the marshes into fields of gold," reads the headline over a dreamy picture of a low-country vista, complete with Spanish moss. "Travel back down South Carolina's Ashepoo, Combahee and Edisto Rivers to the rice plantations that made South Carolina an economic force in a young nation. The planters there grew Carolina Gold—a variety of rice that bestowed great wealth and lavish lifestyles on a few and set the course for the history of the Palmetto State."[24] For me, the useful description in recent decades of the American plantation as a "factory in the field" was only an appropriate first step toward accurately describing what the written records have amply put before us. I would be both surprised and pleased to see *slave labor camp* become an occasional synonym for *plantation*. As Richard Wright once observed, English speakers have traditionally suffered from "a genius for calling things by the wrong names."[25] We need to alter our benign terminology.

My second suggestion is that we make far greater use of comparative modern-day materials. Even as our knowledge of the institution expands steadily, our capacity to empathize—to get inside the process from the perspective of the individual African American who endured it—does not increase accordingly. In part, this is because the task is so formidable; the weight of the burden, the intensity of the storm, is almost too enormous to fathom. But it is also because "them dark days" are long past, and our primary sources are severely limited. How fortunate we are to have Olaudah Equiano's *Travels* and Frederick Douglass's *Life* and an expanding array of slave narratives.[26] And yet how much more engaged we could become with access to thousands of additional firsthand accounts. What if we possessed tapes and transcribed interviews several generations older than the useful Works Progress Administration slave narratives? Imagine if we had hours of real-time film footage and videotapes of participants, situations, and events, allowing us to make an "Eyes on the Prize" series for the eighteenth century.[27]

In 1996, when the television program *20/20* ran a story on current slavery in Sudan, American viewers encountered women whose leg irons had only recently been removed and whose ankles were scarred from the shackles. The century now coming to an end has had no shortage of mass bondage and exploitation in a multitude of forms, and much of it has been documented with cameras and described vividly by survivors. The Holocaust itself, so recent and so imperfectly understood when Stanley Elkins wrote, has been examined from many different angles since his book appeared.[28] Anyone watching the endless deportation trains in Claude Lanzmann's epic 1985 documentary, *Shoah*, while keeping in mind the agonizing one-way flow of the Middle Passage, cannot help but gain new insights into the long-lasting and evil banality of the Atlantic slave trade, as well as the Jewish Holocaust.[29] Sadly, there is no shortage of contemporary evidence with which to "compare and contrast" American enslavement; we have numerous depressing and inspiring situations from which to choose.

In selecting one particular modern saga that students of enslavement could pursue further, in the classroom and beyond, my own choice at present would be the labor camps established in Russia by Josef Stalin.[30] Westerners have had some sense of the "Gulag Archipelago" since the works of Aleksandr Solzhenitsyn and Eugenia Ginzburg were first translated in the mid-1970s,[31] but only with the demise of Soviet communism in the 1980s did firsthand testimony become more widely accessible and verifiable. In 1988, *New York Times* editor A. M. Rosenthal became one of the first foreigners to tour an operating Russian labor camp when he visited Perm 35,[32] and the following year a few Russian and Western historians were given access to the NKVD archives.[33] By 1992 the Felix Travel Agency in Moscow was offering a "Gulag Camp Tour" taking visitors to work camps in Siberia, and by 1995 former prisoners were returning to visit the labor camps where they had once been confined.[34] Additional books and articles are beginning to appear on the experience of the camps and on the social and political atmosphere in which they were created and sustained.[35]

Obviously, there is no simple parallel between eighteenth- and nineteenth-century America and twentieth-century Russia, for differences abound, both large and small: private property versus state labor, regional variety versus bureaucratic sameness, agricultural work versus industry and mining, hereditary bondage versus political incarceration, hot versus cold. The American experience lasted longer and had a larger generational aspect; the Soviet experience involved a higher annual death rate and a greater number of people. The Siberian gulag absorbed more deportees in two generations than all the slave labor camps of the New World absorbed in four centuries. There were roughly seven million persons in Stalin's work camps at the height of the Great Purge in 1938 and roughly twelve million by the time of his death in 1953.[36] Indeed, recent estimates of the number who died in the Gulag Archipelago, "somewhere between 12 million and 20 million people over 74 years,"[37] mirror generally the uncertain modern estimates of total Africans deported to the Americas by the entire European slave trade.

But there is still much to be learned from such a comparison, primarily because we have access to firsthand accounts by survivors—resources that remain all too scarce and fragmentary for American enslavement—now that the rich and tantalizing WPA interviews from the 1930s have been widely examined and explored.[38] When the Polish writer Ryszard Kapuscinski, one of the great journalists of our era, visited the sites of former labor camps in Siberia several years ago, he summarized the physical conditions in terms that journalist Frederick Law Olmsted might have used in touring the nineteenth-century South: "Everywhere, in Vorkuta, in Norilsk, in Magadan, one is struck by the squalor of the camp world, by its extreme shabby poverty, its clumsy, careless provisionality, slovenliness, and primitivism. It is a world stitched together from patches and rags, nailed together with rusted nails driven in with an ordinary ax, tied together with a burlap rope, secured with a piece of old wire."[39]

It is not only the sparse and depressing outer world of enslavement that can be recaptured through these twentieth-century narratives; it is the inner pain and resolution that can be examined as well. In his amazing book titled *The Long Walk*, written in the 1950s about experiences in the 1940s, another Polish writer, Slavomir Rawicz, tells a tale of capture, deportation, deprivation, labor, and escape that sheds revealing light on the psychological experience of enslavement.[40] Like Equiano and Douglass, he is one of the strong and lucky ones: he manages to escape his chains and tell his story.[41] In the process, he helps us think realistically about how large heterogeneous groups adapt to brutal treatment, perverse illogic, and the death of hope—whom to trust and whom to avoid, whom to help and whom to abandon, when to submit and when to resist. His vivid account also reminds us of inner thoughts and feelings—the agonizing recollection of a freshly baked cake, the life-giving force of a sarcastic joke shared among suffering sojourners.

Similarly, Hilda Vitzthum, in her memoir of ten years in a Soviet labor camp, recounts emotional thoughts for which we have few firsthand equivalents in the recollections of African slaves. Vitzthum recalls how, even in the darkest situations, she drew strength from encounters with nature—"moments that briefly diverted us from the despair of our situation." Thrown aboard a prison transport ship, she underwent a harrowing journey suggestive of the Middle Passage. But despite the sheer weariness that overcame her each evening, she "always enjoyed the sight of the glittering stars and the shining moon" before falling asleep at night. Arriving as a stranger at a new slave labor camp, she was "suddenly overwhelmed by the total misery of this compound. . . . What an accursed, puked-on bit of earth! . . . I felt the absolute absurdity, the utter inhumanity of the situation. . . . What all did not go through my head! My whole life passed by my mind's eye." But even as she saw herself "sliding more and more deeply" into "the abyss," she found a token of hope in the natural world.

At that moment all these depressing thoughts and images dominated me with such intensity that I was overcome with deep despair, and my hopes, already weak, seemed to perish utterly. But some spark of defiance must still have remained in my heart. How else could I have noticed the little daisy that has sprouted from this scarred and trampled earth? Instinctively I bent down and loosened the earth around it so that people could see it more readily and not crush it. Had I not just asked myself if there was any purpose in living any longer, since the chance of survival was again reduced and I had nothing but the worst to look forward to? Had this plain little flower, which had grown despite the thousands of footsteps that daily tramped by, become a symbol for me?[42]

For Vitzthum, whose husband had died in the gulag, the tiny daisy foretold an upturn in her bitter fortunes. "I would probably soon have forgotten this little flower," she writes, "had it not formed part of my introduction to a fine human being, such as existed in all camps." A strange man offered her much needed words of encouragement, and this kindred spirit became her partner. "Something that had been completely buried in me came to life again," Vitzthum recalls. "With this day a new chapter had begun in my camp life."[43] Eugenia Ginzburg relates a similar story from her gulag experience, overcoming hesitations to write about the man who shared her tribulations. "The main thing," she remarks, "is that I wanted to show through his image that the victim of inhumanity can remain the bearer of all that is good, of forbearance, and of brotherly feelings toward his fellow man."[44]

Nothing is harder to re-create within the long annals of American enslavement than the complex human dynamics, both depressing and uplifting, that exist within the confines of the slave labor camp experience. We have come a long way in our studies of American slavery, but we have a long way to go. Indeed, only by coming this far can we catch our breath, take stock, and realize that some of the toughest research and most difficult and important discussions still lie ahead. Southern plantations, beyond the carefully maintained elegance and cultivation of the big house, were in fact privately owned slave labor camps, sanctioned by the powers of the state, that persisted for generations; and we may gain insight into those who endured or were crushed under this perverse regime by examining the rapidly expanding record of modern enslavement. Perhaps then Americans can look at the "decorative" Jefferson-Fry cartouche and, instead of seeing "the elegant living of olden times," see a world of perpetual exploitation and incessant degradation built on racist ideology and overwhelming physical force.

Notes

1. William Shakespeare, *The Tempest* (act 5, scene 1).
2. Quoted in Lance Morrow, "The Justice of the Calculator," *Time*, February 24, 1997, 45.
3. Joyce Appleby, Lynn Hunt, and Margaret Jacob, *Telling the Truth about History* (New York, 1994), 154–55. The authors are invoking Mary Douglass. They go

on to remind us that "to speak of the nation as an institution working assiduously to forget experiences incompatible with its righteous self-image is to fudge the issue of whose experiences must be forgotten and for which groups' benefit" (p. 155).

4. An excellent recent essay by Inga Clendinnen discusses the parallel issue of how indigenous cultures were being portrayed by prominent historians in the decade of the Mexican War and the Oregon Trail. She observes that Spain's original "Mexican Conquest as a model for European-native relations was reanimated for the English-speaking world through the marvelously dramatic *History of the Conquest of Mexico* written by W. H. Prescott in the early 1840s, a bestseller in those glorious days when history still taught lessons. The lesson that great history taught was that Europeans will triumph over natives, however formidable the apparent odds, because of cultural superiority." It is hard to dispute her assertion that, for the most part, "historians are the camp followers of the imperialists." Inga Clendinnen, "'Fierce and Unnatural Cruelty': Cortés and the Conquest of Mexico," in *New World Encounters*, ed. Stephen Greenblatt (Berkeley, Calif., 1993), 12, 18.

5. John Frost, *A History of the United States* (Philadelphia, 1837).

6. In his final speech to the U.S. Senate in 1850, Calhoun chastised northerners for "invoking the name of the illustrious Southerner whose mortal remains repose on the western bank of the Potomac. He was one of us—a slaveholder and a planter. We have studied his history, and find nothing in it to justify submission to wrong." *Congressional Globe*, 31 Cong., 1 sess. (March 4, 1850): 454.

7. Once, when Jefferson returned from a long trip to France, the jaunty text continues, "the negroes went to meet his carriage. They walked several miles down the road; when they caught sight of the carriage, they shouted and sang with delight. They would gladly have taken out the horses and drawn it up the steep hill. When Jefferson reached Monticello and got out, the negroes took him in their arms, and, laughing and crying for joy, they carried him into the house. Perhaps no king ever got such a welcome as that; for that welcome was not bought with money: it came from the heart." D. H. Montgomery, *The Beginner's American History* (Boston, 1902), 165–66.

8. Richard Handler and Eric Gambler, *The New History in an Old Museum: Creating the Past at Colonial Williamsburg* (Durham, N.C., 1997), esp. chap. 5.

9. Unable to see American slavery clearly or take it seriously, scholars of the so-called consensus school during the cold war era were quick to generalize. One wrote in 1959, in an assertion that was commonplace for the time: "All historians would agree that, in comparison with Europe, the United States was a relatively classless society." Marcus Cunliffe, *The Nation Takes Shape, 1789–1837* (Chicago, 1959), 168.

10. Gordon S. Wood, "Rhetoric and Reality in the American Revolution," *WMQ* 3d ser., 23 (1966): 27. Robert E. Brown and B. Katherine Brown, *Virginia, 1705–1786: Democracy or Aristocracy?* (East Lansing, Mich., 1964) had appeared two years earlier. The assertion that "tranquility . . . distinguished the politics of Virginia" is repeated in Robert Middlekauff, *The Glorious Cause: The American Revolution, 1763–1789* (New York, 1982), 39–40. For a discerning fresh look at some of Virginia's actual inequalities and why they have long been underestimated, see Holly Brewer, "Entailing Aristocracy in Colonial Virginia: 'Ancient Feudal Restraints' and Revolutionary Reform," *WMQ* 3d ser., 54 (1997):307–46, and the forthcoming book by Woody Holton on Indians, debtors and slaves in the making of the revolution in Virginia.

11. Until his early death at age forty-nine, Peter Jefferson was known not only for his civic energy in Virginia's gentry community but for his physical strength.

According to lore, this huge man could "head," or pull upright, two hogsheads of tobacco at one time, though each weighed more than five hundred pounds. Eyewitnesses said he once pulled down a small outbuilding with a rope, when three slaves were unable to complete the task. Scholars who seek to explain how Thomas Jefferson reconciled a fierce commitment to independence with a willingness to own slaves need only examine the contradictions of this revered father. "A cardinal maxim" of Peter Jefferson was "Never ask another to do for you what you can do for yourself," and yet the master of Shadwell Plantation controlled sixty enslaved Africans at the time of his death. Fawn M. Brodie, *Thomas Jefferson: An Intimate Portrait* (New York, 1974), chap. 1.

12. The obvious absence of women from this representation of mercantile society in the Chesapeake prompts another discussion. Clearly, contemporary representations of the region's women exist in which the dynamics of class and race were represented in a similar manner. See Kathleen M. Brown, *Good Wives, Nasty Wenches, and Anxious Patriarchs: Gender, Race, and Power in Colonial Virginia* (Chapel Hill, N.C., 1996).

13. David Walker, *An Appeal to the Colored Citizens of the World* (Boston, 1829), 69–70, and Peter P. Hinks, *To Awaken My Afflicted Brethren: David Walker and the Problem of Antebellum Slave Resistance* (University Park, Pa., 1997), 210.

14. Angelina Grimké, *An Appeal to the Women of the Nominaly Free States*, 2nd ed., issued by an Anti-slavery Convention of American Women (Boston, 1838), 13–16, 19–23.

15. Stanley M. Elkins, *Slavery: A Problem in American Institutional and Intellectual Life* (Chicago, 1959).

16. Richard Hofstadter, *America at 1750: A Social Portrait* (New York, 1971), 90.

17. I recall vividly an evening when Professor Elkins visited Princeton University in the early 1970s and spoke to students interested in black studies. I was working in the Firestone Library, completing work on a study of early enslavement called "Black Majority," and I attended the talk. When he finished his remarks and the questioning had reached a stalemate, I spoke up from the back of the room, saying that I had recently come across a significant act of slave resistance, then virtually unknown, in Stono, South Carolina, in 1739. As I sketched the details of the Stono rebellion, a black undergraduate in front of me spun around and exclaimed with enthusiasm, "Hey, man, where did you come from?" Serious researchers into eighteenth-century enslavement in the deep South were still rare and surprising creatures.

18. In the wake of Daniel Jonah Goldhagen's controversial recent volume, *Hitler's Willing Executioners: Ordinary Germans and the Holocaust* (New York, 1996), it is possible to imagine an equally provocative volume about the United States entitled "Columbia's Willing Exploiters: Ordinary Americans and African Enslavement." Though unfavorably received in America, Goldhagen's book has swiftly been translated into a dozen languages, and the author received the 1997 Democracy Prize of the *Journal for German and International Politics in Bonn*. The journal praised Goldhagen for providing a generation of young Germans with answers, "which, as a rule, parents and grandparents had denied them," adding that "the answers of German historiography have until now not been able to fill the gap." Debra Bradley Ruder, "Goldhagen wins German prize for Holocaust book," *Harvard University Gazette*, January 9, 1997. Could the same be said of the American historiography of enslavement?

19. Appleby, Hunt, and Jacob, *Telling the Truth*, 296.

20. Alex Gordon, "Activist blazes trail with pointed humor," *Duke Chronicle* February 17, 1997, 5. Dick Gregory knows this long history all too well, of course, and has written about it effectively in *No More Lies: The Myth and Reality of American History* (New York, 1971).

21. "Apology for Slavery," *Poverty and Race* 6, no. 4 (July/August 1997): 4.

22. William Dusinberre, *Them Dark Days: Slavery in the American Rice Swamps* (New York, 1996).

23. William Shakespeare, *The Tempest*, act 1, scene 2, lines 363–65.

24. *Carologue* (summer 1997), inside back cover.

25. Richard Wright, *White Man, Listen!* (1957; reprint, New York, 1995), 57.

26. *Equiano's Travels: The Interesting Narratives of the Life of Olaudah Equiano or Gustavus Vassa, the African,* abridged and ed. Paul Edwards (London, 1996); *Life and Times of Frederick Douglass: His Early Life as a Slave, His Escape from Bondage and His Complete History, Written by Himself* (New York, 1962) and see, for example, the new edition, prepared by David Cecelski and Debi Hamlin, of Allen Parker, *Recollections of Slavery Times* (Worcester, Mass, 1895, reprint forthcoming). For a course syllabus concerning African-American Literature to 1920, devised by Prof. Werner Sollors at Harvard, see his website, complete with useful links to texts, at http://www.courses.fas.harvard.edu/~afam131/syllabus/syllabus.htm.

27. Though such materials can only be imagined, Boston's public television station, WGBH, recently completed a six-hour series on American enslavement. It aired in October 1998 as "Africans in America."

28. See, for example, Terrence Des Pres, *The Survivor: An Anatomy of Life in the Death Camps* (New York, 1976); Elie Wiesel, *Night*, trans. Stella Rodway (New York, 1982); Lawrence L. Langer, *Holocaust Testimonies: The Ruins of Memory* (New Haven, Conn., 1991); Christopher Browning, *Ordinary Men: Batallion 101* (San Francisco, 1991).

29. Claude Lanzmann, *Shoah, an Oral History of the Holocaust: The Complete Text of the Film* (New York, 1985). See also Annette Insdorf, *Indelible Shadows: Film and the Holocaust* (New York, 1983). For a strongly worded restatement of the place of the slave trade in Atlantic history, see the brief but important foreword by Cornel West, "The Ignoble Paradox of Western Modernity," in Madeleine Burnside, *Spirits of the Passage: The Transatlantic Slave Trade in the Seventeenth Century* (New York, 1997), 8–10.

30. In 1987, Peter Kolchin showed us that there is much to be learned from comparing American slavery and Russian serfdom. But a great deal has changed in the decade since then, and we are now beginning to learn about more recent forms of unfree Russian labor. Peter Kolchin, *Unfree Labor: American Slavery and Russian Serfdom* (Cambridge, Mass., 1987).

31. Aleksandr I. Solzhenitsyn, *Gulag Archipelago, 1918–1956: An Experiment in Literary Investigation*, 3 vols. (New York, 1974–78), and Eugenia Ginzburg, *Journey into the Whirlwind* (New York, 1975) and *Within the Whirlwind* (New York, 1981).

32. A. M. Rosenthal, "Into the Heart of the Gulag," *Reader's Digest*, April 1989: 71–76. See also Jean-Pierre Vaudon, "Last Days of the Gulag?" *National Geographic* 177, no. 3 (March 1990): 40–47.

33. Karen J. Winkler, "Opening a Window on Life in Soviet Labor Camps," *Chronicle of Higher Education*, October 30, 1991, A8; R. W. Davies, "Forced Labor under Stalin: The Archive Revelations," *New Left Review* 214 (November–December 1995): 62–81.

34. Deborah Stead, "The Gulag Tour: It Ain't Club Med," *Business Week,* November 16, 1992, 148; Andrew Nagorski, "Back to the Gulag," *Newsweek,* September 25, 1995, 46–48. Gulag is the Russian acronym for the official name of Stalin's vast system of labor camps.

35. See, for example, Irena Ratushinskaya, "En Route to the Gulag," *Commentary* 86, no. 3 (September 1988): 35–41; Leona Toker, "Awaiting Translation: Lev Konson's Gulag Stories," *Judaism: A Quarterly Journal of Jewish Life and Thought* 45 (winter 1995): 119–28; Véronique Garros, Natalia Korenevskaya, and Thomas Lahusen, eds., *Intimacy and Terror: Soviet Diaries of the 1930s* (New York, 1995); Robert W. Thurston, *Life and Terror in Stalin's Russia, 1934–1941* (New Haven, Conn., 1996).

36. Mike Edwards, "The Gulag Remembered," *National Geographic* 177, no. 3 (March 1990): 48–49.

37. Nagorski, "Back to the Gulag," 46.

38. We hope that one day we shall have firsthand accounts of the extensive "Laogai gulag" of forced labor in China. Chinese human rights activist Harry Wu, speaking at a luncheon in his honor sponsored by the Independent Institute in Oakland, California, March 27, 1996, discussed

> . . . the laogai camp system, of which we have identified 1,100 camps. It is also an integral part of the national economy. Its importance is illustrated by some basic facts: one third of China's tea is produced in laogai camps; 60 percent of China's rubber vulcanizing chemicals are produced in a single laogai camp in Shanghai; . . . one of the largest and earliest exporters of hand tools is a camp in Shanghai; an unknown but significant amount of China's cotton crop is grown by prisoners. I could go on and on and on.
>
> Sometimes people ask me, "What are you fighting for?" And my answer is quite simple. I want to see the word laogai in every dictionary in every language in the world. I want to see the laogai ended. Before 1974, gulag did not appear in any dictionary. Today it does. This single word conveys the meaning of Soviet political violence and its labor camp system. Laogai also deserves to become a word in our dictionary. (Harry Wu, "The Outlook for China, Human Rights: The Laogai Gulag," *Vital Speeches* 62, no. 17 [June 15, 1996]: 522)

39. Ryszard Kapuscinski, *Imperium* (New York, 1995), 211.

40. Slavomir Rawicz, *The Long Walk: The True Story of a Trek to Freedom* (New York, 1984); originally published as *The Long Walk: A Gamble for Life* (New York, 1956).

41. Rawiscz, *The Long Walk,* 32–34. Slavomir Rawicz became a runaway slave. He escaped from Camp 303 on the Lena River near the Arctic Circle in the dead of winter, with five companions and a stolen ax; they trekked south across Siberia, Mongolia, the Gobi Desert, and the Himalayan Mountains. It took an entire year for the survivors in the party to reach northern India.

42. Hilda Vitzthum, *Torn Out by the Roots: The Recollections of a Former Communist* (Lincoln, Neb., 1993), 153–54.

43. Ibid., 184–86.

44. Ginzburg, *Within the Whirlwind,* 122.

Philip D. Morgan

RETHINKING EARLY AMERICAN SLAVERY

IN EARLY AMERICA nothing and no one escaped the effects of slavery, an institution forged in the heat of continual, inescapable, face-to-face encounters. Many a white child came into the world in the arms of a black nurse; many a master went out of it on the backs of black pallbearers. Thomas Jefferson's earliest memory was a horseback ride as a two-year-old boy cradled in the arms of a mounted slave. Waking to the sound of black voices, listening to the bustle of black domestics, going to sleep to the snores of black workers were common experiences for slave-owning households. Slave owners populated their figures of speech with slaves: as humble as a slave, as yellow as a mulatto, looking skyward "like a Negro weeding corn," "sleepy like a sugar mill slave," sleeping in one's clothes "like a Negro." Just as slaves invaded the master's everyday world, so they impinged on their unconscious world. A planter in East Florida dreamed that, with a single wave of his hand, his slaves "instantly gathered" huge crops. After a Virginia master lost nine slaves to the British during the revolutionary war, he fancied his runaways returning "most wretchedly meager and wan" to beg his forgiveness. He had to dream on, for his fugitives never returned. White and black, master and slave were inextricably linked, "joined at the hip" in Nathan Huggins's memorable phrase. They shaped each other's destiny.[1]

Slavery was no curious abnormality, no aberration, no marginal feature of early America. Most early Americans found servile labor neither embarrassing nor evil. Rather, slavery was a fundamental, acceptable, thoroughly New World institution, bearing an ancient pedigree to be sure but readily adaptable to American needs and circumstances. In labor recruitment, British America was the land of the unfree. Prior to 1780 three times as many Africans as Europeans crossed the Atlantic to British America. Much of the wealth of early America derived from slave-produced commodities in what was the world's first system of multinational production for a mass market. Slavery defined the structure of a majority of British American regions, underpinning not just their economies but their social, political, cultural, and ideological systems. In classical and Judeo-Christian traditions, slavery was the central paradigm for understanding the nature of liberty. In large measure, conceptions of freedom were the creation of slavery; Jefferson himself once acknowledged that his slaves labored so that he could pursue his own happiness. In everything, then, from dreams to labor recruitment to ideology, slavery must be situated squarely at the center of the early American experience; directly or indirectly, the institution touched everyone. It is the great transforming circumstance of American history.[2]

If slavery is located at the center of the early American experience, why is it in the margins of two recently published books, each in its own way sweeping and expansive, concerning late-eighteenth-century North America? I refer to Gordon Wood's Pulitzer Prize winner on the era of the American Revolution and Stanley Elkins and Eric McKitrick's Bancroft Prize winner on the age of federalism. Both books say very little about the slave experience or the institution of slavery. Granted that a book should be understood and appreciated on its own terms, it is nevertheless discordant to read an account of the transformation of America from 1760 to 1830 without learning anything of the huge expansion of slavery or crystallization of racism that occurred in those years, or an account of the high politics of the 1790s without confronting the fundamental impact of the Haitian revolution. In these two synthetic works, slavery is not just at the margins, it is almost nonexistent.[3]

There are many reasons why it is still possible to marginalize slavery, relegate it to the sidelines, even almost completely ignore it. At one pole are those like Frederick Jackson Turner, who claimed in one of his most celebrated essays that "when American history comes to be rightly viewed it will be seen that the slavery question is an incident." At the other extreme are those who still prefer, in Toni Morrison's words, to forget the unforgettable and to leave the unspeakable unspoken. Or as Fred D'Aguiar's fictional slave, Whitechapel, put it, slavery made him "see without seeing, witness without registering a memory or sensation"; the future was "just more of the past waiting to happen," and memory was "pain trying to resurrect itself." But perhaps the major reason for a failure to grasp slavery's centrality is not scholarly disdain nor induced amnesia but the sheer profusion of new work on the subject, truly an embarrassment of riches. The explosion of books, articles, essay collections, international symposia, research reports, and the like can be gauged in the most comprehensive bibliography of slavery: in 1980 it numbered four thousand items, almost all published since the mid-1950s; today works on slavery cascade from the presses at more than a thousand a year, and the bibliography, I estimate, stands at about sixteen thousand. The proliferation has been so rapid that it is now hard to see the forest for the trees; indeed, in many ways the historiographical landscape might be more accurately represented as a rank thicket of shrubs, saplings, and occasional trees in search of a forest. In short, the study of early American slavery has placed itself in the margins through loss of definition and coherence.[4]

Three central developments in the scholarship of early American slavery have contributed to this loss of focus. First, much of the recent literature has been centrifugal, spinning off in all directions. Conventional Anglo-American boundaries have been expanded to include, for example, the important pioneering and military role that blacks played in early Spanish Florida. The Southwest also clamors for attention, most particularly the rough-and-tumble, violent world of military outposts, Maroon camps, and interracial alliances—one of the most racially flexible societies in the Americas—that emerged in the eighteenth-century Lower Mississippi Valley. In the circum-Caribbean, the scholarly horizons now stretch from the maritime Maroons of the Danish West Indies, a true boat people; to the land-based maroons of Providence Island, who mounted the first slave rebellion in British America; to the Saramaka maroons of Suriname who, in their notion of a First-Time, kept alive memories of wars against the Dutch and their own liberation. Our understanding of early American slavery has been enriched by encompassing its full continental and archipelagic dimensions, its precarious and permeable zones of interaction, its hybrid societies, its mosaic of borderlands where cultures jostled and converged in combinations and permutations of dizzying complexity. But at the same time the temporal and spatial boundaries of the subject are consequently now in flux, which contributes to a loss of scholarly direction.[5]

Another centrifugal force has been the shift in the study of slavery from the plantation heartland to its fringes, from the core to its outer edges. Many slaves, it is now clear, cultivated grains, raised livestock, toiled for the domestic rather than the export market, and worked in every nonagricultural sector. Slavery knew no limits; it penetrated every economic activity, every environment. Slaves lived in temperate highlands as well as in tropical lowlands, on farms as well as on plantations, in cities as well as in the countryside; they worked in fields and in shops, in manual and in skilled occupations, in civilian and in military life, up trees and down mines, on land and at sea. One spotlight has fallen on maritime slaves, forever moving along the edges of the plantation world and connecting one to the other: from the Kru, *grumettes*, and canoe men of the African coast; through the Bermudians and Bahamians who fished the Grand Banks, pursued whales in the North Atlantic, and raked salt and salvaged wrecks in the Caribbean; to the coastal boatmen and offshore seamen who plied up and down the North American coast. Closely connected to maritime slavery was urban slavery, whether black chimney sweeps in New York, the formation of a black community in Philadelphia, or female higglers in Kingston, Jamaica. Another group moving from the shadows into the sunlight are industrial slaves—ironworkers in western Virginia, chemical workers in Baltimore, sugar mill workers in the Caribbean, skilled and unskilled workers in the tanneries, ropewalks, and shipyards of many an Atlantic port town. The attention to the nonplantation world is welcome, attesting to slavery's flexibility and adaptability. But plantations, it should never be forgotten, were the engine that drove the Atlantic slave system. The farms, shops, ships, and manufacturing enterprises may be likened to safety valves that helped keep the great engine running, but the sheer weight of recent scholarship has seemed to give more attention to what regulated rather than what powered the system.[6]

Slavery scholarship has not only spun off outward across old boundaries and to the fringes but turned inward as well. This implosive quality, this thrusting inward to explore the interior of slave life in minute, often microscopic, detail is a second major feature of the recent scholarly literature. Slave heights have been measured, bodies weighed, bones and teeth inspected, hairstyles deconstructed. Clothing has been dissected to describe appearance; faunal remains sifted to explore diet; trash, pots and pans, and tobacco pipes exhumed to provide clues to material and cultural life; graves and root cellars pried open to reveal the slaves' innermost secrets. Evidence has accumulated on everything from comparative stature to the effects of late weaning, from lead content to congenital syphilis. The call has even gone out to exhume Thomas Jefferson and the children of Sally Hemings; only DNA testing can resolve the issue of those children's paternity, it is claimed. To get inside the slaves' minds as well as their bodies, autobiographies and memoirs have been probed, court trials plumbed, newspaper advertisements combed, songs and folktales dissected. The minutiae are by turns fascinating, intriguing, and mind-boggling. As a result, slaves seem in danger of supplanting Puritans in our historiography: we almost know more about them than sane people would want to know.[7]

Slavery scholarship has not only spun off outward and turned inward— something of a gymnastic feat in itself—but has also pirouetted on the fulcrum of marginality, a concept that owes much to the pathbreaking work of Orlando Patterson. Marginality is fascinating. Things that are marginal are ambivalent, simultaneously pointing in two directions. The slave was both physically alive and socially dead; the slave represented the boundary of social existence, the edge of humanity. The slave was a generally dishonored nonperson formally cut off from ancestors, kin, and progeny. Rituals such as hair shaving, branding, and renaming marked off the slave from the recognized classes or castes of organized community. Patterson recognized that the effectiveness of the slave's marginality required some measure of incorporation and hope of eventual manumission, however slight. But for the most part he portrayed the slave as dependent on the master for mediation with the outside world and therefore in a state of formal isolation and liminality. Brilliant as is this argument, there is a danger here of confusing psychology with history, of allowing the search for universal common denominators to become too remote from specific settings, and of minimizing the slaves' subjective sense of lineage and honor.[8]

One unintended consequence, then, of the huge expansion of interest into the byways, interiors, and very marginality of slave life has been a loss of focus, a marginalization, a decentering of the subject. The challenge is how best to put slavery in its rightful place, not in the wings but center stage, not detouring down sidepaths but proceeding along the trunkline, not left behind in the eddies but firmly in the mainstream. Some of the more promising lines of research into early American slavery, I will suggest, derive from perfectly simple yet fundamental historical inquiries, from the obvious yet often ignored questions of where, when, how, and with whom slaves lived—the all-important contextual questions that encourage us to recover the full texture of any people's lives. I conclude by adressing one more question, familiar to all those who attend challenging seminars: so what?

Where?

The *where* question is perhaps the most complex. Any exploration of slavery has to involve spatial comparisons, whether implicit or explicit. This means adopting a wide angle of vision, a broad transoceanic framework, seeing the Atlantic as a single, complex unit of analysis, and breaking out of the national boundaries traditionally set for the study of American slavery. It also means a willingness to sharpen the focus, to examine in-depth specific regions and locales, to embrace particularity. And finally, it means opting for a dynamic diasporic approach, attending to flows, dispersals, and mixtures of people. In short, it means using a telescope, a microscope, and a moving camera.

The most notable example of the telescopic approach is the comparative history of slavery, by far the most extensive and sophisticated comparative literature in American historiography. The bilateral comparisons have been systematic and varied, contrasting race relations in North and South

America, slavery in Virginia and Cuba, white supremacy in the United States and South Africa, unfree labor in America and Russia, two landed elites in the United States and Prussia, and the slaves' economy and material culture on sugar plantations in Jamaica and Louisiana.[9]

Illuminating as these transnational comparisons often have been, legitimate criticisms arise about comparing like with unlike. If the differences between societies seem both numerous and obvious, a comparison might merely validate the predictable contrasts. The ultimate test of a comparative study is that the individual cases appear in a new light when viewed together. But rather than providing constructive commentaries on one another, some comparisons essentially engage in discordant dialogue. As a result, the entities being compared can come away from the encounter looking substantially unchanged. Conjunction serves only to emphasize contrariety. There is a place for more modest comparisons—two varieties of apples, as it were, not apples and oranges. As Raymond Grew explains, there is "no reason to consider the comparison of Chicago and Milan as more comparative than a comparison of Chicago and Baltimore." Richard Dunn's continuing investigation of two plantations—Mount Airy in Virginia and Mesopotamia in Jamaica—is a model, low-key comparison. At once very alike, since they are part of the same Anglophone world, and yet significantly different, since they inhabit different environments, these Virginian and Jamaican slave communities provide intelligent commentaries on one another. My own book explores two regions—the Chesapeake and the low country—within the same Anglophone world. Instead of contrasting divergent legal systems, national cultures, and church-state relations— all too easily highlighted in transnational comparisons—these phenomena are held constant. This constancy allows me to privilege the impact of different ecologies, settlement patterns, demographic regimes, staple systems, and master lifestyles—issues that are too readily ignored when cross-cultural comparisons are made. Not so dissimilar as to produce merely predictable contrasts, these two regions are not so alike as to produce only variations on a theme. Rather, each society looks different in the light of the other; and our understanding of each is enlarged by knowledge of the other.[10]

Far more common than sweeping cross-cultural comparisons in the study of slavery have been investigations of single locales—a region, a colony, a county, a city, a plantation. The advantage of a local study is the heightened specificity that it permits, the opportunity it affords of carrying slavery down to the level of individual slaves. The disadvantage is that typicality and significance can be obscured. Microhistory can easily lead to microthinking. But the best studies of slavery in small places have asked large questions. Edmund Morgan's study of the development of slavery in

Virginia ranged far and wide, beginning in Panama and ending with a vision of America as Virginia writ large. Winthop Jordan's investigation of a slave conspiracy in Adams County, Mississippi, rests on his sense of analogous developments elsewhere in the history of New World slavery. His observations on the whipping of slaves and of the sexual dimensions of slave conspiracy scares are far from parochial and stretch well beyond the confines of Adams County.[11]

My current project is a small-scale study that I aim to press into a larger mold. I am trying to reconstruct what it was like to live in southwestern Jamaica in the second half of the eighteenth century. My goal is to capture the routines and rhythms of everyday life in the region. My main informant is Thomas Thistlewood, a man of no particular distinction except that he kept one of the most detailed records of plantation life in existence. At present, no regional study of slavery exists for eighteenth-century Jamaica, which was certainly no peripheral slave society but rather the most important slave colony in the Anglo-American world, the jewel in Britain's imperial crown. This is the plantation heartland par excellence, and any attempt to come to terms with slavery in its starkest, most intensified form must confront the Caribbean, a part of the world closely connected to but quite different from North America.

One of the larger questions that must be wrestled with is how can a single white man, cloaked in authority, live in isolation among a large number of blacks, working, semistarving, whipping, and raping them at will, yet emerge physically unscathed—although never psychically. In part his resilience is attributable to extraordinarily coercive management techniques; in part to his dependence on a variety of slaves, from whom he learns more than he ever gives; in part to the incentives, indulgences, days off, garden plots, promotions to lighter or more skilled and better rewarded work that he and slaves negotiated; in part to the slaves' restraint; and in part to sheer plain luck. But simple unilinear scales that run from punishment to concessions, from resistance to accommodation, from positive to negative incentives, from subordination to autonomy obscure the daily realities of this world. This Jamaican slave society was starkly polarized, to be sure, but clear-cut dichotomies cannot explain how it functioned. They do a disservice to the tragedy of oppressed people struggling to survive. To understand their survival is to come to terms with engagements and confrontations, concord and conflict. Mechanistic formulas are no help. There is room for a concrete history of slavery, a history that memorializes, by the careful documentation of small events, a remarkable drama of social exchange and cultural survival even under the most oppressive of conditions.[12]

Finally, the moving camera is required to trace the connection between homeland and New World, perhaps the least well studied spatial dimension in slavery scholarship. In this regard, the truly pioneering work is Joseph Miller's *Way of Death*, a close analysis of the connections between two precisely delineated areas on either side of the Atlantic. There have been other attempts to link Africa and America, usually at a high level of generalization, but surely such attempts are premature and must await more carefully contrived regional analyses. I am thinking, for example, of John Thornton's argument that randomization was not a function of the Middle Passage. Thornton and others claim that slave ships drew their entire cargoes from only one or two African ports, that catchment areas were homogeneous, and consequently that most slaves in the Americas perceived themselves as part of communities with distinct ethnic or national roots.[13]

As the slave trade project sponsored by the W. E. B. DuBois Institute for Afro-American Research at Harvard University reaches conclusion, we become able to test such claims. Compiling information on every known individual voyage drawn from the records of all the major European and American slaving powers, the project currently has data on 27,233 voyages, extending from 1562 to 1867. Information exists on perhaps two thirds of all ships that made a transatlantic slave voyage. This project has amassed the largest data set for the study of the long-distance movement of peoples before the twentieth century. As a result, more is already known about the forced migration of Africans than the voluntary migration of Europeans in the early modern era.[14]

The key findings of this consolidated and comprehensive data set concern neither Africa nor the Americas treated alone but rather the connections between the continents. The project makes it possible to view the intercontinental flow of people from both sending and receiving poles. At first glance, some of the preliminary findings seem to support the emerging orthodoxy propounded by Thornton and others. From the vantage point of Africa, most coastal regions funneled a majority of their forced emigrants to one region in the Americas. About 70 percent of Africans from the Bight of Biafra, for example, went to the British Caribbean. And from the perspective of the Americas, some regions, most notably Bahia and South-Central Brazil, drew 80 to 90 percent of their slaves from a single African provenance zone. Yet, even within a single African coastal region, marked shifts occurred in the peoples forcibly expelled, and most American regions received slaves from a wide mix of African peoples. Furthermore, broad summaries of aggregate patterns disguise marked changes over time. A dynamic diasporic approach indicates how slaves came from a changing series of African coastal regions. The aggregate picture masks a fluid reality. Because many African slaves came in tortuous and convoluted ways from the interior to the coast, whatever ethnic identity they originally had was undoubtedly in flux. Similarly, in the New World so-called African ethnic or national identities were often reconstitutions or inventions. Ethnic identities both within Africa and the Americas accordingly should be viewed as fluid and permeable. Heterogeneity, not the homogeneity emphasized by Thornton, is the overriding characteristic of the Atlantic slave trade; and plasticity, not fixity, is the story of ethnic identity in this pan-Atlantic world.[15]

Tracing the transition from particular homelands to particular New World locations, conducting in-depth investigations of single locales with large questions in mind, comprehending both the heart and arteries of the slave system, and exploring explicit comparisons, both cross-cultural and regional, are the kinds of spatial specificity that the study of early American slavery demands. If these interconnected goals can be summarized, it is the need to examine the links, exchanges, and parallels between interrelated segments of an increasingly unified if extended Atlantic system, to integrate the whole and the parts, the general and the particular, and to cross boundaries, in Paul Gilroy's words, "in defiance of classic canonic enclosures."[16]

When?

Just as the study of slavery must be anchored in a close attention to place, so it must be rooted in a precise attention to time—the *when* question. No longer, for example, can a history of slavery in North America begin in the year 1619, because it was 1526 that saw the first contingent of African slaves brought to this continent; the site was not Jamestown but present-day Sapelo Sound in Georgia. Many studies of slavery suffer from a sense of timelessness. In the United States the best exploration of the world the slaves made hinged on a static bargain between master and slave; another recent investigation of slave culture based it on an unchanging African foundation. In the Caribbean, most investigations of slavery are frozen in time: they begin and end in the early nineteenth century. What is often missing from such historical works is, rather surprisingly, the essence of history: emergence, adaptation, adjustment, evanescence—in a word, change. Not all are found wanting, of course, and least so the histories of early American slavery, such as those written by, say, Peter Wood and Stuart Schwartz. Unlike studies of antebellum slavery, such works centrally probe the development and evolution of slave life. Although a general narrative history of early American slavery remains to be written, there probably now exists enough depth in the monographic literature to permit one. What would it look like?[17]

No more than a quick sketch can be offered here, but a few key transitions or critical disjunctures frame the development of slave societies and cultures. One vital watershed that many, though not all, colonial societies experienced was the shift from a society with slaves to a society based on slaves, from a slave-owning society to a slave society, akin to the distinction that some economists make between marketplace economies where commerce occurs and true market economies where commerce reigns supreme. Race relations tended to be more fluid and flexible in slave owning than in slave societies: A slave generally could pass more readily from bondage to freedom, work at a wider range of tasks, and occasionally marry whites in a society where slavery was not the central institution. The emergence of a true slave society was usually accompanied by a large influx of Africans, restrictive and regimented forms of labor, a distancing of white and black, a battery of harsh legal codes, and a battening down of any escape hatches out of slavery. In shaping cultural patterns, the earliest migrants enjoyed certain advantages over later arrivals. They invented many of the rules, created languages, learned how to deal with one another. This early slave-owning phase was a plastic period, a soft moment, an era of malleability, that would later rigidify, harden, and become inflexible.[18]

Another crucial transition is rather more difficult to pinpoint but is perhaps even more important to document. The glitter of first contact inevitably catches the eye, but the long-term historical processes of interracial negotiation of power and meaning, while less glamorous, are absolutely vital to an understanding of an emerging slave society. As masters and slaves became familiar with one another, they found ways to live together. A major turning-point was the emergence of a critical mass of creole or native-born slaves, sometimes with self-sustaining families reproducing themselves demographically and culturally. At the workplace, customary rules and routines emerged. A growing minority of men escaped field labor and began to assume managerial, artisanal, and domestic posts, while slave women increasingly dominated field labor. A code, as much unwritten as written, arose to govern the sexual exploitation of slave women: it ranged from open concubinage in some societies to furtive, secretive interracial liaisons in others. Access to freedom, almost nonexistent in the early years of most full-fledged slave societies, inched wider as time progressed, in large part because some white fathers freed their mulatto offspring.[19]

Another landmark in the history of early American slavery is the era of late-eighteenth- and early-nineteenth-century revolutions, not just political, important as they were, but economic, religious, and intellectual transformations that reshaped the world of white and black and redefined race. For the first time, slavery faced serious challenge: in unprecedented fashion, slaves attacked the general principles justifying their enslavement; the northern states gradually put the institution on the road to extinction. Far more momentously, the slaves of St. Domingue grasped their freedom in the greatest and most successful example of slave resistance in history, with far-reaching and still not fully understood implications for the hemisphere. At the same time as the era marked a new birth of freedom, it also witnessed a great expansion of slavery: the Atlantic slave trade peaked at the end of the eighteenth century, a huge territorial growth of slavery occurred, and racial thought crystallized. A gradual sea change affected master-slave relations as masters began to emphasize solicitude rather than authority, sentiments rather than severity in the governance of their slaves. Island planters began to speak of "amelioration"; mainland planters, of paternalism.[20]

Another watershed occurred when a slave system began to falter. The process of sugar cultivation in the Caribbean has been likened to a relay race, with one island successively relinquishing the baton to another. But once the baton had been passed, how did a slave society cope? How, for example, did Barbadian slavery change once the white-hot fury of the initial sugar revolution had cooled? Similarly, what form did the transformation of slavery in Virginia take once its reliance on tobacco waned? Or how about the consequences of the crisis that occurred in late-eighteenth-century Minas Gerais in Brazil when its gold and diamond mining boom faded? Clearly, all societies to varying degrees diversified, putting slaves to cultivating foodstuffs, producing for local consumption, and engaging in local manufacturing. All three slave societies, again to contrasting degrees, showed signs of vigor. All three, for example, had slave populations that were growing—in two of the three, spectacularly. But were there other features that these societies shared? And what accounts for the differences?[21]

Narrating linear sequences will not be easy. Certain cyclical or broad repeating patterns seem to characterize the ways in which slavery expanded, as, say, the movement from a frontier to a settled state, or from diversified farming to monocultural production and perhaps back again, or from a predominantly immigrant to a predominantly native-born slave population, all of which occurred in successive stages from one slave society to the next. On closer inspection, however, to conceive of the expansion of slavery, a helix may be more appropriate than a repeating circle, for slavery's progression from one society to another—indeed, the progression was often direct, as from Barbados to South Carolina or from the Leewards to the Windwards—could compress, skip almost entirely, perhaps even elongate elements of earlier stages. Thus, a continuous and expanding spiral may be the best way to see slavery expanding from one zone to another. Similarly, cultural development followed no straightforward trajectory of attenuation, death or survival. Rather, complex processes of appropriation, subversion, masking, invention, and revival occurred. The transmission of ethnicity involved reinvention and reinterpretation, discontinuities as much as continuities. In short, the stages of slavery's development were never simple or clear-cut, even if they were part of one overall historical process.[22]

Whatever the narrative complexities, the overall aim must be to historicize slavery, to abandon static analyses of the institution, and to render slaves a people with a history, not outside history, as a people with agency, shaping their own experiences and thereby molding the structures that also victimized them.

How?

Work must be a central element of any attempt to write a chronology of slavery, but for the past few decades slavery scholarship has focused on culture, religion, and family life, obscuring the centrality of work in the lives of slaves. Ironically, just as slavery has been left out of most analyses of American labor, so labor has been left out of most analyses of slavery. But in the last few years this focus has been changing, with work taking center stage where it belongs, for slavery after all was first and foremost an institution of coerced labor. The question of how slaves lived must confront squarely the role of labor in shaping slave life. Black family life, social development, and cultural expression all need grounding in the labor process. The social relations of labor must be the starting point for any examination of the black experience. The basic history of slaves as workers needs to be written.[23]

Not that work alone explains all, of course. Indeed, we might profitably return, in more sophisticated fashion, to U. B. Phillips's concentration on land and labor, environment and workplace, as key influences on slave life. This means coming to terms with some of the more fertile subdisciplines of social history—historical geography, historical archaeology, material culture, ecohistory as some now grandiosely term the study of environmental factors. It means exploring everything from land use to material conditions, from climate to physical landscapes, and the roles they played in framing the lives of slaves. As for labor, it means encompassing the dizzying combinations of modes of work organization, work demands, seasonal rhythms, divisions of labor, hours of work, skill levels, technologies, function by sex and age, and unit size.[24]

Acknowledging the centrality of work offers a useful beginning in the study of slave life, but understanding the slaves' labor cannot stop there. The exploitation entailed in the appropriation of the slaves' labor provides only the barest outline of the lives slaves lived. Most elementally, the work of slaves can be divided into that done for the master and that done for themselves. Slave societies thus involved two interrelated and overlapping economies: one organized by and for masters, the other by and for slaves. The slaves' economy varied in character and extent from place to place. The so-called peasant breach in the slave mode of production was particularly wide in southwestern Jamaica. In 1752 a white resident reckoned that the slaves of his parish spent £20,000 a year, the proceeds of their provision grounds and by-employments. Slaves ran the local market, many possessed livestock, and a sizable minority owned horses. Thistlewood once drafted a will for a slave who bequeathed a cow to his wife's shipmate, a heifer to his wife's daughter, and his horse and the balance of his estate to his wife. He further requested that he be buried at his mother's right hand and that there be no singing around his grave.[25]

As this slave's wishes demonstrate, independent economic endeavors provided a foundation for domestic and community life. They shaped family life, molded the social structure of slave society, provided a material basis for the slaves' distinctive culture, and offered a modicum of power to resist the masters' demands. Slaves laid claim to the fruits of their labor for themselves and their posterity. Traveling about the Chesapeake, one European visitor conversed with slaves to understand their view of the world. They declared "their mind very freely," he noted, saying "as we work and raise all, we ought to consume all." To underline the point, they continued, "Massa does not work; therefore he has not equal right: overseer does not work; he has no right to eat as we do." Caribbean slaves clung to the belief, one estate manager noted, that they had "a right" to their provision grounds on account of their labor on the plantation. The slaves' economy reached deep into all aspects of African-American culture.[26]

Perhaps because studies of slaves have not been fully rooted in the workplace, the pathological character of black life in slavery has been exaggerated and the ability of slaves to shape their own lives underestimated. A more complicated view acknowledges that slaves were unable fundamentally to alter their condition, recognizes that exploitation exacted real costs and engendered long-term harm, and then explores the ability of slaves, often under the most difficult of circumstances, to influence the conditions of their lives and to exercise some control over their day-to-day existence. Work was both the source of the slaves' oppression and the seedbed of their liberation. Work imposed severe constraints, but those limits were in part the product of what was possible to demand or extract from slaves—a result, in other words, of their agency. The aim must be to demonstrate the degree to which slaves contributed to the making of their history, without ever losing sight of the molding power of material forces beyond their control. It can be achieved by demonstrating not only how slaves worked for their masters but how they worked for themselves, not only how they engaged in unrelenting toil for few benefits but how they also derived personal satisfaction and political self-assertion from their work, not only how they were exploited but how they they engaged in numerous and various workplace struggles.[27]

In exploring workplace struggles, much can be learned by comparing and contrasting slave and nonslave workers. Indeed, one of the great virtues of focusing on the importance of work in order to understand slavery is that it should force a confrontation of the relationship of slavery and so-called free labor, a fundamental issue that continues to attract much interest. In early America it is increasingly clear that slave and nonslave (whether free or coerced) labor should be seen, in David Eltis's words, "as part of a continuum" rather than "as polar opposites." Perhaps we are only relearning what Moses Finley taught many years ago, namely, that slavery is a variant of far more general modes of institutionalized unfreedom, that it is "a species of dependent labor and not the genus." Nevertheless, the insights are also deepening: in the recognition that the legal evolution of free labor in early America was an early nineteenth-century development; in the demonstration that some early American labor forces in specific settings and periods were a remarkable mixture of slaves, indentured servants, hired workers, day laborers, and debt servants; in explorations of the reasons why, in certain areas in the Mid-Atlantic and New England, there was a concentration of slaves; in the connections between the "free labor" zones and slave labor zones; and in general accounts that explain why the land-labor ratio in some cases produced slavery and in others did not.[28]

With Whom?

Connecting the slave and the nonslave is necessary in answering the question of with whom slaves lived because it requires paying close attention to the patterns and variations in the endless encounters between the enslaved and the free, white and black. Too frequently, slavery has been seen from an institutional perspective and too often the treatment of slaves has been inferred from statute law, intellectual treatises, or dominant social attitudes. Instead, such perspectives must be supplemented with explorations of actual behavior, of the extensive daily contacts that occurred across the racial divide and that produced almost unlimited permutations of human emotions, infinitely subtle moral entanglements. We need fewer sociologies of the slave institution and more anthropologies of slaves and masters.[29]

The place to start is inside the household, the crucible of social relations in early America. The slave was not simply a factor of production with whom an employer maintained a limited relationship but was a part of the master's household. Not for nothing were slaves termed *famuli* in the ancient world. They were the original *familia*, a group of *famuli* living under the same roof. Anglo-American masters inherited this tradition and referred to their slaves as their "people," their "folks," as part of their "family." Slaves were almost uniformly known by familial not formal names— Jack for John, Sukey for Susanna. The patriarchal outlook, the dominant social ethos of seventeenth and early eighteenth-century Anglo-America, encouraged the use of the familial metaphor.[30]

The appropriateness of patriarchalism to describe eighteenth-century master-slave relations is contentious. Was it not more myth than fact? Were not masters hypocrites, merely capitalist wolves in patriarchal clothing? Surely, selling so-called children cannot be reconciled with any conception of familial governance and must represent the triumph of the capitalistic marketplace over any conceivable ethic of paternal responsibility? The short answer is that patriarchy must be understood in its early modern context. It stressed unswerving obedience and a quick resort to violence when authority was questioned. Although involving protection, guardianship, and reciprocal obligations, patriarchy was an austere code, emphasizing control, discipline, and severity. Patriarchalism cannot be dismissed as mere propaganda or apologetic—though, like all ideological rationalizations, it contained its share of self-serving cant—but was rather an authentic, if deeply flawed, worldview. Its familial rhetoric was not just a smokescreen for exploitation, because it offered no guarantee of benevolence. It was no sentimental self-image, but rather a harsh creed.

Other discourses, other ways of thinking about slaves, unquestionably made their inroads on the patriarchal ideal. Slaves were chattel, and masters thought of and acted toward them using the language of property. Anglo-American masters were profit-conscious, operated in a market economy, and employed the language of commercial capitalism. An economically acquisitive mentality was not, of course, incompatible with the ethics and customs of patriarchy. Indeed, for much of the eighteenth century, neither the discourse of property nor of capitalism overrode, although they certainly encroached on, the masters' sense of slaves as dependents. Being part of a household served to cushion slaves from the full force of free market commercialism. Harsh profit-and-loss purgatives had not yet voided the body politic of its traditional notions of duty and mutuality. To ignore the familial character of slavery, then, is to misconstrue the institution itself. To choose capitalism over patriarchalism is to make an unnecessary choice. The relationship between master and slave received its highest ideological sanction in patriarchalism.

A full anthropology of master and slave, white and black, must move beyond the household to explore the countless human transactions, the everyday encounters, the perpetual contests as well as the continual bargaining, the jostling as well as the mingling that the institution necessarily involved. Perhaps the most important development was the emergence of channels of communication across racial lines. Over time, relations between masters and slaves, blacks and whites became routinized at various connecting points. This active and reciprocal relationship was evident in matters great and small—from the management of a field gang to the running of an errand, from the mediation of an overseer to the intervention of an elderly slave, from trade within the plantation to trade without. Encounters also occurred in different arenas—in the alternating rhythm of truce and violence that characterized the public life of slave societies, in the twisted emotional knot of affection and callousness that bound together white and black sex lives, in the hierarchy and fraternization at recreational events, and in the indifference and enthusiasm at religious meetings. Masters and slaves, whites and blacks created a world that, in Elizabeth Fox-Genovese's words, "could shimmer with mutual affection or . . . shatter in mutual antagonism."[31]

If encounter, that quintessential quincentennial word connoting a measure of mutuality and reciprocity even between oppressor and oppressed, is one concept at the core of early American slavery, it must be considered alongside mastery, which forces a confrontation with the considerable coercive power at the disposal of slave owners, and negotiation, which emphasizes subaltern agency in transactions and interactions.[32] In small compass, these concepts are the essence of the Thistlewood story. Jamaica developed a regime of chattel slavery without parallel in scale, scope, and savagery. Jamaican masters and overseers, a governor once remarked, were schooled in "the diplomacy of the lash," not in the arts of persuasion. Thistlewood's raw and naked mastery is documented in chilling detail: the sadistic, degrading punishments, the regular floggings, the sexual exploitation, the onerous work, the starvation, the high mortality rates. Physical punishment—the fact of it and the threat of it—incidental cruelties, despotic whimsy, and callous brutishness seep through the diary like a running sore. The central tensions in the relations between master and slaves, the lines of battle in an unceasing guerilla war, are also revealed. The conflicts of interest, the pressures toward unthinking and therefore unquestioning obedience, toward loyalty and sabotage, seduction and infidelity, hard work and shirking are all there. The raw nerves of slavery are fully exposed.[33]

Alongside this harrowing story, however, is another side to slavery: a complex give-and-take of gifts and incentives, exchanges and transactions, concessions and bargaining. From this perspective, slavery was less a state of war than a tug-of-war. There were even friendly visits of neighbors, companionable walks about the estate, magic lantern shows, the viewing of eclipses and comets through a telescope, the sharing of folktales—the unremarkable stuff of community living, of mutuality, even of camaraderie, except that all these interactions were between free and unfree, white and black. This was a system of compromises, a series of balances of needs and wills, no matter how unevenly matched and inherently unequal the parties. There was an elusive common ground even in Jamaican slavery, where the minimal demands of masters and slaves were brought into some sort of balance. Masters and slaves contested and negotiated, renegotiated and redefined the terms of their existence in the myriad processes of daily life.[34]

This Jamaican story also suggests a rethinking of a retreat to the margins that seeks to overcome the connotations of passivity associated with plantation slavery. On the margins, away from the greater anonymity of collective agrarian labor, slave life can seem more noble, more meaningful. On the margins, scholars emphasize that slaves controlled more of their own lives, had greater psychological breathing space—"feels as a man," as one observer said of slave sailors—than their plantation counterparts. Thus, ironworkers at Buffalo Forge in West Virginia staked out some precious independence and gained a sense of pride and self-worth from their ability to earn cash; Bermudan sailors working in all-black crews enjoyed considerable autonomy and room for decision making; Belizean log cutters had guns and were entrusted to go into the forest for months at a time; slaves belonging to Moravians in western North Carolina sometimes earned wages, supervised white workers, secured the right not to be sold, and were welcomed with the kiss of peace when they joined the church. These are impressive rights and concessions, hard won and jealously defended, but are they anomalies, the description most beloved by their historians? In the Jamaican plantation heartland, slaves often grew their own food on separate provision grounds, where they worked without supervision, labored in groups of their own choosing, made calculations about what to grow and how much, marketed their products for cash—in sum dramatized their humanity. Is this also a peculiarity? We need to recognize that slaves always tried to turn even the most dismal of circumstances to their advantage, struck bargains to eke out some autonomy, and negotiated the terms of their existence. Some slaves had more bargaining power and a little more room to maneuver than others; but all were subject to a degrading and brutal system, and all had the bittersweet experience of knowing that, whatever the benefits they gained from their slivers of independence, their participation always benefited the master class.[35]

Encounters, mastery, negotiation—these are the currency in which slavery specialists must trade, for they force a turning outward as well as inward, a focus on relationships with whites as well as among blacks, an attention toward structural constraints as well as individual and social agency.

As scholars of working-class life, popular culture, and gender explore the intersection of plebeian and patrician, low and high cultures, women and men, scholars of slavery must continue exploring the same intersections, as well as those between free and unfree, white and black. Yet at the same time that the enslaved and the free were locked into an intimate interdependence, aspects of slave life assumed their characteristic shape within, but to some extent separately from, the masters' social and cultural forms. Slave life, as Sidney Mintz and Richard Price have pointed out, "remained in many ways disengaged from the concerns of masters." Relations among slaves must encompass Africans and creoles, artisans and field hands, family members and solitaries, Christians and non-Christians, but most fundamentally perhaps, men and women. Gender analyses of slavery are an extremely promising line of enquiry.[36]

Consider the slave trade. Women and children actually outnumbered men among Africans arriving in the Americas. True, young men were the single most important component of the slave trade, but when compared to the trade in indentured servants or in convicts, the Middle Passage comprised a remarkably large number of women and children. In fact, the age and sex ratios of the Atlantic slave trade were more similar to free than to contractual migrant flows. The proportion of women also varied markedly both between African regions of embarkation and American regions of arrival and over time. From the perspective of American regions, much larger shares of women were carried to the British areas than elsewhere, with women and men arriving in almost equal numbers in early Barbados and Jamaica, whereas between two and three times more men than women arrived in Cuba and Brazil. Over time, the share of women among African arrivals fell uniformly across African regions. From one region to the next, the proportion of women dropped by well over 50 percent from the seventeenth to the nineteenth century.[37]

This new understanding of the slave trade, coupled with detailed explorations of the demography of particular American slave societies, helps us understand why in some places, even at an early stage in development, women sometimes equaled or even outnumbered men. Furthermore, because slave women were largely denied access to craft and supervisorial positions, the crushing weight of field labor fell disproportionately on their shoulders. Women came to predominate in many a field gang and bore the brunt of increased workloads and ever monotonous drudgery. The large numerical presence of women, their dominance of field labor, the inability of slave men to control women through legally sanctioned marriage, and men's lack of ownership and distribution of property has led some scholars to suggest a measure of equality between the sexes under slavery. Yet slave husbands and fathers often had informal, if not formal, power, as naming practices and the organization of the domestic or slave economy indicates. Slave men monopolized skilled and privileged posts; at a time when authority followed age, husbands tended to be much older than their wives; and slave women were, of course, highly vulnerable to rape and sexual exploitation from white men. Still, working alongside or in place of men in the fields, often raising children unassisted by men, running away far less than men, securing manumission more frequently than men, and serving as the primary transmitters of culture, many slave women were remarkably self-reliant and self-sufficient. An uneasy tension existed in slave life between patriarchal and egalitarian tendencies, with the former uppermost.[38]

Relations between men and women, masters and slaves, whites and blacks acquired meaning only through countless human transactions. Hierarchies of gender, slavery, and race certainly existed: almost all masters, most whites, and many men wielded enormous power and committed manifold acts of blatant oppression. But as much as power originated at the top of the system, it could not be exercised without accounting for the nature of the response from below. Active and reciprocal encounters produced unlimited permutations of human emotions and infinitely subtle moral entanglements.

So What?

Attention to the obvious, deceptively simple, historical inquiries—where, when, how, and with whom slaves lived—encourages us to recover the full context of slave life, to describe the rich texture of past circumstances, and to recapture the fabric of an inescapably varied institution. It is to encompass the spatial dimensions of slavery—traversing along north-south as well as east-west axes, ranging across plantation and farm, heartland and margins, sorting out central and peripheral, majority and minority slave experiences; to re-create the chronology of slavery, its turning points, its watersheds, and most important, its piecemeal growth—the ways in which it was built little by little, step by step; to penetrate to the heart of slavery, work, but then to trace its arteries outward as they radiated into all aspects of black culture; to comprehend the twisted, tangled relations of blacks and whites, the bewilderingly diverse ways in which masters and slaves as well as slave men and women struggled to negotiate their competing interests. Perhaps the best answer to the so what question is to contextualize slavery in all its complexity.

At the risk of sounding old-fashioned and traditional, my summary prescription for the study of early American slavery is what E. P. Thompson once called "the discipline of historical context." Only context can show

that slavery was no static or monolithic institution, but was rather aston-
ishingly diverse and complicated, ever unfolding and dynamic. Only context can show that slaves, above all, worked and that when, where, how,
and with whom they worked determined, in large measure, the course of
their lives. Only context can show that there was no fixed racial divide but
rather a penumbra of negotiability and permeability between masters and
slaves, whites and blacks. Similarly, only context can show that relationships between masters and slaves as well as among slaves were not just a
hierarchy governed by external structures of law and economy but rather
that those visible structures set broad limits within which all people had a
measure of latitude to maneuver in accord with their capacities, opportunities, and interests. Only context can reveal the real evil of slavery. Cruelty
and suffering existed in abundance, but they were not constant and unremitting. Violence was neither ubiquitous nor incidental but above all was
located, was routine, was normal, was part of the everyday fabric of life,
and was all the more brutal for its limitations. As Hannah Arendt has said
in another context, "the normality was much more terrifying than all the
atrocities put together." The normality does not mitigate the evil; it only
places it in context.[39]

The story of slavery is a thoroughly American one of loss and survival,
pain and endurance, damage and ingenuity. Indeed, it is possible to argue
that the concentrated intensity of the slave experience marked blacks as a
truly modern people—literally alienated yet restitching their lives back together, victims of an awesome human tragedy yet defying social death by
insisting on their humanity, driven in regimented fashion beyond endurance yet eking out a degree of freedom, eating imported or rationed foods
yet earning cash in their spare time. It would be an irony if, at a moment
when many, from ordinary folk to artists and novelists, are willing to confront slavery—whether by placing a plaque at the site of a sunken slave ship
off Key West, saving the African Burial Ground in lower Manhattan, celebrating slave ancestors at Mount Vernon, or writing great works of fiction
like *Beloved* or *Sacred Hunger*—historians fail to represent the institution
in all its importance and complexity.[40]

If slavery can be represented fully, its story will be synonymous with
that of America. Racial slavery is, after all, the grim and irrepressible theme
governing the settlement of much of the Western Hemisphere. Many
claims have been made for the single key to understanding America, the
one bedrock on which all else rests—the frontier, the desire for personal
freedom, land speculation, to name only a few—but there is little dispute
about what is America's nightmare, its dark underside. Racial slavery is
early America's haunting original sin. America provided unprecedented
opportunities for some, predicated on the unprecedented exploitation of

others. Liberation and exploitation were the reverse sides of the same coin; they were inextricably joined. Thus, any full accounting of the American revolutionary era or of the high politics of the early republic must reckon with the dramatic expansion of both bondage and liberty, the entrench-ment of southern slavery, the fundamental impact of the Haitian revolu-tion, and the development of northern racism. Slavery was omnipresent in early America, and blacks should be neither invisible nor peripheral but es-sential, crucial, central players in the early American drama.

Notes

1. Henry S. Randall, *The Life of Thomas Jefferson*, 3 vols. (New York, 1858), 1:11; *The Papers of Henry Laurens*, ed. Philip M. Hamer et al., 20 vols. to date (Colum-bia, S.C., 1968–), 3, 553 ("humble"); Josiah Smith to George Austin, Jan. 30, 1773, Josiah Smith Letterbook, University of North Carolina, Chapel Hill ("yellow"); Sam Briggs to Randolph Barksdale, July 22, 1789, Peter Barksdale Letters, Duke University ("skyward"); Stuart B. Schwartz, *Sugar Plantations in the Formation of Brazilian Society: Bahia, 1550–1835* (Cambridge, 1985), 100 ("sleepy"); John C. Fitzpatrick, ed., *The Writings of George Washington from the Original Manuscript Sources, 1745–1799*, 39 vols. (Washington, D.C., 1931–1944), 1, 17 ("sleeping"); F. G. Mulcaster to [?], Nov. 6, 1768, Manigault Family Papers, South Caroliniana Li-brary, University of South Carolina, Columbia ("East Florida"); Jack P. Greene, ed., *The Diary of Colonel Landon Carter of Sabine Hall, 1752–1778*, 2 vols. (Char-lottesville, Va., 1965), 2, 1064 ("Virginia"); Nathan I. Huggins, "The Deforming Mirror of Truth: Slavery and the Master Narrative of American History," *Radical History Review* 49 (winter 1991): 25–46; also published, with other fine essays, in *Revelations: American History, American Myths*, ed. Brenda Smith Huggins (Ox-ford, 1995), 252–83.

2. David Eltis, "Free and Coerced Transatlantic Migrations: Some Compari-sons," *AHR* 88 (1983): 251–80; John J. McCusker and Russell R. Menard, *The Econ-omy of British America, 1607–1789* (Chapel Hill, N.C., 1985); Orlando Patterson, *Freedom*: vol. 1, *Freedom in the Making of Western Culture* (New York, 1991); Lucia Stanton, "'Those Who Labor for My Happiness': Thomas Jefferson and His Slaves," in Peter S. Onuf, ed., *Jeffersonian Legacies* (Charlottesville, Va., 1993), 147–80. The reader will note that early America is usually British America in what follows. I confine myself in this way for two reasons: I know British America better than I do French, Spanish, Portuguese, or Dutch America, and I have not the space for a more general treatment. Nevertheless, I draw on non-British experiences, and I believe many of my arguments have wider application. I therefore have not re-stricted the geographic scope of my title.

3. Gordon Wood, *The Radicalism of the American Revolution* (New York, 1992); Stanley Elkins and Eric McKitrick, *The Age of Federalism: The Early American Republic, 1788–1800* (New York, 1993). For a study that puts slavery at the forefront of early national politics, see Robert Pierce Forbes, "Slavery and the Meaning of America, 1819–1837" (Ph.D. diss., Yale University, 1994).

4. Frederick Jackson Turner, *The Frontier in American History* (New York, 1920), 24; Toni Morrison, "Unspeakable Things Unspoken: The Afro-American

Presence in American Literature," *Michigan Quarterly Review* 28 (1989): 1–34; Fred D'Aguiar, *The Longest Memory* (London, 1994), 1, 4–5, 138. The most complete and up-to-date bibliography is Joseph Miller, *Slavery and Slaving in World History: A Bibliography, 1900–1991* (Milford, N.Y., 1993), with annual updates in the journal *Slavery and Abolition*, the most recent of which is Joseph C. Miller and Janis M. Gibbs, "Slavery: An Annual Bibliographical Supplement (1995)," *Slavery and Abolition 17*, no. 3 (1996), 270–339.

5. Jane Landers, "Gracia Real de Santa Teresa de Mose: A Free Black Town in Spanish Colonial Florida," *AHR* 95 (1990): 9–30; Gwendolyn Midlo Hall, *Africans in Colonial Louisiana: the Development of Afro-Creole Culture in the Eighteenth Century* (Baton Rouge, La., 1992); Daniel H. Usner Jr., *Indians, Settlers, and Slaves in a Frontier Exchange Economy: The Lower Mississippi Valley before 1783* (Chapel Hill, N.C., 1992); Neville A. T. Hall, *Slave Society in the Danish West Indies: St. Thomas, St. John and St. Croix* (Baltimore, 1992); Karen Ordahl Kupperman, *Providence Island 1630–1641: The Other Puritan Colony* (New York, 1993); Richard Price, *First-Time: The Historical Vision of an Afro-American People* (Baltimore, 1983).

6. For examples of the range, see John C. Inscoe, *Mountain Masters, Slavery, and the Sectional Crisis in Western North Carolina* (Knoxville, Tenn., 1989); Wayne K. Durrill, "Routine of Seasons: Labour Regimes and Social Ritual in an Antebellum Plantation Community," *Slavery and Abolition* 16 (1995): 161–87; Patience Essah, *A House Divided: Slavery and Emancipation in Delaware, 1638–1865* (Charlottesville, Va., 1996); W. Jeffrey Bolster, *Black Jacks: African-American Seamen in the Age of Sail* (New York, 1997); Paul A. Gilje and Howard B. Rock, "'Sweep O! Sweep O!': African-American Chimney Sweeps and Citizenship in the New Nation," *WMQ* 3d ser., 51 (1994): 507–38; Gary B. Nash, *Forging Freedom: The Formation of Philadelphia's Black Community, 1720–1840* (Cambridge, Mass., 1988); Lorna Simmons, "Slave Higglering in Jamaica, 1780–1834," *Jamaica Journal* 20, no. 1 (1987): 31–38; Charles B. Dew, *Bond of Iron: Master and Slave at Buffalo Forge* (New York, 1994); T. Stephen Whitman, "Industrial Slavery at the Margin: The Maryland Chemical Works," *Journal of Southern History 59* (1993): 31–62; Robert S. Starobin, *Industrial Slavery in the Old South* (New York, 1970); Peter J. Parish, *Slavery: History and Historians* (New York, 1989), 97–123; Philip D. Morgan, "Black Life in Eighteenth-Century Charleston," *Perspectives in American History, n.s.* 1 (1984), 187–232; Shane White, *Somewhat More Independent: The End of Slavery in New York City, 1770–1810* (Athens, Ga., 1991); White, "'It Was a Proud Day': African Americans, Festivals, and Parades in the North, 1741–1834," *JAH* 81 (1994), 13–50; Franklin W. Knight and Peggy K. Liss, eds., *Atlantic Port Cities: Economy, Culture, and Society in the Atlantic World, 1650–1850* (Knoxville, Tenn., 1990). For a different view of the shift to the "margins," see Jon F. Sensbach, "Charting a Course in Early African-American History," *WMQ* 3d ser., 50 (1993): 394–405, esp. 397–98.

7. A massive literature exists on these subjects. For a few examples, see Robert W. Fogel, *Without Consent or Contract: The Rise and Fall of American Slavery* (New York, 1989), 138–43; Shane White and Graham White, "Slave Hair and African-American Culture in the Eighteenth and Nineteenth Centuries," *Journal of Southern History* 61 (1995): 45–76; Shane White and Graham White, "Slave Clothing and African-American Culture in the Eighteenth and Nineteenth Centuries," *Past and Present* 148 (1995): 149–86; Matthew C. Emerson, "Decorated Clay Tobacco Pipes from the Chesapeake: An African Connection," in *Historical Archaeology of*

the Chesapeake, ed. Paul A. Shackel and Barbara J. Little (Washington, D.C., 1994), 35–50; Jerome S. Handler and Frederick W. Lange, *Plantation Slavery in Barbados: An Archaeological and Historical Investigation* (Cambridge, Mass., 1978); Jerome S. Handler and Robert S. Corruccini, "Weaning among West Indian Slaves: Historical and Bioanthropological Evidence from Barbados," *WMQ* 3d ser., 43 (1986): 111–17; Jerome S. Handler, Arthur C. Aufderheide, and Robert S. Corruccini, "Lead Contact and Poisoning in Barbados Slaves: Historical, Chemical, and Bioanthropological Evidence," in *The African Exchange: Toward a Biological History of Black People*, ed. Kenneth F. Kiple (Durham, N.C., 1988), 140–66; Paul Finkelman, "Thomas Jefferson and Antislavery: The Myth Goes On," *Virginia Magazine of History and Biography* 102 (1994): 196. For good, up-to-date accounts, see Patricia Samford, "The Archaeology of African-American Slavery and Material Culture," *WMQ* 3d ser., 53 (1996): 87–114; *I, too, Am America: Studies in African American Archaeology*, ed. Theresa A. Singleton (Charlottesville, Va., forthcoming); and *The Archaeology of the African Diaspora in the Americas*, Guides to the Archaeological Literature of the Immigrant Experience in America, no. 2, ed. Theresa A. Singleton and Mark D. Bogard (Ann Arbor, Mich., 1995).

8. Orlando Patterson, *Slavery and Social Death: A Comparative Study* (Cambridge, Mass., 1982); David Brion Davis, "At the Heart of Slavery," *New York Review of Books* 43 (Oct. 17, 1996): 51–54.

9. Frank Tannenbaum, *Slave and Citizen: The Negro in the Americas* (New York, 1946); Herbert S. Klein, *Slavery in the Americas: A Comparative Study of Cuba and Virginia* (Chicago, 1967); Carl N. Degler, *Neither Black nor White: Slavery and Race Relations in Brazil and the United States* (New York, 1971); George M. Fredrickson, *White Supremacy: A Comparative Study in American and South African History* (New York, 1981); Peter Kolchin, *Unfree Labor: American Slavery and Russian Serfdom* (Cambridge, Mass., 1987); Shearer Davis Bowman, *Masters and Lords: Mid-Nineteenth-Century U.S. Planters and Prussian Junkers* (Oxford, 1993); Roderick A. McDonald, *The Economy and Material Condition of Slaves: Goods and Chattels on the Sugar Plantations of Jamaica and Louisiana* (Baton Rouge, La., 1993).

10. Raymond Grew, "The Comparative Weakness of American History," *Journal of Interdisciplinary History* 16 (summer 1985): 95; Richard S. Dunn, "A Tale of Two Plantations: Slave Life at Mesopotamia in Jamaica and Mount Airy in Virginia 1799 to 1828," *WMQ* 3d ser., 34 (1977): 32–65; Philip D. Morgan, *Slave Counterpoint: Black Culture in the Eighteenth-Century Chesapeake and Lowcountry* (Chapel Hill, N.C., 1998). See also Michael Mullin, *Africa in America: Slave Acculturation in the American South and the British Caribbean, 1736–1831* (Urbana, Ill., 1992).

11. Edmund S. Morgan, *American Freedom—American Slavery: The Ordeal of Colonial Virginia* (New York, 1975); Winthrop D. Jordan, *Tumult and Silence at Second Creek: An Inquiry into a Civil War Slave Conspiracy* (Baton Rouge, La., 1993). For a later period, see *Plantation, Town and County: Essays on the Local History of American Slave Society*, ed. Elinor Miller and Eugene D. Genovese (Urbana, Ill., 1974), and Charles Joyner, *Down by the Riverside: A South Carolina Slave Community* (Urbana, Ill., 1984). For general reflections, see Darrett B. Rutman with Anita H. Rutman, *Small Worlds, Large Questions: Explorations in Early American Social History, 1600–1850* (Charlottesville, Va., 1994).

12. For Thistlewood, see J. R. Ward, "A Planter and His Slaves in Eighteenth-Century Jamaica," in *The Search for Wealth and Stability: Essays in Honour of Michael W. Flinn*, ed. T. C. Smout (New York, 1979), 1–21; Douglas Hall, *In Miserable*

Slavery: Thomas Thistlewood in Jamaica, 1750–86 (London, 1989); and Philip D. Morgan, "Slaves and Livestock in Eighteenth-Century Jamaica: Vineyard Pen, 1750–1751," *WMQ* 3d. ser., 52 (1995): 47–76.

13. Joseph C. Miller, *Way of Death: Merchant Capitalism and the Angolan Slave Trade, 1730–1830* (Madison, Wis., 1988); John Thornton, *Africa and Africans in the Making of the Atlantic World, 1400–1680* (New York, 1992), esp. 195–97. For arguments similar to those of Thornton concerning ethnicity, see Hall, *Africans in Colonial Louisiana,* 159; Mervyn C. Alleyne, *Roots of Jamaican Culture* (London, 1988), ix, 18; Mullin, *Africa in America,* 160. For a nuanced attempt to explore these issues, see Paul E. Lovejoy, "The African Diaspora: Revisionist Interpretations of Ethnicity, Culture, and Religion under Slavery," Boston University African Studies Center Working Papers, 1996.

14. For some analyses deriving from the project, see David Eltis and Stanley L. Engerman, "Was the Slave Trade Dominated by Men?" *Journal of Interdisciplinary History* 23 (1992): 237–57; David Eltis and Stanley L. Engerman, "Fluctuations in Sex and Age Ratios in the Transatlantic Slave Trade, 1663–1864," *Economic History Review* 46 (1993): 308–23; David Eltis, "The Volume and African Origins of the British Slave Trade before 1714," *Cahiers d'Etudes africaines* 138 (1995): 617–27; *Routes to Slavery: Direction, Ethnicity and Mortality in the Transatlantic Slave Trade,* ed. David Eltis and David Richardson (London, 1997); Stephen D. Behrendt, "The Annual Volume and Regional Distribution of the British Slave Trade, 1780–1807," *Journal of African History* 38 (1997): 187–211; David Richardson, "The British Empire and the Atlantic Slave Trade, 1660-1807," in *The Oxford History of the British Empire:* vol. 2: *The Eighteenth Century,* ed. Peter Marshall (New York, 1998); David Eltis et al., *The Trans-Atlantic Slave Trade: A Database on CD-ROM* (New York, 1998).

15. For a detailed discussion and elaboration, see Philip D. Morgan, "The Cultural Implications of the Atlantic Slave Trade: African Regional Origins, American Destinations, and New World Developments," *Slavery and Abolition* 18 (1997): 122–45; and Sean Hawkins and Philip Morgan, "Patterns of Cultural Transmission: Diffusion, Destruction, and Development in the African Diaspora" (paper presented at a workshop on "The African Diaspora and the Nigerian Hinterland: The Research Agenda," York University, Toronto, February 1996). See also Stephan Palmie, "Ethnogenetic Processes and Cultural Transfer in Afro-American Slave Populations," in *Slavery in the Americas,* ed. Wolfgang Binder (Wurzburg, Germany, 1993), 337–63.

16. Paul Gilroy, *The Black Atlantic: Modernity and Double Consciousness* (Cambridge, Mass., 1993).

17. Eugene D. Genovese, *Roll, Jordan, Roll: The World the Slaves Made* (New York, 1974); Sterling Stuckey, *Slave Culture: Nationalist Theory and the Foundations of Black America* (New York, 1987); B. W. Higman, *Slave Populations of the British Caribbean, 1807–1834* (Baltimore, 1984); Peter H. Wood, *Black Majority: Negroes in Colonial South Carolina from 1670 through the Stono Rebellion* (New York, 1974); Schwartz, *Sugar Plantations.* For other admirable works of early American slavery, see Allan Kulikoff, *Tobacco and Slaves: The Development of Southern Cultures in the Chesapeake, 1680–1800* (Chapel Hill, N.C., 1986), and Lorena Walsh, *From Calabar to Carter's Grove: The History of a Virginia Slave Community* (Charlottesville, Va., 1997).

18. Philip D. Morgan, "British Encounters with Africans and African-Americans, circa 1600–1780," in *Strangers in the Realm: Cultural Margins of the First British*

Empire, ed. Bernard Bailyn and Philip D. Morgan (Chapel Hill, N.C., 1992), 157–219; Ira Berlin, "From Creole to African: Atlantic Creoles and the Origins of African-American Society in Mainland North America," *WMQ* 3d ser., 53 (1996): 251–88. Why slavery arose in particular places at particular times merits much closer investigation. For a good introduction to the subject, see Russell R. Menard and Stuart B. Schwartz, "Why African Slavery? Labor Force Transitions in Brazil, Mexico, and the Carolina Lowcountry," in *Slavery in the Americas*, ed. Binder, 89–114, and Russell R. Menard, "Transitions to Slavery in British America, 1630–1730: Barbados, Virginia, and South Carolina," *Indian Historical Review* 15 (1988–1989): 33–49.

19. I explore some of these themes in my *Slave Counterpoint*. I believe that the privileged Atlantic "creoles," so well explored by Berlin in "From Creole to African," had little long-term influence.

20. *Slavery and Freedom in the Age of Revolution*, ed. Ira Berlin and Ronald Hoffman (Charlottesville, 1983); Sylvia R. Frey, *Water from the Rock: Black Resistance in a Revolutionary Age* (Princeton, N.J., 1991); David Brion Davis, *The Problem of Slavery in the Age of Revolution, 1770–1823* (Ithaca, N.Y., 1975). There has been some useful recent work on the Haitian revolution and its impact, esp. Carolyn Fick, *The Making of Haiti: The Saint Domingue Revolution from Below* (Knoxville, Tenn., 1990), and Alfred N. Hunt, *Haiti's Influence on Antebellum America* (Baton Rouge, La., 1988). But we will know a great deal more when David Geggus and Julius Scott publish their full-length studies on the subject.

21. Eric Williams, *Capitalism and Slavery* (Chapel Hill, N.C., 1944), 8. There is as yet no detailed study of Barbadian slave society in the eighteenth century, although Jerome Handler has limned the story in many articles. For an excellent sketch of Chesapeake developments, see Lorena S. Walsh, "Slave Life, Slave Society, and Tobacco Production in the Tidewater Chesapeake, 1620–1820," in *Cultivation and Culture: Labor and the Shaping of Slave Life in the Americas*, ed. Ira Berlin and Philip D. Morgan (Charlottesville, Va., 1993), 170–99, although more work is required on the shift to grains. Minas Gerais has turned into a cottage industry; see, for the beginning of the debate, Amilcar Martins Filho and Roberto B. Martins, "Slavery in a Non-Export Economy: Nineteenth-Century Minas Gerais Revisited," *Hispanic American Historical Review* 63 (1983): 537–68; Robert W. Slenes, Warren Dean, Stanley L. Engerman, and Eugene D. Genovese, "Comments on 'Slavery in a Non-export Economy,'" idem., 569–90; and Martins and Filho, "'Slavery in a Non-export Economy': A Reply," idem., 64 (1984): 135–46.

22. I explored the issue of how to characterize the trajectory of Chesapeake slavery from Tidewater to Piedmont in "Slave Life in the Virginia Piedmont, 1720–1790," in *Colonial Chesapeake Society*, ed. Lois Green Carr, Philip D. Morgan, and Jean B. Russo (Chapel Hill, N.C., 1988), 433–84. For a good account of the surprising twists and turns of one black people's cultural development, see Sally Price and Richard Price, *Afro-American Arts of the Suriname Rain Forest* (Berkeley, Calif., 1980). The formation of creole languages provides a great deal of insight into the complexities of reinvention and reinterpretation, simplification and elaboration; the literature is vast, but see *Pidginization and Creolization of Languages: Proceedings of a Conference Held at the University of the West Indies, Mona, Jamaica, April 1968*, ed. Dell Hymes (Cambridge, 1971); Mervyn C. Alleyne, *Comparative Afro-American: An Historical-Comparative Study of English-based Afro-American Dialects of the New World* (Ann Arbor, Mich., 1980); and John A. Holm, *Pidgins and Creoles*, 2 vols. (Cambridge, 1988).

23. Stuart B. Schwartz, *Slaves, Peasants, and Rebels: Reconsidering Brazilian Slavery* (Urbana, Ill., 1992), x–xi, 39–59. This and the suceeding paragraphs draw from Berlin and Morgan, eds., *Cultivation and Culture*, 1–45. For attempts to put slavery and racism back into studies of American labor, see Alexander Saxton, *The Rise and Fall of the White Republic: Class Politics and Mass Culture in Nineteenth-Century America* (London, 1990); and David R. Roediger, *The Wages of Whiteness: Race and the Making of the American Working Class* (London, 1991); "Race and the Working-Class Past in the United States: Multiple Identities and the Future of Labor History," *International Review of Social History* 38 (1993): 127–43; and *Towards the Abolition of Whiteness: Essays on Race, Politics, and Working Class History* (London, 1994), esp. 30–34.

24. Ulrich Bonnell Phillips, *Life and Labor in the Old South* (Boston, 1929). For some examples of sensitivity to the environmental context of slavery, see B. W. Higman, *Jamaica Surveyed: Plantation Maps and Plans of the Eighteenth and Nineteenth Centuries* (Kingston, Jamaica, 1988), esp. 5–18, 80-230, 243–76, 291; and Mart A. Stewart, *"What Nature Suffers to Groe": Life, Labor, and Landscape on the Georgia Coast, 1680–1910* (Athens, Ga., 1996).

25. Dec. 26, 1752, Mar. 21, 1758, diaries of Thomas Thistlewood, Monson MSS 31/1-37, Lincolnshire County Record Office. For the so-called peasant breach, see Berlin and Morgan, eds., *Cultivation and Culture*, 3, 303–4 n. 4; also Berlin and Morgan, eds., *The Slaves' Economy: Independent Production by Slaves in the Americas* (London, 1991); Larry E. Hudson Jr., *Working Toward Freedom: Slave Society and Domestic Economy in the American South* (Rochester, N.Y., 1994); and B. J. Barickman, "'A Bit of Land, Which They Call Roca': Slave Provision Grounds in the Bahian Reconcavo, 1780–1860," *Hispanic American Historical Review* 74 (1994): 649–87.

26. Richard Parkinson, *A Tour in America, in 1798, 1799, and 1800 . . .* 2 vols. (London, 1805), 2:432–33; Sidney W. Mintz and Douglas Hall, *The Origins of the Jamaican Internal Marketing System*, Yale University Publications in Anthropology, no. 57 (New Haven, Conn., 1960): 4, 17, 22; Woodville K. Marshall, "Provision Ground and Plantation Labor in Four Windward Islands: Competition for Resources during Slavery," in Berlin and Morgan, eds., *Cultivation and Culture*, 215–17.

27. C. E. Walker, *Deromanticizing Black History* (Knoxville, Tenn., 1991); Richard J. Ellis, "The Social Construction of Slavery," in *Politics, Policy, and Culture*, ed. Dennis J. Coyle and Richard J. Ellis (Boulder, Colo., 1994), 117–35. For an antiromantic view of laborers, see Peter Way, *Common Labour: Workers and the Digging of North American Canals, 1780–1860* (Cambridge, 1993), and "Labour's Love Lost: Observations on the Historiography of Class and Ethnicity in the Nineteenth Century," *Journal of American Studies* 28 (1994): 1–22.

28. David Eltis, "Labour and Coercion in the English Atlantic World from the Seventeenth to the Early Twentieth Century," in *The Wages of Slavery: From Chattel Slavery to Wage Labour in Africa, the Caribbean and England*, ed. Michael Twaddle (London, 1993), 207–26; M. I. Finley, "Between Slavery and Freedom," *Comparative Studies in Society and History* 6 (April 1964): 247–48; Robert J. Steinfeld, *The Invention of Free Labor: The Employment Relation in English and American Law and Culture, 1350–1870* (Chapel Hill, N.C., 1991); Christine Daniels, "Gresham's Laws: Labor Management on an Early Eighteenth-Century Chesapeake Plantation," *Journal of Southern History* 62 (1996): 205–38; Christopher Hanes, "Turnover Cost and the Distribution of Slave Labor in Anglo-America,"

Journal of Economic History 56 (1996): 307–29; Thomas Dublin, *Transforming Women's Work: New England Lives in the Industrial Revolution* (Ithaca, N.Y., 1994), 34n, 49–50; David Richardson, "Slavery, Trade, and Economic Growth in Eighteenth-century New England," in *Slavery and the Rise of the Atlantic System*, ed. Barbara L. Solow (New York, 1991), 237–64; Solow, "Slavery and Colonization," in *Slavery and the Rise of the Atlantic System*, 21–42; Philip D. Morgan, "Bound Labor: The British and Dutch Colonies," in *Encyclopedia of the North American Colonies*, ed. Jacob Ernest Cooke et al. (New York, 1993), 2:17–32.

29. Winthrop D. Jordan, "Planter and Slave Identity Formation: Some Problems in the Comparative Approach," in *Comparative Perspectives on Slavery in New World Plantation Societies*, ed.Vera Rubin and Arthur Tuden, vol. 292 of the New York Academy of Sciences *Annals* (New York, 1977), 37.

30. Morgan, *Slave Counterpoint*, 258–59, 268–71, 273–84; Carole Shammas, "Anglo-American Household Government in Comparative Perspective" and accompanying "Forum," *WMQ* 3d ser., 52 (1995): 104–66; Robert C.-H. Shell, *Children of Bondage: A Social History of the Slave Society at the Cape of Good Hope, 1652–1838* (Hanover, N.H., 1994); Kenneth A. Lockridge, *On the Sources of Patriarchal Rage; The Commonplace Books of William Byrd and Thomas Jefferson and the Gendering of Power in the Eighteenth Century* (New York, 1992); William James Booth, *Households: On the Moral Architecture of the Economy* (Ithaca, N.Y., 1993), esp. 95–106. Although for a later period, particularly instructive is Eugene Genovese, "'Our Family, White and Black': Family and Household in the Southern Slaveholders' World View," in *In Joy and in Sorrow: Women, Family, and Marriage in the Victorian South, 1830–1900*, ed. Carol Bleser (New York, 1991), 69–87.

31. Elizabeth Fox-Genovese, *Within the Plantation Household: Black and White Women of the Old South* (Chapel Hill, N.C., 1988), 27. The preceding paragraphs draw on my "Three Planters and Their Slaves: Perspectives on Slavery in Virginia, South Carolina, and Jamaica, 1750–1790," in *Race and Family in the Colonial South*, ed. Winthrop D. Jordan and Sheila L. Skemp (Jackson, Miss., 1987), 37–79, and *Slave Counterpoint*, pt. 2. See also Mechal Sobel, *The World They Made Together: Black and White Values in Eighteenth-Century Virginia* (Princeton, N.J., 1987); *Black and White Cultural Interaction in the Antebellum South*, ed. Ted Ownby (Jackson, Miss., 1993); and Robert Olwell, "'A Reckoning of Accounts': Patriarchy, Market Relations, and Control on Henry Laurens's Lowcountry Plantations, 1762–1785," in *Working toward Freedom*, ed. Hudson, 33–52.

32. Jack P. Greene, "Beyond Power: Paradigm Subversion and Reformulation and the Re-Creation of the Early Modern Atlantic World," in *Interpreting Early America: Historiographical Essays* (Charlottesville, Va., 1996), 17–42, esp. 40.

33. W. L. Burn, *Emancipation and Apprenticeship in the British West Indies* (London, 1937), 176–79; I have been heavily influenced by Keith Hopkins, "Novel Evidence for Roman Slavery," *Past and Present* 138 (1993): 3–27.

34. I am presently writing this story. See also n. 12, above.

35. James Kelly, *Voyage to Jamaica . . .* (Belfast, 1838), 29–30; Dew, *Bond of Iron*, 108–11, 114–21, 162, 182–85; Michael Jarvis, "'In the Eye of All Trade': Maritime Revolution and the Transformation of Bermudian Society, 1612–1800" (Ph.D diss., College of William and Mary, 1998); O. Nigel Bolland, *The Formation of a Colonial Society: Belize, from Conquest to Crown Colony* (Baltimore, 1977), 28–32, 54–57, 60–61, 77; Jon F. Sensbach, *A Separate Canaan: The Making of an Afro-Moravian World in North Carolina, 1763–1840* (Chapel Hill, N.C., 1997), 96–97, 114–15, 152–53, 155–56, 171–72. For negotiation, see Mary Turner, ed., *From Chattel Slaves to*

Wage Slaves: The Dynamics of Labour Bargaining in the Americas (Kingston, Jamaica; Bloomington, Ind., 1995); Hudson, ed., *Working toward Freedom*; Mintz and Hall, *Origins of the Jamaican Internal Marketing System*, 3–26. For the relationship of agency and structure, I have found useful Eric Wolf, "Perilous Ideas: Race, Culture, and People," "Comments," and "Reply," *Current Anthropology* 35 (1994), 1–12; some of the contributors in *Slave Cultures and the Cultures of Slavery*, ed. Stephan Palmie (Knoxville, Tenn., 1995); and Schwartz, *Slaves, Peasants, and Rebels*, esp. ix, 162–64.

36. Sidney W. Mintz and Richard Price, *The Birth of African-American Culture: An Anthropological Perspective* (Boston, 1992 [orig. publ., Philadelphia, 1976]), 38.

37. See n. 14.

38. Marietta Morrissey, *Slave Women in the New World: Gender Stratification in the Caribbean* (Lawrence, Kans., 1989); Richard S. Dunn, "Sugar Production and Slave Women in Jamaica," in *Cultivation and Culture*, ed. Berlin and Morgan, 49–72; Brigitte Kossek, "Racist and Patriarchal Aspects of Plantation Slavery in Grenada: 'White Ladies,' 'Black Women Slaves' and 'Rebels,'" in *Slavery in the Americas*, ed. Binder, 277–303; Emilia Viotti da Costa, *Crowns of Glory, Tears of Blood: The Demerara Slave Rebellion of 1823* (New York, 1994), 191–93; Verene Shepherd, Bridget Brereton, and Barbara Bailey, eds., *Engendering History: Caribbean Women in Historical Perspective* (Kingston, 1995), esp. essay by Brereton; *More than Chattel: Black Women and Slavery in the Americas*, ed. David Barry Gaspar and Darlene Clark Hine (Bloomington, Ind., 1996), esp. essays by Robertson, Gaspar, Moitt, and Geggus; *Discovering the Women in Slavery: Emancipating Perspectives on the American Past*, ed. Patricia Morton (Athens, Ga., 1996); *The Devil's Lane: Sex and Race in the Early South*, ed. Catherine Clinton and Michele Gillespie (New York, 1997); James Sidbury, *Ploughshares into Swords: Cultural Appropriation, Racial Identity, and Resisance to Slavery in Gabriel's Virginia, 1750–1810* (New York, 1997), esp. chaps. 2 and 7.

39. E. P. Thompson, "Anthropology and the Discipline of Historical Context," *Midland History* 1, no. 3 (1972): 41–55; Hannah Arendt, *Eichmann in Jerusalem: A Report on the Banality of Evil* (New York, 1963), 253.

40. *New York Times*, Apr. 2, 1995; Barry Unsworth, *Sacred Hunger* (New York, 1992); Toni Morrison, *Beloved* (New York, 1987). Other recent works of fiction that explore slavery include Charles Johnson, *Middle Passage* (New York, 1990), Caryl Phillips, *Cambridge* (New York, 1992), and Fred D'Aguiar, *Feeding the Ghosts* (London, 1997). On slaves as modern people, see, for example, Sidney W. Mintz, *Goodbye, Columbus: Second Thoughts on the Caribbean Region at Mid-Millenium*, Walter Rodney Memorial Lecture (Coventry, 1993), 10, and Gilroy, *Black Atlantic*, ix, 221–23.

Gary B. Nash

THE CONCEPT OF INEVITABILITY IN THE HISTORY OF EUROPEAN– INDIAN RELATIONS

IT IS COMMONPLACE nowadays to observe, as J. H. Plumb wrote a quarter century ago, that history "has always been a vital strand in the ideology of all ruling classes."[1] Nowhere is this more evident than in the way historians have explained Indian-European relations in North America. For nearly three hundred years historians have included Indians in a grandiose nationalist narrative, mainly as the foils for the European invaders' ceaseless march of progress. "Bound inextricably in a primitive past, a primitive society, and a primitive environment to be destroyed by God, Nature, and Progress to make way for Civilized Man," as Roy Harvey Pearce put it many years ago, the Indian appears on stage primarily as bloodthirsty savage or insensate victim of a superior people.[2] This essay argues that in this triumphalist recounting of the past a key element is the idea of inevitable historical outcomes. Moving from providential to secular explanations of historical causation, historians have constructed a subtext in which the history of interracial conflict and the dispossession of Indian lands seems inexorable, unalterable, and foreordained. In a narrative structure with the promise of America as the controlling theme, the deployment of the notion of historical inevitability is virtually obligatory. It is also a subtle, powerful, and (for most white readers) comforting explanation about the European settlers' mastery of North America. By presenting Indian peoples as innately inferior, the keepers of the past have scripted an encounter between the people of two cultures that could have only one main outcome. The notion of inequality woven into the inevitabilist argument is a silent way of loading the dice in favor of conquering Europeans in the Americas.

The idea of historical inevitability is as old as the tales told by conquerors. In the case of North American Indian history it can be found in the earliest Puritan writings of the late seventeenth century. For Puritans, who saw themselves establishing God's outpost on the western edge of the Atlantic, history was the intricate working out of God's master plan for the human race. In such a providential view, every cataclysmic event—ferocious war, ravaging epidemic, pestilence, flood, and famine—demonstrated the work of the intervening hand of an angry God. By the same token, an abundant harvest or victory in a war against infidels or against the popish French signified an approving God.[3] Men were but the puny instruments of God's will, and history was the story of destinies dictated from on high.

In this vein, the first Puritan scribes saw conflict with Algonkian tribes as divinely directed. The ultimate outcome, therefore, was predestined. Writing of the Puritans' burning of the Pequot fort near Mystic River in 1636, where hundreds of Pequots—mostly women and children—were incinerated, John Mason, one of the leaders of the Mystic Fort attack, wrote that the genocidal attack was God-directed: "God was above them, who laughed at his enemies and the Enemies of his People to Scorn, making them as a fiery Oven. Thus were the Stout Hearted spoiled, having slept their last Sleep. . . . Thus did the Lord Judge among the Heathen, filling the Place with dead Bodies." It was the same for John Underhill, another militia captain, who justified the killing of women and children as biblically authorized: "Sometimes the Scripture declareth women and children must perish with their parents. Sometimes the case alters; but we will not dispute it now. We had sufficient light from the word of God for our proceedings."[4] In a book issued sixteen weeks after the Puritan soldiers hung and quartered Metacomet, Wampanoag leader in King Philip's War (1675–76), Increase Mather's published account of the war explained that "it hath not been brought to pass by our number, or skill, or valour, we have not got the Land in possession by our own Sword, neither did our own arm save us, But God hath wasted the Heathen, by sending the destroying Angel among them, since the War began."[5] In his section on King Philip's War, Cotton Mather continued his father's providential story, recounting that Mount Hope "was the seat where Philip was kennell'd with the rest of these horrid salvages" and that later an English commander drove "the 'beasts of prey' back to their dens, after he had first sacrificed many scores of them unto the divine vengeance." Though it may not have seemed so for Puritan soldiers, these wars were later depicted as unequal contests, with God on the English side.[6]

It is doubtful that these presentations of God's plan for the extermination of indigenous people had much influence on the public; Mather's

Magnalia Christi Americana (1702) and Mason's account, first published in 1736, were not widely available. Underhill's account made no American appearance until 1837. But the twin ideas about Indian inferiority and the Puritans' godly work in the wilderness were so widespread that the inevitability rationale for the rapid Indian depopulation in eastern North America was undoubtedly the common view. In the two generations before the Civil War, as the public school movement began to bring basic education to American youth, the first textbook characterizations of early European–Indian relations drove home this theme of inevitability promulgated by earlier Puritan annalists. As distinct from a generalized view of historical outcomes when Europeans and Indians met, now the first schoolbooks enshrined the idea of historical inevitability. For example, the first American geography schoolbook, Jedidiah Morse's *Geography Made Easy* (1791), instructed children that the rapid mortality of New England Algonkians was God's undertaking. Paraphrasing John Winthrop, Morse explained that "the hand of Providence is noticeable in these surprising instances of mortality among the Indians to make room for the English. . . . They waste and moulder away; they in a manner unaccountable disappear."[7] It was the same with the expropriation of Indian land. A schoolbook published during the War of 1812 assured students that "the religion of nature, the light of revelation, and the pages of history, are combined in the proof, that God has ordered that nations shall become extinct, and that others shall take their places." Authors sometimes included poems and essays with romanticist titles such as "Melancholy Fate of the Indians," but it took students little effort to see that it was God's will, rather than human agency, that was destroying Indian peoples.[8]

Many antebellum textbook writers softened their view of Indians, perhaps partaking of the widespread New England sympathy for the five "civilized" tribes of the Southeast in an era when their removal to the West was a hot topic of discussion; but they continued to instruct schoolchildren in the doctrine of destiny. Schoolbook writers such as Samuel Willard, Charles Goodrich, and Charles Prentiss were no less certain than Cotton Mather that the Indians were of a lower human order, using the terms "Indians," "savages," and "aborigines" interchangeably. They also assumed that, as savages, the Indians were inherently warlike and that bellicosity, along with the Indians' racial inferiority, fueled the early wars in New England and Virginia.[9]

Yet in evincing a sympathetic interest in Indian culture that sharply distinguishes their narratives from those of seventeenth-century Puritan writers, these writers purveyed a contradictory image of the Indian. They described Native Americans not as beasts of prey or dogs to be kenneled but as wholly human if religiously misled creatures. Instructing children on the

"general character" of Indians, Goodrich spoke of their intelligence, cour-
teousness, eloquence, and gravity in councils and commended their bravery in war. In treating King Philip's War of 1676–77, both Goodrich and
Prentiss pointed to the English encroachment on Indian land as a cause of
the hostilities. Many schoolbooks quoted Washington Irving's description
of Philip as a romantic noble savage: "a patriot, attached to his native soil;
a prince true to his subjects, and indignant of their wrongs; a soldier, daring in battle, firm in adversity, patient of fatigue, of hunger, of every variety of bodily suffering, and ready to perish in the cause he espoused."[10]
Prentiss, in addressing the ghastly burning of Pequot women, children,
and old men in the earlier war of 1637, felt the need to justify English behavior by claiming, with no evidence, that the Indians had earlier acted in
the same way. The most sharp-witted student might have noticed the
contradiction in the presentation of Indians with both savage and noble
qualities; but it is unlikely, given the abysmal condition of the Indian rem-
nants in the Northeast in this era, that young students would discern that
the war with Indians was not inevitable after all.

If these textbook authors found much to admire in the bravery and nobility of Indians, there was still much to deplore. Particularly, textbooks
dwelled on their cruelty and bloodthirstiness. Students learned that Indians
were a "savage foe, whose delight was cruelty"; they "listened to the cries of
their victims with pleasure"; they demonstrated "a diabolical thirst of
blood" and indulged in their "lust of murderous deeds."[11] Whether describing Indians as treacherous foes or noble savages, the antebellum textbooks left the message in the minds of young learners that the outcome of
a collision of European and Native American peoples was preordained.

By the mid-nineteenth century the search for a scientific history brought
forth a new secular version of inevitability reasoning. An angry Jehovah
did not dictate the course of history, but larger forces did, whether environmental and geographic, moral and political, or economic and social.
The view arose, as Isaiah Berlin has written of modern history in general,
that "the behaviour of men is . . . made what it is by factors largely beyond
the control of individuals."[12] Thus, the writing of the late nineteenth and
early twentieth centuries became suffused with terms such as "the march of
events," the "spirit of the age," the "laws of history," "manifest destiny,"
the "tide of human affairs"—all phrases connoting the inevitability of
events, the irresistible rhythms of human life, and the unswervable forces
that dictate the way humans act, individually and collectively.

Looking back on providential history, we modernists speak sympatheti-
cally of explanations understandable to those living in a different age. But
modern-day historians who have placed the responsibility for what happened in history on impersonal or superpersonal forces have thus far gone

unchallenged. Amid the rise of "scientific history," when the first generation of American professional historians abandoned providential interpretations of history, little comment emerged on causative schemes that not only described Indian–white conflict in deeply Eurocentric terms but justified the decimation of indigenous peoples by implying that "the individual's freedom of choice is ultimately an illusion."[13] In narrating the course of early Indian–white relations, late-nineteenth- and twentieth-century historians have presented students with a logical contradiction. On the one hand, students have been stirred by the heroic exploits of explorers and Indian fighters such as Meriwether Lewis and William Clark, Daniel Boone, Davy Crockett, Jim Bridger, and Kit Carson. These larger-than-life heroes epitomize individual willpower; they are men who make history rather than succumb to larger forces. But on the other hand, the narratives have largely eliminated the notion of individual responsibility in the larger course of interracial contact. The formula for telling the broader story of savagery versus civilization conforms to Berlin's critique that "the explanation, and in some sense the weight of responsibility, for all human action is (at times with ill-concealed relief) transferred to the broad backs of these vast impersonal forces — institutions, or historical trends — better made to bear such burdens than a feeble, thinking reedlike man."[14] Inevitability becomes the salve of a troubled national conscience.

In post–Civil War history books written for schools, colleges, and the general public, historians planted "mental depth-charges," to use James Axtell's telling phrase. Axtell reminds us how loaded words, "when heard or read . . . quickly sink into our consciousness and explode, sending off cognitive shrapnel in all directions, . . . showering our understanding with fragments of accumulated meaning and association."[15] This aptly describes the furtive power of words such as *inevitable, inexorable,* and *unstoppable* — or in Isaiah Berlin's elegant formulation, the transferring of guilt about sordid parts of our history to cosmic forces beyond the power of individuals to alter:

No sooner do we acquire adequate "natural" or "metaphysical" insight into the "inexorable" or "inevitable" parts played by all things animate and inanimate in the cosmic process, than we are freed from the sense of personal endeavour. Our sense of guilt and of sin, our pangs of remorse and self-condemnation, are automatically dissolved; the tension, the fear of failure and frustration disappear as we become aware of the elements of a larger "organic whole," of which we are variously described as limbs or elements.[16]

Adopting a secularized version of inevitability, historians found a mighty new intellectual arsenal to draw on in the work of early anthropologists. Led by the phrenologist Samuel George Morton, leading scientists in the rapidly expanding nation convinced most Americans that nature had created distinct branches of the human species, endowing each race un-equally and unalterably. Whatever the original moving force, Caucasians had been endowed with the largest crania, the bone cage of the brain, fol-lowed in order by the Mongolians, the Malays, the American Indians, and—the least endowed—Africans. Even before the phrenological frenzy of the 1840s and 1850s, the school texts had begun to grasp this truth. "Na-ture has formed the different degrees of genius, and the characters of na-tions, which are seldom known to change," according to one of the first American schoolbooks published in 1793. But after the 1850s, this general rule was elevated to the status of scientific fact, becoming latent, if not ex-plicitly expressed, in virtually all of the schoolbooks.[17]

In the decades bracketing the Civil War, when the first multivolume his-tories of the United States reached the public, the view of American In-dians darkened distinctly, and the presumption of inevitable conflict and conquest came strongly to the fore. George Bancroft's epic history of the United States, which began appearing in 1856, casually dismissed Indian culture. The native people were "ignorant of the arts of life" and suffered from "the hereditary idleness of the race." Yet Bancroft made clear that in both of New England's seventeenth-century wars, Indians fought tena-ciously to protect their land. Still, given the inferiority of native culture, English victories were to be expected when the two cultures clashed.

Postwar historians, writing in an era when wars against Great Plains tribes made newspaper headlines, echoed Bancroft. John Gorham Palfrey, whose *Compendious History of New England* began to appear in 1873, spent an early chapter depicting the Indians as biologically inferior, insolent, and lacking in mental capacity. Influenced by the general acceptance of phreno-logical certitudes, which posited a hierarchical ordering of the various branches of the human family, Palfrey blamed the Pequots entirely for the war of 1637. For Palfrey, unprovoked atrocities by Pequots made war nec-essary. As for King Philip's War two generations later, Palfrey insisted that land was not a point of contention; instead, as in 1637, unprovoked Indian attacks initiated the war. The English had come to Massachusetts, he argued, "and found a vacant domain, on which, without intrusion on any predecessors, they built and planted."[18] For John Fiske, popular lecturer in the centennial year of 1876, nature's arrangement of the races made geno-cide defensible. "As a matter of practical policy, " he wrote, "the annihila-tion of the Pequots can be condemned only by those who read history so incorrectly as to suppose that savages, whose business is to torture and slay, can always be dealt with according to the methods in use between civilized peoples."[19] John Bach McMaster's *History of the People of the United States* (1888) taught that the Indian "was never so happy as when, in the dead of night, he roused his sleeping enemies with an unearthly yell, and massacred them by the light of their burning homes." The "idle, shiftless savage" was almost subhuman, "as superstitious as a Hottentot negro and as unreasonable as a child."[20]

The postbellum schoolbooks drove home the iron rule of "the races of men." Not yet imbibing Darwin's evolutionary theory, Arnold Guyot, one of the leading geographers of this era, instructed students that "certain physical features and mental characteristics . . . have remained unchanged from a time anterior to all history."[21] This view underpinned the pivotal understanding that nature decreed European ascendancy over Native Americans. "The law of nature" had replaced "God's wise providence." Imbued with the scientific racism of the late nineteenth century, textbook writers harped on the lesson that Indian decline, which in fact was occurring rapidly after the Plains Wars of the 1870s and 1880s, was caused by the Indians' own inability to rise above the lesser endowments bestowed by nature. "The Indian will not learn the arts of civilization, and he and his forest must perish together," children read in turn-of-the-century textbooks. "With the advance of the white man," they learned, "the red race is rapidly passing away in accordance with a well-established law of nature, that causes an inferior race to yield to a superior when one comes in contact with the other."[22]

These books conform closely to Berlin's description of modern historiography: "Acts hitherto regarded as wicked or unjustifiable are seen in a more 'objective' fashion—in the larger context—as part of the process of history which, being responsible for providing us with our scale of values, must not therefore be judged in terms of it; and viewed in this new light [our historical actions] turn out no longer wicked but right and good because necessitated."[23] At a time when a swiftly increasing percentage of the nation's youth received a basic education in American history, their textbooks were explaining that the American government and white settlers in general were blameless in the rapid decline of the Indian population.

By the late nineteenth century, schoolchildren were encouraged to consider the plight of Native Americans in relation to the situation of the millions of African Americans recently released from slavery. Textbooks consistently pictured the innate degradation of Indians and African Americans alike. Both suffered from behavioral defects acquired at birth. Before the Civil War, schoolbooks spread the belief that people of African descent were "destitute of intelligence," that "their mental powers, in general, participate in the imbecility of their bodies," or that they came from a continent where "human nature is nowhere exhibited in a more rude and disgusting attire."[24] After the Civil War, textbooks were nearly as gloomy on the capabilities of African Americans. Since nature had arranged the races of men hierarchically, who could argue with the consignment of dark-skinned people to the lowest positions in society? American children grew up with the understanding that in a democracy the portioning out of unequal opportunities and rewards according to race was perfectly natural because nature had endowed Americans of different skin hues unequally.

If nineteenth-century science taught children that Indians and blacks were irredeemably inferior, history books encouraged young learners to reach different conclusions about the future of Indians and African Americans. Their textbooks told them that while nature condemned freed blacks to hauling water and splitting wood, it instead consigned Indians to extinction. This fit nicely with the commonsense view of white Americans that the brawn of black Americans was hardly expendable but that Native Americans were decidedly dispensable. Even before Lincoln's Emancipation Proclamation, "the dominant scientific position," Reginald Horsman wrote, "was that the Indians were doomed because of innate inferiority, that they were succumbing to a superior race, and that this was for the good of America and the world."[25] The new state of California in the 1850s elevated this scientific position to the level of policy. Following years of brutalization and extermination of California Indians under both Spanish and American governments, Governor Peter H. Burnett announced in 1851: "That a war of extermination will continue to be waged between the two races until the Indian race becomes extinct, must be expected; while we cannot anticipate this result with but painful regret, the inevitable destiny of the race is beyond the power and wisdom of man to avert."[26] In the following decades, as the Indian population continued to plummet, the public view was that the demise of Indians was inevitable, almost as if a cosmic snowball, careening downhill and gathering mass, was beyond the ability of human agency to stop.

To be sure, a few dissenters raised their voices, creating counternarratives that told of grasping whites in search of land rather than destiny as the cause of the Indians' plight. Foremost among the dissenters were Native Americans. We will never know how many Indians passed on stories contradicting the victor's tale of how culturally inferior people inevitably lost their lives and land to superior and more enlightened people. But it can be easily imagined that Indians were as unlikely to tell their children of the inevitability of their forced removal or dispossession of ancient homelands as Jewish parents would tell their children about the inevitability of the Holocaust.

If we cannot recover much of Indian oral history in the years before about 1800, it is possible to recapture the Indians' anti-inevitabilist rendition of history from the first published Indian narratives issued in the era of antebellum reform. William Apess's autobiographical account, *A Son of the Forest* (1829) and his historical work, *Eulogy on King Philip* (1836), are cases in point. A Pequot with white and probably African blood in his veins, Apess not only led a Mashpee campaign for tribal self-government but conducted a war of words with white authors. Employing the rhetoric of abolitionist writers, Apess attacked white racism, oppression, and treaty violations and defended Indian character against white charges of inescapable degeneration. This implicitly anti-inevitabilist message, however, found no place in the schoolbooks of the antebellum era.[27]

If the work of Apess and other Indian writers, such as Elias Boudinot and George Copway, made little headway with the public, a much larger audience read an anti-inevitabilist version of Indian history from the hand of the indomitable Helen Hunt Jackson. A transplanted easterner, Jackson's life in the West moved her to write *A Century of Dishonor*, issued in blood-red covers in 1881.[28] Rather than writing about early Indian–white relations, Jackson excoriated the federal government's Indian policies in the century following the ratification of the Constitution. Hers was perhaps the first book to expose the genocidal policies of the government as the cause of the Indians' demise. Sharply contesting the notion that the Indian must inexorably vanish from the continent, Jackson attacked the related notion that the victors had no responsibility for the vanquished.

Jackson's *Century of Dishonor*, which played a role in the establishment of the Indian Rights Association in 1882, might have led to a reconsideration of textbook treatments of Indian–white relations. But Jackson's books hardly moved members of the budding historical profession. More to their liking, however, was one of their own—the Harvard-trained Theodore Roosevelt, whose highly popular *Winning of the West* (1924) was a classic of inevitabilist argument. In this multivolume tableau, Roosevelt organized all of American history around "a series of mighty movements" that began in the Saxon forests of the previous millennium. All history moved teleologically toward the dominance of the English race. Tied to this premise, all Indian wars, from the early seventeenth century through the post–Civil War clashes on the Great Plains, were part of the inexorable "race-history of the nations," as Roosevelt called it.[29]

Contemptuous of Indians as a racial type, Roosevelt described the Plains wars in the trans-Mississippi West as an updated version of the early colonial wars in which European settlers had reduced the once powerful Indian tribes to "a horde of lazy, filthy, cruel beggars always crowding into their houses, killing their cattle, and by their very presence threatening their families."[30] If genocide was the fate of irredeemable Indians, "the conquest and settlement by the whites of the Indian lands was necessary to the greatness of the race and to the well-being of civilized mankind. It was as ultimately beneficial as it was inevitable."[31] Those who dallied with Jackson's *Century of Dishonor*, which Roosevelt called "thoroughly untrustworthy from cover

to cover," were simply "amiable but maudlin fanatics" and "foolish senti-
mentalists" who "not only write foul slanders about their countrymen, but
are themselves the worst possible advisers on any point touching Indian
management." For Roosevelt, it was "wholly impossible to avoid conflicts
with the weaker race." Moreover, the extermination of Indians, in any
event unstoppable, should be acknowledged with national pride because
"the most ultimately righteous of all wars is a war against savages," for it establishes "the foundations for the future greatness of a mighty people."[32]

Writing in the same era, when the idea of the manifest destiny of white
Americans to dominate the continent was in full flood, R. A. Brock, among
the first professional historians of Virginia, justified the wars against Algonkian peoples in the Chesapeake region in 1622, 1644, and 1675 as utterly
unavoidable, given the fact that the Indians were "determined upon the
utter extinction of the [English] colony" from the beginning. Brock's depictions of native people were peppered with words such as "cunning,"
"treacherous," and "revengeful."[33] For Woodrow Wilson, at the time a
professor of political science at Princeton, the early colonial wars in his
home state of Virginia had something to do with "unwise" and "unjust"
behavior by the colonists. But more important was the innate character of
the "savages who lurked within [North America's] forests." He quickly explained the Pequot War of 1637: "The Pequots had grown very hot against
the English crowding in. No Englishman's life was safe anywhere . . . because of them." Thus provoked, the settlers "set themselves ruthlessly to
exterminate the tribe. A single bloody season of fire and the sword, and the
work was done."[34]

In what we know as the Progressive era, the limited admiration for some
aspects of Indian culture that had surfaced in some pre–Civil War textbooks nearly disappeared except in elementary schools, where teachers still
assigned such titles as Clara Kern Bayliss's *Two Little Algonkin Lads* (1907),
Mary Catherine Judd's *Wigwam Stories* (1906), and Ella M. Powers's *Stories of Indian Days* (1912).[35] Examining a number of textbooks for this period, Frances FitzGerald writes that their "characterization of the Indians
crystallized into a precise and unvarying formula, which, once set, did not
change for thirty years."[36] Among the most widely read textbooks was Edward Channing's *History of the United States.* Published in 1905, it was
fiercely unsympathetic to Indians. Channing made no attempt to specify
why Powhatan's people attacked the Virginians in 1622 or why the Pequot
War erupted in New England in 1637. Inevitability coursed resoundingly
through his prose. "The New England colonists undoubtedly did their best
to deal fairly with the Indians; but native intrigues and policies were too
involved for their simple English understandings." After English attempts
to convert Indians to Christianity and a civilized style of life failed, war

became all the more inevitable as Indians stubbornly "relapsed" into their old ways.[37]

The emerging textbook titan of the Progressive era, when American high schools for the first time were enrolling a majority of teenage Americans, was David Saville Muzzey. A Massachusetts Brahmin from a long line of teachers and preachers, his lively prose and firm grip on the new scholarship, at least in some areas, brought a more mature history to the nation's classrooms. His plainly titled textbooks—*An American History* (1911), *The United States of America* (1922), *History of the American People* (1927), and *A History of Our Country* (1937)—arguably were read by more school and college students than any books in the history of the world. Selling briskly into the 1950s, they influenced millions of Americans growing up in the modern era. Muzzey was stunned by the attacks on his books in the early 1920s as "treason texts" that would contaminate the minds of young learners and rattle the foundations of American democracy. Muzzey subscribed to Progressive beliefs that democracy needed refurbishing and that the rise of smokestack America, fueled by massive immigration from southern and eastern Europe, had destabilized the old Protestant regime. He was critical of the growing gap between the rich and poor, detested the Mexican War because it expanded slave territory, and wanted children to know that slavery was a cancer—"a damnable cause the South fought for."[38] Yet Muzzey was thoroughly patrician in his distaste for labor organizing and labor conflict in the industrial period. And he partook of the conventional theories of innate racial inferiority of American Indians, African Americans, and others of lesser stock than Anglo-Americans.

When it came to Indian–white relations, Muzzey varied only slightly from earlier textbook interpretations and seemingly approved of Roosevelt's indictment of Indian character. Like his predecessors, he conditioned his readers to see Indian–white relations as predetermined. In his first textbook he taught students about the "stolid stupidity [of Indians] that no white man could match" and that they "loved to bask idly in the sun, like the Mississippi negro of to-day." On the second page of *History of the American People* he wrote that while Indians were a diverse lot in North America, "nowhere had they risen above the stage of barbarism." Most were "sunk in bestial savagery." In the twentieth century, he advised students, Indians were "a picturesque object of study" who "have contributed almost nothing to the making of America." Indians, anyway, were hardly to be found when the Europeans arrived. "The New World," he wrote, "was a virgin continent for the European discoverers and their descendants to make of it what they would."[39]

Millions of American schoolchildren learned manifest destiny history in undiluted form from Muzzey's books. "It was impossible," he wrote, "that these few hundred thousand natives should stop the spread of the Europeans over the country. That would have been to condemn one of the fairest lands of the earth to the stagnation of barbarism." Indians were "now immovable as a rock, now capricious as an April breeze." What the Indians *did* have to contribute to the making of America was a stimulus to create a new kind of man—Frederick Jackson Turner's "self-reliant, resourceful, and remarkably courageous" American bred on the frontier, where settlers struggled "to subdue the wild forest and the wilder savages."[40]

Muzzey had his difficulties with patrioteers after World War I, who condemned his textbook coverage of the American Revolution and the War of 1812 as pro-British. He had poisoned the American "loving-cup" by discounting revolutionary heroes and presenting the English side of the argument in the constitutional dispute that blew up after the Seven Years War. Chief among the wretched "revisionists" who "minimize or omit many of the vital principles, heroes, and incidents of the Revolution, hitherto held sacred in American history," Muzzey was lambasted in the Hearst press for several years before the controversy blew over. But nobody criticized Muzzey over his depiction of Native Americans or his message that Indian–white relations could not have occurred differently.

By the late 1920s, when the furor over Muzzey's textbooks subsided, the treatment of Indian–white relations began to fade from the textbooks.[41] "In the nineteen-thirties," writes Frances FitzGerald, "the only [school] texts that even mentioned the Indians were those for lower grades, whose authors clearly intended to interest children with tales of a colorful, exotic people who behaved, as one book put it bluntly, just like children."[42] To judge by Charles and Mary Beard's *The Rise of American Civilization* (1927), college textbooks were also jettisoning the Indian and Indian–white relations as a topic worthy of study. In their best-selling volume, the Beards gave scant treatment to Native Americans. The Pequot War rated just one statement—that "under the indomitable John Mason, they [the New England colonists] fell upon the neighbouring Pequods, exterminating them by sword and fire." King Philip's War, which cost the New Englanders a higher proportion of their population than any war in our history, received no mention at all. From the Beards' textbooks, students learned only that Indians were an impediment to westward expansion and an unpliant labor force, a people too fierce and proud of spirit to subject themselves to the settlers.[43]

The "pragmatic revolt" in historical writing, which posited that historical judgments should be tentative and that presenting more than one perspective on the past is fairer to the variety of people involved in any historical situation, brought new approaches to Indian–white relations in the 1930s. Leading the way was Harold Rugg, a previously inconspicuous man who wrote a series of twenty history and social studies textbooks for middle and high school students. A ninth-generation New Englander, who worked as a weaver in a Massachusetts textile mill in order to understand industrial work and acquire a firsthand knowledge of life at the bottom of American society, Rugg drank deeply from the wells of progressive educators as he reached for ideas and pedagogical strategies to stimulate creative ability in young learners. He lamented his own constricted educational experience. In New England, "life was thin and arid like the soil; norm domineered over the spirit. All social forces—home, community, and education—made for acquiescence, molding my contemporaries and myself to the standards of adult life. Independence of thought was minimized; loyalty was canonized."[44]

By dint of his progressive pedagogy alone, Rugg urged teachers and students to reconsider the inevitability of the depopulation of Indian peoples and the dispossession of their lands. In his *Teacher's Guide and Key* he insisted that "pupils must learn critically about modern problems," that they must acquire the indispensable quality of "open-mindedness" and "critical mindedness." He advised teachers to pursue the goal of "tolerant understanding" by making constant use of phrases such as "Why do you think so?" "Are you open-minded about the matter?" "What is your authority?" "Have you considered all sides of the case?"

By rethinking customary constructions of Indian–white relations, Rugg brought a freshness to his schoolbooks. Far in advance of his fellow textbook writers, he asked students to ponder such questions as "In what spirit did the Indians and the Europeans receive each other?" "Did the white man buy the Indians' land that they settled upon?" "Or did they ruthlessly conquer it as the Spaniards had done in Central and South America?" "Consider also the ethical problem: Was it right for the more numerous Europeans to drive back the scattered tribes of Indians?" Despite his efforts to get students to explore familiar historical events afresh, one of Rugg's culminating questions betrayed his sense of the inevitable fate of American Indians. "Ask yourself," he told students, "whether it was possible for two widely differing civilizations to live side by side in the same region."[45] In the conclusion of a chapter titled "The Struggle between White Man and Red Man," he reminded students that "we have learned how impossible it was to prevent misunderstandings because of ignorance of each other's languages and the sharp difference between the civilizations of the two races."[46]

Rugg's books were nearly banished from the schools in the late 1930s when he came under attack by ultraconservatives, who charged he was infatuated with "collectivism" and was "Sovietizing our children." The American Federation of Advertising took offense at Rugg's comments that one of the purposes of advertising was "to persuade the purchaser to buy whether he wants to or not." But more broadly, he was attacked for treasonous textbooks that perpetrated anti-Americanism. "For a generation now," charged the president of the National Association of Manufacturers, "our free institutions and the heroes of the American republic have been derided and debunked by a host of puny iconoclasts, who destroy since they cannot build."[47] Mrs. Elwood Turner, corresponding secretary of the Daughters of the Colonial Wars, blasted Rugg's books for trying "to give a child an unbiased viewpoint instead of teaching him real Americanism. All the old histories taught my country right or wrong. That's the point of view we want our children to adopt. We can't afford to teach them to be unbiased and let them make up their own minds."[48]

After World War II, in which American Indians enlisted in large numbers and played important roles, textbooks began to tone down the descriptions of degraded and irredeemable Indian character, but the notion that the history of Indian–white relations was foreordained continued. At times, historians such as Henry Steele Commager and Samuel Eliot Morison, who wrote the most widely used college textbook of the World War II period, drew back from earlier inflamed descriptions of Indian culture as irredeemably savage, speaking more moderately of "lower cultures" and usually eliminating the word *savage*. In *The Growth of the American Republic*, first issued in 1930, Morison and Commager even argued that "American culture has been greatly enriched by the Indians' contribution." But the only contribution they specified was the courageous fighting qualities of Indians, which made the colonizers "pay dear for the mastery of a continent" and thus bred in the American a fighting quality, as Teddy Roosevelt had argued, that led to greatness.[49]

Substituting "lower cultures" for "savages" changed Morison's fundamental message very little. In 1958, introducing the first scholarly book on King Philip's War by Douglas Leach, Morison wrote in the preface: "In view of our recent experiences of warfare, and of the many instances today of backward peoples getting enlarged notions of nationalism and turning ferociously on Europeans who have attempted to civilize them, this early conflict of the same nature cannot help but be of interest."[50] The civilization versus savagery theme, with overtones of inevitability, was hardly disguised by using "backward peoples," though Morison might have noticed that the people with "enlarged notions of nationalism" were, by the late 1950s, the victors in overturning centuries of European colonialism.

What is particularly revealing about the enduring pattern of casting the history of early Indian–white relations as inevitably hostile and inexorably resolved in the Europeans' favor is the studied inattention to the dramatic counterexample of how Indian–white relations in North America could work out differently. William Penn and his Quaker followers, who streamed into New Jersey and Pennsylvania and in the early 1680s, were entering a maelstrom of bloody racial conflict that had reached a peak just a few years earlier, when wars between colonizers and Indians devastated New England, Maryland, Virginia, North Carolina, and South Carolina. But unlike other colonists, Quakers came with peace on their mind; as pacifists, they categorically forswore violence. Along with Penn's pledge not to allow one acre of land to be settled until he had purchased it from the local Lenni Lenape chiefs, pacifism made the crucial difference. As long as the Quaker peace testimony and friendly relations with the Indian peoples of the region held sway, interracial relations in the Delaware River Valley, while not frictionless, remained peaceful. Unprecedented in a century of Indian–white relations, several tribes moved into an English colony seeking a sanctuary from the violent attacks of other settlers.

It is telling that historians have largely ignored Indian relations in Quaker Pennsylvania and how little young Americans learn from their textbooks about Quaker–Indian comity. It is almost as if this case study of interracial relations shaped by human desire, by values held and choices made, rather than by forces beyond the reach of man, must be hidden from view. Some historians, such as Channing, Morison, and Commager, while portraying European–Indian conflict as inevitable, ignored the fact that no blood was spilled for nearly three quarters of a century of Quaker settlement in the land of the Lenni Lenape and Susquehannock. Others mention this in passing; for example, Prentiss in the 1840s wrote simply that Penn, "having previously made a treaty with the Indians purchased of them large tracts of land, and, by a beneficent deportment towards them, secured their lasting friendship."[51] Prentiss did not consider, however, how this compromised his earlier statements about the inevitability of conflict in New England and Virginia.

Other historians struggled with this contradiction and then offered fragmentary or spurious answers that would have puzzled the most astute young students. For example, Woodrow Wilson explained that the New Englanders "had sought to be just with the redmen; but the Quakers sought to add a gentle kindliness to justice, and their peace was more lasting than that of the English." This stopped short of saying that the Quakers' gentle kindliness was actually pacifism—a refusal to make war. Wilson then explained away the Quakers' success: "And yet not even the fine temper and quick spirit of justice could have so steadily held the restless redskins off from mischief had not the fates of the forest made their borders a place of peace. The Indians they [the Quakers] dealt with were not the men who had once made that wilderness a place of dread and caution. . . . There were none but the humble Delaware to be dealt with in Mr.

Penn's province."⁵² In this description, the "redskins" are temperamentally "restless" and full of "mischief"; but only fate—that which is beyond human control—brought peace. The Delawares' weakness and humbleness, rather than Quaker pacifism and fair dealing, avoided conflict. Muzzey, by contrast, told students of Penn's "scrupulous and fair dealing with the Indians," which "saved the colonies from the horrors of savage raids and massacres."⁵³ Rugg explained that Penn dealt fairly with the Indians, that in return "the Indians loved him with real affection," and that for more than half a century Penn's colonists "lived in peace with them."⁵⁴

If most textbook writers glided smoothly by the Quakers' nonviolent encounters with native peoples, Daniel Boorstin tried to make sure that students would never forget the Quakers. But his message was that the Quakers' relatively peaceful relations with Native Americans for three generations was a sickening mistake that non-Quaker settlers would have to pay for. Published in 1958, Boorstin's *The Americans: The Colonial Experience* set up this cynical view of Quaker pacifism by depicting Indians as everlastingly violent and always the cause of conflict. "The Indian was omnipresent; he struck without warning and was a nightly terror in the remote silence of backwoods cabins. . . . Every section of the seacoast colonies suffered massacres. . . Such nightmares shaped the military policy of settlers until nearly the end of the eighteenth century."⁵⁵ Facing Indian massacres almost everywhere from their first arrival, all settlers except the Quakers responded logically and correctly. The idea of inevitability rings resoundingly in Boorstin's description "How Quakers Misjudged the Indians." The Quakers

. . .view of the Indian was . . . unrealistic, inflexible, and based on false premises about human nature. . . . The increasing, west-flowing population of the Province [Pennsylvania] was passing like a tidal wave over Indian lands. The troubles of the Indians could no longer be reduced to niceties of protocol, to maxims of fair play, or to cliches of self-reproach. Here was one of those great conflicts in history when a mighty force was meeting a long-unmoved body; either the force had to be stopped or the body had to move.⁵⁶

The writing of history as inevitably determined, Indian–white relations as unalterably violent, and the demise of American Indians through no fault of the European colonizers began to change slowly after World War II, though many textbooks perpetuated the story of innate Indian bloodlust and settler blamelessness.⁵⁷ With the G.I. Bill enabling millions of Americans to go to college for the first time, the gates of the historical profession gradually opened to people of diverse class, religious, and racial backgrounds. Influenced by the civil rights movement, some historians began to reexamine the history of Indian–white relations. Although known as the period when the "consensus school" of American history emphasized the homogeneity of American society and its lack of conflict, the postwar decades also produced new interpretations of early Indian–white relations.

George F. Willison's *Saints and Strangers* took a refreshing new stance on early Indian–white relations in New England. Beginning from the premise that Indians had a viable and worthy culture, Willison showed that without Indian cooperation the early settlements could not have survived. He also argued that New England's tribes had legitimate reasons for quarreling with the intruders. Simply by abandoning the savagery–civilization paradigm, Willison found his way to alternative explanations, with little ring of inevitability, of the Anglo–Indian conflicts. Willison had reduced the scale of causation from cosmic force to prosaic human desire. At the heart of the struggles was land.[58]

Tens of thousands of post-war high school and college students who read Richard Hofstader, William Miller, and Daniel Aaron's *American Republic*, first published in 1959, imbibed a more realistic, less self-justifying treatment of early Indian relations that might have shocked their parents, weaned on a different set of lessons about what happened when Europeans and Indians met. "The Indians," wrote this author team, "were confronted by a people who would be satisfied with nothing less than complete ownership of land and for whom a contract was a contract." If the colonizers could not purchase land, "they did not hesitate to claim new territory by right of conquest when the Indians resisted their advances; in fact, they acted as if divine law required them to do so." King Philip's War and many subsequent wars followed a certain cycle of events: "first, friendly overtures from the Indians, then open war, and finally the expulsion or extermination of the natives."[59]

If *The American Republic* was a big step forward in abandoning inevitabilist interpretations of Indian–white relations, plenty of textbook writers clung to hoary versions of the story. Between 1965 and 1973, four scathing critiques of textbooks made it clear that all but a few were filled with the disparagement of Indian cultures, had huge silences on Indian history and Indian–white relations, and were riddled with errors that tilted the story to the victor's side.[60] Yet books were changing. The statement in John Garraty's best-selling college textbook, *The American Nation*, first published in 1966, was a far cry from the books of the previous century and a half. "The settlement of America," Garraty charged, "ranks among the worst examples of naked aggression in human history." "English settlers described the Indian as being of 'a tractable, free, and loving nature, without guile or treachery,' yet in most instances they exploited and all but exterminated them." "Naked aggression," human behavior elevated to state policy, rather than God's intervening hand or nature's unstoppable course, directed the flow of history.[61]

As contingency rather than inevitability began to undergird explanations of early European–Indian contact, as culpability rather than moral justification filtered into the stories, some historians reverted to timeworn ways of explaining early Indian–white relations. Alden Vaughan's *New England Frontier*, first published in 1965, included no references to savages but portrayed early Puritan–Indian relations as all too inevitably determined. Vaughan insisted that the Puritans did not push the Algonkian peoples off their land, they did not "deplete the food sources of the native," they did not "kill off the Indians in a series of protracted military actions," and they did not "drive the Indian to despair through repeated injustices and cruelties." While arguing that the Puritans set a standard for fair play that other colonists could not match, Vaughan ignored Indian relations in Quaker Pennsylvania. The root of the friction between Puritan and Indian was "the nature of the two societies that met. . . . One was unified, visionary, disciplined, and dynamic. The other was divided, self-satisfied, undisciplined, and static." Vaughan steered students reading the book, which was widely assigned in college courses, to the proper conclusion. "It would be unreasonable to expect," he calmly pointed out, "that such societies could live side by side indefinitely with no penetration of the more fragmented and passive by the more consolidated and active."[62] Reading key words that loaded the dice and perhaps unconsciously swayed by the revealing sexual metaphor at the end of this statement, students understandably would conclude that Puritan–Algonkian contact could have only one outcome. Growing up in the civil rights era, when the American Indian Movement urgently pressed its case, students may have unconsciously read the book with relief (as did many reviewers). Isaiah Berlin's wisdom applies: "The growth of knowledge brings with it relief from moral burdens, for if powers beyond and above us are at work, it is wild presumption to claim responsibility for their activity or blame ourselves for failing in it."[63]

Some historians ably criticized Vaughan, most notably in a long book in which Francis Jennings tried to invert the story of New England settlers' encounters with the various tribes of the region. Breathing fire, Jennings implicitly rejected inevitable outcomes when Puritans met Algonkians, assuming that "human persons do have some power of choice over their own conduct."[64] As Jennings's book title indicates, he was as adept as Vaughan in scattering semantic shrapnel. More important, these two books fueled a pivotal debate, already simmering, on moral judgment in the writing of history.[65] For our purposes, what is most trenchant in this ongoing argument is that those who have held the colonists largely blameless for the result of Indian–white contact have built their argument around the notion of inevitability. "In truth, as a historical phenomenon," writes Bernard W. Sheehan, "the Indian disintegrated; as an Indian he was not annihilated but he faded culturally into another entity. The crime, if there ever was one, was the *inexorable* breakdown of the native's cultural integrity, in part the result of conscious policy and in part the *inevitable* consequence of competition between two disparate ways of life. . . . The American aborigine was the victim of a *process*."[66] James Axtell's response, published fourteen years later, insisted that historians must look at the "plural choices that historical actors enjoyed," and argued that "to say that their choices were inevitable . . . is to deny the existence of free will and to drift into the bog of historical determinism."[67]

History's victors do not give up their accumulated property in history without a fight, and the contest about interpreting European–Indian relations will go on for a long time. A steady stream of critiques about the textbook inaccuracies, distortions, and silences detailed earlier have brought about changes in what young students learn about the past.[68] Most of the new college textbooks written after World War II stopped promoting the notion that the unequal treatment of different groups in contemporary society was based on the inherent inferiority of American Indians, African Americans, and other groups—the insidious message of nature's unchangeable sorting out of intellectual and social capabilities. Moreover, most of the textbooks published in the past decade have largely abandoned explanations about the inevitable fate of American Indians. These improvements have trickled down to the schoolbooks as well, partly through effective protests by Indian people and partly through the coming of age of a more sensitive generation of scholars. Almost all textbooks admit voracious European land hunger, brutality, and treaty violations and place blame on both sides for cultural misunderstanding and violence. Virtually all now launch the story of American history with a chapter on pre-Columbian indigenous societies. Fifth-graders typically get their first lesson in American history by reading a chapter titled "The First Americans" in which they learn of the populousness of the Americas before the Columbian voyages, the broad diversity of indigenous cultures, and the ways in which Indian peoples often were as skilled in water engineering, agriculture, and town planning as Europeans of the fifteenth century. If they lacked literacy, Native Americans passed stories from generation to generation. If they had no written laws, indigenous people had codes of conduct. If they lacked Iron Age technology, gunpowder, and compasses, Indians conducted intracontinental trade over vast territories.[69] In approaching American history in this way, the vast cultural gap portrayed in the polar opposites of civilization and savagery—the incubator of inevitabilist thinking—yields to a meeting of cultures where almost nothing was inexorably determined and almost everything was contingent, negotiated, and in the end, the result of human agency.

Among the many ironies of the history wars of the 1990s, one is particularly relevant to this essay. In attacking the voluntary National History Standards urged by the nation's governors in 1989 and funded by the National Endowment for the Humanities and the federal Department of Education, conservative op-ed writers employed historical revisionism, including attempts to reach a fairer judgment about the nature of Indian–white relations, as a growling epithet. The scores of teachers and academic historians involved in constructing the standards cringed to hear that they were "history bandits" and "history thieves," antipatriots who were "hijacking American history." For Newt Gingrich, "there has been a calculated effort by cultural elites to discredit the [American] civilization and replace it with a culture of irresponsibility that is incompatible with American freedoms as we have known them." Bob Dole, running hard for the Republican presidential nomination in 1995, agreed that today's historians were members of "intellectual elites who seem embarrassed by America."[70] Writing in *U.S. News and World Report*, John Leo grimaced at the occasional mentions of American Indians in the suggested framework for studying history in the schools. "By allocation of the text," he fumed, "America today seems to be about 65 percent Indian with most of the rest of us black, female or oppressive." This disciple of Lynne Cheney, who let the attack on the history standards, sneered at the mention of Speckled Snake in a teaching example on Cherokee resistance to forced removal during Andrew Jackson's presidency.[71] In fact, Americans of the 1830s knew the name well enough since Speckled Snake was a powerful leader of one of the nation's most populous Indian nations.

A few historians, more academically inclined, objected to the notion of young students studying the convergence of Indian, African, and European peoples in the Americas because the very notion of colliding and interacting cultures would undermine the primacy of European ideas and institutions in the shaping of American culture. Jack Diggins argued that the notion of interacting societies not only detracts from an emphasis on Western values transported to North America but is inherently bankrupt. Allowing that students might appropriately study the culture of West Africans and indigenous people in anthropology classes, presumably in college, he maintained that such exotic cultural understandings "may have no bearing on teaching students how to think historically" because African and Native American societies had nothing to do with the unfolding of American history. The notion of convergence, he argues, sets students to "studying past cultures whose people reproduced their own bondage to rites and rituals."[72]

The history wars of the 1990s indicate that revisions of the history of Indian America and Indian–African–European relations will be attacked for a long while. This is typical of historical discourse in a large, democratically disposed society. But it is equally likely that schoolbooks will not revert to earlier depictions of Indian "savages," insist that Indians had little to contribute to the American mosaic, place the blame for three centuries of intercultural violence on inherent Indian characteristics, or insist that outcomes were dictated from the first moment when Europeans clambered off wooden ships in the Americas. What is now known cannot be easily forgotten. The tolling bell is not easily unrung.

Notes

I gratefully acknowledge research assistance from James Drake, Samantha Holtkamp, Richard Olivas, and Edie Sparks. Frederick Hoxie gave expert advice, and the editors of this book have provided sensitive suggestions.

1. Quoted in Gary B. Nash, *Race, Class, and Politics* (Urbana, Ill., 1986), xviii.

2. Roy Harvey Pearce, *Savagism and Civilization: A Study of the Indian and the American Mind* (Berkeley and Los Angeles, 1988), 4. The book was first issued in 1953 as *The Savages of America: A Study of the Indian and the Idea of Civilization*.

3. For a masterful exploration of this explanatory paradigm, see John Demos, *The Unredeemed Captive: A Family Story from Early America* (New York, 1994); an important earlier essay is Richard S. Dunn, "Seventeenth-Century English Historians of America," in *Seventeenth-Century America: Essays in Colonial History*, ed. James M. Smith (Chapel Hill, N.C., 1959), 195–225.

4. Quoted in Richard Drinnon, *Facing West: The Metaphysics of Indian-Hating and Empire-Building* (Minneapolis, 1980), 43. John Mason's *A Brief History of the Pequot War* (Boston, 1736) and John Underhill's *Newes from America; or, A New and Experimental Discoverie of New England* (London, 1638) were republished by the Massachusetts Historical Society; see *CMHS* 2d ser., vol. 8 (1819): 120–53; 3d ser., vol 6 (1837): 1–28.

5. *A brief History of the Wars with the Indians in New-England. From June 24, 1675. (When the first Englishman was murdered by the Indians) to August 12, 1676, when Philip, alias Metacomet, the principal author and Beginner of the War, was slain* (London, 1676), 50–51.

6. Cotton Mather, *Magnalia Christi Americana*, 2 vols. (Hartford, Conn., 1853), 2:561, 564.

7. Quoted in Ruth Elson, *Guardians of Tradition: American Schoolbooks of the Nineteenth Century* (Lincoln, Neb., 1964), 76.

8. Joseph Richardson, *The American Reader*, 2d ed. (Boston, 1813), 122, quoted in Elson, *Guardians of Tradition*, 79.

9. Charles A. Goodrich, *A History of the United States of America, on a Plan Adapted to the Capacity of Youth and Designed to Aid the Memory by Systematick Arrangement and Interesting Associations* (Bellow Falls, Vt., 1832); [Charles Prentiss], *History of the United States of America . . . For the Use of Schools and Families* (Keene, N.H., 1823); Samuel Willard, *The General Class-Book* (Greenfield, Mass., 1828).

10. Quoted in Elson, *Guardians of Tradition*, 72.

11. Quoted from various antebellum textbooks in Elson, *Guardians of Tradition*, 73.

12. Isaiah Berlin, *Historical Inevitability* (London, 1954), 7.

13. Ibid, 20.

14. Ibid., 38–39.

15. James Axtell, "Forked Tongues: Moral Judgments in Indian History," in *After Columbus: Essays in the Ethnohistory of Colonial North America* (New York, 1988), 35. In the following analysis, I draw upon representative books widely read in the era of their publication rather than an exhaustive list of books.

16. Berlin, *Historical Inevitability*, 39.

17. J. Hamilton Moore, *The Young Gentleman and Lady's Monitor and English Teacher's Assistant* (New York, 1793), 300, quoted in Elson, *Guardians of Tradition*, 66.

18. John Gorham Palfrey, *A Compendious History of New England from the Discovery by Europeans to the First General Congress of the Anglo-American Colonies*, 2 vols. (Cambridge, Mass., 1873), 1:131–32, 184–86, 194; 2:122.

19. John Fiske, *The Beginnings of New England or the Puritan Theocracy in Its Relation to Civil and Religious Liberty* (New York, 1889), 134.

20. Quoted in Virgil J. Vogel, *The Indian in American History* (Evanston, Ill., 1968), 5.

21. Arnold Guyot, *Physical Geography* (New York, 1866), 114, cited in Elson, *Guardians of Tradition*, 66.

22. James A. Bowen, *English Words as Spoken and Written* (New York, 1900), 90, and Henry E. Chambers, *A Higher History of the United States* (New Orleans, 1889), 82, quoted in Elson, *Guardians of Tradition*, 80.

23. Berlin, *Historical Inevitability*, 39–40.

24. Roswell C. Smith, *An Introductory Geography*, 13th ed. (New York, 1851), 157; *The American Class Book*, 2d ed. (Philadelphia, 1815), 139; John C. Rudd, *A Compendium of Geography* (Elizabethtown, N.J., 1816), 91, quoted in Elson, *Guardians of Tradition*, 87–88.

25. Reginald Horsman, *Race and Manifest Destiny: The Origins of American Racial Anglo-Saxonism* (Cambridge, Mass., 1981), 191.

26. Quoted in Horsman, *Race and Manifest Destiny*, 279.

27. On Apess, see Bernd C. Peyer, *The Tutor'd Mind: Indian Missionary-Writers in Antebellum America* (Amherst, Mass., 1997), 117–65.

28. Helen Hunt Jackson, *A Century of Dishonor: A Sketch of the United States Government's Dealings with Some Indian Tribes* (Boston, 1881).

29. Theodore Roosevelt, *The Winning of the West*, vol. 10 of *The Works of Theodore Roosevelt*, 11 vols. (New York, 1924), 8.

30. Quoted in Thomas G. Dyer, *Theodore Roosevelt and the Idea of Race* (Baton Rouge, La., 1980), 72.

31. Roosevelt, *Winning of the West*, in *Works*, 11:388–89.

32. Ibid., 11:275.

33. R. A. Brock, *Virginia and Virginians*, 2 vols. (Richmond, Va., 1888), 1:286–94.

34. Woodrow Wilson, *A History of the American People* (New York, 1901), 1:154.

35. John W. Wayland, the author of *How to Teach American History: A Handbook for Teachers and Students* (New York, 1916), held to the view that "for small children Indian life and the life of the white pioneers afford many appropriate subjects and incidents for dramatic reproduction." Creative teachers should have children reenact Indian braves stalking deer with bows and arrows, with "dark tresses

unbraided and fair faces daubed with some harmless paint, with a few rather loud ornaments donned for the occasion." This would help students "rush swiftly back across the years and deep into the primeval forest" (pp. 156–57). I have not seen any discussion of how children engaged in such reenactments might have negotiated the grim lessons they would learn about Indian barbarity and degeneration in high school.

36. Frances FitzGerald, *America Revised: History Schoolbooks in the Twentieth Century* (Boston, 1979), 91.

37. Edward Channing, *A History of the United States*, 2 vols. (New York, 1905), 1:402; 2:77.

38. Muzzey to Carl Becker, Oct. 16, 1920, quoted in Peter Novick, *That Noble Dream: The 'Objectivity Question' and the American Historical Profession* (New York, 1988), 229.

39. David Saville Muzzey, *An American History* (Boston, 1911), 25, 23; *History of the American People* (Boston, 1927), 2.

40. Muzzey, *American History*, 25; *History of the American People*, 228.

41. In the first volume of his *The United States of America*, 2 vols. (Boston, 1922), Muzzey excised Indians altogether in the section on the planting of the English colonies.

42. FitzGerald, *America Revised*, 92. However, FitzGerald ignores Rugg's books, as detailed below.

43. Charles Beard and Mary Beard, *The Rise of American Civilization* (New York, 1927; reprint, 1930), 58. In other textbooks, even through revised editions published as late as 1958, the Beards completely ignored Jackson's removal policies as noted in Vogel, *Indian in American History*, 2. Likewise, Carl Becker's *The United States Experiment in Democracy* (New York, 1920), ignored the Pequot War.

44. Harold Rugg, *That Men May Understand* (New York, 1940), 173.

45. Harold Rugg, *A History of American Civilization* (New York, 1930), 198; *Teachers Guide*, 80–83. In *The Conquest of America: A History of American Civilization: Economic and Social* (Boston, 1937), Rugg ruminated that "perhaps the warfare that developed out of disputes over land could not be avoided because the civilizations of the red man and the white man differed so greatly" (p. 185).

46. Rugg, *History of American Civilization*, 217.

47. "Book Burnings," *Time*, Sept. 9, 1940; *New York Times*, June 6, 1940, Sept. 23, 1940; S. Alexander Rippa, *Education in a Free Society*, 5th ed. (New York, 1984), 298–99.

48. Quoted in Peter F. Carbonne Jr., *The Social and Educational Thought of Harold Rugg* (Durham, N.C., 1977), 28.

49. Henry Steele Commager and Samuel Eliot Morison, *The Growth of the American Republic* (New York, 1950), 12. In earlier editions in 1930, 1940, and 1942, the authors began their account of American history in 1763.

50. Douglas Edward Leach, *Flintlock and Tomahawk: New England in King Philip's War* (New York, 1958), vi. Leach was as firmly an inevitabilist as Morison, his mentor. The first two sentences of his book told readers: "From the day when the first English settlers landed on New England shores and built permanent homes there, King Philip's War became virtually inevitable. Here in the wilderness two mutually incompatible ways of life confronted each other, and one of the two would have to prevail."

51. [Prentiss], *History of the United States of America*, 76–77.

52. Wilson, *History of the American People*, 312–13.

53. Muzzey, *History of the American People,* 65.

54. Rugg, *Conquest of America,* 179–80. None of the textbooks that I have consulted used the words *pacifism* or *peace testimony* in describing Quaker Indian policy. From the Spanish American War to World War II, members of the Society of Friends were embroiled in court cases about religious objections to conscription, and textbook writers—or their publishers—apparently did not dare introduce such terms.

55. Daniel J. Boorstin, *The Americans: The Colonial Experience* (New York, 1958), 348.

56. Ibid., 354.

57. In his *American History for Colleges* (1943), Muzzey began to incorporate material on Indians. He touched briefly on the Bering land bridge migration and the fur trade, for example. His tone also changed. He wrote of Europeans as "invaders of their [Indian] lands," of "Indian atrocities . . . in revenge for the treatment they received from the white man who regarded them as devils to be exterminated" and of the "merciless" treatment of Indians that "forms a rather disgraceful chapter in our history" (pp. 23–25).

58. George F. Willison, *Saints and Strangers* (New York, 1945).

59. Richard Hofstader, William Miller, and Daniel Aaron, *The American Republic* (Englewood Cliffs, N.J., 1959), 33.

60. William Brandon, "American Indians and American History," *The American West* 2, no. 2 (1965): 14–25; Vogel, *Indian in American History;* Jeannette Henry, *Textbooks and the American Indian,* ed. Rupert Costo ([San Francisco], 1970); Robert Berkhofer, "Native Americans and United States History," in *The Reinterpretation of American History and Culture,* ed. William H. Cartwright and Richard L. Watson Jr. (Washington, D.C., 1973). None of these critiques raised the use of inevitability in accounts of Indian–European conflict and the outcome of cultural interaction.

61. John Garraty, *The American Nation: A History of the United States* (New York, 1966), 10.

62. Alden T. Vaughan, *The New England Frontier: Puritans and Indians, 1620–1675* (Boston, 1965), 323. In a revised edition published in 1979, Vaughan retreated from this formulation but still concluded with statement that the Puritan–Indian outcome was inevitable.

63. Berlin, *Historical Inevitability,* 39.

64. Francis P. Jennings, *The Invasion of America: Indians, Colonialism, and the Cant of Conquest* (Chapel Hill, N.C., 1975), ix.

65. The literature on this is large. It is carefully documented by one of the main contestants in the argument: James Axtell, "A Moral History of Indian-White Relations Revisited," in *After Columbus,* chap. 1.

66. Bernard Sheehan, "Indian-White Relations in Early America: A Review Essay," *WMQ* 3d ser., 26 (1969): 269 (emphasis added).

67. Axtell, "Moral History of Indian-White Relations," 15. This essay was first published in *The History Teacher* 16 (1983).

68. Fred Hoxie, *The Indians versus the Textbooks: Is There Any Way Out?* (Chicago, 1984); James Axtell, "Europeans, Indians, and the Age of Discovery in American History Textbooks," *AHR* 92 (1987): 621–36; Patricia Nelson Limerick, "The Case of the Premature Departure: The Trans-Mississippi West and American History Textbooks," *JAH* 78 (1992): 1380–94; James A. Hijiya, "Why the West Is Lost," *WMQ* 3d ser., 51 (1994), 276–92; James Loewen, *Lies My Teacher Told Me:*

Everything Your American History Textbook Got Wrong (New York, 1995). In a chapter titled "Red Eyes," Loewen begins: "Historically, American Indians have been the most lied-about subset of our population" (p. 91). Loewen's book is based on a survey of twelve widely-used high school textbooks, but only two of them were published later than 1987.

69. Three recent schoolbooks that begin with "The First Americans" are Herman Viola, *Why We Remember: United States History through Reconstruction* (Menlo Park, Calif., 1977); Joyce Appleby, Alan Brinkley, and James MacPherson, *The American Journey* (New York, 1997); and Sarah Bednarz et al., *We the People: Build Our Nation* (Boston, 1997). All of these books give very limited space to American Indian history after the first chapter, but they do not plant in the minds of schoolchildren "a story of the inevitable triumph by the good guys," as Loewen puts it (*Lies My Teacher Told Me*, 129).

70. Gingrich, *To Renew America* (1995), excerpted in *Los Angeles Times*, July 31, 1995; Robert Dole speech in Indianapolis, Sept. 4, 1995, transcript from Federal Document Clearing House, 5.

71. John Leo, "The Hijacking of American History," *U.S. News & World Report*, Nov. 14, 1994, 36; John D. Fonte, "Rewriting History," *San Diego Union-Tribune*, Nov. 6, 1994.

72. Jack Diggins, "The National History Standards," *American Scholar* 64 (1995), 501–2; for a discussion of this controversy, see Gary B. Nash, "Early American History and the National History Standards," *WMQ* 3d ser., 54 (1997): 579–600, and responses to Diggins by seven historians and teachers: William Cronon et al., "Teaching American History," *American Scholar* 67 (1998): 91–106.

 *Afterword*

Richard S. Dunn

REMINISCENCES OF GARY B. NASH

GARY NASH AND I go back more than forty-three years, to the fall of 1954. In attempting to reconstruct as accurately as possible a long association that I greatly treasure, I have done what every good historian does: I have checked my sources. And in my file drawers I have found a sheaf of letters and papers that document in skeletal fashion the contours of our friendship during four decades. This evidence, when pieced together, gives a somewhat skewed picture of Gary Nash's evolving career. Like all good historical evidence, it highlights friction points: the occasions when Gary and I have differed, sometimes quite sharply, over how to interpret the historical past. No doubt there is too little of Gary and too much of me in the account that follows. I offer it as my tribute to a colleague who has never entirely seen eye to eye with me, but who has influenced me enormously as he has championed more forcibly than any other contemporary scholar a fundamental reinterpretation of early American history.

I first met Gary in September 1954 when he was a twenty-one-year-old senior at Princeton and I was a twenty-six-year-old graduate student attempting to lead the weekly discussion meetings, known as precepts, in History 306, which was Professor Frank Craven's undergraduate course in American colonial history. At the time, I was finishing my doctoral dissertation under Frank's supervision, and I felt specially privileged to be sitting in on Craven's lectures and assisting him in his course. Precepting at Princeton was, however, a new experience for me and a daunting one. In a typical precept, eight young males (there were no female students then at Tigertown) would enter my long narrow office, sit four on each side of the room facing each other, and start tossing the conversational ball back and forth. They generally talked so glibly about the book assigned for discussion that I was hard-pressed to tell whether any of them had actually read it. Gary Nash quickly won my gratitude because he did his homework and kept the discussion on target. I still have my gradebook for History 306. In those days Princeton used an eccentric grading system that ranged from 1 (high A) to 7 (low F). The record shows that I awarded Gary the top grade in his precept, a grade of 1–. Many years later he told me that my A was one of the few he received at Princeton. Gary stands out in my memory in another way: he was a sandy-haired, clean-cut youth who wore his snappy naval uniform to my class because his NROTC drill session took place during the preceding period. He seemed from my profoundly pacifist civilian perspective to be predestined for a dashing military career.

In 1954 I knew all too little about the young cadet who came to my precept once a week. Years later Gary told me that he grew up in the suburbs of Philadelphia in a family with minimal interest in intellectual pursuits. Yet he frequented the local library during summer vacations as a child and developed a love of reading. He claims to have entered Princeton with no career in mind and drifted into history—in his words, he was "reeled in with many aimless fish"—because it was the least objectionable major available. A senior thesis was required of all history majors at Princeton, and Gary chose to examine the Anglo-German naval pact of 1935 as his topic. His thesis adviser was the commander of the NROTC unit on campus, who was perhaps more proficient at drilling his cadets than at showing them how to do historical research. Gary did rather poorly on his senior comprehensive exam. "My interest," he says, "was in squash, partying, the yearbook—in about that order."[1] I still like to think, however, that his performance in my American colonial history precept was a portent of things to come.

Three years of duty from 1955 to 1958 in the recently desegregated U.S. Navy did a lot to shape Gary's future. Aboard a North Atlantic destroyer he observed white-black race relations close up. The prejudice and bigotry that he witnessed firsthand touched a raw nerve, and he instinctively sided with the underdog. Here, no doubt, was the initial impetus for Gary's decision, once he became an establish professional historian, to focus his attention on the theme of social inequality in early America. Returning to Princeton in 1959, still without clear career plans, he secured a low-level administrative job as assistant to the dean of the Graduate School. In 1960 he first exchanged letters with me. "I am indeed your former student in History 306," he wrote and went on to say that he had secured permission to take one graduate seminar in history per term at Princeton as an incidental student "to determine whether I am properly motivated to graduate work and a professorial career."[2] His first graduate seminar was with Frank Craven. He supposed at this point that he had no chance of admission to the Princeton history graduate program as a Ph.D. candidate because of his mediocre undergraduate record, so he asked about the possibility of enrolling for summer school courses at the University of Pennsylvania, where I had recently begun to teach.

A few months later he wrote again. By this time Gary knew that he wanted to enter graduate school full-time in 1961, and he was applying to a variety of history programs. He asked me to recommend him for fellowship support since most of his other undergraduate history teachers "have long since forgotten me." But he was in a buoyant mood. He was taking a mix of American and European history courses at Princeton and enjoying all of them. "This term I am getting a good dose of Gordon Craig—a seminar on domestic German history from 1870. It goes better and better and I am really quite excited at the prospect of getting at this full time." In fact, it was going so well that Princeton admitted him as a Ph.D. candidate. By 1962 he was starting to plan his doctoral dissertation under Frank Craven's supervision, and he came to Philadelphia to talk to my wife, Mary, and me about his topic: the structure of politics and society in early Pennsylvania. Laying plans for this visit, he wrote: "I am looking forward to seeing you again, Mr. Dunn, after some seven or eight years, and to meeting your wife." For our part, we were very much interested in Gary's dissertation project, since Mary had recently finished her own doctoral dissertation on William Penn's political thought and I was supervising a dissertation by Joe Illick on William Penn's relations with the British government.[3]

In retrospect, Gary's dissertation opened up most of the chief topics and issues that would absorb him for the next thirty years. He chose to study Pennsylvania, a colony that had heretofore receive vastly less attention than Massachusetts or even Virginia. His topic was the impact of social structure on politics. He wasn't yet fully into what would become his signature theme of inequality because he studied the founding of Pennsylvania from the top down. But he emphasized the class divisions within early Pennsylvania, and his unflattering portrayal of William Penn and other well-heeled Quakers and his exposé of their property disputes and power grabs left the alert reader in little doubt as to his egalitarian sympathies.

Working rapidly, Gary completed his dissertation in two years and received his Ph.D. in 1964. Soon after, he submitted his dissertation manuscript to Princeton University Press, and they asked me to review it, perhaps because I had recently published my first book, *Puritans and Yankees*, with Princeton. I agreed to read the manuscript and played the role of mentor to Gary once again. In time-honored avuncular fashion, I told the Princeton press that Gary's manuscript was provocative and full of interest and should be published—but not until he had reorganized and revised it very thoroughly. I complained that "in many passages, Nash is too evidently leading us on a tour through his note-cards," so I recommended that he cut one hundred pages and consolidate his ten chapters into seven, which, in fact, Gary proceeded to do. And I noted that the book, when published, "may irritate chauvinistic Pennsylvanians, fond of the 'Holy Experiment' legend, but this won't hurt sales." Gary accepted my strictures in good spirit and even thanked me for making him prune his narrative detail. "You forced me to do what needed to be done and I am grateful to you for it." Giving it a second review, I strongly recommended publication.

Princeton issued this book in 1968 under the title *Quakers and Politics: Pennsylvania, 1681–1726*.[4] It was priced at $8.50, according to the tattered dust jacket of my copy. There was no paperback edition until many years later, which was a pity, because *Quakers and Politics* was quickly recognized as the book to start with for any student of early Pennsylvania. At the time I thought, as I still do, that Gary was rather rough on William Penn and not as interested as he should have been in Quaker ideals and values. But his approach was deliberately provocative and highly illuminating. He rejected the generally accepted view that the founders of this colony were liberal idealists engaged in a noble "holy experiment"; he argued instead that the Quakers were extraordinarily fractious, that they didn't know how to compromise, and that in consequence they created the most unstable political system in English America. His interpretation of early Pennsylvania was a lot less bland and pietistic than anything I had read before, and by emphasizing the economic divisions and political tensions that disrupted this utopian community he brought the Quaker colony into line with the rest of English America.

Gary was appointed assistant professor of history at Princeton in 1964 and then moved to the University of California, Los Angeles, in 1966 at the same rank. I continued to see him from time to time after he resettled in California, because he came east to do archival research. Just about the time of his move west he found a magnificent series of tax lists for Chester County, Pennsylvania, running from 1693 to 1802. This was a revelatory discovery because Gary immediately saw, as he later wrote to me, "how the shrouds could be lifted from 18th-century mid-Atlantic society in ways that people would jump out of the past and present themselves, if very imperfectly, to our view and our (re)consideration." During his first year at UCLA he collaborated with James Lemon to write a seminal article on the Chester county tax lists, which was published in the *Journal of Social History* in 1968. A little later he found a 1767 tax list for Philadelphia, which triggered his interest in urban slaveholding in colonial America and led to his path-breaking article on Philadelphia slaves and slave owners, published in the *William and Mary Quarterly* in 1973.[5]

As he began to work on this new line of research, Gary asked me to support his application for a Guggenheim Fellowship, which he received in 1970. "As you will see, the proposal is somewhat imprecise. I am no model-builder, for which I make no apologies, and I thought it best to be frank about the fact that it is only through total immersion in the materials that I will find out exactly what I am about."[6] In fact, Gary knew from the start pretty well what he was about. He was charting the maldistribution of wealth in Philadelphia, Boston, and New York. He was tracking the growth of African-American slavery in an urban setting. He was looking for evidences of social dislocation and class conflict. And he was exploring the efforts of the struggling urban poor to rise up against their elite oppressors. In sum, he was studying the causes and consequences of inequality in eighteenth-century urban America.

Once Gary was installed at UCLA, he rose rapidly through the ranks, with promotion to associate professor in 1968 and to professor in 1972. The chairman of the UCLA department wrote to me on February 8, 1972, asking me to serve as an outside evaluator and adding that the decision on whether to promote Nash to professor "will be taken in two weeks' time, so I must ask for your letter as soon as you can conveniently get it to us." On February 9, Gary wrote to say that he was sending a packet of his latest work, two articles in press and a third in draft, and asked me to be sure to comment on these pieces in my evaluation and to "write as soon as possible after receiving them." The transcontinental mail must have moved uncommonly fast, and I must have responded with unaccustomed alacrity, because I find in my files a carbon copy of my letter to the UCLA chairman dated February 13, 1972, in which I comment very positively on Gary's forthcoming *William and Mary Quarterly* article, "The Image of the Indian in the Southern Colonial Mind," and on his forthcoming *Journal of American History* article, "The Transformation of Urban Politics, 1700–1765."[7] In pushing for Gary's promotion, I predicted that "he will continue to be aggressive and argumentative in his scholarship, seeking to deflate time honored myths and to expose latent tensions in early American history." In a separate letter of the same date to Gary, I offered him some free advice on his projected book on prerevolutionary urban politics in Philadelphia, Boston, and New York, hoping that he would explain to us "why Boston was such an active revolutionary center in the 1760s and 1770s and Philadelphia and New York were so comparatively passive." Gary thanked me politely for my "eminently sane comments" without pointing out that I was utterly clueless about the argument that he was in the process of developing for *The Urban Crucible*.[8]

During the 1970s, while working on his second big book, Gary was also widening his focus appreciably. For one thing, he began to produce a series of short books designed for classroom use: textbooks and documentary sourcebooks. The most significant and widely used of these was his textbook on colonial race relations, *Red, White, and Black: The Peoples of Early*

America, first published in 1974 with two subsequent revised editions. Here, Gary was inspired to a considerable degree by the example of his mentor Frank Craven, who took more interest in Native Americans and African Americans than did most other colonial historians of the 1950s and 1960s. One of Craven's last publications was a little volume in 1971 titled *White, Red, and Black: The Seventeenth-Century Virginian*. Gary not only improved on Frank Craven's title, he composed a much broader narrative, and he argued his case far more belligerently. *Red, White, and Black* rejects the standard textbook portrayal of European colonists settling an empty wilderness and replaces it with a strikingly different account of triracial interaction among Indians, Africans, and Europeans. Gary set out to show how Indians and Africans were, in his words, "actively and intimately involved" in the creation of colonial America.[9] The whites' brutal exploitation of the reds and blacks is strongly emphasized, but Gary describes a world in which everything is contested, where people are always trying to compel other people to act according to their own wishes but often cannot do so. His primary purpose was not to besmirch the English colonists but to demonstrate to the modern college student that America has been an actively multicultural society for four hundred years and that today's social potentialities and problems are rooted in our colonial period. And he underlined this point by discussing the internal class divisions within white society, the miseries of the large white servant class, and the growing gap between rich and poor. Here is popular history without the Pilgrim Fathers escaping from Old World persecution or pioneers forging into the trackless wilderness or Paul Revere's ride. Gary finds room for Pocahontas, to be sure, but not for Betsy Ross.

At the same time that Gary was writing history for the classroom, he was continuing and expanding his scholarly research. Though he lived three thousand miles from his sources, he did more digging in the Philadelphia, Boston, and New York archives during the 1970s than any Philadelphia-, Boston-, or New York–based colonial scholar. As he studied the economic, social, and political development of those three towns, he uncovered striking evidence of social dislocation and class conflict in all three places. And he produced a series of probing articles. "Care to play the critic?" he asked Mary and me in 1974 as he sent us a draft of "Urban Wealth and Poverty in Pre-Revolutionary America," which appeared two years later in the *Journal of Interdisciplinary History*.[10] Despite or maybe because of all his eastern forays, Gay became a committed Angelino. During one of his Philadelphia visits in the mid-1970s, I took him to a basketball game between Penn and St. Josephs at the Palestra. I was a little hesitant about doing so, since UCLA was then the perennial national basketball champion. But the game we saw proved to be a thrilling contest that went into overtime before Penn pulled out a one-point victory. As the frenzied crowd was howling around us, Gary remarked to me that he thought my Quakers might be able to put up a pretty good fight against one of the LA high school teams.

In 1977, Mary and I asked Gary to write on our behalf to the National Endowment for the Humanities, to endorse our application for a grant to edit *The Papers of William Penn*. He did so and at the same time reported that "my book on the cities may yet see the light of print. I had a good summer of writing and have completed 10 of the 12 chapters." *The Urban Crucible* was nearing publication. A few months later, at Gary's urging, Harvard University Press sent me the ten completed chapters for review. Once more I offered plenty of advice. I told the Harvard press that *The Urban Crucible* was an important and innovative book, completely superseding Carl Bridenbaugh's celebratory account of colonial American urban life in *Cities in the Wilderness* and *Cities in Revolt*. I recognized that Gary was not only correcting Bridenbaugh but also countering Bernard Bailyn's *Ideological Origins of the American Revolution*, by emphasizing the social and economic factors at play in the 1760s and 1770s and by arguing that the revolution was no mere war of words. In my review for Harvard, I especially praised Gary's effort to penetrate into the inarticulate ranges of town life and to delineate the attitudes and actions of the artisans and laboring poor. At the same time, I worried that his emphasis on class struggle was overdrawn and that his delight in the crowd attacks on patricians like Hutchinson was excessive. In a separate letter to Gary, I complained that he found too little room in his story for religious beliefs and political ideas; I found him too much of an economic determinist. Gary immediately replied: "I'm bemused by your comment about economic determinism. I got the same comment from Al Young. I'll keep it in mind as I revise, of course, but . . ." And he then proceeded to hammer me with arguments reaffirming his own position.[11]

In early 1979, I read the final three chapters of *The Urban Crucible* for the Harvard press, and at this point my differences with Gary became sharper. I thought his argument for extreme urban poverty in the 1760s and 1770s was exaggerated, and I was dissatisfied with his presentation of the coming of the revolution in Boston. I didn't understand why the Boston poor, if they were as oppressed by their local elite leaders as he claimed, should have joined Sam Adams and John Hancock so wholeheartedly in the Whig campaign against British rule. And I didn't understand why Gary should dismiss all of the revolutionary anti-British action that took place in Boston from 1767 to 1775 as irrelevant to his purpose and dwell instead on the class conflict he found in Philadelphia and New York. "I am quite sure," I told the Harvard press, "that Gary will agree with few, if any, of these strictures. I really throw them out only to suggest how much I have enjoyed reading and arguing with this book." This time Gary didn't bother to respond. He was doubtless tired of my Whiggery, and he had already pointed out to me that he was no more condemnatory of the prerevolutionary urban elite than I was of the West Indian planter class in my book *Sugar and Slaves*. Without further significant revision, *The Urban Crucible: Social Change, Political Consciousness and the Origins of the American Revolution* appeared in print a few months later.[12]

Starting in 1978, when I became director of the Philadelphia Center for Early American Studies at the University of Pennsylvania, I began to witness at firsthand Gary Nash's prowess as a trainer of graduate students. At the PCEAS, I initiated a fellowship program designed to help graduate students from other universities who needed or wanted to come to Philadelphia for a year to work on their doctoral dissertations. To date, five of Gary's UCLA students—Sharon V. Salinger, Billy G. Smith, David Lehman, Rosalind Remer, and James Pearson—have won PCEAS dissertation fellowships, and all of them have reflected in distinctive and creative ways their mentor's interests and research techniques during their time at the Philadelphia Center. Gary himself took part in a conference that the PCEAS presented in 1981 to celebrate the publication of the first volume of *The Papers of William Penn*, and his essay was published in the conference volume that Mary and I edited, *The World of William Penn* (1986).[13] In addition, Gary has presented several other papers at the PCEAS seminar in order to get feedback on draft articles or book chapters.

During the 1980s, Gary and I found ourselves working on somewhat parallel research projects. He was studying the emancipation of African-American slaves in the northern cities during and after the revolution, and I was studying African-American plantation slave life in Jamaica and Virginia. We both gave papers at a conference on slavery and emancipation in the revolutionary era organized by Ronald Hoffman and Ira Berlin in Washington; these essays were published in *Slavery and Freedom in the Age of the American Revolution* (1982). Shortly afterward, we both delivered broader papers surveying recent scholarship on early American history at a conference organized by Jack Greene and Jack Pole in Oxford; these essays were published in *Colonial British America* (1984).[14] Gary then invited me to contribute a brief foreword to a volume of his collected essays on American colonial and revolutionary society, published under the title *Race, Class, and Politics* (1986). I did so with great pleasure, using the occasion to summarize my view of his scholarship. Our relations now began to border on the incestuous. I chaired a session at the Organization of American Historians devoted to Gary's work. And Gary reciprocated by helping to organize a conference on the occasion of my retirement from the Penn history department and contributed an essay summarizing and analyzing my work.[15]

In many ways, Gary's new research in the 1980s built naturally on two of his previous books. In *The Urban Crucible* he had explored the possibilities of history from the bottom up by examining the role played by oppressed urban whites in the revolutionary era. In *Red, White, and Black* he had pictured eighteenth-century America as a triracial society. So it was appropriate for him to follow up with an investigation into the experiences of urban blacks during and after the American Revolution. In 1982 he published a striking essay on the black emancipation experience in Boston, New York, and Philadelphia, and in 1988 he produced what seems to me his finest book to date, *Forging Freedom: The Formation of Philadelphia's Black Community, 1720–1840.*[16] Here, taking another long look at the city of brotherly love, Gary brings out both the achievement and the heartache of black Philadelphians as they escaped from slavery during and after the revolution, forming the largest free black community in the new nation, only to find that they were restricted at every turn by a color line that demonized and ghettoized them. The blacks who figure in this book have active agency. Many of them liberate themselves during the revolutionary era and then resourcefully build up their businesses, churches, schools, and social support network. Religion plays a far more positive role in *Forging Freedom* than in Gary's earlier books; the black church is at the heart of his story. And the book closes on a bleak note with the burning of Pennsylvania Hall, newly opened by radical abolitionists, in 1838. When I asked Gary why he ended his story in 1840, he told me that the negrophobic rioting by white mobs that took place in Philadelphia during the following twenty years was too painful to write about. But he did join Jean Soderlund in writing a companion volume, titled *Freedom by Degrees: Emancipation and Its Aftermath in Pennsylvania, 1690–1840* and published in 1991, in which the two authors demonstrate how very limited and very grudging the white commitment to emancipation was in this supposedly antislavery state.[17]

In the late 1980s and 1990s, Gary has moved from academic scholarship into almost full-time pedagogy. He has published college-level and school-level U.S. history textbooks, and he is currently helping to manage the National Center for History in the Schools and the National History Standards Project. One of his most imaginative recent achievements, in my opinion, was the exhibit he designed titled "Finding Philadelphia's Past: Visions and Revisions," which was on display at the Historical Society of Pennsylvania from 1989 to 1997. Selecting from the HSP's collection of ten thousand art works and historical artifacts, most of which were donated to the society by patrician benefactors as testimonials to their high culture,

Gary managed to create an exhilarating display that illuminated all aspects of Philadelphia life over two centuries. It focused as much on the humble as on the elite and reminded the viewer of shameful episodes (such as the Civil War race riots) as well as prideful achievements from the past. This exhibit, it seems to me, was emblematic of Gary's entrée into the culture wars. He showed how one could take a fresh look at traditional historical materials, find ways of presenting familiar events from the bottom up as well as the top down, and thereby create a vibrant new vision of the past.

It is not my purpose to follow Gary into the culture wars. But I do want to point out that the man I am memorializing is a person of extraordinary consistency. He is a straight-shooting scholar with a strongly held set of beliefs, which are plain to behold in all of his books and in his current prescriptions for history reform in the schools. He has always been a champion of the underdog and has undertaken the arduous task of rescuing from obscurity some of those many early Americans who never did get a fair shake when they were alive. He doesn't see the need to bow down and worship the founding fathers or any other tin gods from our past. He is a bear for documentary research, and he has done everything in his power to encourage school and college students to learn about history directly from the sources. And he is a provocative and argumentative writer, which makes him consistently stimulating to read. Here's to Gary Nash!

Notes

1. Gary Nash to Richard Dunn, June 6, 1996.
2. Gary Nash to Richard Dunn, February 1, 1960.
3. Gary Nash to Richard Dunn, November 7, 1960; November 12, 1960. Later published as Mary Maples Dunn, *William Penn: Politics and Conscience* (Princeton, N.J., 1967); and Joseph E. Illick, *William Penn, the Politician: His Relations with the English Government* (Ithaca, N.Y., 1965).
4. Richard S. Dunn, *Puritans and Yankees: The Winthrop Dynasty of New England, 1630–1717* (Princeton, N.J., 1962). Richard Dunn, reader's report to Princeton University Press, August 31, 1966. Gary's proposed title for his book was "Seed of a Nation," which I thought an unfortunate choice since "we already have too many germinative titles in this field." Gary Nash to Herbert Bailey, director, Princeton University Press, September 22, 1967; Nash to Richard Dunn, March 7, 1968. Gary B. Nash, *Quakers and Politics: Pennsylvania, 1681–1726* (Princeton, N.J., 1968).
5. Gary Nash to Richard Dunn, June 6, 1996. James T. Lemon and Gary B. Nash, "The Distribution of Wealth in Eighteenth-Century America," *Journal of Social History* 2 (1968): 1–24. Gary B. Nash, "Slaves and Slaveowners in Colonial Philadelphia," *WMQ* 3d ser., 30 (1973): 223–56.
6. Gary Nash to Richard Dunn, October 23, 1968.
7. Robert Wohl to Richard Dunn, February 8, 1972; Gary Nash to Richard

Dunn, February 9, 1972. Gary B. Nash, "The Image of the Indian in the Southern Colonial Mind," *WMQ* 3d ser., 29 (1972): 197–230; "The Transformation of Urban Politics, 1700–1764," *JAH* 60 (1973): 605–32.

8. Richard Dunn to Robert Wohl, February 13, 1972; Richard Dunn to Gary Nash, February 13, 1972; Gary Nash to Richard Dunn, February 24, 1972.

9. Gary B. Nash, *Red, White, and Black: The Peoples of Early America* (Englewood Cliffs, N.J., 1974), 3.

10. Gary Nash to Richard Dunn and Mary Dunn, September 10, 1974; Mary Dunn to Gary Nash, October 9, 1974. Gary B. Nash, "Urban Wealth and Poverty in Prerevolutionary America," *Journal of Interdisciplinary History* 4 (1976): 545–84.

11. Gary Nash to Richard Dunn and Mary Dunn, December 21, 1977; Richard Dunn to Aida Donald, Harvard University Press, March 8, 1978. Carl Bridenbaugh, *Cities in the Wilderness: The First Century of Urban Life in America, 1625–1742* (New York, 1938), and *Cities in Revolt: Urban Life in America, 1743–1776* (New York, 1955); Bernard Bailyn, *The Ideological Origins of the American Revolution* (Cambridge, Mass., 1967). Gary Nash to Richard Dunn, March 12, 1978; May 30, 1978.

12. Richard Dunn to Aida Donald, February 15, 1979. Richard S. Dunn, *Sugar and Slaves: The Rise of the Planter Class in the English West Indies, 1624–1713* (Chapel Hill, N.C., 1972); Gary B. Nash, *The Urban Crucible: Social Change, Political Consciousness, and the Origins of the American Revolution* (Cambridge, Mass., 1979).

13. Some of these dissertations have subsequently been published, see Sharon V. Salinger, *"To Serve Well and Faithfully": Labour and Indentured Servants in Pennsylvania 1682–1800* (Cambridge, 1987); Billy G. Smith, *The "Lower Sort": Philadelphia's Laboring People, 1750–1800* (Ithaca, N.Y., 1990); and Rosalind Remer, *Printers and Men of Capital: Philadelphia Book Publishers in the New Republic* (Philadelphia, 1996). Also see J. David Lehman, "Explaining Hard Times: Political Economy and the Panic of 1819 in Philadelphia" (Ph.D. diss., UCLA, 1992); Jim Pearson is still working on his dissertation. Gary B. Nash, "The Early Merchants of Philadelphia: The Formation and Disintegration of a Founding Elite," in *The World of William Penn,* ed. Richard S. Dunn and Mary Maples Dunn (Philadelphia, 1986), 337–62.

14. Gary B. Nash, "Forging Freedom: The Emancipation Experience in the Northern Seaports, 1775–1820," in *Slavery and Freedom in the Age of the American Revolution,* ed. Ira Berlin and Ronald Hoffman (Charlottesville, Va., 1983), 3–48; "The Social Development of Colonial America," in *Colonial British America: Essays in the History of the Early Modern Era,* ed. Jack P. Greene and J. R. Pole (Baltimore, 1984), 233–61.

15. Gary B. Nash, "The Work of Richard Dunn," in *Empire, Society and Labor: Essays in Honor of Richard S. Dunn,* ed. Nicholas Canny, Joseph E. Illick, Gary B. Nash, and William Pencak, in a special supplemental issue of *Pennsylvania History* 64 (summer 1997): 11–25.

16. Nash, "Forging Freedom"; *Forging Freedom: The Formation of Philadelphia's Black Community, 1720–1840* (Cambridge, Mass., 1988).

17. Gary B. Nash and Jean R. Soderlund, *Freedom by Degrees: Emancipation in Pennsylvania and Its Aftermath* (New York, 1991).

Contributors

RICHARD S. DUNN is the Roy F. and Jeannette P. Nichols Professor Emeritus of American History at the University of Pennsylvania and Director of the McNeil Center for Early American Studies. His work on inequality in early America includes *Sugar and Slaves: The Rise of the Planter Class in the English West Indies, 1624–1713* (1972); "Servants and Slaves: The Recruitment and Employment of Labor," in *Colonial British America,* ed. Jack P. Greene and J. R. Pole (1984); and more recently, a series of articles on slave life and labor in two plantations: Mesopotamia in Jamaica and Mount Airy in Virginia.

SYLVIA R. FREY is Professor of History at Tulane University and served as Pitt Professor of American History at the University of Cambridge in 1997–1998. A social historian of the American revolutionary era, her work focuses on the collective histories of groups whose past is largely unknown—working men, African Americans, and women. Her publications include *The British Soldier in America: A Social History of Military Life in the Revolutionary Era* (1981); *Water from the Rock: Black Resistance in a Revolutionary Age* (1991); and, with Betty Wood, *Come Shouting to Zion: African American Protestant Christianity in the American South and the British Caribbean to 1830* (1998).

THOMAS N. INGERSOLL's dissertation is forthcoming under the title *Mammon and Manon: The Earliest Slave Society in the Deep South, New Orleans, 1718–1819.* He has published preliminary findings in *WMQ, Law and History Review,* and elsewhere. He is currently working on a book about racial intermixture in early North America. His understanding of inequality began with an apprenticeship in the working class as a farmhand in Michigan, a hospital janitor in Wichita, a cabdriver and desk-jockey in San Francisco. During the last two decades the study of popular radicals in early New England and slaves in colonial Louisiana has refined his analytical framework. Ingersoll is currently on the history faculty at the Université de Montréal.

PHILIP D. MORGAN is editor of the *William and Mary Quarterly* at the Omohundro Institute of Early American History and Culture and Professor of History at the College of William and Mary. He is the author of *Slave Counterpoint: Black Culture in the Eighteenth-Century Chesapeake and Lowcountry* (1998) and editor (with Bernard Bailyn) of *Strangers Within the Realm: Cultural Margins of the First British Empire* (1991) and (with Ira Berlin) of *Cultivation and Culture: Labor and the Shaping of Slave Life in the Americas* (1993). Most of his research has been about New World slavery.

GARY B. NASH is Professor of History at the University of California, Los Angeles. The author of numerous books and articles, his research and teaching have explored inequality in early America, in many of its various forms, for over thirty years. Nash is currently director of the National Center for History in the Schools at UCLA. He is completing *Forbidden Love: The Secret History of Mixed-Race America*, a book on mixed-race identity and attitudes toward interracial marriage, to be published by Henry Holt & Company in 1999.

MARY BETH NORTON is the Mary Donlon Alger Professor of American History at Cornell University. She is the author of *Liberty's Daughters: The Revolutionary Experience of American Women, 1750–1800* (1980, 1996); and *Founding Mothers and Fathers: Gendered Power and the Forming of American Society* (1996). Both books and her article in this volume reflect her continuing interest in exploring the gendered nature of inequality in early America, which arises from her awareness of the persistence of such inequality (though often in very different forms) into our own day.

J. RICHARD OLIVAS received his Ph.D. degree in early American history from UCLA in 1997. Upon graduation he became a Presidential Postdoctoral Fellow at the University of California. When Olivas chose to study with Gary Nash, he did not expect inequality to have played a role in the Great Awakening. Only late in the dissertation-writing stage did he discover that partiality had permeated Boston awakening. The relationship between revivalism and the socioeconomic standing of those who participated in the revival is now an important concern of his.

CARLA GARDINA PESTANA earned her Ph.D. degree at UCLA in 1987, writing a dissertation on religious sectarianism that was later published as *Quakers and Baptists in Colonial Massachusetts* (1991). She has also published a number of articles related to an ongoing project on the Quaker executions of 1658–61. Currently she is completing a book manuscript on Anglo-America during the English revolution, 1641–61. Much of her research and teaching pivots on issues of radicalism and dissent, but until working on this conference and volume, she had not grappled with inequality in a sustained way. She is an Associate Professor of History at the Ohio State University.

SHARON V. SALINGER is on the faculty of the Department of History and an associate dean of the College of Humanities, Arts, and Social Sciences at the University of California, Riverside. She received her Ph.D. degree from UCLA in 1980 and first ventured into the field of inequality in colonial America with her dissertation, supervised by Gary Nash. It was published as *"To Serve Well and Faithfully": Labor and Indentured Servants in Pennsylvania, 1682–1800* (1987). She has also published articles on wealth and housing inequality in eighteenth-century Philadelphia. Salinger's book on early American taverns as gendered spaces is due out later in 1999.

NEAL SALISBURY, Professor of History, Smith College, completed his dissertation at UCLA under Gary Nash's direction (1972). He has since published *Manitou and Provience: Indians, Europeans, and the Making of New England* (1982), *The Enduring Vision: A History of the American People* (with Paul S. Boyer et al.; 3d ed.; 1996), an edition of Mary Rowlandson, *The Sovereignty and Goodness of God*

(1997), as well as chapters, articles, and essays on Native American history in colonial North America, especially New England. He is currently working on *The Transformation of Anglo-Indian New England, 1637–1689*; a textbook on Native American history with R. David Edmunds and Frederick Hoxie; and *The Blackwell Companion to Native American History*, with Philip J. Deloria. His approach to the study of inequality embraces the distribution of not only material resources and formal political power but also the power to identify and represent selves and others across boundaries of culture and ethnicity.

RONALD SCHULTZ is Professor of History at the University of Wyoming. He is the author of *The Republic of Labor: Philadelphia Artisans and the Politics of Class, 1720–1830* (1993), a study of working-class formation in the Quaker City, as well as several essays on artisans and the transition to capitalism in America. Most recently, he is editor, with Jacquelyn Miller, of *Constructing Class: Alternative Meanings of Class in Early America* (forthcoming), a collection of essays exploring alternative formulations of class in eighteenth- and nineteenth-century America. His current research focuses on the role of inequality in cross-cultural exchanges in the Atlantic world.

BILLY G. SMITH is Professor of History at Montana State University. His research has focused on issues of inequality, class, race, and resistance in early America. He is author of *The "Lower Sort": Philadelphia's Laboring People, 1750–1800* (1990). He edited *Life in Early Philadelphia: Documents from the Revolutionary and Early National Periods* (1995) and co-edited *The Infortunate: The Voyage and Adventures of William Moraley, an Indentured Servant* (1992), and *"A Melancholy Scene of Devastation": The Public Response to the 1793 Philadelphia Yellow Fever Epidemic* (1997).

STERLING STUCKEY is the author of *Slave Culture* (1987) and *Going Through the Storm: The Influence of African American Art in History* (1995). His interest in the relationship of art to history has led him to publish a number of essays on Herman Melville's *Benito Cereno*. His latest essay on that novella was published in *The Cambridge Companion to Herman Melville* (spring, 1998). He is Professor of History and Cooperating Faculty, Dance Department, the University of California, Riverside.

LAUREL THATCHER ULRICH is James Duncan Phillips Professor of Early American History at Harvard University. In her first scholarly article, "Vertuous Women Found: New England Ministerial Literature, 1668–1735," published in *American Quarterly* in 1976, she probed the relationship between the spiritual equality and social inequality of women and men. Over the past twenty years she has pursued related themes in numerous articles and two books. *Good Wives: Image and Reality in the Lives of Women in Northern New England, 1650–1750* (1982); and *A Midwife's Tale: The Life of Martha Ballard Based on Her Diary, 1785–1812*, which received the Pulitzer Prize for History in 1991. Her essay in this volume is drawn from a work in progress on New England's "age of homespun."

PETER H. WOOD earned his Ph.D. degree from Harvard in 1972. His dissertation project, published in 1974 as *Black Majority: Negroes in Colonial South Carolina from 1670 through the Stono Rebellion*, taught him a great deal about inequality in early America. Before graduate school he spent several years at Oxford University on a Rhodes Scholarship, and afterward he worked for several years as a Humanities Officer for the Rockefeller Foundation. These experiences also obliged him to confront relations between the "haves" and the "have-nots" in the world, past and present. Since 1975 he has taught colonial history (and more recently, Native American history) at Duke University. He is the co-author, with Karen Dalton, of *Winslow Homer's Images of Blacks: The Civil War and Reconstruction Years* (1988) and a co-editor of *Powhatan's Mantle: Indians in the Colonial Southeast* (1989). His most recent book, part of a series for young readers on African-American history, is titled *Strange New Land: African Americans, 1617–1776* (1996).

Index

UNIVERSITY PRESS OF NEW ENGLAND
publishes books under its own imprint and is the publisher for Brandeis
University Press, Dartmouth College, Middlebury College Press, University of New Hampshire, Tufts University, and Wesleyan University Press.

Library of Congress Cataloging-in-Publication Data

Inequality in early America / Carla Gardina Pestana and Sharon V. Salinger, editors.
     p.   cm. — (Reencounters with colonialism—new perspectives on the Americas)
Includes bibliographical references and index.
ISBN 0–87451–926–8 (cloth : alk. paper). — ISBN 0–87451–927–6 (pbk. : alk. paper)
1. United States—History—Colonial period, ca. 1600–1775. 2. United States—History—
Revolution, 1775–1783. 3. United States—History—1783–1815. 4. Equality—United
States—History—17th century. 5. Equality—United States—18th century. 6. United
States—Social conditions—To 1865. 7. United States—Race relations. 8. Social classes—
United States—History—17th century. 9. Social classes—United States—History—18th
century.
I. Pestana, Carla Gardina. II. Salinger, Sharon V. (Sharon Vineberg) III. Series
E1888.5.I54 1999
973.2—dc21   99–25050

DATE DUE
